St. Mary's High School

WOMEN IN CHRIST

D1124780

WOMEN IN CHRIST

Toward a New Feminism

Edited by

Michele M. Schumacher

WILLIAM B. EERDMANS PUBLISHING COMPANY
GRAND RAPIDS, MICHIGAN / CAMBRIDGE, U.K.

Originally published in French under the title
Femmes dans le Christ: Vers un nouveau féminisme.
© 2003 Éditions du Carmel, Toulouse, France.

This English edition
© 2004 Wm. B. Eerdmans Publishing Co.
All rights reserved

Wm. B. Eerdmans Publishing Co.
255 Jefferson Ave. S.E., Grand Rapids, Michigan 49503 /
P.O. Box 163, Cambridge CB3 9PU U.K.

Printed in the United States of America

08 07 06 05 04   7 6 5 4 3 2 1

Library of Congress Cataloging-in-Publication Data

Women in Christ: toward a new feminism / edited by Michele M. Schumacher.
        p.   cm.
    Includes bibliographical references and index.
    ISBN 0-8028-1294-5 (pbk.: alk. paper)
    1. Feminism — Religious aspects — Catholic Church.
    I. Schumacher, Michele M.

    BX1795.F44W66   2004
    230′.082 — dc22

                                                    2003058384

www.eerdmans.com

Contents

Part II: Theological Anthropology

Part III: Ethical and Practical Consequences

Foreword

I will give thanks to the LORD with my whole heart;
I will tell of all thy wonderful deeds.
I will be glad and exult in thee,
I will sing praise to thy name, O Most High.

PSALM 9:1-2 RSV

It is only appropriate that the opening words of this book — which are, in fact, the last ones written — be words of thanks and praise to the Lord of all goodness and mercies. Only by his grace has this work been accomplished, although it admittedly remains a mere introduction to a topic meriting continuous reflection and ongoing dialogue. I am extremely grateful for the opportunity of contributing to this important subject, thanks to the discalced Carmelite fathers of the Province of Avignon-Aquitaine and Father Marie-Bruno Borde among them, who not only invited me to edit this volume in the original French edition, but also supplied the encouragement and moral support I needed to push forward despite the various obstacles I have faced. I am also grateful to Fr. Borde and to Fr. Jean-Gabriel Rueg, O.C.D., for permission to print this book in English. My respect and appreciation for the various contributors to this volume is profound. Each exposé entails a true gift of self, as is apparent in the author's engagement with the topic of his or her reflection. Far from a distanced and detached account of Christian anthropology, this volume represents — it seems to me — the fruit of a profound involvement of each author's very person. My gratitude to Sr. Prudence Allen, R.S.M., is double: not only because she has contributed twice, but also because of her generosity in offering suggestions, advice, references, and encouragement. Fr. Francis Martin has also been very helpful in this regard, even before I took on this project. The translators of the French and German texts, Sr. Allison Braus, O.C.D., and Grant Kaplan respectively, also merit many thanks for their painstaking efforts and precision. Finally, I am thankful for my wonderful family, especially my mother-in-law, Emma Schumacher, and my husband Bernard, who so graciously cared for our children so that I could engage in this work. More than this, I deeply appreciate the constancy of Bernard's help and encouragement. I am also indebted to my beautiful children — Myriam, Sophia, Teresa, and the child I now carry in my womb — for having awakened my maternal spirit, whereby I have come to appreciate more fully my own femininity. This book is dedicated to them.

MICHELE M. SCHUMACHER

An Introduction to a New Feminism

Michele M. Schumacher

The challenge of founding and articulating a *new feminism* has barely been taken up, at least not in a theoretical way, since it was first launched by Pope John Paul II in his 1995 encyclical *Evangelium vitae:* "In transforming culture so that it supports life, *women* occupy a place, in thought and action, which is unique and decisive. It depends on them to promote a 'new feminism' which rejects the temptation of imitating models of 'male domination,' in order to acknowledge and affirm the true genius of women in every aspect of the life of society, and overcome all discrimination, violence and exploitation."[1] In this goal of overcoming the discrimination, violence, and exploitation of women, a new feminism is not unlike the "old" brand of feminism, which I refer to as "traditional" or mainstream feminism, although I am thereby referring to the more recent forms of feminism — those associated with the women's liberation movement — and not necessarily those of the nineteenth and early twentieth centuries. It must furthermore must be admitted that there are an almost endless number of different strands of feminism today. The difference between these old "feminisms" and

---

1. Encyclical letter on the gospel of life, *Evangelium vitae* (March 25, 1995), #99. For the sake of accuracy, it is worth noting that the term "new feminism" was already employed in 1975 by Mary Aquin O'Neill ("Toward a Renewed Anthropology," *Theological Studies* 36 [December 1975]: 725-36) with reference to the women's liberation movement (for clarification of the connection, see Margaret A. Farley's article in the same issue: "New Patterns of Relationship: Beginnings of a Moral Revolution," pp. 627-46) and by *Les cahiers protestants* in their December 1979 issue entitled "Vers un nouveau féminisme." O'Neill in particular makes an important correlation between this "new" feminism and an adequate theological anthropology, noting most especially that sexual differentiation "demands that the perspective of each sex, with all the experience, history, insight, and imagination which is its own, contribute to the description of [the] human being and of God which grounds a theological anthropology" (p. 725).

the new feminism lies, Sr. Prudence Allen will explain, in their respective percep-tions of women's responsibility to herself and to society, in, that is to say, the en-dorsement or denial of the proposition that "the dignity of human life should be supported toward its full development for the common good" (p. 98). To the ex-tent, she will argue, that this conviction is maintained and even fostered by a given feminism, it may be considered an authentic humanism. The obvious ethi-cal implications of this conviction which are explored by Jean Bethke Elshtain, Marguerite Léna, and Elizabeth Fox-Genovese are, it is maintained, necessarily founded upon a solid anthropology which, in turn, may be fostered by the ethical questions connected to feminism: questions related, for example, to freedom, to rights, and to responsibilities, and thus ultimately to the connection between the personal and the social, or between the individual and the community, and ulti-mately — as Fox-Genovese insists — between theory and practice. As such, they also point to the nature of sexual difference and even to nature itself, especially in its more or less dynamic or determinant relation to culture, an area of contro-versy exposed by Hanna-Barbara Gerl-Falkovitz and Michele M. Schumacher. Fr. Francis Martin will therefore meet harmonious voices when he notes: "By inte-grating what is true in the efforts of the rights-oriented feminism into the ques-tion, 'Who is a woman?' we will arrive at a genuine development of doctrine in the area of Christian anthropology." Indeed, the new feminism "represents," he maintains, "a definitive shift from a consideration of women's rights to reflection on the very nature of woman herself" (p. 141).

A New Feminism: Anthropological Foundations

The thirteen contributions to this volume seek to articulate an integral philo-sophical and theological anthropology on the basis of which this new feminism might enter into a meaningful dialogue with what I have called traditional or mainstream feminism, on the one hand, and so-called patriarchy, on the other. Our goal is not to thereby mediate between the two, nor to judge the validity of their often ideological claims; far less to correct their errors. Without avoiding these valid and even worthy objectives — which are addressed to some extent by many of the authors — our primary purpose is to forge a way through the im-passe that these ideologies have created in Western society and, more positively, to rise above an often degraded cultural vision of the human person in general and of women in particular: a vision which calls into question the transcenden-tal, or metaphysical, foundation of his or her existence, of his or her divine ori-gin and end, and thus ultimately of his or her spiritual childhood. As such our intention is to seek an honest response to the questions which emerge from the depths of the human heart: "What is man [i.e., the human person]? . . . What can man [and woman] contribute to society? What can he [and she] expect from it? What happens after this earthly life is ended?"[2] More specifically in the case at hand, it is a question of woman's place beside man, of the foundation of her equal dignity, of her shared responsibility for the earth and its inhabitants, of her likeness to him, and ultimately of her originality: her specific, metaphysical differences from man — as distinguished from differences between women themselves — including what John Paul II refers to as "the true genius of women."[3]

By instinctively directing these inquiries within the light of Christian revelation, our *Christian anthropological approach* — which, as such, is more properly a philosophical and theological anthropology (where God is the "measure" of man) than an anthropological philosophy or theology (where man is the measure of God) — points to both the power and the limits of cultural determinism, to culture's own conditioning by the transcendental realm, which is no small matter given the significance that cultural determinism assumes within traditional feminist arguments.[4] This means that authentic self-realization should be understood vertically as well as horizontally, an understanding which requires a certain balance between nature and culture (nurture) on the one hand and nature and grace on the other. Indeed, if even on a natural level human nature requires "guidance" — social stimulation, direction, and influence — all the more reason that our divine calling should require grace for its realization. Instead of flattening the transcendental dimension in an effort to preserve human freedom, a new feminism thus proposes an elevation of freedom itself. Contrary to an understanding of freedom as autonomy in promotion of individualism, ours is therefore a presentation of freedom as enabling us to break out of the confines of sin alienating us from other persons, human and divine.

From this perspective the cultural effect of patriarchy is more than "matched" by the communal effects of grace and redemption, and the relational meaning of nature — what Elshtain refers to as "sociality," as opposed to "socialization"[5] — is itself raised to a new level. Proposed for the new feminism is thus

2. Vatican Council II, Pastoral Constitution on the Church, *Gaudium et spes*, #10.

3. See, for example, *Evangelium vitae*, #99, and his Angelus reflection of July 23, 1995. Both excerpts and other interesting insights on the same may be found in John Paul II, *The Genius of Women* (Washington, D.C.: United States Conference of Catholic Bishops, 1997).

4. On this, see my contribution to this volume: "The Nature of Nature in Feminism, Old and New."

5. "Socialization" is, she explains, "learning to conform to the ways of one's group or society," including, for example, women's conformity to the expectations set for them by patriarchy. "Sociality," on the other hand, means "that human beings are social creatures from birth" ("'Thank Heaven for Little Girls': The Dialectics of Development," in Elshtain, *The Family in Political Thought* [Brighton, Sussex: Harvester Press, 1982], pp. 288-351, cited at p. 289).

a reformulation of the important axiom that expresses the false dichotomy of the nature-nurture debate at the heart of "traditional" (mainstream) feminism: the individual forms the community, and the community forms the individual. Replacing the hero of modernity — the "self-made" man — is, within the context of this new feminism, the hero and heroine of a new civilization: the man and woman realized and given in communion with other persons, human and divine. In this way the "consciousness-raising" of traditional feminism, whereby the "sin" of patriarchy is overcome by the rightful refusal to play by its rules, is matched by the consciousness of oneself not only *as relational* — that which is characteristic of at least one major strain of traditional feminism[6] — but also *as loved:* loved with an eternal love in virtue of which the human person not only exists, but exists as one enabled to love, as one endowed with the capacity to discover and realize himself or herself "through a sincere gift of self."[7]

This important phrase of the Second Vatican Council, which Pope John Paul II maintains "sum[s] up *the whole of Christian anthropology,*"[8] is also *at the heart of the new feminism* presented here. As such, this new feminism might join traditional feminism in its option for an experiential, and thus a relational, perspective, as I will demonstrate (see Schumacher's essay on experience in this volume, pp. 169-200). The experience it is based on, however, is love: human love, of course, but also and most profoundly divine love, whereby the failures of human love, from which we all suffer both as victims and as perpetrators, are redeemed. It is the experience of a relation with the living God who is Love and who loves the human person, each and every human person, into being by creation and into action by the liberating power of redemption and the call to mission. This "divinely stimulated" action might, in turn, be conceived as a participation in the *communication of love* whose goal is — for the self and the beloved "other" — a participation in the *communion of Love* (divine life).

The authentically liberated woman is, therefore, one who experiences herself as eternally loved and forgiven, and thus as authentically free. "Self-possessed" in this sense, she is really capable of giving herself to God and to other human persons; for one cannot truly give what is not in one's possession, what is not one's own, even where the possession is one's identity itself. To the extent, more specifically, that she gives herself to God, she is capable of loving

6. On this, see Karen Offen, "Defining Feminism: A Comparative Historical Approach," *Signs: A Journal of Women in Culture and Socity* 14, no. 1 (1988): 119-57. See especially p. 136. See also Alice Jardin, "Prelude: The Future of Difference," in *The Future of Difference,* ed. Hester Eisenstein and Alice Jardine (Boston: G. K. Hall, 1980), pp. xxv-xxvii.

7. Vatican Council II, *Gaudium et spes,* #22.

8. John Paul II, encyclical letter "On the Holy Spirit in the Life of the Church and the World," *Dominum et vivificatem* (May 30, 1986), #59; emphasis John Paul's.

her neighbor without necessarily seeking her own good thereby. Ironically, it is in fact by giving of herself without seeking in return that she actually fulfills herself in accord with God's own manner of being and acting. Far from constraining women to an "eternal essence," the dynamic Christian anthropology proceeding from this vision and proposed in this volume insists upon the right and the responsibility of each woman to realize herself in perfect Christian freedom.

An Integrating Task

Implied in this vision of the new feminism is thus the mutual enrichment of theology, philosophy, and the social sciences, which is not to acknowledge a certain "authority of secular perspectives" in contact with Christian orthodoxy, as Elaine Graham puts it,[9] but rather to regard the natural realm as revelatory of the divine, for it is illuminated and permeated by the divine "order" of grace, where this is understood in its etymological sense of *gift*.

To admit to this is not to grant that the philosopher and social scientist are fundamentally theologians. It is, however, to suggest that all academic sciences might — indeed should — be conducted with what John Paul II refers to as *"a contemplative outlook"*: "It is the outlook of those who see life in its deeper meaning, who grasp its utter gratuitousness, its beauty and its invitation to freedom and responsibility. It is the outlook of those who do not presume to take possession of reality but instead accept it as a gift, discovering in all things the reflection of the Creator and seeing in every person his living image (cf. Gen 1:27; Ps 8:5)."[10] By contemplating women within, more specifically, the mystery of Christ who "reveals man [that is to say, man and woman] to himself [or herself],"[11] we seek to

9. See Elaine Graham, *Making the Difference: Gender, Personhood, and Technology* (New York: Mowbray, 1995), p. 5. She notes as "a perennial dilemma" the question of the extent to which "the changes around us (ought) to be absorbed into the life of the church as evidence of God at work in the world; or has [she asks] Scripture and the accumulated teaching of tradition provided sufficient authority to guide the affairs of the Christian community in matters of human relationships?"

10. John Paul II, *Evangelium vitae*, #83. In this it is directly opposed to what Francis Martin refers to as characteristic of feminist foundationalism: "the conviction, influenced by Kantianism, that any act of knowledge in which the subject is receptive is a diminishment of the subject." This, he explains, "derives from the Enlightenment identification of causality with domination" (Francis Martin, *The Feminist Question: Feminist Theology in the Light of Christian Tradition* [Grand Rapids: Eerdmans, 1994], p. 165).

11. Vatican Council II, *Gaudium et spes*, #22. The explicit role of this contemplation may, of course, be conceived differently for philosophers than for theologians, although both may be equally inspired by faith.

direct the cultural vision of women beyond the male standard against which they have historically — according to the feminist critique of patriarchy — too often been measured. It is Christ, this new feminism teaches, who reveals *woman* to herself by inviting her to participate in his own mission of revealing the Father and his love. In the encounter with the beloved Bridegroom of the church — in union, that is to say, with Christ, who is both her principle and her end — woman (each and every woman) discovers her true identity: the true meaning of her humanity and of her femininity.

In light of the foregoing, the task of developing a theoretical foundation for a new feminism is manifest primarily as integrating or harmonizing — without denying or "alleviating" — the various tensions, relations, or irreducible differences that characterize human existence as such: the relations, first of all, *within the person himself or herself,* especially that between his or her body and soul (see Vollmer Coles), or — more recently in philosophical thinking — between bodily "matter" and subjectivity (see Gerl-Falkovitz). From here there also arises the relation, on the one hand, between the physical and the spiritual, or the sign value of the human body as a "sacrament" of the person (see Schumacher on the body and Elshtain, who treats this in passing), and on the other hand between the human, the sexual, and the personal dimensions of his or her being and vocation (see von Streng). Secondly, it concerns the relation *between the individual and the community,* including the more fundamental relation — which is the proper relation of our investigation but remains inseparable from the others — between man and woman (see especially the two contributions of Allen) and thus also between difference and equality (see Elshtain and Fox-Genovese). This sphere of relation also includes the important correlation between personal dignity and social — including familial — responsibilities, between anthropology and ethics (see Léna; Elshtain) and thus also between theory and practice (see Fox-Genovese). In the properly theological realm, it includes the relation between the personal and communal dimensions of the church (see Pelletier and Schumacher on experience). Implied in this individual-communal relation is also the "tension" between nature and culture and, even more fundamentally, between nature and grace (see Schumacher on nature) which is itself a form of the relation between the human person and God,[12] who is "himself" a communion of "complementary" and irreducible persons. Hence also the question of the relation among the three states of human existence: the state of innocence, the fallen state, and the state of redemption, foreshadowing the state of glory (see Martin).

---

12. Grace is here understood as a participation in divine (and thus triune) life.

All these important relations characterizing human life are, for the Christian, integrated within the larger and all-encompassing relation of the human person to the triune God by actually participating in his life. It is, as Jean Mouroux expresses, "the supremely unifying relationship in human life, that which tends more than anything else to realize the living vocation for which the human person is made, from the beginning to the end of his life — in short, as the relationship that inaugurates the highest form of communion with Being and all lesser beings."[13]

Notes for the Reader

Several things stand out as significant in directing the reader of this volume. To begin, it seems important to comment on our understanding of the word "gender." Initially I had objected to the obviously metaphysical content assigned by many of the authors to the word. This seemed, I reasoned, to somehow contest the apparently valid intention of traditional feminists to identify that which may be attributed to social and cultural, rather than natural, influences in the differences between the sexes and in one's own sexual identity. Certainly, my reasoning continued, it could not be denied that culture and education — what is commonly rendered "nurture" — really do have a more or less determinant influence upon sexual distinctions. What I failed to recognize, however, is that it is relatively impossible to draw a line between what, in sexual differences, is attributable to nature and what to education and culture. To categorically set certain aspects of human nature outside the influence of nature is, it now seems to me, objectionable at best. It ironically betrays an almost mechanistic conception of the human person, or one that would make of this being a Frankenstein: a "monster" created by the human person but now beyond his or her range of power or control. It is thus best to admit a certain caution in approaching the term so as not to read too much nor too little into any author's use thereof.

Second — and this point lies in continuity with the previous one — it seems important to acknowledge that although a certain critical distance is often assumed by the various contributors vis-à-vis traditional feminism, many, if not most, have honestly sought to engage feminist arguments and to grant a sympathetic hearing whenever possible. This willingness to meet the "other" on "her" own terms is, it seems to me, critical to the success of both the new

---

13. Jean Mouroux, *The Christian Experience: An Introduction to a Theology,* trans. George Lamb (New York: Sheed and Ward, 1954), pp. 8-9.

evangelization and the new feminism, if it is worthy of the name.[14] Also note-worthy (as my third point) is the fact that despite the editorial distinction — in the organization of the texts — between philosophical anthropology and theo-logical anthropology, the authors have themselves achieved a marvelous inte-gration of the two, as is typical of their properly Catholic approach. For the same reason, the various contributions are highly complementary of one an-other, although each may be read independently of the others. Fourth, it seems important to admit that while the general aim of the new feminism is above all practical — and this, I insist, need not be understood as opposed to or even as differing (i.e., by necessity) from the spiritual — our aim is primarily *theoreti-cal:* the laying of a solid foundation from which there may proceed an intelli-gent and faith-filled praxis. It follows that the final section, dedicated to the ethical and practical consequences of the anthropology developed in the prior sections, is *itself* of a theoretical nature. Great is the challenge of developing a new feminist ethic, of discerning the proper integration of the public and the private-domestic spheres of women's action, of distinguishing and integrating maternity and paternity (both physical and spiritual), of discerning the minis-terial roles of women in the church and society and of educating girls and women toward this end, to name but a few of the areas implicated. These more practical concerns — which are, admittedly, the proper end of a new feminism — are, however, best discerned in a properly contemplative fashion, which is to say that priority is awarded to receptivity over activity and that one does well, in accord with the popular maxim, to think — and, I might add, to pray — before one acts.

14. On the unity of the two, see Joyce A. Little, "The New Evangelization and Gender: The Remystification of the Body," *Communio* 21 (Winter 1994): 776-99.

PART I

PHILOSOPHICAL ANTHROPOLOGY

Gender Difference: Critical Questions concerning Gender Studies

Hanna-Barbara Gerl-Falkovitz   Translated by Grant Kaplan

With the arrival of the new millennium, the question no longer concerns the dualism between mind and nature, of the mind's own corporality and whether it is conditioned by the body (Körper). Instead this matter has been resolved and the body (Körper) itself has now become a focus of concern. The postmodern dissolution of the boundary between interior and exterior, organic and inorganic, masculine and feminine, mind and matter, culminates in the loss of the distinction between bodily representation and bodily reality. The desire for the fragmentary and the heterogeneous has shed the straitjacket imposed by modernity but also opened the door to a nihilistic disintegration. Human bodies (Körper) function as mere objects of art . . . , they form living sculptures, fluctuating loci of action, or they are simply "undifferentiated matter." As a cultural artifact, the body loses its rigidity and stability. The notion of a social construct is taken literally and arises with the attempt to make one's own existence no longer dependent on the previous contingency of the body to which it belongs, but instead to self-consciously reform itself and to re-engineer itself at will.[1]

How do we arrive at such a claim?

1. Heike Christina Ludwig, "Der Körper — eine Insel im Reich des Möglichen? Leiblichkeit in philosophischen Positionen des 20. Jahrhunderts" (master's thesis, Dresden Technische Universität, 2000), pp. 56ff. Certain claims in my essay owe their origin to this work.

The Integral Compatibility of the Body,[2] Soul, and Mind: Edith Stein's Phenomenology

The question about the "essence of the woman" has been taboo at least since Simone de Beauvoir.[3] The "woman" becomes a woman because she is "made" to be so. Therefore clever definitions like Gertrude von le Fort's typical formulation for the thirties — that the essence of the woman is surrender [*Hingabe*] — have been deemed nonsense.[4] Most scholarship concerning gender does not ask "What is a woman?" but "How does one become a woman?" From such a standpoint, ontological expressions or phenomenological analyses of essence appear to be excluded or relegated to normative futility.

The student of Husserl and temporary women's rights advocate, Edith Stein (1891-1942) sought in the 1920s and 1930s to approach the question of woman from a phenomenological standpoint. More specifically, she sought to examine in her own life the "phenomena" of female corporality and to use these phenomena as analytic points of departure for expressions of essence. Stein's statements are more expansive than can be articulated in this essay.[5] This said, her formulation, a valuable alternative to the present debate about gender, is oriented quite clearly toward a natural basis, namely, the corporality of the body.

Stein applies as a principle the old scholastic maxim *anima forma corporis* — the soul is the form of the body. Of course, the correlate of this statement means that the body is the bearer and expression of something interior. In order to determine at least to some extent how women differ from men, the observation of the body serves as a principle of the female soul and mind. Naturally Stein does not define the woman only in terms of what makes her different from a man.[6] Rather she repeatedly attempts to clarify an "essential" distinction

2. Translator's note: Both *Leib* and *Körper* mean body in German. For this essay, *Leib* is always translated as "body" and *Körper* as both "matter" when possible and "body" more often than not. In the latter case, the German will follow in parentheses.

3. Simone de Beauvoir, *Le deuxième sexe* (Paris: Gallimard, 1949); ET, *The Second Sex*, trans. and ed. M. Parshley (New York: Vintage, 1989).

4. Gertrud von le Fort, *The Eternal Woman*, trans. Placid Jordan (Milwaukee: Bruce, 1962).

5. See Sophie Binggeli, introduction to *Die Frau. Fragestellung und Reflexionen*, by Edith Stein, ed. Maria Amata Neyer (Freiburg: Herder, 2000), p. 13.

6. Prescinding from the theologically foundational personality of both sexes, the *common call* of the commission in Genesis is decisive for both the man and the woman. The redemption of man and woman is likewise bound together. See Hanna-Barbara Gerl, *Unerbitterliches Licht. Edith Stein. Philosophie — Mystik — Leben* (Mainz: Mathias Grünewald Verlag, 1998), pp. 55-64.

of the sexes through their bodily difference. From such an analysis she seeks to locate more precisely the unique dignity *(Selbstwürdigung)* of the woman.

Stein begins with the fundamental and natural features of *corporality* which most clearly define a woman: readiness to receive (also to be understood as partnership with man) and motherhood (in relation to children) as capacities conditioned by the body of the feminine *species*. Both qualities lead to statements about a soul-like "inside."

> The primary calling of the woman is the procreation and raising of children; for this, the man is given to her as protector. . . . With the woman there are capabilities of caring, protecting, and promoting that which is becoming and growing. She has the gift thereby to live in an intimately bound physical compass and to collect her forces in silence; on the other hand, she is created to endure pain, to adapt and abnegate herself. Psychically she is directed to the concrete, the individual, and the personal: she has the ability to grasp the concrete in its individuality and to adapt herself to it, and she has the longing to help this peculiarity to its development.[7]

Stein articulated these points in an interview: "I emphasize motherhood to define the form of the female psyche. While the female psyche is not bound to corporeal motherhood, we cannot lose this model of motherhood, regardless of where we stand. The malady of our time is the relinquishing of this motherhood."[8] Corporeal guidelines decisively form the psychological as well as the spiritual realms. In the *psychological* this formation results essentially in a specific "empathy" — the faculty of a relationship with a man. This faculty extends to the artistic and scientific realm, in the empathy for the weak as for the strong. In this, women manifest a lofty and diverse availability, a support for fostering life other than one's own, a protection of the human in humanity-threatening areas like technology. The fundamental strength of the woman lies in the faculty for such "emotion." This emotion is aroused by everything human, especially in relation to the beautiful as well as the true. The woman's strength lies in these emotions, "where this world experiences the mysterious force and pull of another world."[9] Stein asserts that such a situation explains the spontaneous female awe toward everything great or consid-

---

7. Edith Stein, *Essays on Women,* vol. 2 of *The Collected Works of Edith Stein,* trans. Freda Mary Oben, 2nd rev. ed. (Washington, D.C.: ICS Publications, 1996), pp. 100-101.

8. Edith Stein, "Diskussion zum Vortrag 'Grundlagen der Frauenbildung,'" in *Die Frau,* p. 245. (Trans. — this discussion is not translated in the English edition.)

9. Stein, *Essays on Women,* p. 102. Parenthetical page numbers in the following text are to this work.

ered great — an awe that must be tempered by a responsible feminine formation (p. 97).

Such conclusions result in some dubious claims to be regarded as conditioned by their time. In addition, Stein's claims indicate that a single (corporeal) principle, namely, motherhood, should not be applied too liberally. Stein
claimed in 1932: "Epoch-making achievements by women are relatively scarce,
and this may be explained in terms of woman's nature. Yet, the feminine gifts of
empathy and adjustment enable her to participate, understand, and stimulate;
she does so outstandingly as an assistant, an interpreter, or a teacher" (p. 115).
Derived exclusively from the corporality of the woman, a similarly disquieting
result runs as follows:

> The body of the woman is fashioned "to be one flesh" with another and to
> nurse new human life in itself. A well-disciplined body is an accommodat-
> ing instrument for the mind which animates it; at the same time, it is a
> source of power and a place of dwelling for the mind. Just so, woman's soul
> is designed to be subordinate to man in obedience and support; it is also
> fashioned to be a shelter in which other souls may unfold. Both spiritual
> companionship and spiritual motherliness are not limited to the physical
> spouse and mother relationships, but they extend to all people with whom
> woman comes into contact. (p. 132)

Stein engages here in the type of narrow thinking that she seeks to critique in other writings. Biological capacities are confused with historical developments (*gender* in today's lingo) and taken as a norm. An analysis of phenomena does not de facto prevent this confusion.

The attempt to locate the specifically feminine form of the mind *(Geist)*
becomes noticeably difficult. For Stein the primary importance of the female
mind consists in "a longing to give love and receive love, and in this respect a
yearning to be elevated from narrow, day-to-day existence into the realm of a
higher being" (p. 93). The border between active and passive in the female intel-
lectuality consists just as much in its own growth as in "stimulating and furthering the desire for perfection in others; this yearning can emerge in the most
diverse forms and some of these forms may appear distorted, even degenerate.
Such yearning is an essential aspect of the eternal destiny of women" (p. 94).

These speculations by Stein seem too general, or one could even say too
abstract. This stems from the fact that her claims demand further anthropological and psychological research, and Stein never had a thorough command of
these fields. It helps to remember that her own discipline of phenomenology
had difficulty actually distinguishing man and woman on the basis of "essential" mental characteristics. What appears obvious in corporality becomes less

easily deduced in the conception of the soul, and appears forced in the defining of the mind.

Almost in spite of herself, Stein broadened the parameters of phenomenological characterization whenever she analyzed the *history* of women or developed wide-ranging approaches to women's education. The education of women involves the transition from education by others to self-formation. As a rule Stein emphasizes the plurality of these general guidelines, which are perhaps too general. Before every person lies the particular task of developing what has been given to her in her own unique way. Further, such a task requires great skill, and the possibility of failure always looms. Stein articulates the particularity of women most clearly when she places the female essence within human (personal, free, self-identical) essence. She remarks concerning Ibsen's Nora, "She knows that before she is able to try again to be a wife and a mother, she must first become a person" (p. 91). She also writes, "Indeed, no woman is only *woman*" (p. 49). From a *historical* perspective she observes that the realization of personhood in Europe occurred through the education of women by women, embodied in such visionary, religiously motivated school founders as Mary Ward and Angela Merici. Stein also sees such a realization in the efforts of the modern liberal women's movement since the nineteenth century. Even so, corporality — that the soul is embodied — remains essential:

> That the human soul is within a material body . . . is not inconsequential. The body [*Lieb*] is characterized as such, and it is distinguished from the pure material body [*Körper*] that also co-constitutes it. All of the body's conditions and everything that happens to it is sensed or can be sensed. Everything corporeal has an interior element. Where the body is, there is also an inner life. It is not only a *material body* (Körper) *that feels*, but belongs essentially as a body to a subject who thereby (i.e. through the body) senses, whose exterior form is thereby represented, who is thereby posited in the exterior world, who is thereby able to be creatively engaged, who thereby grasps his own condition.[10]

The "female eunuch" is not yet in view.[11]

---

10. Stein, "Die ontische Struktur der Person und ihre erkenntnistheoretische Problematik," in *Welt und Person,* Edith Stein Werke, vol. 6 (Louvain: Herder, 1962), p. 172. This fascinating essay will be published in the forthcoming critical edition in the collected works under its proper title, "Natur, Freiheit, Gnade." The essay further thematizes the possibility of a far-reaching bodily freedom on the basis of an interior psychological development.

11. Germaine Greer, *The Female Eunuch* (New York: McGraw-Hill, 1971).

Bodiless Philosophy — Lifeless Philosophy? Thought in the Wake of Reduced Anthropology

In the following section we will examine whether the current female self-definition remains virtual. Certain elements of the contemporary discussion reveal a deficient understanding of the body, and this understanding has been prevalent for some time. Beauvoir's "classic" definition has been reinterpreted by Regula Giuliani as the transitional body: "The body has become . . . an inert object imprisoned by material, a mere instrument and tool that serves to realize mental desires more (with a male body) or less (with a female body) adequately."[12] The purpose of being human is an individual one, described as "the way from me to myself." It is established independently of the body and of sex, and employs a new form of essentialism.

Such a disengagement from the body takes place not only in the male-dominated history of philosophy, but also within contemporary deconstructionism and the philosophical feminism that employs the postmodern framework. The marginal role given the body indicates that philosophy has never placed much importance on the theme of the body and sex. The omission, reduction, and minimalization of the body, all hallmarks of Descartes's philosophy, bear traces in the present era as well. This modern reductionism introduces a quantification and mechanization of the world, and at the same time leads to a geometrization of the person.[13] Freud on the other hand diagnoses as a "sickness" the affirmative modern consciousness that is distanced from the body. Consciousness is infiltrated by a subconscious drive and impulsive action that stems from the body. One can detect an unresolved tension in the Freudian theory, for it does not stress the integration of a natural desire, but instead understands this cultural repression as necessary for society. For Freud the body and mind remain in cultural tension. With the help of the "great reason of the body," Nietzsche's transvaluation of all values also lays the groundwork for twentieth-century reflections.

The depreciation of the body through a residual ambivalence — is the body a stabilization or limitation of identity? — in no way demonstrates an esoteric, secondary matter of inquiry but instead leads to valuable and essential questions concerning the present constitution of subjectivity. Even if no present consensus can be formulated regarding the body as a foundation of iden-

---

12. Regula Giuliani, "Der übergangene Leib," *Phänomenologische Forschungen*, n.s., 2 (1997): 110.

13. See Hanna-Barbara Gerl-Falkovitz, *Einführung in die Philosophie der Renaissance* (Darmstadt: Wissenschaftliche Buchgesellschaft, 1995; reprint, Dresden, 2001).

tity, there is no doubt a new "somatism" to combat a total negligence of the body. This new somatism fluctuates between a "self-definition" unable to distinguish between the person and the body, and a virtual reformation and even disintegration of the body in cyberspace.

The distinction between body and matter can serve as a linguistic demonstration for the problem at hand. The literature prefers for the most part "matter" to an already "animated" body. Such a preference places an accent on matter as a quantitative mechanism, as a *res extensa*. However, some phenomenological efforts articulate the experience of having a body as an integral principle for subjectivity. French phenomenology acknowledges the body as an indispensable constituent of human existence. Certainly Sartre does not overcome the antagonism between the body *(Körper)* "for myself" and the body *(Körper)* "for others." The internal and external (mediated by society) experience of the body are two different matters for Sartre. The phenomenal, matter-of-fact unity of the body is theoretically undone.[14] On the other hand Merleau-Ponty defines matter as a transcendental "being to the world" in contrast to Cartesianism that thinks of matter as prior to all thought.[15] In some analyses this "being to the world" is relegated by double reduction to mere consciousness or mechanistic reflex. The existential analysis demonstrates much more the original intentionality of the body. It is always oriented to the world and to the individual, and both the world and the body experience this orientation before all reflection. But the body maintains an indivisible tension through its outer-directedness and interiority, which cannot be reduced to a monism of mere corporality.

The two German terms *Leib* (body) and *Körper* (matter) refer to a fundamentally different perception of the individual. There is no doubt that the intersubjective "construction" of the body pushes it to the interface between nature and culture, while the constructivist reflections attempt to eliminate the raw naturality of the body. At any rate, there remain two possibilities in need of a methodological investigation: first, the phenomenological perception of the body; second, the situation in which the body *(Körper)*, becoming distant to the individual, is seen as socially conditioned, a status that leads to radical postmodern virtuality.

14. Jean-Paul Sartre, *Being and Nothingness*, trans. Hazel Barnes (New York: Washington Square Press, 1984). See esp. chap. 3, pt. 2: "The Body," pp. 401-70.

15. Maurice Merleau-Ponty, *The Structure of Behavior*, trans. Alden Fischer (Boston: Beacon Press, 1963).

HANNA-BARBARA GERL-FALKOVITZ

Gender Research and the Distancing from and Deconstruction of the Body

An exemplary illustration of the second thesis emerges in the current volatile combination of postmodernism, deconstructionism, and philosophical feminism. Lyotard identifies the postmodern as the consent of the heterogeneous subjectivity and cultivation of difference in reflection. Feminist thought does not always coincide with postmodernism, as in the dispute about what "otherness" means. However, both camps oppose the ideas of absolute and transcendental reason. While quasi-neutral, such notions of reason suppose a latently masculine overcoming of the world by transcending the empirical. Feminism incorporates the deconstructionism formulated by Derrida, which abolishes "essentialist" categories such as sex.

For the first time feminist deconstructionism in the nineties purported that sex is not given, but constructed as well. Such a claim initiated the debate about whether the assumed difference between men and women is socially conditioned. Sex as a biological component was reduced to "gender," a culturally conditioned reality, and exposed as a social need, thus making it available for deconstruction. The Berkeley professor of rhetoric Judith Butler is one of the leading exponents of this position.[16] She believes to have discovered a contradiction in earlier feminist claims: on the one hand, sex results from social circumstances and is therefore conditioned; on the other, sex is biologically determined and thus not conditioned. Butler resolves the contradiction by asserting that the "natural" body *(Körper)* as such does not exist "before" the language and meaning of cultures. Language cultivates different bodily sex differences. One can arrive at the radical conclusion that the difference between sex and gender is a question of interpretation. Stated simply, even biology is a matter of culture. In order to liberate oneself as a women, one can subjectively "engineer" one's open-ended sex.

Jane Flax articulates this point: "Postmodernists wish to destroy all essentialist conceptions of human being or nature. . . . In fact man is a social, historical, or linguistic artifact, not a noumenal or transcendental Being. . . . Man is forever caught in the web of fictive meaning, in chains of signification, in which the subject is merely another position in language."[17] Feminists are thus the first to claim that biological principles are not ultimate and replace

16. Judith Butler, *Gender Trouble: Feminism and the Subversion of Identity* (New York: Routledge, 1990).

17. Jane Flax, *Thinking Fragments: Psychoanalysis, Feminism, and Postmodernism in the Contemporary West* (Berkeley: University of California Press, 1990), pp. 32ff.

these principles with gender roles. Ontology, which had always served as the basis for an anthropology of the sexes, is viewed as merely a construct of hidden, phallo-centric power.[18]

The explosive result of such concepts is considerable. For example, the visual arts readily apply open-ended notions of the body *(Körper)* or of "fluid identity." A hypothetical collection of works by young Swiss artists employs these seemingly theoretical ideas and serves to demonstrate the waves of this resonance.[19] The exhibition spoke against the "irritating game of gender categories and sexual disposition." It declared further, "In order to be defined, the body is produced, and thus transcends the boundary of the artificial."[20]

In a similar vein the novelist Barbara Vinken perceives fashion as an arena of caricature and transvestism. "Fashion mocks and parodies gender roles. It thwarts or appropriates the purpose of gender roles."[21] The fundamental theme of this process is "construction," and the male sex also gets caught up in the same freedom and coercion of construction. Only through anticharacteristics does one arrive at the stereotypes of masculinity. One only abides in these stereotypes through revulsion from the shock of "the ideal of androgynous corporality seen in the techno, pop and cyber culture, as well as in deconstructive gender theory."[22] At this point one is not far from the theory of a third sex that first arose in 1900.[23]

This "new femininity" no longer defines itself in distinction from masculinity but instead underlies the opposition between masculine and feminine. Concretely, an employment of *all* sexual possibilities, especially lesbianism, can liberate one from previous gender constructions. The true foundation of sex hierarchy is the "forced heterosexuality" which now can be exposed as nothing but a ploy for power (Monique Wittig). Whether physiological or psychological, transvestism and sex change are now not only conceivable but desirable.

18. See Seyla Benhabib, Judith Butler, Drucilla Cornell, and Nancy Frazer, eds., *Feminist Contentions: A Philosophical Exchange* (New York: Routledge, 1995).

19. Gallery Glarus, Switzerland, 1996.

20. Carole Gürtler, "Pickel, Narben, Spitzendeckchen," *Basel Zeitung,* October 14, 1996, p. 34.

21. Kathrin Hönig, "Frau als Mann als Frau," *Neue Zürcher Zeitung* 132 (June 11, 1997): 32.

22. Christina von Braun, "Der Stroh-Mann. Zur Konstruktion moderner Männlichkeit," review of *Das Bild des Mannes. Zur Konstruktion der modernen Männlichkeit,* by George L. Mosse, *Neue Zürcher Zeitung* 129 (June 7, 1997): 53.

23. This term is understood in different ways: first as homosexuality, as in the work of Magnus Hirschfeld. Second as the desexualized leveling of sex through the increasingly technologized world of employment, as in Seigfried Kracauer in 1927 or through the National Socialist de-eroticism seen in Ernst Jünger's "The Worker." See Franziska Meier, "Das dritte Geschlecht. Ein 'merkwürdiger Gedanke,'" *Neue Zürcher Zeitung* 129 (June 7, 1997): 53.

Sex life becomes fabricated and the individual adorns a particular gender mask, but "in fact this mask does not hide any individual."[24]

The easily parodied themes have been present in literature for many years. One such example is Virginia Woolf's 1928 *Orlando*. In it a narcissistic young nobleman sails through numerous affairs over four centuries. In the course of his affairs he transforms into a woman. This fictional portrayal about the indeterminacy of sex contains certain neurotic elements. Yet if one judges by the success of the play, this theme of hermaphroditism still resonates with audiences.[25]

Postmodern feminists seek to replace the notion of body *(Körper)* through the concept of the "cyborg" or cyberorganism in a manner no less exotic than the theme of fluid identity treated above.[26] The American feminist Donna Haraway proposes a new model of thought

> in which the concepts of body *(Körper)* and individuality are subject to a new terminology. In this new realm one takes as a starting point a continual *process* in which streams of information and codes intersect continually and form new ephemeral meanings. Body *(Körper)* and soul no longer conceived as ontologically-based entities. Traditionally viewed as the material aspect of the human being, the body *(Körper)* paradoxically creates a semiotic materiality that is neither a biological given nor a purely cultural creation. . . . The "object" always emerges in a specific language, practice and historical context.[27]

When biology no longer describes identical bodies *(Körper)*, but instead becomes a discourse *on* the body *(Körper)*, one can no longer speak of a given identity of this body *(Körper)*. Under such a rubric the problem of organ transplants is approached anew. Haraway calls every organism a "cyborg" that needs a foreign organ to survive. By cyborg she implies an organism no longer identi-

---

24. Seyla Benhabib, "Feminism and Postmodernism: An Uneasy Alliance," in *Feminist Contentions*, p. 22.

25. For example, Gina Thomas's commentary on the 1996 performance at the Edinburgh Festival: "The actress [Miranda Richardson] employs her body like it were made of rubber and engages in astonishing vocal acrobatics. She accomplishes the transformation from a precocious young boy into a capricious woman in different levels, like a cocoon that becomes a butterfly. Her hair is transformed from a normal cut for a man into an ambiguity. One side the audience sees soft curls hanging down, while on the other side the haircut remains short" (in *Frankfurter Allgemeine Zeitung*, September 3, 1996, p. 36).

26. Donna Haraway, *Woman, Simian, and Cyborgs: The Reinvention of Nature* (London, 1991).

27. Lieke van der Scheer, "The *Human Body?* in the Work of Donna Haraway" (presentation at the Robert-Bosch Society, Stuttgart, May 4-6, 1995), pp. 4ff.

cal with itself. After the transplant such a cyborg has a partial identity in common with the donor. The relationship between donor and recipient creates a fluid identity between the two. Such a symbiotic relationship can also occur between a cyborg and a machine, as in dialysis. According to Haraway, doctors should no longer make decisions about transplants based on traditional medical criteria, for such criteria presume a definite concept of the body. Instead they should decide according to a partiality between the recipient and the giver. For example, an anencephalis enters into relation with an organ recipient and is "accepted" by the recipient.

As seen above, a variety of artificial claims has been purported so as to incite the dissolution and re-creation of the body *(Körper)* as a continually manufactured identity. This identity rescinds the presumed rigidity of the understanding of the body *(Körper)* as well as its previous differentiation from a machine. Such a process happens fictively in the virtual world and actually through operation. The vision of the human being as his own software — complete with the obligation to be continually transformed — indicates the neglect, if not the destruction, of a comprehensive notion of the body as it is philosophically presented by Edith Stein.

Conclusion

The outbreak of interdisciplinary material regarding the anthropology of gender in the last twenty years brought about a plethora of radical innovations (or at least calls for innovation) that was not necessarily well measured. One cannot rashly summarize such material and decide it is either "progressive" or not worthwhile. Instead one can view it in the context of the development of the notion of the body *(Körper)* from antiquity through modernity. When one views the problem from such an angle, one sees the inherited yet still significant shortcomings and deficiencies of the entire phenomenon, beginning with Descartes, that understood the body *(Körper)* no longer as *my* body, as an appearance of *my* subjectivity. Philosophers too often gloss over the paradigm shift between such an understanding and the Christian understanding based on the incarnation.[28] In this we might discover a connection, although possibly *e contrario,* to Nietzsche and even to phenomenology (more specifically to Edith Stein or Gabriel Marcel). One must also newly consider other, nonmechanistic conceptions of the body (not every mind-body dualism must be *eo ipso* hostile to the body). The

---

28. A medieval example of the Christian understanding of the body can be seen in the "body-friendly" thought of Hildegard von Bingen.

previous focus on the mechanical concept of the body proposes only *one* (selective) philosophically and historically determined development resulting in the self-production of the body *(Körper)* seen today. This one-sided historical development demonstrates, in any case, that the strange and even destructive claims made today result from a certain trajectory, and such a trajectory is not immune to a critical examination and reflection. A critical and analytic approach to these authors and the above-cited texts opens the possibility of developing a substantial critique that is not imported from but rather immanent to feminist arguments. Exemplary are the theories of the body by Simone de Beauvoir, Judith Butler, and Donna Haraway. By carefully following their premises, one arrives at subliminal contradictions. All three authors purport (perhaps unwillingly, but in any case an unspoken) denigration of the (female) body, be it in Beauvoir's instrumentalization, Butler's divorce from actuality (deontologization), or Haraway's denaturalization in her technologized cyborg.[29]

An engagement with gender theory requires a familiarity with arguments from ancient to modern European philosophy. It requires a heightened attentiveness to problems and the ability to follow this complex theme carefully through its different variations without losing sight of or simplifying the central argument. One can neither dismiss nor uncritically harmonize the claims made by such phenomenologists as Stein. For one must observe that even within the feminist discussion not everyone shares the belief in a merely constructed corporality. For instance, Lyndal Roper develops the thesis that the body (whether male or female) is not socially or discursively constructed, but instead determined through physical characteristics.[30]

Once one interprets reality as mere role playing — regardless of whether it is deconstructed or newly constructed — both identity and the valid expression of this identity become lost. And if the body is merely a semiotic system of variable meanings, then one must undertake an investigation based on its actions to determine in what language game "the body" *(Körper)* belongs. Even transitory characteristics need a transporter. Compared to the variable "role playing" and the dissolution of the subject in a "product of male enlightenment," Stein's concept of the person can be considered once again. This concept first arose in the sixth century in Boethius's definition inspired by Christianity. He managed to investigate the difference between the sexes without eliminating them through an exploration of their common personality.[31]

29. Ludwig, pp. 49-56.

30. Lyndal Roper, *Ödipus und der Teufel. Körper und Psyche in der Frühen Neuzeit* (Frankfurt am Main: Fischer, 1995).

31. See the investigation of the notion of the person in Robert Spaemann, *Personen. Versuche über den Unterschied zwischen 'etwas' und 'jemand'* (Stuttgart: Reclam, 1996).

One can counter the thesis concerning the physical or psychological transformation from one sex to another with the claim that — excluding cases of biological deformity or hermaphrodites — every person is a whole person, although possessing only one-half of the human sex. In one's sexual and additional differentiation, one does not experience a merely limited portion of human possibility, for these specific limitations afford us the perception of the whole of humanity.

In view of the notion that reality is "given," it is undoubtedly necessary to rethink personal subjectivity/identity/self-constitution. A given *(datum)* need not become a fact *(factum)* in order to be accepted. Such questions are not merely the focal point of philosophy, but of society as well. Therefore we need a critical, intellectual engagement as proposed above.

To repeat, "No woman is only a woman" — she is *also* a woman. For the current reflections we will not discuss the matrix of questions or the tensions that Stein outlined as fundamental, for the current debate is not familiar with this problematic. Stein sketched the base relation of corporality ("nature") to personal self-conception including the social classification ("culture"), and as a *superadditum* the relation of *Dasein's* origin and end. This account is sadly and unfairly ignored in most feminist discourse, for the matter of existence concerns the question of a creative "corollary" and the origin of existence. Stein defines the particularity of woman through biblical texts. She views the natural essence of the woman as subordinate to redeemed humanity, i.e., personal, free, and identical to itself. "Humanity is primary, femininity is secondary."[32] Stein is not so much concerned with gender-based subjectivity as with personal profile. The particular life tension which recognizes oneself and the other as distinctive and unalterable by God's will, and which even intentionally orders oneself as such, is — through the vitality of the individual created state — contained within the foundational model of creation. Stein developed a meaningful theory of human freedom that provides an alternative to the theory whereby one supposedly frees oneself from God. "One must be free so that one can be liberated."[33] Stein develops the relationship between Kantian autonomy and freedom. "We must begin with nature, given as male or female. . . . The closer one approximates Christ, the more man and woman become similar. As in St. Benedict's rule: the abbot is the father and the mother. Thus the domination that happens through gender is canceled by the Spirit."[34]

No doubt much of the contemporary discussion of gender would skepti-

---

32. Stein, "Diskussion zum Vortrag 'Grundlagen der Frauenbildung,'" p. 246.
33. Stein, *Die ontische Struktur der Person,* p. 139.
34. Stein, "Diskussion zum Vortrag 'Grundlagen der Frauenbildung,'" pp. 246, 248.

cally approach the foregoing, especially when physical traits are claimed to contribute to a normative essence and normative guidelines that are extrapolated therefrom *(ought* from *is)*. However, Stein modifies nature through historical and personal factors on the basis of her theological reflection: nature itself is not intact *(heil)*, but needs divine liberation, the supernatural salvation *(Heilung)* achieved in cooperation with one's own action. The dynamic between nature as the realm of the embodied spirit, of a personal formation, and the divine will contributes an important methodological and substantial alternative to the merely virtual self-definition of contemporary postmodernism.

The Nature of Nature in Feminism, Old and New: From Dualism to Complementary Unity

Michele M. Schumacher

> *Man's design is not to repeat himself in time: it is to take control of the instant and mold the future. It is male activity that in creating values has made of existence itself a value; this activity has prevailed over the confused forces of life; it has subdued Nature and Woman.*
>
> SIMONE DE BEAUVOIR[1]

As if commenting on Beauvoir's own observation, Jean Bethke Elshtain notes that the "nature-made women" is, dialectically speaking, "the perfect companion to the 'self-made man' whose tough, pragmatic, no-nonsense code is 'free choice,' 'no constraints,' and 'my life is my own.'"[2] Both authors point to what, in my estimation, is a central problematic addressed either directly or indirectly (i.e., as a reaction) by much — if not all — feminist literature: the *dualistic conception of nature* which is itself, many feminists claim, a product of the "divide-and-rule" mentality of Enlightenment thought and "androcentric logic."[3] Like women who are set off from the normative male as

1. Simone de Beauvoir, *The Second Sex*, trans. H. M. Parshley (New York: Vintage, 1989), p. 65.

2. Jean Bethke Elshtain, "'Thank Heaven for Little Girls': The Dialectics of Development," in *The Family in Political Thought,* ed. Elshtain (Brighton, Sussex: Harvest Press, 1982), p. 299.

3. See Ina Praetorius, "In Search of the Feminine Condition: A Plea for a Women's Ecumene," *Concilium* (1991/6): 3-10, cited at p. 3. For a critique of the feminist rejection of the

With much gratitude to my husband Bernard and to Fr. Francis Martin and Sr. Prudence Allen, R.S.M., for their excellent and very helpful commentaries.

"Other"[4] (and thus different), nature — the argument continues — is presented as unintelligent or subhuman creation opposed to that which is human; the uncultivated opposed to the cultured; the natural opposed to the artificial and technical; the biological opposed to the sociological; the controlled, manipulated, governed opposed to the controller, manipulator, governor; the body opposed to the mind; matter opposed to spirit.[5] From here the opposition proceeds further to mark the difference between the private or domestic and the public;[6] the immanent and the transcendent;[7] the nongraced or even sinful and the divinized or redeemed;[8] the inferior, and thus subordinated, and the superior with the upper hand.[9] In each case it is woman who is traditionally within

Enlightenment, see Elizabeth Fox-Genovese, *Feminism without Illusion: A Critique of Individualism* (Chapel Hill and London: University of North Carolina Press, 1991). On dualism and the Enlightenment, see Susan Hekman, "The Feminization of Epistemology: Gender and the Social Sciences," in *Feminism and Epistemology: Approaches to Research in Women and Politics*, ed. Maria J. Falco (New York and London: Haworth Press, 1987), pp. 65-83.

4. Perhaps the most classic argument among feminists on this is Beauvoir's: "She [woman] is defined and differentiated with reference to man and not he with reference to her; she is the incidental, the inessential as opposed to the essential. He is the Subject, he is the Absolute — she is the Other" (Beauvoir, p. xxii).

5. See, for example, Pamela Dickey Young, *Feminist Theology/Christian Theology: In Search of Method* (Minneapolis: Fortress, 1990), p. 66.

6. See Jean Bethke Elshtain, *Public Man, Private Woman: Women in Social and Political Thought* (Oxford: Martin Robertson; Princeton: Princeton University Press, 1981); Elshtain, "Aristotle, the Public-Private Split, and the Case of the Suffragists," in *The Family in Political Thought*, pp. 51-65; Joan B. Landes, ed., *Feminism, the Public and the Private*, Oxford Readings in Feminism (Oxford and New York: Oxford University Press, 1998); Rosemary Radford Ruether, "Home and Work: Women's Roles and the Transformation of Values," *Theological Studies* 36 (1975): 647-59; Virginia Held, *Feminist Morality: Transforming Culture, Society, and Politics* (Chicago and London: University of Chicago Press, 1993), esp. pp. 127-30; Miora Gatens, "Toward a Feminist Philosophy of the Body," in *Feminisms and the Critique of Knowledges*, ed. Barbara Caine, E. A. Grosz, and Marie Lepervanche (Sydney, Wellington, London, and Boston: Allen and Unwin, 1988), pp. 59-70 (esp. p. 68).

7. See the critique of Hedwig Meyer-Wilmes, "Woman's Nature and Feminine Identity: Theological Legitimations and Feminist Questions," *Concilium* (1987): 93-101 (esp. pp. 96-98).

8. Mary Frohlich faults Mark E. Frisby for holding this view in his article, "Lonergan's Method in Ethics and the Meaning of Human Sexuality," *Proceedings of the American Catholic Philosophical Association*, 1990, pp. 235-56. See Frohlich, "From Mystification to Mystery: Lonergan and the Theological Significance of Sexuality," in *Lonergan and Feminism*, ed. Cynthia S. W. Crysdale (Toronto: University of Toronto Press, 1994), p. 176. See also Daphne Hampson, "On Power and Gender," *Modern Theology* 4, no. 3 (April 1988): 234-50, esp. p. 236.

9. See Hampson, "On Power and Gender," and Michelle Zimbalist Rosaldo, "Woman, Culture, and Society: A Theoretical Overview," in *Woman, Culture, and Society*, ed. Michelle Zimbalist Rosaldo and Louise Lamphere (Stanford: Stanford University Press, 1974), pp. 17-42 (esp. pp. 20-21).

a patriarchal society aligned — at least metaphorically — with nature on the left side of each of these opposed pairs. It is she who, whether with good reason or simple prejudice,[10] is identified with nature which, in turn, has been conceptually transformed by patriarchic thought from its former status as mother, *mater,* into soulless and manipulated (because "manipulatable") *matter.*[11]

While traditional Western (and more "academic")[12] feminism thus advances a solid critique of nature as viewed from a modern, dualistic, and arguably patriarchal perspective, it ironically falters, I will argue, in the same regard. More specifically, in its rightful refutation of the reductionist claim that anatomy is destiny, it has deprived nature of any "real" (essential) content and thereby accepted the "patriarchal" division of nature and culture which denies nature of its traditional metaphysical dimension. This is a consequence, I will argue, of the larger cultural separation of nature and grace, which is to say that nature is no longer regarded as gifted at its creation, if it be regarded as created at all; nor is it consequently perceived as the principle of meaningful actions: actions ordered by a given nature — human or other — that is itself intrinsically ordered, or orientated, toward a more or less well defined end, an end which is, in the case of human beings, nonetheless freely chosen.

The way out of this feminist quandary is, it seems to me, to insist upon

10. Sherry B. Ortner, in her very influential (much cited) article, concludes: "Ultimately, it must be stressed again that the whole scheme is a construct of culture rather than a fact of nature. Woman is not 'in reality' any closer to (or further from) nature than man — both have consciousness, both are mortal. But there are certainly reasons why she appears that way. . . . The result is a (sadly) efficient feedback system: various aspects of woman's situation (physical, social, psychological) contribute to her being seen as closer to nature, while the view of her as closer to nature is in turn embodied in institutional forms that reproduce her situation. The implications for social change are similarly circular: a different cultural view can only grow out of a different social actuality; a different social actuality can only grow out of a different cultural view" ("Is Female to Male as Nature Is to Culture?" in *Woman, Culture, and Society,* pp. 67-87, cited at p. 87; reprinted in *Feminism, the Public and the Private,* pp. 21-44, cited at p. 42).

11. In this, Rosemary Radford Ruether recognizes what she calls "the big lie." See Rosemary Radford Ruether, *Sexism and God-Talk: Toward a Feminist Theology,* 2nd ed. (Boston: Beacon Press, 1993), p. 265. For a more detailed explanation, see Carolyn Merchant, *The Death of Nature: Women, Ecology, and the Scientific Revolution* (San Francisco: Harper and Row, 1980); Susan Bordo, *The Flight to Objectivity: Essays on Cartesianism and Culture* (Albany: SUNY Press, 1987); Evelyn Fox Keller, *Reflections on Gender and Science* (New Haven: Yale University Press, 1985). See also the critique of these authors by Kathleen Okruhlik: "Birth of a New Physics or Death of Nature?" in *Women and Reason,* ed. Elizabeth D. Harvey and Kathleen Okruhlik (Ann Arbor: University of Michigan Press, 1992), pp. 63-76.

12. The precision comes from Candace Vogler of the University of Chicago, to whom I am grateful.

neither the social construction of nature that would refuse essential differences between men and women nor an "essentialist" view of nature when interpreted as the de facto isolation of women from the larger male-dominated polis, one precluding them from any "substantial" contribution to the common good, any "transcendent"[13] goal. A *new feminism* ought rather, I will argue, to accept and even welcome these sexual differences within a relational model of human nature. Far from being at odds with the transcendental character of the human person — with his or her self-determination and the ongoing "project" of self-development and self-fulfillment which are integral to human existence as such — the return to a more classic presentation of nature (whether of the Greek or Latin tendency)[14] would actually preserve this dimension within the larger context of personal self-fulfillment and thus of vocation, where "vocation" is itself understood in terms of and as a response to love. In this sense transcendence would be understood in a supernatural sense, which is to say that human nature would itself be understood as open to — if not actually orientated toward — grace: a participation in divine life. Strictly opposed to biological determinism, nature thus understood is that whereby the human person is "equipped" to freely enter into relations with other persons, human and divine. In this sense, neither man nor woman is simply controlled by others, not even by the divine Other; nor is he or she so constituted as to seek his or her own good at the expense of others, as Hobbes would have it.[15] The human being — male and female — is instead, I will argue, relational *by nature,* which is to say that his personal good — far from being opposed to the common good — is actually achieved through his participation in and contribution to this common good. In this sense self-fulfillment is as much a communal effort as a personal one. Nature both requires culture and contributes to culture.

In this effort to lead feminism back to a classic presentation of nature — one which preserves the social or relational element of human nature, including nature's dynamic relation to culture, within the larger transcendental relationship between the human person and his or her Creator and thus between

---

13. In much feminist thought the term is used in a strictly human (horizontal) rather than divine (vertical) sense, a transcendence divorced of (what I consider) an authentically transcendental realm. This is particularly apparent in the writing of Simone de Beauvoir, for example: "Thus the paternalism that claims women for hearth and home defines her as sentiment, inwardness, immanence. In fact every existent is at once immanence and transcendence; when one offers the existent no aim, or prevents him from attaining any, or robs him of his victory, then his transcendence falls vainly into the past — that is to say, falls back into immanence" (Beauvoir, p. 255).

14. On the distinction between the two tendencies, see n. 65 below.

15. See Thomas Hobbes, *Leviathan* (Cambridge: Cambridge University Press, 1991).

nature and grace — I will begin with a brief introduction to this important problematic in Western feminism. From there I will demonstrate the dualisms apparent in a feminist appraisal of nature and the almost universal assumption among Western feminists that nature is without an essence, its "content" being reduced to that of a social construction. Within what is esteemed by these feminists as a cultural climate of patriarchy, I will demonstrate how nature, so conceived, poses a terrible threat to women's freedom of self-realization. In virtue of this same argumentation (that nature threatens freedom), the division between nature and culture is, I will argue, extended to the realm of nature and grace. With reference to these divisions and the concrete challenge of formulating a new feminism, I will reassess a traditional metaphysical presentation of nature as meeting the demands posed by human freedom. This is accomplished, I will argue, by setting freedom within the context of authentically Christian love in virtue of which we realize ourselves in communion with other persons: human and divine. Against this background I will then address the specific question — so central to the Western feminist debate — of whether it is possible to speak of a particularly feminine nature. Finally, as part of my effort to present a truly integral vision of nature — one which overcomes the dualisms that this feminism ironically both rejects and promotes — I will address the question of the relationship between nature and vocation within the larger question of the human person's orientation to God and thus of nature's orientation to grace.

Introduction to the Problematic

Although Western (American and European) academic feminism has, with good reason, advanced a strong critique of the dualistic conception of nature, typical of Enlightenment philosophy and patriarchal culture, it has not escaped the snares of the nature-nurture problematic characterizing the social sciences in general. The question, for example, of whether the individual is a tabula rasa fully determined by the environment — especially social-cultural practices and conventions — or the impact of the environment upon the individual builds upon something more fundamental[16] has been appropriated by the feminist movement within its overriding concern for women's liberation. The nature-nurture question as raised by Western feminists is whether specifically feminine characteristics — hitherto marginalized or repressed by a patriarchal society —

---

16. By this I mean to suggest, most especially, a base disposition otherwise known as nature or essence.

must be liberated or whether women themselves must be liberated from a constrained image of femininity and thus also of women's roles in society and the church. In the first case a particular feminine "nature" is sometimes maintained; in the second it is presumably denied. The "male-dominated" culture of patriarchy regards women, it is argued, within the framework of a biological determinism deriving their vocation from their "nature," their *ought* from their *is*. Woman's freedom to self-determination is thus hindered at best by her predetermined and often very limited "place" in the family, the church, and the society.

Within this context the term "gender," unavoidable in contemporary feminist discourse, was coined to distinguish what in sexual differences is determined by education, social norms, and/or culture — and thus by patriarchy — from what is biologically or physiologically determined, the latter being known as "sex." The distinction enabled feminist scholars to argue that women's subordination was the result of socially constructed, and not naturally occurring, patterns of gender division. The debate over whether gender identity should be presented in terms of an intrinsic similarity and "equality" of women and men or in terms of differences nonetheless continued within the larger debate over how best to theorize women's political interests. Gender studies have thus moved away from their initial concentration upon the empirical examination of sex differences toward a theoretical analysis of Western culture and society with the result that gender distinctions have increasingly been understood as historically, rather than naturally, based.[17] Sociobiology — the study of social conduct as explained by biology — is, as a scientific theory, ridiculed by contemporary feminists who nonetheless take its political implications very seriously. Rather than thinking of men and women as existing in separate ontological spheres, it is argued that theirs is a relationship of "negotiation, transcendence and transformation; a constant interplay between practical labour, symbolic construction and social structure."[18] Resulting from this reasoning is a radical questioning of the relation between biology and gender, of course, but even of biology as such. Because feminists think scientific inquiry into sexual difference is influenced by cultural interpretations of masculinity and femininity as well as by power relations between men and women, they challenge the objectivity of its method. Biology, no less than gender, is — the argument continues — socially constructed and subject to patriarchal ideologies.

17. What many contemporary feminists refer to as a typically "feminine" epistemology is, for example, claimed to reveal shared experiences among women rather than a common womanly nature. See my essay "Feminist Experience and Faith Experience," pp. 169-200 below.

18. See Elaine Graham, *Making the Difference: Gender, Personhood, and Technology* (New York: Mowbray, 1995), p. 76; see also pp. 11-34 and 83-84.

Not surprisingly, the famous Beauvoirian phrase "One is not born a woman; one becomes a woman" has been presented as the very hallmark of feminism.[19] Practically speaking, this means feminism has fallen victim to what Jane Roland Martin describes as "a chilly research climate" and even "a kind of dogmatism on the methodological level" whereby any talk of essence is "essentially" forbidden.[20] Even Elaine Graham, who endorses Robin George Collingwood's argument to curtail the manipulation of natural resources through a reunification of science and philosophy, advocates a view of nature as existential — by which she means "contingent and contextual" — rather than essential.[21] In contemporary feminist thought, sexual differences are consequently claimed — if at all — not as a natural state, but as a simple matter of social convention or even as a reaction to the standardized male bias in accounts of a "shared" human nature. To include women in this "false universalism" is, according to the claim, to de facto deny them what they hope to thereby obtain.[22]

Ever so subtly — unperceived even by many feminists themselves — its argumentation has thus evolved from the social construction of *gender* to the social construction of *nature*. The recent trend in feminism is to argue for a reversal of the "patriarchal" ordering of the relationship between culture and nature, politics and physiology, "so that the constructs of human *culture* may be seen as defining our concepts of *'nature,'* and not the other way around."[23] The delicate balance between nature and nurture — already upset (if we accept the feminist critique) by patriarchy's reduction of the former to the physiological realm — is further threatened (this time in the other direction) by feminism's insistence upon the overbearing power of culture. A majority of feminists to-

19. This insight, Donna Haraway claims, originated all modern feminist accounts of gender. See "'Gender' for a Marxist Dictionary: The Sexual Politics of a Word," in Haraway, *Simians, Cyborgs, and Women: The Reinvention of Nature* (New York: Routledge, 1992), p. 131.

20. Jane Roland Martin, "Methodological Essentialism, False Difference, and Other Dangerous Traps," *Signs* 19 (1994): 630-57 (cited at p. 654).

21. See Graham, pp. 223, 150. See also Robin George Collingwood, *The Idea of Nature* (Oxford: Clarendon, 1945).

22. For a more qualified explanation, see Susan F. Parsons, "The Dilemma of Difference: A Feminist Theological Exploration," *Feminist Theology* 14 (January 1997): 51-72; Catherine Keller, "Seeking and Sucking: On Relation and Essence in Feminist Theology," in *Horizons in Feminist Theology: Identity, Tradition, and Norms,* ed. Rebecca S. Chopp and Sheila Greeve Davaney (Minneapolis: Fortress, 1997), pp. 54-78 (esp. p. 61).

23. Graham, p. 84. Graham makes reference here to S. Cucchiari, "The Gender Revolution and the Transition from Bisexual Horde to Patrilocal Band: The Origins of Gender Hierarchy," in *Sexual Meanings: The Cultural Construction of Gender and Sexuality,* ed. Sherry B. Ortner and Harriet Whitehead (New York: Cambridge University Press, 1981), pp. 31-79.

day no longer regard human nature as *human* — and thus as the seat of self-determination — except in its origin: the human being who creates himself and thus his nature. Within the context of a male-dominated society, it is reduced to a patriarchal construct designed to keep women in their "place." Can it be surprising that much of contemporary feminism has thus denied it?

The Nature-Nurture Divide in Traditional Feminism

Certainly feminists are correct in arguing that many aspects of gender — what is commonly referred to as femininity or masculinity — are to some (perhaps even a large) extent culturally determined. To ipso facto conclude that gender identity is therefore exempt from biological and even metaphysical influence — that there is no "real" relation between nature and gender — is, however, to fall into the same dualistic trap they (many contemporary Western feminists) purport to deny: the social is set at odds with the natural, the human with the animal. The logic of our conventions is consequently presented as based solely upon our own manipulative intentions, as is particularly evident, according to feminist argumentation, within the realm of a patriarchal society.[24] Dominant "malestream" epistemologies, for example, are presented by feminists as created for the benefit of men: they "function to oppress and belittle those who are other than the white, privileged men in charge of knowledge."[25] The portrayal of "male rationality" as standard effectively "polices" thoughts, bringing them into strict conformity.[26] Despite the possible validity of such claims of patriar-

24. See the excellent critique of modern Western feminist reasoning by Carol McMillian, *Women, Reason, and Nature: Some Philosophical Problems with Feminism* (Princeton: Princeton University Press, 1982).

25. Rebecca Chopp, "Eve's Knowing: Feminist Theology's Resistance to Malestream Epistemological Frameworks," *Concilium* (1996/1): pp. 116-23, cited at p. 117. Mary Hawkesworth, whose article, although dated, presents an excellent survey of the field, as the title suggests, cites certain functionalist arguments (those of Greer and Barrett) maintaining that epistemological theories valorizing (what is regarded as) male styles of thinking (i.e., as opposed to those of women) are part of a larger sexist ideology serving the interests of men. See Hawkesworth, "Feminist Epistemology: A Survey of the Field," in *Feminism and Epistemology;* Germaine Greer, *The Female Eunuch* (New York: McGraw-Hill, 1971); Michele Barrett, *Women's Oppression Today: Problems in Marxist Feminist Analysis* (London: Verso, 1980).

26. Jane Flax, "Political Philosophy and the Patriarchal Unconscious: A Psychoanalytic Perspective on Epistemology and Metaphysics," in *Discovering Reality: Feminist Perspectives on Epistemology, Metaphysics, Methodology, and Philosophy of Science,* ed. Sandra Harding and Merrill B. Hintikka (Dordrecht, Boston, and London: D. Reidel, 1983), pp. 245-81. Sandra Harding (*The Science Question in Feminism* [Ithaca, N.Y.: Cornell University Press, 1986]) argues that atomistic conceptions of knowledge, for instance, further the goal of capitalism.

chal manipulation, when social convention is thought to entirely influence "natural" behavior, the delicate balance between nature and nurture is destroyed. The meaning of the former is consequently reduced to something far less than the dynamic and interactive, or relational, one it has traditionally assumed within the Christian philosophical tradition, as we shall see.

This reduction, as advocated by a nature-nurture dualism, is particularly apparent in the writings of Simone de Beauvoir, who categorically rejects — as a "doctrine whose foundations have long since been thoroughly undermined" — what she refers to as a psychophysiological parallelism. Granted, it is woman's "misfortune," Beauvoir argues, to have been "biologically destined" to transmit life whereby she is closer to the animal realm, "more enslaved to the species," than is man. She challenges women, however, to rise above the "animal" act of *giving* life so as to share in the masculine act of *risking* life. In so doing, they transcend the natural realm and enter into the properly human sphere. It is in woman's possibilities — which Beauvoir contrasts to her actual state — that she is comparable to man who, Beauvoir maintains, is a historical idea rather than a natural species.[27] Shulamith Firestone, who dedicates her book to Beauvoir, takes her argument one step further. She too accepts the nature-culture divide, but rather than seeking to transcend the natural realm, she wishes to destroy it. "Humanity has begun to outgrow nature: we can no longer justify the maintenance of a discriminatory sex class system on grounds of its origins in Nature. Indeed, for pragmatic reasons alone it is beginning to look as if we *must* get rid of it."[28] More specifically, she advocates not merely that women regain full "ownership" of their bodies, but that they also gain at least temporary control of human fertility and of "the social institutions" of childbearing and child rearing. Ultimately she has in mind the elimination of sex *distinction* itself, which is to say that biological sex would carry no cultural value and artificial reproduction would replace natural reproduction and destroy the "tyranny of the biological family."[29]

There are, of course, feminists who have reacted against this uncritical acceptance of "masculine" logic setting nature at odds with culture. Ecofeminists, for example, argue that men are wrong to oppose themselves to nature and that women do best to reclaim their affinity with it. As a case in point, Adrienne Rich criticizes modern childbearing for having become technologically controlled by men, and modern child rearing, which has become increas-

27. This Beauvoir maintains in reference to Merleau-Ponty. See Beauvoir, pp. 33, 64, 255, 34. To assimilate woman to nature is, Beauvoir argues, "simply to act from prejudice" (p. 255).

28. Shulamith Firestone, *The Dialectic of Sex: The Case for Feminist Revolution* (New York: Bantam Books, 1970), p. 10.

29. Firestone, p. 11.

ingly entrusted to the direction of male "experts" who challenge women's "natural" right and competence for it.[30] Although eco-feminists thus argue against an unqualified division between nature and culture and the subsequent control and manipulation of the former by the latter, they also overlook what I believe to be the critical point of the nature-culture division. They and a majority of academic, Western feminists assume that whatever nature *is,* it is not human. There is, it is argued, no such "thing" as specifically *human* nature,[31] unless of course it is presented as simply a social convention. Such is the conclusion of Elaine Graham, who, proceeding from the notion of gender as a form of social relations, argues for "a model of human nature as profoundly relational, requiring the agency of culture to bring our personhood fully into being."[32] Within this context it is not surprising that the theoretical distinction between essentialism and social constructionalism has been called into question on its own theoretical grounds,[33] nor that contemporary feminists are flocking to poststructuralism wherein differential relation makes concrete meaning — however obscurely that word be understood — possible. *Woman,* according to this recent philosophical trend, is known only in terms of what she is not: it is the differential relation between herself and her opposite, *man,* which gives meaning to her "being." In this we are far removed from anything that signals human reality — male or female — for there is "no fixed knowledge base in poststructuralism . . . , no explanation that is not subject to destabilization."[34] The path from Beauvoir's "Other" has thus led to "an-other" that almost literally calls everything into question but dualism itself.

30. Adrienne Rich, *Of Woman Born: Motherhood as Experience and Institution* (New York: Bantam Books, 1977). The classification of Rich as an eco-feminist is contested, but the example remains pertinent, it seems to me.

31. This particular and vital point comes to a head in Virginia Held's criticism of feminists on both sides of the division for failing to distinguish between the distinctively human and the natural components of human reality. "Experiences of choice, consciousness, and imaginative representation are distinctively human; that calcium is a component of human bones is not" (Held, p. 124).

32. Graham, p. 223. See also Alison M. Jaggar, "Human Biology in Feminist Theory: Sexual Equality Reconsidered," in *Beyond Domination: New Perspectives on Women and Philosophy,* ed. Carol C. Gould (Totowa, N.J.: Rowman and Allanheld, 1984), esp. pp. 37-38.

33. See, in this regard, Diana Fuss, *Essentially Speaking: Feminism, Nature, and Difference* (New York: Routledge, 1990), and Janet Sayers, *Biological Politics: Feminist and Anti-Feminist Perspectives* (London: Tavistock Publications, 1982).

34. Mary McClintock Fulkerson, "Contesting the Gendered Subject: A Feminist Account of the *Imago Dei,*" in *Horizons in Feminist Theology,* pp. 104, 105.

Nature's "Threat" to Human Freedom

In this ironic search for meaning in the context of poststructuralism, we confront the central problematic addressed by the feminist refusal of nature: the infringement that social (especially patriarchal) conditioning imposes upon women's freedom in the name of (under the pretext of) "nature."[35] This is especially the case when the latter is interpreted as biological determinism. Sylvie le Bon, for example, argues against certain "antifeminist" interpretations of the famous Beauvoirian maxim that one is not born but becomes a woman, according to which she (woman) achieves femininity by "rejoining" her feminine essence.[36] Similarly, Mary Daly argues that "the characteristics of the eternal woman are opposed to a developing, authentic person, who will be unique, self-critical, self-creative, active and searching. By contrast with these authentic personal qualities, the eternal woman is said to have a vocation to surrender and hiddenness; hence the symbolism of the veil. Selfless, she achieves not individualization but merely generic fulfillment in motherhood, physical, or spiritual."[37] In the feminist claim that one "becomes a woman" lies a protest to what Michelle Zimbalist Rosaldo has noted as a cross-cultural phenomenon distinguishing the "natural" woman from the "achieved" man: "A woman becomes a woman by following in her mother's footsteps, whereas there must be a break in a man's experience. For a boy to become an adult, he must prove himself — his masculinity — among his peers. And although all boys may succeed in reaching manhood, cultures treat this development as something that each individual *has achieved*." In contrast to womanhood as a natural category or criterion — woman being regarded as "naturally" what she is — manhood is "a cultural product" achieved within a complex social structure including "elaborate systems of

---

35. Susan Frank Parsons (*Feminism and Christian Ethics* [Cambridge: Cambridge University Press, 1996]) presents as a "constant feature" of the debate between traditional and feminist versions of the naturalist paradigm "the question of how to distinguish the humble receptiveness to meaning, by which what transcends human choice or perspective is acknowledged, from the arrogant imposition of meaning upon the world, by which advantage is gained for those who name this reality" (p. 154).

36. "Far from being at history's starting point, woman's reality is situated at its completion. It is always praxis, singular ideologies that have modeled this completely historical reality which is proposed as an Idea, a Being, a Fact" (Sylvie le Bon, "Le deuxième sexe, l'esprit et la lettre," *L'Arc* 61 [1975]: *Simone de Beauvoir et la lutte des femmes*, p. 56).

37. Mary Daly, *The Church and the Second Sex*, 3rd ed. (Boston: Beacon Press, 1985), p. 149. See also Daly, *Pure Lust: Elemental Feminist Philosophy* (Boston: Beacon Press, 1984). Here she argues that Christian asceticism, emblematic of patriarchal religious practice, is "sado-ritual": self-denial is glorified as the means of becoming someone other than oneself.

norms, ideals, and standards of evaluation" whereby men compete and order relationships among themselves.[38]

This analysis echoes Beauvoir's own point of contention. In contrast to the "terrible misfortune" of women being biologically "destined" to give life, she insists upon the "transcendent goal" of all human life: "Within humanity, the reasons to live are more important than life itself, the project of man being not that of repeating himself in time, but of surpassing life by existence."[39] What is sought, in the name of all women, is not simply the right to think — and thus to act — humanly, but to think and act *for oneself,* which apparently requires our liberation from the bondage of present patriarchal structures: a break from nature as man has conceived it. Yet in woman's "own" battle cry, man has not so inconspicuously left his mark. In Beauvoir's claim to fame — "one is not born a woman; one becomes a woman" — is there not echoed Sartre's own "existence precedes essence"?[40] This, in turn, is but a natural progression from Descartes's mechanistic (nonessentialist) conception of nature and the Kantian development setting nature at odds with reason. For Beauvoir, as for Sartre, a nature opposed to reason — and thus freedom — is a nature which must be denied; and when nature is lost, all that remains is freedom itself. The human being *is* freedom: a freedom whose only goal is to will itself. Freedom invents its own values and gives meaning to a life having no a priori meaning.[41] The feminist denial of nature in the name of women's freedom to self-determination is thus part, it seems to me, of a much larger problematic: one which, in the final analysis, may well be rooted in the Protestant opposition between nature and grace, as we shall see.

A Nature-Grace Divide

For Sartre there can be no human nature because there is no Creator to conceive of it. As for Beauvoir, she also denies female nature,[42] because woman

38. Michelle Zimbalist Rosaldo, "Woman, Culture, and Society: A Theoretical Overview," in *Woman, Culture, and Society,* p. 28, emphasis mine.

39. Beauvoir, as summarized by le Bon, p. 60. Cf. Beauvoir, p. 64.

40. Man, according to Sartre, is at first "nothing. Only afterward will he be something, and he himself will have made what he will be.... Not only is man what he conceives himself to be, but he is also only what he wills himself to be after this thrust toward existence. Man is nothing else but what he makes of himself.... Man is at the start a plan ... nothing exists prior to this plan ... man will be what he will have planned to be" (Jean-Paul Sartre, *Existentialism and Human Emotions,* 2nd ed. [New York: Citadel Press, 1985], pp. 15, 16).

41. See Georges Cottier, "Nature et nature humaine," *Nova et Vetera* (1999/4): 57-74.

42. See Sr. Prudence Allen's discussion, p. 271 (and n. 63) and p. 101 (and n. 139) in this volume.

"naturally" aspires beyond the limitations set for her by her own body and the "first" sex. In the first example is manifest the ageless "problem" of the interaction between divine and human wills, of the perceived threat that divine providence and divine (creative) agency pose to human freedom; in the second, the threat of the "demiurge": the threat that one created freedom poses for another, "lesser" freedom. Ironically, this secular denial of nature — because of its affiliation with divine grace — parallels the religious emptying of nature of its properly human content: its capacity for self-realization based upon free will. When nature, more specifically, is overpowered by grace — as in properly Lutheran thought whereby it, in the absence of grace, is capable of nothing but evil — the pendulum swings toward the overpowering of grace by nature or even the denial of any divine influence upon human nature; for to grant the divine prerogative would be, presumably, to sacrifice human nature to the "gods." Abandoned, instead, to human governance — by which it is left entirely to its own resources without the "intervention" of divine grace — nature ironically returns to its "fallen" state. Its "natural" orientation to the good — in accord with traditional metaphysics and Catholic doctrine — is called into question, especially when it is perceived by feminists as controlled by a patriarchal society that is itself intrinsically corrupt. Nature becomes that which "man" wishes it to be: a manipulative tool whereby he achieves his sovereign rule over women and "lesser" men.

Such a dishonorable intention might understandably be attributed to Luther when he argues: "The fact that pregnancies wear women out and in the end lead them to death is not serious. Let the pregnancies kill them; they are here for that."[43] Setting aside the question of Luther's possibly misogynist tendencies, the more profound question which emerges in this passage is that of human freedom and thus of the possibility of a Christian vocation, as such. "As little as it is in your power not to be a woman, no more is it your prerogative to be without a husband," he argues. "It is not a question left to free will or to counsel but a necessary and natural thing that every man must have a wife and every woman must have a husband."[44] If, then, Luther were to grant with Saint

---

43. Martin Luther, "Judgment on Monastic Vows," quoted by Georges Chantraine, "Woman as Deprived of the Spirit: An Aspect of Luther's Thought on Woman," *Communio* (English edition), Fall 1983, pp. 244-45.

44. Luther ("Judgment on Monastic Vows") quoted by Chantraine, "Women as Deprived," p. 244. Chantraine comments: "Here as elsewhere [in Luther's writing], the idea of necessity excludes that of free will. In the divine work creating man and woman, no vocation is inscribed, or at least no attraction to a vocation. The idea of nature excludes that of free choice. What is natural is not voluntary nor can it be. To accept one's body as divine work is not to accept it as a gift, but as an indestructible law."

Paul that women are somehow "saved" through childbirth (cf. 1 Tim. 2:15), this would not be to accord them a meritorious "work" in cooperation with grace; on the contrary, they are abandoned to the "natural" (i.e., biological) realm in which is manifest, it is maintained, the Creator's intention and will.[45]

The "natural," to summarize, cannot in properly Lutheran thought be free. Nor can it be destined for holiness. In his attempt to preserve the salvific prerogative of grace, Luther deprives nature — that is, properly *human* nature — of any predetermined orientation to the good, even to the extent that it is deemed incapable of anything other than evil. Whatever is not Christ and his grace is — for the father of the Protestant Reformation — impiety, and whoever is not in Christ "is like unto Satan."[46] To be sure, it is not creation as such that Luther regards as evil. This, in fact, remains good in his eyes even after the fall. It is rather *human* nature that is problematic for him. His contention with the scholastic presentation of the relationship between nature and grace, for example — especially its important formulation that grace does not destroy but perfects and completes nature[47] — resides in his interpretation of the latter (nature) as "humanity's attempt to attain grace by its own power or as a reward for its own goodness."[48] Hence, even the act of justifying faith is not — he argues — to be considered free; if such were the case, it would be a human act in virtue of which no one can be freed from sin.[49] In the final analysis, Luther's quarrel is with human freedom: "this is only the servant of sin, death and Satan"; it "does nothing nor is capable of anything, except evil."[50] Only God is free, for he alone "can and does."[51] The human being, in contrast, is "servile

---

45. Maternal (or any) suffering is, it would seem, "efficacious" only in the sense that grace is thereby "king," i.e., unhindered by human action which, as such, is necessarily corrupt.

46. Georges Chantraine, *Erasme et Luther. Libre et serf arbitre* (Paris: Lethielleux, 1981), p. 219.

47. See, for example, Thomas Aquinas, *Summa theologica* I, q.1, a.8, ad. 2.

48. Russell Kleckley, "'Omnes Creaturae Sacramenta': Creation, Nature, and the World View in Luther's Theology of the Lord's Supper" (Dissertation zur Erlangung der Doktorwürde der Ludwig-Maximilians-Universität München, Evangelisch-Theologische Fakultät, 1990), p. 225. "Nature," Kleckley reasons, is here understood as "works."

49. Ironically, however, Lutheran faith in not a supernatural reality *in* the soul, a habitus. "What is emphasized here almost exclusively," notes Jean Borella, "is the human dimension of faith, faith as the human act, the human will within mercy. It is a faith *felt* by the believer, faith reduced to the subjective experience of faith and not properly a *theological* faith in which spiritual reality is by no means perceptible to ordinary consciousness" (Jean Borella, *The Sense of the Supernatural*, trans. G. John Champoux [Edinburgh: T. & T. Clark, 1998], p. 155).

50. Chantraine, *Erasme et Luther*, p. 158. Erasmus accuses Luther of exaggerating and amplifying original sin to the extent that even grace, when it acts in the human being, can work nothing other than sin. See p. 220.

51. Chantraine, *Erasme et Luther*, p. 164.

and captive" whether to God or to Satan, which is to say that his servitude (of the One or the other) is a work of predestination. Even the justified human being is incapable of accomplishing the divine precepts without divine intervention.[52] Lacking in Lutheran theology is thus the notion that the human person is, whether by creation or redemption, really capable of a good act; hence the Lutheran denial of inhering grace as the formal cause of justification, even within the context of the contemporary Catholic-Lutheran dialogue.[53] So too, the Lutheran refusal of Christian vocations when these are understood as an active — even if God-given — participation in the universal mission of Christ. Simultaneously just and sinner, the human being is unable to contribute to his own salvation, let alone to that of his neighbor and the world.

Ironically, this attempt to preserve grace of human influence by granting it virtually full dominion over nature may have effectively led to its (grace's) estrangement from the natural realm. "By Lutheran decree, divine grace has been forbidden to *take root* in our human earth. Henceforth our world is cleared of the sacred."[54] To be sure, humanism — at least in the secular variety — has been championed by those far less sympathetic to Catholic teaching than the great defender of the church, Erasmus.[55] The feminist denial of nature is, simply stated, not without precedent. In feminism, as in secular humanism, an artificial wedge is driven not only between nature and culture, but also and consequently between nature and grace. The former is, more specifically, deprived of its previous status as a divine creation. Nature is no longer regarded as revelatory of God; creation no longer points to the Creator. Concretely this has resulted in the estrangement of faith and theology from the contemporary dialogue between nature and culture.[56] Biology and the social sciences, it is often argued, may (indeed should!) influence theology, but theology is denied any influence in their regard. Rather than considering, for example, how theology

52. See Chantraine, *Erasme et Luther*, pp. 163, 189-90, 156. Luther (in *Contra Scholasticam theologiam*), Chantraine notes, argues that the best and "infallible" preparation for grace is divine and eternal election and predestination. See pp. 120-21.

53. On this point see Christopher Malloy, "The Nature of Justifying Grace: A Lacuna in the *Joint Declaration*," *Thomist* 65, no. 1 (January 2001): 93-120.

54. Borella, p. 154.

55. Erasmus, in fact, insisted most especially upon the Catholic teaching that "the freedom of the free will is inadmissible. This first gift is constitutive: man cannot lose it without losing his spiritual nature" (Chantraine, *Erasme et Luther*, p. 361). Erasmus reproached Luther for not having known "any other manner of exalting the grace of the Redeemer than of making of man Satan or even more impious if possible; he [Luther] forgets that that good which remains in man is a gift of Christ" (Erasmus, as quoted by Chantraine, p. 217).

56. As regards this phenomenon in feminism, see Rebecca S. Chopp, "Theorizing Feminist Theology," in *Horizons in Feminist Theology*, p. 230.

might contribute to the interdisciplinary debate over sexual differences, feminists such as Elaine Graham argue for the integration of contemporary theories of gender into theological studies and Christian practice.[57] Even for many feminist theologians, the primary question is not how our knowledge of God might affect our conception of human (and thus female) persons, but how feminist conceptions and experiences — especially the experience of oppression — affect our conception of the divine.[58] Ironically this means that although feminists are quick to fault traditional theology for what is judged an attempt to explain sexual differences by means of an extrapolation from biological and sociological data,[59] they have not moved far from the same.[60] More specifically, there is denied in this feminist conception of human nature any metaphysical content that is not directly attributable to something or someone other than human agency. Whatever in human nature (if there be such a thing!) that cannot be reduced to the human body is perceived as reducible to the human mind. Hence the challenge, in the context of a new feminism, to reintroduce grace into the natural realm and God into creation.

In confronting this challenge, I propose that we examine the nature-nurture problematic at the heart of feminism — the question of the delicate

57. See Graham, p. 4.

58. See, for example, the critique of Daphne Hampson, *Theology and Feminism* (Oxford and Cambridge: Blackwell, 1990), pp. 116-18.

59. See Margaret A. Farley, "New Patterns of Relationship: Beginnings of a Moral Revolution," *Theological Studies* 36 (December 1975): 627-46 (cited at p. 634). For the accusation that the magisterium has traditionally argued from biology to archetype, see also Patrick Snyder, *La femme selon Jean-Paul II. Lectures des fondements anthropologiques et théologiques et des applications pratiques de son enseignement* (Québec: Fides, 1999); Kari Elisabeth Börresen, *Subordination et équivalence. Nature et rôle de la femme d'après Augustin et Thomas d'Aquin* (Paris: Mame, 1968); Börresen, "Image ajustée, typologie arrêtée," in *Penser la foi. Recherches en théologie aujourd'hui*, ed. Joseph Doré and Christoph Theolbald (Paris: Cerf, 1985); Hedwig Meyer-Wilmes, "Woman's Nature and Feminine Identity: Theological Legitimations and Feminist Questions," *Concilium* 194 (1987/6): 93-101; Elisabeth Gössmann, "The Construction of Women's Difference in the Christian Theological Tradition," *Concilium* 238 (1991): 50-59; Jean-Marie Aubert, *La femme. Antiféminisme et christianisme* (Paris: Cerf & Desclée, 1975); Mary Aquin O'Neill, "Toward a Renewed Anthropology," *Theological Studies* 36 (1975): 725-36; Theodor Schneider, "Mann und Frau — Grundproblem theologischer Anthropologie? Thematische Einfuhrung," in *Mann und Frau — Grundproblem theologischer Anthropologie*, ed. Theodor Schneider (Freiburg: Herder, 1989), pp. 11-24.

60. "I have argued that attention to both biology and socio-cultural factors ought to be part of a feminist theological redefinition of human nature. This would mean that differences between men and women, and differences between women, shape the starting-point of our theory-building" (Katherine Zappone, "'Women's Special Nature': A Different Horizon for Theological Anthropology," *Concilium* [1991/6]: 87-97, cited at pp. 91-92).

but absolutely necessary balance between nature, conceived as an essential reality, and nature, conceived as a socially determined reality — within the context of the larger question of the relationship between nature and grace. From my own perspective, our primary concern should be to maintain the essential harmony between the latter two (nature and grace) such that there is preserved the integrity of both without collapsing the one into the other.[61]

Toward a New Feminism: A Nature-Grace Reunion

Foreign to the feminist perspective of nature, as portrayed above, is the idea of its (nature's) ordination to anything other than what is willed by human "freedom." Ironically, however, when freedom is named master over itself and human nature, it forfeits its own reign: one man's freedom is easily sacrificed to that of another. Survival of the fittest becomes law of the land, and freedom is reduced to its lowest terms: that whereby one protects his or her own interests in the face of certain corruption. In such a world there is no room for love whereby one's own good is recognized as existing in that of the other, whereby one is even "fulfilled" in giving of himself or herself to another. Instead, each one's good is conceived as independent of — even opposed to — the good of the other who, in turn, is regarded as a potential enemy rather than a potential friend. The only "real" relationship is that of utility. Mothers become wombs for babies; babies are playthings for mothers. Women are sex objects for men, and men are, as it were, the very incarnation of evil, at least for some women. Relationships, far from being received or humbly welcomed as that toward which nature is itself intrinsically ordered, are created with one's own interest in mind. In the powerful words of Hans Urs von Balthasar, this is "a world without women, without children, without reverence for love in poverty and humiliation — a world in which power and the profit-margin are the sole criteria, where the disinterested, the useless, and purposeless is despised, persecuted and in the end exterminated — a world in which art itself is forced to wear the mask and features of technique."[62]

Ironically, a feminist strategy for overcoming this mentality has been to accept it on its own terms. Even among those feminists who hold a relational

---

61. Such is the case, on the one hand, of Pelagianism and Semipelagianism, which underestimate the need for grace in obtaining salvation (consequently overstepping the boundaries of nature) and, on the other hand, of Baianism and Jansenism, which overemphasize the power of grace over nature (consequently diminishing the latter's integrity).

62. Hans Urs von Balthasar, *Love Alone*, trans. Alexander Dru (New York: Herder and Herder, 1969), p. 115.

model of the human person, there is strong objection to the idea of a woman being perceived or presented in terms of her relationships with others: her "status" as daughter, wife, mother, etc. In order to be truly free, she must — it is reasoned — be thought of as an independent being, as her "own" person. As such, she is thought of as related to others only in virtue of her *own choice*.[63] Hence, although relationality remains an important concept in feminist thought,[64] it is in no way to be mistaken as constitutive of, or essential to, the human (and thus the feminine) person as such. The person, in most feminist thought, is always prior to and ultimately free with regard to these relationships which — it bears repeating — remain a consequence, or product, of his or her choosing.

Such a feminist and patriarchal vision of the human person and human freedom is at odds with a classic metaphysical presentation of nature:[65] one in which human nature exists harmoniously with divine influence, or grace, in virtue of which it is properly ordered to the good of both the individual and the community without being thereby any less freely chosen.[66] The individual within this classical approach is free *by nature* and even freer by grace. This means, on the

63. An important example may be found in the work of Carol Gilligan (*In a Different Voice: Psychological Theory and Women's Development* [Cambridge: Harvard University Press, 1982]), who has revolutionized moral thinking by insisting upon the typically feminine category of "attachment" (opposed to the traditional, "masculine" emphasis upon separation) as marking authentic moral development. Gilligan's "ethic of care," which takes as its "central insight" the idea that "self and other are interdependent," supposes that self-care be integrated with care for the other whereby is challenged "the logic of self-sacrifice in the service of a morality of care" (pp. 74, 82; cf. p. 93). In its practical application, this means a sort of balancing of interests, such that the "needs" or interests of the woman herself, the child's father, the woman's other dependent children, and her parents, for example, are regarded as possibly greater than a child's right to life. The language of rights is, however, foreign to this properly feminine ethic, belonging instead to the domain of a "masculine" ethic based on justice.

64. See my contribution to this volume, "Feminist Experience and Faith Experience."

65. Distinction might, of course, be made between the Greek and Latin, or more properly Christian, presentation of nature. On the other hand, as Louis Dupré has effectively demonstrated, Saint Thomas follows Aristotle in using a purely philosophical concept of nature which, although lacking the support of revelation, "has nothing in common with the *natura pura* which sixteenth-century theologians abstracted from the concrete reality of the fall and redemption. Aquinas's philosophical *nature* is not a nature without grace, but human nature as we concretely find it, when considered independently of what revelation teaches about grace. It possesses a transcendent openness to grace and some thomists would claim a *desiderium naturale* toward a fulfillment in grace" (Louis Dupré, "Nature and Grace: Fateful Separation and Attempted Reunion," in *Catholicism and Secularization in America*, ed. David L. Schindler [Huntington and Notre Dame, Ind.: Our Sunday Visitor and Communio Books, 1990], pp. 52-73, cited at p. 57).

66. See Peter Kwasniewski, "The Inseparability of Freedom, Goodness and Final End in Saint Thomas," *Aquinas Review* 5, no. 1 (1998): 50-69; Yves Simon, *Traité du libre arbitre* (Fribourg: Editions Universitaires Fribourg Suisse, 1951, 1989).

other hand, that "the will cannot be entirely 'free' (in our accustomed sense) if we are to act freely! For it has no *choice* — which we spontaneously identify with freedom — about its orientation to 'the good'; that belongs to it *naturally*."[67] The human person, to continue our exposition of a classic anthropology, "freely" fulfills himself or herself in and through his or her actions, provided that these are morally good as judged by conscience. This in turn presupposes that the notion of good is not simply relative — that it is not invented by the human subject — but that one is able to judge one's actions in reference to a transcendent value: the *true* good. The power of volition is, in other words, held "in check" by that of the intellect; the intellect, in turn, by its proper object. The human "I" is nonetheless accomplished in and through personal actions, but only to the extent that this subject transcends himself or herself in tending toward the good (as measured by the truth) which surpasses him or her, all in remaining within his or her intellectual and volitional "grasp." "I do not fulfill myself because I accomplish an act, but only because I become good when the act is morally good."[68]

In virtue of this transcendent value,[69] the individual is able to contribute to the common good and thus also to the culture and community of which he is a part, and this contribution is that whereby he or she simultaneously "constructs" or realizes his or her human "I." The community, on the other hand, assures, or protects, the good of each of its individual members, especially the most vulnerable. In this way human nature is conceived as intrinsically ordained to communion: communion with the world, with other human persons, and ultimately and fundamentally with God, the source of each one's being.[70] This, it is important to specify, is not to say that personhood is constituted by relations formed by the human person himself, as Elaine Graham would have it,[71] nor that personhood can be denied by the simple refusal of a relationship, as in the "logic" of abortion.[72] Rather, certain essential rela-

67. See David B. Burrell, "Freedom and Creation in the Abrahamic Traditions," *International Philosophical Quarterly* 40, no. 2 (June 2000): 161-71, cited at p. 166.

68. Karol Wojtyla, "The Person: Subject and Community," *Review of Metaphysics* (December 1979): p. 287.

69. By this I mean a value which is not simply conferred by choice — as Sartre would have it — but *given* as an object of knowledge: it is good because it is true.

70. In Thomistic thought, being, which is good in itself, nonetheless "strives towards complete goodness, by which it is related as it should be to everything outside itself *(ut debito modo se habent ad omnia quae sunt extra ipsum)*, by which it is perfected in relation to other things" (Jan Aertsen, *Nature and the Creature* [Leiden: Brill, 1988], p. 354; cf. Thomas, *De veritate* 22.7).

71. See Graham, p. 233; see above, n. 32. See also the critique of Harriet A. Harris, "Should We Say That Personhood Is Relational?" *Scottish Journal of Theology* 51, no. 2 (1998): 214-34.

72. See Joyce A. Little, "The New Evangelization and Gender: The Remystification of the Body," *Communio* 21 (Winter 1994): 776-99, esp. p. 793.

tionships (Creator-creature, soul-body, individual-community, male-female, etc.) are *given* a priori with personhood itself,[73] and the natural gift of human freedom enables the person to accept, welcome, and even foster these as an act of self-fulfillment, or self-realization. When, moreover, these relations exist between persons, the willing appropriation — which cannot be other than by an act of love, i.e., a gift of self — transforms the seemingly static *relation* into a dynamic *relationship*.[74]

Even for subhuman and inanimate beings, their unity ought not be understood, insists Kenneth Schmitz, "as *ens indivisum,* but as *conatus,* that is, as the drive for self-expression. Each being *in-sists, re-sists,* and *ex-sists* in relation to others," profiting from an integrity which it "receives from its source, namely, the 'freedom' to be itself *(ens per se).*"[75] Even the smallest particle, Schmitz points out, "is possessed of its own pattern of activity," which means that "a certain self-affirmation lies at the root of existence."[76] This "power" to self-affirmation, this "freedom to be itself," does not, however, permit a being to close in upon itself; for this particular dynamism is the capacity "to develop in accord with the received potential for its fullness," i.e., in virtue of its received nature. Hence, "the fundamental character of receptivity resonates throughout each created being."[77] In practical, although metaphysical, terms, this means that being precedes act (at least in the created realm), even to the extent of marking the particular essential character of a given act: *ordo essendi est ordo agendi.* It follows that being is not created in and by consciousness. Instead, it not only precedes but also "constitutes . . . consciousness and the reality of human action as conscious."[78] Thus is refuted the "mind over matter" mentality according to which all things — not excluding the human body — can be determined by the manipulative power of the human will. "This notion that I can become anything in general rests upon the assumption that I am not already something in particular. For if I am already something in particular, then what I can or cannot become will be determined to a very large extent by what I already am. In short, this notion that I, in the essential givenness of my being, am

---

73. Ultimately this means that the person does not create himself or herself.

74. Jean Mouroux distinguishes, for example, between the ontological and the spiritual aspects of our relation with God. See Mouroux, *The Christian Experience: An Introduction to a Theology,* trans. George Lamb (New York: Sheed and Ward, 1954), pp. 18-19.

75. Kenneth L. Schmitz, "The Solidarity of Personalism and the Metaphysics of Existential Act," *Fides Quaerens Intellectum* 1, no. 1 (summer 2001): 196. Here there is particularly evident the influence of Gabriel Marcel and his notion of the basic generosity of being.

76. Schmitz, "The Solidarity of Personalism," p. 198.

77. Schmitz, "The Solidarity of Personalism," p. 196.

78. Wojtyla, p. 278.

defined by nothing I need take seriously is fundamentally nihilistic, since it assumes I am intrinsically a cipher signifying absolutely nothing."[79] The metaphysical approach, on the contrary, points to a "fixed"[80] nature that provides the fundamental base, the determined foundation, from which the human self is realized through his actions.[81]

In this we encounter, once again, the graced nature of nature itself, where grace is understood in its etymological sense as *giftedness:* a giftedness which, in the case of the human person, is both crea*ted* and crea*tive*. As created, nature (coming from the Latin *nascor,* to be born) implies a principle;[82] as creative, it implies a purpose or end.[83] The resulting dynamic is "so much a part of the actual core of 'nature'" that it cannot be grasped apart from it. "In determining the meaning of nature, the circle of finality is just as important as the actuating dynamic-active potentialities that are brought about in this circle and 'formed' in it."[84] Human actions are thus "determined" (in the sense of "directed" or "orientated") by an immanent specifying principle — what Schmitz refers to as "spirit" — which is also "the first principle of human becoming." In virtue of this principle, we develop and grow as persons. That is to say, our personal being is increased through knowledge and enhanced through what we love, provided, of course, that we love what is good *for us* as is determined by that same specifying power of the spirit.[85]

79. Little, p. 788; see also p. 792.

80. The term ought not be understood as "static."

81. See Bernard N. Schumacher, *Une philosophie de l'espérance. La pensée de Josef Pieper dans le contexte du débat contemporain sur l'espérance* (Paris: Cerf, 2000), chap. 1. ET: *A Philosophy of Hope: The Thought of Joseph Pieper in the Context of the Contemporary Debate on Hope* (New York: Fordham University Press, 2003), chap. 1.

82. "Thus the generator and the generated are as it were one thing. Therefore, because the name 'nature' is derived from 'nascor' (to be born), those are said to be by nature of which the principle is within themselves" (Thomas Aquinas, *In III Sent.* 8, 1; cf. Aquinas, *Summa theologica* I, q.115, a.2).

83. "The thing's nature, which is the end of generation, is further ordained to another end, which is either an operation, or some product of operation, to which one attains by means of operation" (Aquinas, *Summa theologica* I-II, q.49, a.3). "Determinative of what is appetible for a being is its nature. For nature is the principle of motion. The first condition for the attainment of an end is therefore a nature that is proportionate to it. What is meant by this proportion to the end: Nothing other than that in the principle a certain beginning of the end *(inchoatio finis),* an orientation, pre-exists" (Aertsen, p. 343).

84. Hans Urs von Balthasar, *The Theology of Karl Barth: Exposition and Interpretation,* trans. Edward T. Oakes (San Francisco: Ignatius/Communio Books, 1992), p. 274.

85. In virtue of the same logic, distorted love can actually count as a personal loss. According to Schmitz, there are "three kinds of quasi-mutation that enter into the movement of the human spirit": (1) spiritual enhancement or gain, (2) loss caused by nonspiritual condi-

This, of course, brings us back to the important question at the heart of feminism: If the dynamism of human existence, which we have here attributed to nature, is in fact that of the spirit, then ought we not maintain that it is the same for women as for men? In other words, since the spiritual realm presumably transcends the physical, can we not conclude that sexual differences do not touch upon human nature as such? Or is it in fact possible to maintain that women differ from men not only in body but in spirit as well?

One Nature, Two Modes

The assumption that women differ only bodily from men — that sexual differences remain confined to the biological domain, which is to say that there is no essential connection between body and spirit — is nastily divisive. More specifically, we thereby return to a dualistic concept of nature as is popularly associated with Enlightenment thought and attributed by many feminists to patriarchy. The spirit invoked by Schmitz is not in fact to be understood primarily in terms of the German tradition (so as to be rendered *Geist*), a tradition which, he maintains, tends to reduce the concepts of interiority and immateriality to subjectivity and thus to the human dimension. Instead, he refers to spirit in the Latin sense of *spiritus*, whereby some kind of interiority, or immateriality ("spirit"), is rightfully attributed to all beings, even those that are subrational. Indeed, traditional metaphysics — of both the Greek and Latin tendencies — held that within all material beings there is present not only "primary matter" (the passive and potential factor within them) but also certain nonmaterial factors: form, finality, and "participation in the cosmic web of existence."[86] In this sense, spirit might be understood as permeating the physical realm. Especially among living things, it is possible to speak of "an 'intelligent' organizing and creative force" by which a being is ordained with a "constant regularity towards a precise determined end, i.e., the ultimate development of its nature."[87] On the other hand, Schmitz invites us to recall that the human person is no pure spirit, which is to say that both the material and immaterial modalities are integral to him. Even when engaged in such spiri-

---

tions such as aging, forgetfulness, brain damage, etc., and (3) properly spiritual loss, such as moral failures, the loss of the sense of meaning, indifference and apathy, etc. See Schmitz, "The First Principle of Personal Becoming," *Review of Metaphysics* 47 (June 1994): 757-74, cited at pp. 772-73.

86. See Schmitz, "First Principle," pp. 766-67.
87. Bernard Schumacher, p. 44 (French ed.).

tual activities as knowing and loving, the physical aspects of his being are operative. That "becoming" which is proper to the human person is "mixed with mutations to eye and ear and body, but the becoming is not to be identified simply with those mutations."[88]

To return to the question, then, of whether women might differ from men in their spirits, it would seem that so long as there are bodily differences, these might in some way entail spiritual differences as well, although the extent of those differences lies beyond the scope of this article. We ought not, however, thereby conclude that men and women should be considered as possessing separate natures. To so reason is to avoid one dualism by promoting another. On the other hand, it seems important to acknowledge that the essential relationship within traditional metaphysics between nature and act — and thus between nature and vocation, as we shall see — has certain questionable implications for women. More specifically it is often maintained that this very connection, which feminists esteem as part of the social construction of nature, has significantly limited their possibilities of contributing to the common good and ultimately of realizing themselves.[89] Indeed, without denying that the divine benevolence is always greater than our sinfulness, it can be admitted — as does Pope John Paul II with sincere apology for certain "sons of the Church" — that some women really have suffered from patriarchal divisions between men and women's "natural" roles within society, even to the point of being "marginalized," or worse, "reduced to slavery."[90] Women's freedom of self-determination, including their right and responsibility to contribute to the common good, has thereby been significantly hampered. Rather than questioning the connection between nature and act (and thus nature and vocation),

88. Schmitz, "First Principle," pp. 771-72.

89. Both Ann Loades and Anne E. Patrick object, for example, to what they consider the linking of women's nature and vocation in the conciliar document *Gaudium et spes*, n. 60. "It seems to be understood (given the association of women, rather than men, with nature)," Loades writes, "that women's nature is both well defined and limiting, though there was also an implicit concession to new possibilities in the need for everyone to 'acknowledge and favour the proper and necessary participation of women in cultural life,' to which they may not have contributed. . . . Real exasperation was provoked by the closing messages of the council, messages to men (males) regarded in terms of their diversified contributions to society, with women having a message addressed to them alone, and with reference to their sexual states" (Ann Loades, "Feminist Theology," in *The Modern Theologians: An Introduction to Christian Theology in the Twentieth Century*, vol. 2, ed. David F. Ford [Oxford: Blackwell, 1989], pp. 235-52, cited at p. 239). See also Anne E. Patrick, "Women and Religion: A Survey of Significant Literature, 1965-1974," *Theological Studies* 36, no. 4 (1975): 738-39.

90. John Paul II, "Letter to Women," on the occasion of the Fourth World Conference on Women in Beijing (June 29, 1995), in *Origins* 25, no. 9 (July 27, 1995): #6.

however, women ought — it seems to me — to challenge the division of human nature along sex lines.

In answer to whether there is a specifically "female" nature, I suggest we respond in the negative. There are not, in my sense, two human natures, but one nature that necessarily exists in one of two modes or "expressions":[91] the female mode and the male mode. This means, on the one hand, that no one sex points to, or represents in itself, the human "whole": the male can never — no more than the female — be the standard against which "the human" is measured. Without denying that both woman and man are, each in themselves, fully human, we must therefore insist that humanity cannot be fully represented by one sex alone. The human is, as such, both male and female. The fact that human nature exists in two modes means, on the other hand, that sexual differences are *essential*, which is not, I repeat, to admit that these modes represent different natures; rather, I mean to argue that *it is of the very nature* of the human being to be sexual, to exist in one of these two modes.[92]

These essential expressions of being human also point to the "naturally" communal character of this nature, to the fact that the human person is a social animal, as Aristotle characterized him, for example.[93] In the case of man and woman existing as two modes of one (human) nature, there is a mutual reference of the one to the other, "a personal otherness *(Gegenüber)* and relatedness *(Zueinander)*" whereby each is, in the words of Karl Lehmann, "indispensably linked" to the other.[94] The human person "always has before himself the other way of being human, which is to him inaccessible." In the man-woman relation is manifest "the contingent character of the human creature: the 'I' needs the other and depends upon the other for his fulfillment."[95] This essential relatedness of man and woman is particularly manifest in the fruit of their sexual union. Far surpassing the "self-realization" of two isolated individuals, this union creates a "transcendent" community: that "greater We" of the child and the family. Similarly on the spiritual plane, the complementary differences of man

---

91. See Dietrich von Hildebrand, *Man and Woman: Love and the Meaning of Intimacy* (Manchester, N.H.: Sophia Institute Press, 1966), p. 37. Similarly, Karl Lehmann refers to a "double issue" *(Doppelausgabe)*: see "The Place of Women as a Problem in Theological Anthropology," *Communio* (English edition), fall 1983, pp. 219-39, cited at p. 234.

92. I realize that this statement is challenged by the difficult problematic of the androgyne (dual sexuality in a single being), but this exceptional example is indeed exceptional: beyond normal biological development.

93. See Aristotle, *Politics* 1.2.1253a2-3; *Nicomachean Ethics* 1.7.1097b11.

94. Lehmann, p. 237.

95. Angelo Scola, "The Dignity and Mission of Women: The Anthropological and Theological Foundations," *Communio* 25 (spring 1988): 42-56, cited at p. 46.

and woman serve their mutual enrichment and mitigate the dangers to which each sex is prone when deprived of the other's influence.[96]

Within this context of the spiritual nature of the human person and that of our aim of promoting an integral vision of human nature securing the authentic interests of women, we might address the question of transcendence beyond the merely human dimension such that "spiritual" is understood theologically. Hence we also address the question of the integration of a theological vision and a philosophical vision of the human person, including their complementarity.

Nature and Vocation: Theological Considerations

Without insisting upon an exclusively theological vision of human nature — which would, I believe, amount to a de facto acceptance of the Protestant opposition between faith and reason, nature and grace — an authentically integral vision of this nature ought to, it seems to me, at least entertain the question of the human being's orientation to God.

Although in traditional Thomistic thought God alone is essentially good,[97] creatures are good to the extent that they participate in divine goodness, i.e., by assimilation. On the one hand, it is in tending toward its own good or perfection that the creature actually tends toward the divine likeness; on the other hand, it tends to its own good precisely *because* it tends to the divine likeness.[98] God thus moves the creature to perfection as both an efficient and final cause,[99] which is to say that we have been made *by* God and *for* God. In the eloquent words of Augustine: "You have made us for yourself, Oh Lord, and our hearts are restless until they rest in you."[100] Within the context of Thomas's *exitus-reditus* schema — according to which the "raw" human creature is sent forth from his Creator with the mission to return to him — divine likeness is

96. These dangers are addressed at length in the work of Edith Stein. See the contribution of Sibylle von Streng to this volume: "Woman's Threefold Vocation according to Edith Stein," pp. 105-40.

97. Aquinas, *Summa theologica* I, q.6, a.3.

98. See Thomas Aquinas, *Contra Gentiles* 3.24, ad. 6; *Compendium theologia* 103.

99. See Aquinas, *In I Sent.* d.34, q.2, a.1, ad. 4: the good is said to be diffusive in the manner of a final cause, as it is said that the end moves the efficient cause. "There is a concurrence of movements in the dynamics towards perfection, in which the origin becomes the end," explains Jan Aertsen of Thomas. "Every being strives in its own way to become God-like. 'Perfect' has the character of 'ultimate.' In this perfectionism may be found the ultimate 'ratio' of Thomas' way of thought" (Aertsen, p. 335).

100. Augustine, *Confessions* 1.1.

not merely *given,* it is also *achieved.* The image of God in the human person thus varies according to degree: the *imago creationis,* whereby the human person has the capacity to know and love God, is perfected in the *imago recreationis* inasmuch as he or she, by grace, "actually or habitually knows and loves God, though imperfectly." This, in turn, is fully realized in the *imago similitudinis,* whereby the human being knows and loves God perfectly "in the likeness of glory."[101] Similarly for the church fathers,[102] the distinction in Genesis 1:27 between the divine "image" *(selem)* and "likeness" *(demut)* is interpreted as that between nature and divine assimilation.

In accord with the demands of human freedom, the image of God in the human person is thus presented as both a gift and a task, which is to say that the gift of being is accompanied by the invitation and the mission to cooperate or collaborate with the "project" the human person always already *is* for God. "Being a person means striving towards self-realization (the Council speaks of self-discovery), which can only be achieved *'through a sincere gift of self.'*"[103] The "beginning" evoked by Genesis 1:27 is thus "naturally" related to the "end": the "fundamental inheritance" belonging to all humanity, our destination in Christ.[104] Created in the image of Christ, the Alpha, we are not yet "realized" except in our return to him (the Omega), by way of the initial momentum which sent us forth from him and our own willing cooperation: our mission, which is a participation in Christ's own mission of revealing the Father and his love. "We love because he first loved us" (1 John 4:19). Far from limiting freedom, such a concept of nature actually guarantees its authenticity by anchoring it in certain a priori relations constitutive of the human self: relations to the world, the body, and God. Freedom in this sense is not formulated as an absence of constraint (it is not *liberum arbitrium,* which is primary here); nor is it understood as "an empty 'form' before it is a 'content'" so as to be "more basi-

101. Aquinas, *Summa theologica* I, q.93, a.4 (Benziger Brothers, 1947). Similarly, Thomas argues that just as in a natural generation the engendered is similar *(in similitudine)* to the engendering (i.e., according to its species) only at the final stage of its generation, so also there is not an immediate union to God through the first effects by which we have substantial being *(per primos effectus quibus in esse naturae subsistimus),* but only by the last effect by which we adhere to him as to our last end *(sed per ultimos quibus fini adhaeremus).* See *In I Sent.* d.14, q.2, a.2.

102. Such is the case of Irenaeus, Origen, Basil, and Maximus the Confessor, for example. See Hans Urs von Balthasar, *Theo-Drama: Theological Dramatic Theory,* vol. 2, *Dramatis Personae: Man in God* (San Francisco: Ignatius, 1992), pp. 318, 327-30.

103. John Paul II, apostolic letter on the dignity and vocation of women, *Mulieris dignitatem,* August 15, 1988, #7; cf. Vatican Council II, Pastoral Constitution on the Church, *Gaudium et spes,* #24. The tension between the *already* and the *not yet* character of our salvation is often evoked with reference to 1 John 3:1-3.

104. See John Paul II, *Mulieris dignitatem,* #2.

cally a freedom *from* (the other) than a freedom *for* (or a response to the other)."[105] On the contrary, it is an enabling power — a positive potentiality — to not only recognize oneself as a gift, but also to *become* one, to make of oneself a gift for the other, and in so doing to realize one's fullest potential: the potential that is love.

The Aristotelian formula *ordo essendi est ordo agendi* is thus so elevated in Christian teaching that human nature is — by reason of its own freedom — thought of as directed toward and realized in union with the divine.[106] For although all properly human action is motivated by love — whether perverse or authentic, as measured by its ordination to the highest, or most perfect, good — love is itself "a kind of union or connaturality of the lover and the beloved."[107] This supposes that grace is not merely the fact of God "not counting their trespasses against them" (2 Cor. 5:19), but is also and especially the means of our transformation, or assimilation, to the eternal Word-made-flesh. This, in turn, points to the *admirabile commercium* of salvation, that "marvelous exchange"[108] in which "the Word became man so as to accustom man to receive God and to accustom God to dwell in man";[109] and more radically still, the becoming "sin" of him "who knew no sin, so that in him we might become the righteousness of God" (2 Cor. 5:21; cf. 8:9). Justification, then, is a "making" just, and not merely declaring it. This, in turn, is accomplished not by God averting his angry glance — so as to see not our sins but rather the face of his innocent Son handed over for those sins — but by actually giving us the capacity to *be* just. As such it may be considered either a habit or an act: "according as man is made just by becoming possessed of the habit of justice" or "according as he does works of justice," as he executes justice. This does not make of justification any less a gift, for although the acquired virtue is caused by works, so the infused virtue is caused by God himself, i.e., by his grace.[110] The justified actually

105. David L. Schindler, "The Meaning of the Human in a Technological Age: *Homo Faber, Homo Sapiens, Homo Amans*," *Communio* (English edition) 26 (1999): 80-103, cited at p. 94.

106. See Balthasar, *Theology of Karl Barth*, pp. 267-69. For the important distinction between the natural and the supernatural ends of the human person, see Steven A. Long, "On the Possibility of a Purely Natural End for Man," *Thomist* 64 (2000): 211-37.

107. Aquinas, *Summa theologica* I-II, q.32, a.3, ad. 3. See q.27, a.4.

108. Cf. Antiphon I, Evening Prayer, January 1: "O Marvelous Exchange! Man's Creator has become man, born of a virgin. We have been made sharers in the divinity of Christ who humbled himself to share in our humanity."

109. "Verbum Dei quod habituit in hominis factus est ut adsuesceret hominem percipere Deum et adsuesceret Deum habitare in homine secundum placitum Patris" (Irenaeus, *Adversus haereses* 3.20.2; Sources chrétiennes 211, 390, 392).

110. Aquinas, *Summa theologica* I-II, q.100, a.12.

participate in God's own justice, or righteousness, whereby they *act* justly (righteously); they practice justice.[111] It follows that salvation is not merely something that happens *to us;* it is a real participation in God's saving action.

Within the realm of this dynamic and integral conception of nature, we properly address the subject of vocation (from *vocare,* "to call") and mission (from *missio,* "to send"), which recognizes the a priori relation of the self to God as key to the full flowering or "becoming" of the human person. As the source of authentically human actions, nature is of course influential in that which concerns the question of vocation. The nature here in question is, however, more fundamentally human than it is feminine or masculine. Vocation, on the other hand, is both personal and "personalizing,"[112] which is to say that it implies a spiritual identity. Hence it is possible to address both a natural human vocation and a specifically personal one, which is to say that the universal call to holiness in union with Christ — the call to make of oneself a gift — is lived in a unique manner by each and every individual.

Within the context of the feminist concern for women's liberation, there still remains, however, the important question of whether there might be *a particularly "feminine" vocation:* one which would lie somewhere between the general (human) and the specific (personal) vocation of any given woman. Although this question is addressed in a very thorough manner in this volume by Sibylle von Streng, our specific concern in this context is to determine the relation between vocation and nature. In this we must of course insist that vocational classifications based upon a restricted view of nature (especially "female" nature) — such as that which would equate it with corporeality, for example —

111. Even in the Old Covenant the commandments are presented as a sort of commentary on what it means to be the people of God: "I am the Lord your God who brought you out of the land of Egypt, out of the house of bondage. You shall . . ." (Exod. 20:2ff.; cf. Deut. 5:6ff.). More explicitly in Leviticus, likeness to the Lord is required of those chosen for his service: "For I am the Lord who brought you up out of the land of Egypt, to be your God; you shall therefore be holy, for I am holy" (11:45; cf. 19:2; 20:26). In practical terms this means: "Yahweh your God is God of gods and Lord of lords, the great God, triumphant and terrible, never partial, never to be bribed. It is he who sees justice done for the orphan and the widow, who loves the stranger and gives him food and clothing. Love the stranger then for you were strangers in the land of Egypt" (Deut. 10:17-19). As for the New Testament, the command to exercise justice in the manner in which one has received it is so strong that the disciples are actually taught to pray, "forgive us our debts, as we also forgive our debtors" (Matt. 6:12). Within the context of the Lord's Prayer and Matthew's Sermon on the Mount, these words are themselves a concrete expression of what it means to "be perfect as your heavenly Father is perfect" (5:48, RSV).

112. That is to say, in virtue of one's vocation willingly received and lived, the individual becomes more authentically himself or herself. This is an important insight of Hans Urs von Balthasar. See his *Theo-Drama: Theological Dramatic Theory,* vol. 3, *Dramatis Personae: Persons in Christ* (San Francisco: Ignatius, 1992), especially the third part.

are justifiably suspect. Far from a model of biological determinism which would read into woman's bodily structure the full mystery of her person and her vocation, an authentically Christian model of nature actually frees her potentialities by setting them in the context of love, the ultimate meaning of freedom positively perceived. "God has honored man by bestowing freedom upon him," explains Gregory of Nazianzus, "so that the good properly belongs to the one who chooses it, no less than to the One who deposited the premises of the good in nature."[113] In the most extreme case, this act may require the renouncing of one's own will,[114] but in such a way that freedom is itself set free (cf. Gal. 5:1) within the kingdom of love. "For you were called to freedom; only do not use your freedom as an opportunity for the flesh, but through love be servants of one another" (v. 13). The Christian, Paul insists, has been set free from sin, but in such a way as to become a "servant" of God whereby he or she is sanctified and promised a share in eternal life (cf. Rom. 6:22).

The question of whether we might speak of a specifically feminine vocation, then, ultimately amounts to whether there might be a *specifically feminine manner of loving* in union with and in response to the love of Christ. The answer, it seems to me, cannot be separated from the formula expressed above: one (human) nature, two modes of expression (the male and female). If, more specifically, my reader is willing to grant that there is no particularly "feminine" nature but rather one human nature that is equally, and necessarily, manifest in feminine and masculine persons, then it would seem logical to conclude that there is, corresponding to the one nature, one vocation manifest in two different modes. In other words, we might argue for *a common human vocation* shared by man and woman: not in the sense that they contribute to a common goal or interest as two independent and autonomous individuals, but in that each does so in union with the other. Together they form a communion of persons which is also a community of action, even to the extent that each is personally realized in union with the other. "[C]alled from the beginning not only to exist 'side by side' or 'together'" but also *"to exist mutually one for the other,"*

---

113. Gregory of Nazianzus, *Oratio XLV, In sanctum Pascha*, in *Patrologia Graeca*, 36:632C. Quoted by Paul Evdokimov, *Woman and the Salvation of the World: A Christian Anthropology on the Charisms of Women*, trans. Anthony P. Gythiel (Crestwood, N.Y.: St. Vladimir's Seminary Press, 1994), p. 48.

114. Here it may be helpful to distinguish with Evdokimov between freedom and will. "Freedom is the metaphysical foundation of the will. The will remains linked to nature; it is subject to necessity and immediate goals. Freedom depends upon mind, the person. When we become supremely free by renouncing our own will, we freely desire only the true and the good. In the *plērōma* to come, the good and the true will correspond to the image of the divine freedom and to its desires" (Evdokimov, p. 50).

they simultaneously realize themselves and their communion: that "unity of the two" whereby they "mirror in the world the communion of love that is in God" (i.e., as a trinity of persons).

> To be human means [Pope John Paul II teaches] to be called to interpersonal communion. The text of Genesis 2:18-25 shows that marriage is the first and, in a sense, the fundamental dimension of this call. But it is not the only one. The whole of human history unfolds within the context of this call. In this history, on the basis of the principle of mutually being "for" the other, in interpersonal "communion," there develops in humanity itself, in accordance with God's will, the integration of *what is "masculine" and what is "feminine."*[115]

Such a communion of persons need not — it bears repeating — be understood as existing exclusively between husband and wife, nor even between man and woman. On the other hand, the metaphysical — as opposed to the merely biological — differences between them enable each to enter more profoundly in communion with the other than is the case of a communion formed by members of the same sex. It is perhaps for this reason that Paul addresses the *mysterion* (cf. Eph. 5:32) of the Christ-church union with reference to the marital union of husband and wife.

In precisely this context the bridal character of the church's vocation meets that of women in general, which is to say that women have a particularly "prophetic vocation."[116] More specifically, the "bridal" gift of self whereby the woman "realizes" herself as a wife and mother or as a consecrated bride of Christ[117] is, as John Paul II maintains, symbolic of the general human vocation — i.e., the vocation of *men and women* alike — to be, in the church, the "bride" of Christ by accepting his (Christ's) gift of himself in the form of redemption and divine life and by responding "with the gift of his or her own person."[118] The mutual self-gift of man and woman in marriage whereby they realize themselves in their commu-

---

115. John Paul II, *Mulieris dignitatem*, #7.

116. See Michele M. Schumacher, "The Prophetic Vocation of Women and the Order of Love," *Logos* 2, no. 2 (spring 1999): 147-92. With regard to Eph. 5:21-33, the pope writes: "The analogy of the Bridegroom and the Bride speaks of the love with which every human being — man and woman — is loved by God in Christ. But in the context of the biblical analogy and the text's interior logic, it is precisely the woman — the bride — who manifests this truth to everyone" (John Paul II, *Mulieris dignitatem*, #29).

117. These, the pope teaches, are "two particular dimensions of the fulfillment of the female personality," "two dimensions of the female vocation" (John Paul II, *Mulieris dignitatem*, #17).

118. John Paul II, *Mulieris dignitatem*, #25.

nion of persons is thus an image of and a participation in the more profound un-ion of Christ and the church, of course, but also an image of this divine "Bride-groom" and the human person — each and every human person, whether male or female — created in his image and called to be his "bride" by means of a sin-cere gift of self in response to Christ's gift of himself, even unto death. In this sense, then, women — precisely in their bridal love for their husbands, whether as wives and mothers or as consecrated brides of Christ — might be said to reveal to all people the universal Christian vocation par excellence: the vocation to be given fully to Christ, the divine Bridegroom of the church. Because, furthermore, one can be fully given in an almost endless number of ways, this specifically feminine vocation is not at all limiting of women, as is often the feminist accusation. What women are called most fundamentally to do and, more importantly, to *be* is in fact common to all of God's children, male and female. There nonetheless re-mains a certain "feminine privilege in the love of Jesus." What a man must realize with a certain "symbolic abstraction," as François-Marie Léthel notes,[119] a woman is able to express "immediately and fully," namely, the love of a bride and mother for the divine Bridegroom and the infant Jesus.

Conclusion

Rather than a form of divine determinism, the universal vocation to holiness in union with Christ is actually an invitation to direct freedom toward responsi-bility. As such, it supposes an important premise of the "new feminism," namely, that women really *are* responsible agents in charge of their own lives and not merely victims of oppression or creatures restricted by a patriarchal view of nature.[120] Ours, no less than that of men, is a vocation to self-realization through the dynamic of love: a love which calls forth love, because we love in response to and by the grace of Christ's liberating love for us.[121] To

119. Léthel explains that this abstraction may be realized either in that a man uses certain feminine symbols to refer to himself, as for example, when Saint John of the Cross addresses his soul as the bride of Christ, or in that certain feminine symbols are evoked with reference to Christ, as when Saint Francis refers to himself as the knight of Lady Poverty or when Saint Louis-Marie de Montfort refers to himself as the bridegroom of divine Wisdom. See François-Marie Léthel, *Théologie de l'amour de Jesus. Écrits sur la théologie des saints* (Venasque: Éditions du Carmel, 1996), p. 184.

120. On this point, see Elshtain, "Thank Heaven," pp. 301-2; and Margaret O'Brien Steinfels, "Obstacles to the New Feminism: Look Before You Leap," *America*, July 6, 1996, pp. 16-21.

121. See Michele M. Schumacher, "The Prophetic Vocation of Women and the Order of Love." It is worth noting that we love as a response to Christ's love even when this is uncon-scious, as when one loves without thinking of Christ, but also when one loves another in a truly

the statement "God is love" (1 John 4:16) there corresponds, in the words of the Orthodox theologian Paul Evdokimov, "the human being's *Amo, ergo sum* ('I love, therefore I am')."[122] United to the primal source of both being and love, the man and woman, fulfilled in Christ, love with Christ's own love. "God is Love, and he who remains in love remains in God, and God remains in him" (1 John 4:16; cf. 3:24).

Directed toward Christ in virtue of our very constitution as beings fashioned in his image,[123] we are all the more so by reason of redemption whereby our selfish wills are turned away from ourselves to be more perfectly orientated toward him as the "object" of our fulfillment.[124] At the same time, we are challenged to recognize his presence in our neighbor, even to the extent that one's union with one's spouse is an "icon" of his or her union with Christ and ultimately of the church's union with Christ.[125] This identification of God and neighbor in the person of Christ — who is himself the "one mediator between God and men" (1 Tim. 2:5) — is that whereby the nature-grace divide is finally dissolved. In him, the descent of God to human being is met with the ascent of human being to God. "He who is the 'image of the invisible God' (Col. 1:15)" is — according to the fathers of the Second Vatican Council — "himself the perfect man who has restored in the children of Adam that likeness to God which had been disfigured ever since the first sin." All that is "natural" in this man is touched and transformed by grace. "For, by his incarnation, he, the Son of God, has in a certain way united himself with each man. He worked with human hands, he thought with a human mind. He acted with a human will, and with a human heart he loved. Born of the Virgin Mary, he has truly been made one of us, like to us in all things except sin."[126] Whatever "determination" might remain within this presentation of nature and grace is freely chosen and achieved

---

selfless manner without having explicit faith in Christ, for all are touched by his grace. See Vatican Council II, *Gaudium et spes*, #22.

122. Evdokimov, p. 64.

123. And this, it is important to insist, is true of women no less than men.

124. In this we might cite Augustine's famous phrase, "amor Dei usque ad contemptum sui." See *De civitate Dei* 14.28; *Œuvres de Saint Augustin*, 35: *La Cité de Dieu*, livres XI-XIV: *Formation des deux cités* (Paris: Desclée de Brouwer, 1959), p. 464. See also above, n. 100.

125. On this see Francis Martin's contribution to this volume, "The New Feminism: Biblical Foundations and Some Lines of Development," pp. 141-68, as well as Michele M. Schumacher, "An Inseparable Connection: The Fruitfulness of Conjugal Love and the Divine Norm," *Lugano Theological Review* 4 (1999): 465-84, reprinted in the English edition of *Nova et Vetera*, fall 2003; and Michele M. Schumacher, "The Eucharistic Meaning of Marriage," *Anthropotes: Rivista di Studi sulla Persona e Famiglia* (Rome) 10, no. 2 (December 1994): 161-76.

126. Vatican Council II, *Gaudium et spes*, #22.

as a collaboration with the Almighty, who "has done great things for us" (cf. Luke 1:49).[127]

With these words we are reminded that we can hardly do better than to look for our own fulfillment in imitation of the one who, even in accord with her own prophecy, has been lauded throughout "all generations" (Luke 1:48). "Totally dependent upon God and completely directed towards him," she is "at the side of her Son . . . *the most perfect image of freedom and of the liberation* of humanity and of the universe. It is to her as Mother and Model, that the Church must look in order to understand in its completeness the meaning of her own mission."[128]

The archetypical Marian qualities here presented for imitation are of course those which many feminists object to as serving the social, domestic, and ecclesial subordination of women to men.[129] It is important to recall, however, that while Mary is "completely directed" toward Christ, he in turn is completely directed toward the Father, in perfect obedience, and toward the church, in perfect service: "I do as the Father has commanded me, so that the world may know that I love the Father" (John 14:31); "Greater love has no man than this, that a man lay down his life for his friends" (John 15:13). In looking to Christ as a woman looks to her bridegroom, the church sees in him the same qualities she recognizes in Mary, her archetype and mother.

In his assumption of human nature, the eternal Son — we conclude — also assumed the complementary and communal value (i.e., as sexed and gendered) of this same nature: Christ is not only man *(homo)* but also male *(vir)*. As such (fully human and fully male), he is "naturally" and "obediently" orientated to woman as his partner in humanity. The standard and "measure of everything human in all its dimensions,"[130] Christ exists within what Balthasar calls "a human constellation," including, most especially, his mother Mary.[131]

127. "All of God's actions in human history at all times respects the free will of the human 'I.' And such was the case with the Annunciation at Nazareth" (John Paul II, *Mulieris dignitatem,* #4).

128. Congregation for the Doctrine of the Faith, *Instruction on Christian Freedom and Liberation,* March 22, 1986, #97.

129. See, for example, Elizabeth Johnson, "Mary, Friend of God and Prophet: A Critical Reading of the Marian Tradition," *Theology Digest* 47, no. 4 (winter 2000): 317-25; Maurice Hamington, *Hail Mary? The Struggle for Ultimate Womanhood in Catholicism* (New York and London: Routledge, 1995); Jaroslav Pelikan, *Mary through the Centuries: Her Place in the History of Culture* (New Haven and London: Yale University Press, 1996).

130. Hans Urs von Balthasar, *Does Jesus Know Us? Do We Know Him?* (San Francisco: Ignatius, 1983), p. 39. Balthasar also refers frequently throughout his writings to Christ as the "concrete universal" and the "concrete *analogia entis.*"

131. See Hans Urs von Balthasar, *The Office of Peter and the Structure of the Church* (San Francisco: Ignatius, 1986), esp. pp. 136-45. "Christ's mission has an archetypal quality — it is

Born of a woman, as are all human beings, he also subjected himself to her in filial obedience (cf. Luke 2:51) and willingly depended upon her "spousal" collaboration (i.e., as archetype of the church)[132] for the accomplishment of his mission; a mission which began with her fiat granting him "entry," through the flesh, therein.[133] The bridal obedience and submission of Mary is, on the other hand, dependent upon the filial obedience (cf. Heb. 10:7; John 14:31) and spousal sacrifice of Christ (cf. Eph. 5:25), which is to say that her own immaculate fiat is, as it were, formed within his own. More specifically, her immaculate conception — that which "equips" her for her extraordinary bridal (i.e., virginal) and maternal vocation — is itself the fruit of his redemptive merit.[134] In the filial-maternal relationship of Mary and Jesus and in the spousal relationship of Christ and the church there is thus revealed the fact that we can have "no adequate hermeneutic of man, of what is 'human,' without appropriate reference to what is 'feminine.'" More specific to our context, "we cannot omit" from the mystery of Christ "the mystery of 'woman': virgin-mother-spouse."[135]

Again, it is worth mention that such a presentation of "woman" — as virgin-mother-spouse — is refused by many feminists as significantly limiting her possibilities for self-realization and, in virtue of the same, for contributing to the good of society and the church.[136] The pope, however, actually recog-

---

identical with the acting person — and, as we have repeatedly said, it is from this center that human conscious subjects are allotted personalizing roles or missions (charisms)" (Balthasar, *Theo-Drama*, vol. 3, p. 258).

132. Mary is, in the words of Balthasar, the "archetypical Bride of Christ." See "Maria und der Geist," *Geist und Leben* 56 (1983): 173-77, cited at p. 174. The *"typos"* of the church, Mary is also its "*Realsymbol* and epitome" (*Theo-Drama*, vol. 3, p. 333). On the bridal and maternal qualities of Mary vis-à-vis her Son, see p. 323.

133. Her fiat, Thomas argues, is sought by the Lord "on behalf of all human nature." See *Summa theologica* III, q.30, a.1, ob. 4. Similarly, Augustine presents the Virgin's womb as a wedding chamber in which is united the eternal Word and human nature: "Verbum enim sponsus et sponsa caro humana; et utrumque unus Filius Dei, et idem filius hominis: ubi factus est caput Ecclesiae, ille uterus virginis Mariae thalamus ejus, inde processit tanquam sponsus de thalamo suo . . ." (*In Joannis evangelium* 7.2.4: *Homélies sur l'Evangile de Saint Jean*, Bibliothèque Augustinienne 71 [Paris: Desclée de Brouwer, 1969], pp. 474-76: *Patrologia Latina*, 35:1452).

134. "From the first moment of her conception the Blessed Virgin Mary was, by the singular grace and privilege of Almighty God, and in view of the merits of Jesus Christ, Saviour of mankind, kept free from all stain of original sin" (Pius IX, Bull *Ineffabilis Deus*, December 8, 1854).

135. John Paul II, *Mulieris dignitatem*, #22.

136. See, for example, Elisabeth von der Lieth, "Die Zeit der Frau? Das Apostolische Schreiben Mulieris Dignitatem Papst Johannes Paulus II," in *Auch wir sind die Kirche. Frauen in der Kirche zwischen Tradition und Aufbruch*, ed. Veronika Straub (Munich: Verlag J. Pfeiffer, 1991), p. 97.

nizes in this relational presentation of women a fundamental characteristic of the human person in general — indeed one which, as he puts it, enters into the very "definition of the person":[137] the fact that the human being can only realize himself in giving himself. The bridal gift of self which is expressed in the vocations of marriage and consecrated celibacy — and thus in the image of woman as virgin-mother-spouse and the complementary image of man as virgin/priest-father-spouse — far from limiting one's possibilities for self-actualization, is that whereby she or he most profoundly realizes the inner "truth" of her or his person.

In his "revelation of man to himself,"[138] Christ — we might conclude — reveals the "meaning" of human nature as given and achieved, as male and female, as relational in both its origin and end. As such, he points beyond the nature-culture and nature-grace dualisms which have marked human history throughout its long search for meaning and fulfillment: in feminism no less than in patriarchy. The gifted nature of the human self — the fact that it is given to him or her to become a gift, that there is inscribed within his or her inner being the call to realize himself or herself in precisely this, and no other, way — is revealed just as much in Christ's relationship with his mother Mary and with his bride the church as in her/their relationship with him: a relationship which is of course effected by his grace but which nonetheless remains freely her/their own. The "fullness of grace" that was granted to Mary as the mother of God "also signifies" — by the fact that grace does not destroy or "replace" nature but rather perfects and elevates it — "the fullness of the perfection of 'what is characteristic of woman,' of 'what is feminine.' Here we find ourselves in a sense, at the culminating point, the archetype, of the personal dignity of women."[139]

137. John Paul II, *Mulieris dignitatem*, #18.
138. Vatican Council II, *Gaudium et spes*, #22.
139. John Paul II, *Mulieris dignitatem*, #5.

New Feminism: A Sex-Gender Reunion

Beatriz Vollmer Coles

T he arrival of a new millennium has been a good occasion to reassess many
cultural trends: feminism is one that needs thorough reevaluation. Pope
John Paul II has been a strong advocate of a greater and more respected role of
women in the church and in society, and he has asked Catholic women to contribute to this important endeavor.

During the twentieth century feminism led itself into its own crisis by
succumbing to ideology and politics, neglecting a rigorous philosophical and
anthropological background. Today it has almost as many tendencies as sup-
porters, with a conflicting and contradictory concept of the human person.
One of the most significant developments by a recent movement of feminists
has been the radical distinction and separation of sex and gender, which has
fragmented the dignity of woman and man. This division was made explicit in
the 1990s, but only as a consequence of earlier feminist theories. While the original meaning (in English) of the term "gender" refers to the grammatical distinction between masculine and feminine nouns, pronouns, and adjectives,
common usage in the past twenty years has shifted its meaning to individual
sexual identity. Feminists rightly claimed that not all of human sexuality is
found in the body, and they adopted "gender" to denote the intangible aspect of
sexuality. They added that patriarchy had alienated women from their sexual
identity owing to social expectations and pressures, thus making gender a social
construct capable of being modified.

Wittgenstein states that the meaning of a word is the use it is given in language; I do not thus presume to alter the feminist meaning of gender, but only
to take it a few steps further toward a significance that does not jeopardize human dignity nor any transcendental aspect of the human person. More specifically I will argue that the intangible aspect of sexuality, which feminists have

called "gender" — perhaps unbeknown to them — includes a transcendent dimension, accounting for all that surpasses biological, social, and cultural influences.

I propose reuniting sex and an enriched concept of gender in order to launch a new feminism for the new millennium. In the first section I will expose a brief historical background of feminism that led to the sex-gender division and describe the opposing extremes that developed, in the second and third sections. In the fourth part I will try to compare by analogy the sex-gender relationship with that of body and soul, and I will conclude by arguing that the self-fulfillment of women, rightfully advocated by feminists, is not accomplished by separating sex from gender but by acting in consonance with their true selves, whereby is revealed their gendered being.

The Progression of Feminist Thought

Perhaps the greatest threat to the dignity and identity of women has been what feminists themselves have imposed on all of humanity: the separation of sex and gender. Driven by ideological and political interests, they neglected the rigor and discipline needed to create a solid, lasting basis upon which future generations of feminists could build. Instead, they have split into two contradictory positions with one goal that unites them.

The women's liberation movements of the eighteenth century began with noteworthy cultural differences, and these developed into the opposing theories they represent today. The Anglo-Saxon approach to the equality of the sexes differed from that of the French, although their goal was essentially the same: the attainment of equal opportunities for all people. Anglo-Saxon women tended toward reducing sex-based role differences in society, while the continental European approach was more inclined to highlight the feminine and to claim more recognition for women. This subtle difference lasted for almost two hundred years and only began to develop into separate philosophies after 1950.

The publication of *The Second Sex* by Simone de Beauvoir in 1949 marked a turning point for the "women's movement" and triggered a new phase named *feminism,* having different goals and even different methods than those of the original movement. Today's feminist concept of gender as a social construct in fact derives from her famous statement that one is not born a woman but becomes one. The notion of equality of the sexes also developed and became a matter of *legal* equality after 1960.

Not content with legal equality, more recent feminists have argued that the "real" problem for women is the persisting differentiation, which ends by influencing women's careers, professions, salaries, and lifestyles. Catherine MacKinnon speaks for many American feminists, affirming that their issue is not "gender difference but *the difference gender makes*."[1] This persisting differentiation has also marked the beginning of philosophical inquiry for some feminists. What is the specific difference (if any) between male and female? How do I exercise my profession as a woman or as a man? What is different in my activities or in how they are achieved if I am a man or a woman? The question has shifted from legal equality to *ontological* difference or sameness. It is not the opportunities, the education, the salary that they seek; these have already been achieved by their predecessors. What they desire is either to be the *same* as men in all respects or so different as to have separate ethics and epistemologies.

The second half of the twentieth century was marked by the spread of feminism and women's studies; feminism has proliferated so much in its meaning that it is difficult to find points of convergence within the various currents of feminism. Guy Bouchard, a specialist in feminist history and theory, has made the ambiguity and the discrepancy evident by presenting feminism as a utopian theory and stating that the "common denominator" of the different feminisms is "the conviction that women, as a collectivity, have always been treated unjustly in patriarchal societies. This originary conviction is at the source of a very complex semantic, ideological and praxeological field which includes at least 630 different tendencies."[2]

Having studied the different definitions of feminism and the enormous number of separate tendencies, Bouchard identified eighteen varieties, which he has discussed in several other works. These varieties are determined by feminists who consider their ideology (a) a theory and/or a practice, (b) of an individual and/or of a collective order, (c) having to do only with women or with both women and men. Added to these defining options, the hypothetical cause of women's oppression further distinguishes the various tendencies. These causes can be one or a combination of either gender differences, social class, or race. In his extensive analysis of feminisms, Bouchard has observed that the proposed solutions for overcoming this oppression are equally manifold, ranging from the maintenance of existent social structures with improved conditions for women (abstract equality) to the overturning of this society and any signs of sexual domination (concrete equality).[3]

1. See Catherine MacKinnon, *Feminism Unmodified: Discourses on Life and Law* (Cambridge: Harvard University Press, 1988), p. 23.

2. Guy Bouchard, "L'hétéropolitique féministe," *Laval théologique et philosophique* 45 (1989): 95-120; cited at pp. 100-101.

3. Bouchard, p. 101.

Because twentieth-century feminism has had no solid philosophical foundation, it has been driven to skepticism if not absurdity. There has been no other goal, standard, or concept than "war against patriarchy"; and even then, there is ambiguity as to what feminists mean thereby. Some feminists wish to redefine the relationship between the sexes by transforming society. Their ambition ranges from a mere reform to an all-encompassing revolution. Some would like to eradicate what they see as the social construction of gender by starting over on a "desert island" without prejudices or by influencing society in that direction. By this they intend to illustrate today's "undesirable" relationship between man and woman as a product of patriarchal society.

Feminism up until the 1960s promoted equal rights and opportunities, and in this way was similar to its founding impetus: the women's movement of the eighteenth and nineteenth centuries. This initial stage is often called *liberal feminism,* because women sought various freedoms such as suffrage, education, and employment opportunities. It has since gradually changed its focus, however, from a mostly practical to a theoretical agenda.

Feminist theory continued its shift with an adaptation of Marxist theory in the 1970s. Commonly known as *radical feminism,*[4] it rejected liberal feminism for being too "soft" on patriarchy and for not achieving satisfactory goals. Radical feminism called for revolution, a sex-class struggle, which is not meant to be a rebellion against a particular government but a cultural transformation. This reform would do away with religious beliefs, taboos, moral principles, and anything "fundamentalist," and according to this theory would offer tolerance, political correctness, and above all a sex-neutral society.

Due to the recent failure of communism and an ever-increasing valuation of freedom, radical feminists were not as triumphant as they had hoped; instead their goals have been moderated and developed. In the 1980s and 1990s radical feminism was renamed *gender feminism.* This new form redefined "equality" to no longer refer to dignity, rights, and opportunities; instead its meaning was reduced to mathematical equality for statistical ends. Its political lobby even pushed some governments to impose quotas and affirmative action in an attempt to pervade all spheres, including the home.

---

4. Without going into detail about each one, there are different currents implied in radical feminism which include Marxist feminism, socialist feminism, ideological feminism, difference feminism, lesbian and matriarchal separatists, and so on. For more on these, see Christina Hoff Sommers, *Who Stole Feminism? How Women Have Betrayed Women* (New York: Simon and Schuster, Touchstone, 1995), and Dale O'Leary, *Gender: The Deconstruction of Women, Analysis of the Gender Perspective in Preparation for the Fourth World Conference on Women, Beijing, China,* published with assistance of *Hearth Magazine,* Providence (R.I.), 1995. For more by radical feminists, see Shulamith Firestone, Judith Butler, Kate Millet, and Alison Jagger.

It is in consonance with the purest Marxist theory that women are seen as the oppressed class and men as their oppressors. Life will only be fair after a class struggle resulting in a classless (sexless) society. Gender feminists believe that as long as there are families — with explicit husbands and wives, fathers and mothers, brothers and sisters, rather than any combination of couples, parents, and siblings — the male half of humanity will exploit the female half. It is precisely the sex-based division of labor and traditional family structures that are the main obstacles to equality in society. Gender feminists do not accept discussions on "essential differences" between the sexes because these "static" descriptions promote stereotypes and social constructs.

Gender feminists get their name because they instituted "gender" as a feminist term meaning individual sexual identity as a product of social pressures. Their intention was to help dissociate woman from the place nature and nurture had set aside for her. Carole Pateman explains how the meanings of words have been manipulated to suit the needs of the feminist agenda.

> "Sex" was declared the province of nature, of biology, of physiology, and bodily differences between women and men. "Sex," or the natural male and female forms, was separated from "gender," or the social constructions and meanings that constitute the masculinity and femininity of "individuals." There were good political reasons for such a terminological strategy in the early days of the revival of the organized feminist movement in the late 1960s, and the assumption underlying the sex/gender distinction, that the body is socially and politically neutral, fits in with the language of "sex roles" of the period.[5]

It is by linguistic misuse that gender feminists formally separated sex from gender for their own political ends. Before this time "sex" encompassed all the nuances of human sexuality, and "gender" was a grammatical term. From this moment on "sex" signified the physical aspect and "gender" the existential or metaphysical aspect of human sexuality, or rather "the masculinity and femininity of individuals." Gender feminists also introduced the belief that the differences between the sexes are socially constructed. Physical differences, which are allegedly socially and politically neutral, leave total freedom to choose a partner. Homo-, hetero-, and bisexuality are all equally valuable and are a matter of preference. They affirm that differences between male and female have no relation to natural or biological causes, but are due to social impositions. From this belief derives the new claim to "equality" not only in public and private ac-

5. Carole Pateman, "Sex and Power," *Ethics* 100, no. 2 (1989-90): 398-407; cited at pp. 401-2.

tivities, but also in the matter of reproduction. Gender feminists insist upon sexual and reproductive "rights," including the right to abortion (on demand), contraception, and all fertility treatments for single women, adolescents, and lesbians. Gay rights and sexual liberation are direct results of radical and gender feminism.

Late structuralists of a Marxist slant, such as Derrida, Lacan, and Foucault, are the background philosophers for today's gender feminists. These adopted Derrida's definition of the deconstruction of philosophy and started a movement that used that term as their weapon against patriarchy, social roles, religion, tradition, education, politics, and so on. "To 'deconstruct' philosophy, thus, would be to think — in the most faithful, interior way — the structured genealogy of philosophy's concepts, but at the same time to determine — from a certain exterior that is unqualifiable or unnamable by philosophy — what this history has been able to dissimulate or forbid, making itself into a history by means of this somewhere motivated repression."[6] In the context of feminism, this unnamable, dissimulated, forbidden, and repressed is woman/she: the purported abhorrence of woman has made patriarchal philosophy possible. Despite their opposite origins and cultural differences, feminists have recently made the deconstruction of gender and a genderless society their common goals.

While the term "gender" increased in significance in the feminist agenda, the greatest innovation of gender feminism has been the radical severance of sex and gender in the human person: if sex is an indifferent biological reality and gender a social construct, the alleged inferior situation of women must be due to a malfunctioning society, i.e., patriarchy. Their possible advancement, according to feminists, thus requires that society be freed from this social construction so that men and women will finally be "the same." Gender feminists — following the tracks of poststructuralist philosophers — are interested in deconstructing, among other things, language, family relationships, reproduction, sexuality, work, religion, government, and culture in general. Difference is to be avoided if not eliminated. If gender identity is constructed, it is flexible and can always change.

Gender feminists should get credit for creating a word indicating an aspect of sexuality that goes beyond the body. Before their time, this intangible dimension was only implied in the all-encompassing term "human sexuality." In this sense their contribution of the term "gender" has been valuable, but in

6. James Robert Quick, "*Prenom* 'She': Luce Irigaray's Fluid Dynamics," *Philosophy Today* 36, no. 3 (1992): 199-209; cited at p. 200, from Jacques Derrida, *Positions,* trans. Alan Blass (Chicago: University of Chicago Press, 1981), p. 6.

my opinion incomplete, and the sex-gender separation advocated by feminists is a new form of dualism which, as we know, attacks human dignity. If the body (and with it a specific sex) is made more important than the soul (and with it a specific gender), or vice versa, the resulting polarity leads to a limiting concept of the human being.

Today's Extremes: The Separation of Sex and Gender

The eighteenth- and nineteenth-century women's movement employed arguments for equality that never questioned the "ontological" aspect of the human being; it almost took for granted the fact that women and men are equally human, although it permitted different roles. Its goal was the attainment of legal and political equality. Over the decades, however, the idea of "women being equally human" slowly degenerated into "women are equal to men," and eventually into "women are identical to men." Implied was the idea that women must be "the same as men" in order to be "equal" to them. This careless use of concepts has recently led some women to a fierce resentment against "patriarchy." The male "class" must stop behaving the way it does so that the female "class" can feel comfortable, and this can only be realized by force: a legal and political revolution.

Today feminism ranges between two extreme and opposing poles. On one side gender feminists, daughters of the Anglo-Saxon approach, claim that men and women are born identical and that all differences between them, other than the obviously physical ones, are constructed by society. The opposite pole, the more continental European line, considers male and female as irreconcilably different and all communication and understanding between them as mere chance, or worse, an illusion. Elisabeth Badinter distinguishes these by referring to the deconstructionist or gender tendency as "blown up masculinity" *(la masculinité éclatée)* and to that which emphasizes difference as "the eternal masculine" *(l'éternel masculin)*. She also points out that the contemporary debate in feminism is not between old and modern, traditional and liberal, but between two vehemently opposed currents, both aiming at the equality of the sexes. One is based on the *absolute dualism* of genders (the European slant); the other on the resemblance of the sexes and the *infinite variations* of human genders (the Anglo-Saxon one).[7] The defining element of these extremes is based upon very

7. "Contrary to appearances, it is not only the old debate between the ancients and the moderns, traditionalists against liberals; it is also that which apparently opposes two contemporary feminist currents claiming — both of them — to ground the equality of the sexes: the one

basic anthropological presuppositions: (a) If more value is placed on the *mind*, it would seem that male and female differences are socially constructed. In other words, if the mind is what matters, being male or female is accidental to the true being of the person. This approach is strongly influenced by Marxist theory such that the social distinction between male and female is seen as oppression and alienation. The ultimate goal, therefore, is a "genderless" society in which there are a myriad of masculine and feminine identities. (b) If, on the other hand, the *body* is given more value for the evident differences between male and female, differences are highlighted over and above similarities. The result has brought about a postmodern dualism, exalting one sex over the other, but it has also encouraged homosexual lobbies, new witchcraft, and other extreme ideologies, which exist almost exclusively in contemporary Western culture.

Highlighting the Mind or Eliminating Differences

The goal, then, of Marxist- and poststructuralist-oriented feminisms is a new model of the ideal person in society: the androgyne, or rather, the genderless being. Structures, such as the family, in which genders are constructed, must be dismantled. The irony of this ideology is that if structures resist, *force and coercion* are a legitimate means of enabling all people to develop their personal identities in *freedom*.[8] Obviously this has gone far beyond the goal of equal opportunity in politics, education, and labor.

Extreme gender feminism claims that men and women are fundamentally and in all respects the same; it rejects any ontological concept of essence and any given structure, thus denying differentiation beyond that which is strictly biological. The tragedy of this tendency, and what most critics of this line of feminism reject, is that it easily reduces maleness to the model and standard for women. Nietzsche and Georg Simmel objected to women becoming malelike in view of their liberation more than a century ago. Similarly, Hans Urs von Balthasar argued that while fighting for equal rights in a "predominantly male-oriented, technological civilization," this form of feminism either antagonizes civilization as such or claims its place within it. According to him, the profound tragedy of our times is that women wish to become unnaturally masculine or

---

upon the absolute dualism of the two genders, the other upon the resemblance of the sexes and the infinity of human genders" (Elisabeth Badinter, *XY de l'identité masculine* [Paris: Ed. Odile Jacob, 1992], p. 42).

8. See Patricia Donohue-White, "Who Is Woman That You Should Be Mindful of Her? Confronting Feminism and Christian Personalism" (thesis for the Licence, Pont. Inst. John Paul II for Studies on Marriage and Family, Rome, 1995), p. 33.

try to reduce the difference between the sexes to its minimal expression.[9] Ironically, these women are yearning for permanent competition with men in areas in which they may be less capable of succeeding, rather than highlighting differences and accepting gender-specific strengths.

The denial of difference is thus actually a denial of the feminine, which is to say that feminine characteristics are most under attack by these feminists. The masculine remains the implicit norm for what is considered fulfilled sexuality in the human being. Because masculinity if it is not to be meaningless and sexless must, logically speaking, have femininity as its counterpart, gender feminists tend to eliminate sexual differences by moving toward a masculine stereotype. The resulting ideal of the sexless or genderless person (wrongly termed "androgynous") is intended to be one without masculine or feminine distinctiveness but in reality corresponds to the autonomous, ambitious, economically and professionally successful male, commonly referred to as a "yuppie" (young upward-moving professional).

Underscoring the Body or Eliminating Similarities

The opposite extreme of the feminism that claims radical equality of the sexes is that which *exalts the difference.* This second tendency derived from the nineteenth-century Continental form of feminism which saw the Anglo-American direction as "unwomanly." Motherhood, femininity, womanliness are considered, by this extreme, among the greatest values. Rousseau's influence encouraged women to stress sexual differentiation by valuing, above all, their roles as mothers. It eventually led some to believe that women are morally superior to men (reversed sex polarity).

The late 1970s witnessed the beginning of this new branch of feminism when the followers of Simone de Beauvoir saw that women, who had fought for equality, had only gained twice the work. By having a job outside the home, added to the regular chores they were not spared, theirs was a "double slavery." On top of that, they were usually paid less than men. In trying to become men's equals, women had to renounce their feminine nature and become pale copies of their "masters." Badinter observes that in losing their feminine identity, they lived the worst of alienations and gave masculine imperialism its final victory, by mistake.[10]

9. Hans Urs von Balthasar, "Women Priests? A Marian Church in a Fatherless and Motherless Culture," *Communio* 22, no. 1 (1995): 164-70. See esp. pp. 164-65.

10. Badinter, *XY de l'identité masculine*, p. 44.

Biology and sociobiology were the starting point of this tendency. It was thought that if "biology is destiny," the masculine and feminine essences are evident. Sociobiology, which began as a new discipline with E. O. Wilson in 1975, was understood as the systematic study of the biological foundations of all social conduct. According to this theory, the sexes were not made to relate to each other, but only to reproduce. Contrary to the theory of deconstructionist feminism, it held that all the differences between the sexes could be retraced to biological phenomena.

Difference feminists today can also be called *maximalist feminists,* because they want to maximize the differences between the sexes, as opposed to *minimalists,* who wish to eliminate them. Maximalists eventually advocate feminist epistemologies or, in extreme cases, "sexual solipsism." In search of a specific feminine essence, they part from physical differences, usually exalting maternity above any other feminine quality, because it is one that men cannot share with women. Many followers of this extreme, such as Luce Irigaray, Adrienne Rich, and numerous feminist lesbians in the United States, even claim the superiority of women, which may not however be "acknowledged" by society until they achieve absolute equality. These feminists speak of the mother-daughter relationship as the quintessence of the human couple, the foundation of the force and friendship among women, and the first answer to patriarchy.[11] Ironically, it is not only patriarchy that must be repressed, according to difference feminists, but even — at the extreme — masculinity itself. Not surprisingly, this strand has led to lesbianism and matriarchal separatism, which they consider authentic feminine values.[12]

After analyzing the extremes into which feminism has developed, it is almost comic to note that the representatives of both prefer to overlook their differences and basic presuppositions in favor of "women's interests" and the destruction of patriarchy. The downfall of "old feminism" is that it is based more on ideology for political ends than on the sciences that can sustain it throughout time.

A Conceptual Dilemma

Because "feminism" has become an ambiguous term in an ideological battle, it has lost impact. "Feminism" as a movement per se is rarely found today; it is

---

11. See Badinter, *XY de l'identité masculine,* p. 45.

12. Some of the extreme propositions they make include witchcraft as a female counterpart to male priesthood, artificial insemination so as to minimize the contact and dependency upon men, goddess worship, etc. See, for example, the various works of Luce Irigaray.

usually accompanied by modifiers such as "liberal," "socialist," or "maximalist" which explain its background and frame it within a context. Critics of current feminism and feminists themselves reject the fact that it seems to depend on other theories that endorse it. Many agree that it has become a loose collection of factors and complaints that describe women's misfortunes, rather than a systematic analysis of a state of affairs with a proper theory to support it.

According to Badinter, the last important step in the liberation of women has been the mastery of their own body. As soon as women took charge of their fertility, and maternity became a matter of choice, their position in relation to men necessarily changed. The 1920s introduced this last step with the concepts of family planning and birth control, and since the 1960s the main subject of feminist debate has been procreation. Badinter observes that the question is no longer which of the sexes plays a greater role in reproduction, but which *controls* it.[13] This empowerment over fertility has affected the relationship between the sexes in ways we cannot yet fully measure, but it has clearly done away with patriarchy: the male has lost his supremacy and the female has changed her status. "If once, patriarchy was defined as [men's] control over women's fertility and a sex-based division of labour, the last twenty years are marked by a double feminine conquest: the mastery over their fertility and sharing the economic world with men."[14] Indeed, the man-woman relationship has changed radically in the past twenty years. Women can no longer claim to be "objects." By taking on jobs outside the home, they have put an end to the millennial sex-based division of labor, and equal education for both boys and girls has aided in this achievement. While continuing to care for the family as well as earning a salary, women have not only ended patriarchy, they have also challenged men's traditional roles as "breadwinners." This has demanded a redefinition of masculinity and of the role of men in society, from both men and women.

Although feminism's embers still glow as a political lobby, the roaring fire that it once was has now dissipated. Lacking a rigorous methodology supporting their ideology, many feminists have seen their goals come to nothing. Some are content competing with men on a professional level, others are happy with the achievement of "reproductive freedom," and still others are willing to spend a lifetime coercing men to do more at home.

The great failure of twentieth-century feminism has been its careless manipulation of concepts and its disregard of human dignity. One extreme overemphasized the physical differences, thus reducing womanhood to the mere ca-

---

13. See Elisabeth Badinter, *L'un est l'autre*, 5th ed. (Paris: Ed. Odile Jacob, 1995), pp. 220ff.
14. Badinter, *L'un est l'autre*, p. 224.

pacity of childbearing, while the other stressed the social influence on gendered behavior, leaving the differentiation between male and female to the malleability of the mind. Both groups neglected the metaphysical and transcendental aspect of human existence.

Reuniting Sex and Gender

Having fleetingly analyzed the nature and progression of twentieth-century feminism, I believe the key to a new and more enriching feminism for this new millennium lies in the reunion of sex and gender. By adopting a new perspective of the human person, or rather, by taking a new look at the age-old theory of composite beings, we enter the heart of this reunion. I would like to present an audacious analogy between the body-soul relationship and that of sex and gender, for I believe that just as the body has a metaphysical dimension in virtue of the soul, our sex has a metaphysical dimension in virtue of our gender. This, however, is more an invitation to discussion than a statement of definitive truth!

The basic assumption behind this analogy is that the body and the soul coexist and are inseparable during the life of a person. In other words, our souls are embodied within us. Human embodiment communicates meaning and is implicit in every human relationship. All our expression and fulfillment derive from it: love, masculinity, femininity, human activity, openness to society, personal relation with God, and much more. A human body can *only and always* be either male or female, so that embodiment necessarily implies a sex. Sexuality is necessarily an essential aspect of being human.

Saint Thomas Aquinas explains the makeup of composite beings in *De ente et essentia (On Being and Essence)*. In this short but thorough work, he illustrates how all tangible beings are made of matter and form; the matter being the principle of individuation, the form accounting for substance. The human being is classified in the highest category of these beings because our souls, which transcend the physical world in which we exist, are the substantial forms of our bodies, which in turn account for our matter.

For the sake of a better understanding of the entire being, Aquinas follows Aristotle in stating that matter and form cannot be separated in composite beings, but should be distinguished. He further explains that a form cannot come into existence without matter, and a soul cannot come into existence without a body. If by way of analogy I superimpose *sex* on the tangible, material, bodily side of the human composite and *gender* on that of transcendence, form, and soul, it does not seem possible that a gender (masculine or feminine) could come into existence without a specific sex (male or female).[15]

Also helpful in this comparison is the distinction between the *universal substance* (man or woman), which has no real existence outside of the mind, and the *individual substance* (this woman — Jane — or this man — Peter), in which case the individual matter and the substantial form are unique and the composite being is real. If the analogy is followed through, a person's gender would seem to be individual but conditioned in its possibilities by a given sex. The feminist request for "freedom to choose" among several genders thus seems absurd. Although there is room for individual variance, sex and gender are and will remain interdependent. Remaining is, however, the question of how much each one determines the other and whether external influences, such as family, society, and even divine grace, make a difference to the final composite.[16]

In answer we might turn again to Saint Thomas, who states that it is the form that perfects matter. Once again superimposing gender upon the soul (form) and sex upon the body (matter), we see that neither the one nor the other can ever be considered static; instead we can only grow toward our own fulfillment or perfection by the very fact of having a transcendent dimension to our embodied (material) existence. This dynamic relationship given in us as human beings seems to give our lives not only a direction for fulfillment but also a meaning to existence. We must acknowledge that both the soul and gender are influenced by grace, culture, family, individual experience, and much more; so they are both at least partially "constructed" rather than inborn. A "genderless" society, as desired by certain feminists, then seems impossible; it would be a soulless society.

Possibilities

The coexistence of sex and gender within the human person can still be taken a few steps further, although these might extend beyond the scope of this essay. I would like to "borrow" one more contribution from yet another great philosopher and adapt it to my interpretation of sex and gender. Karol Wojtyla distinguishes between "man-acts" and "what happens in man," as described in his en-

---

15. Perhaps the awareness of gender begins to exist long after the sex does, but I think it is safe to say that, like the soul, it "grows" with the person from the very beginning.

16. It is important to remember that soul and gender, body and sex are not intended to be the same, but they belong on the same levels of existence: the transcendent and the immanent, respectively.

lightening book *The Acting Person*. What happens in man requires and involves no freedom; it is passively received as a given. In this sense what happens in man pertains to the realm of matter or potency, awaiting form or action. Man-acts, on the other hand, pertain to the form and involve what Wojtyla calls "efficacy" or awareness of one's actions. It is the substantial form which "acts" upon matter. Reflexive knowledge of our actions is embodied and potentially social because we know we are acting and could affect others.

For our purposes a physical sex can be understood as "what happens in man," as we have no choice in its determination; it just "is." Just as Wojtyla explains that action reveals the person, the same action reveals the *gendered* person. It is through the actions of an embodied person that we can perceive his or her metaphysical dimension, and this includes his or her gendered nature. Wojtyla links fulfillment to action, whereby action is more perfect than what happens. Following this theory, he takes the term through to its usage today: self-fulfillment. "In the notion of 'felicity' there is something akin to fulfillment, to the fulfillment of the self through action. To fulfill oneself is almost synonymous with felicity, with being happy. But to fulfill oneself is the same thing as to realize the good whereby man as the person becomes and is good himself."[17]

Felicity, or happiness, is not pleasure, because the latter *happens* in man whereas the former is a result of a person's actions. Being more perfect and more perfecting than what happens, actions are also more fulfilling. Wojtyla points out that felicity, as a result of intentional good actions, is a characteristically human emotion, while pleasure remains a mere sensation.[18] The ever-yearned-for self-fulfillment and happiness of women can only be reached, then, as a result of their actions as persons, not by liberating themselves from family or other obligations.

If women wish to "fulfill" themselves particularly as women, they must first define what they understand as their common "self." Are given facts, such as embodiment and spiritual endowment, considered the entire or only a part of the self? This is where the issue of a "feminine essence" comes into our argument. Since the 1960s there has been a generalized refusal of any suggestion of a feminine essence. But if certain feminists presume to find a *standard* of fulfillment for women, as many indeed do, they must first find constant, unvarying elements common to all women. Not only should these elements lie beyond cultural, religious, and educational differences, but also over and above what

17. Karol Wojtyla, *The Acting Person*, Analecta Husserliana, vol. 10 (Dordrecht: D. Reidel, 1979), p. 174.

18. Wojtyla, p. 177.

happens in woman or her sex. These common elements must be found objectively in actions that are exclusive to women. An "essence of the feminine," which is more likely to be found than a "feminine essence," must be searched for in the transcendent area of human embodiment: in the gendered spirit of woman.

Feminism has had a fascinating development during the twentieth century. Although feminists have not attained all their ideals, their efforts have had wide social consequences, including the achievement of a more favorable world for many women. Not only has feminism served to develop sociology and social consciousness, it has also greatly influenced philosophy and anthropology.

At the dawn of a new millennium there is hope that feminism will take on a new direction by pointing all women toward true fulfillment. "Gender-neutrality," "liberation," and other confrontational terms implied in feminist discourse should be concepts of the past, as evidence has proven that men and women are equal but different. Whether married or not, with children or not, employed or not, women should have the privilege of knowing that it is primarily their actions that will lead to their fulfillment and happiness, and in this men and women are identical.

Philosophy of Relation in
John Paul II's New Feminism

Sr. Prudence Allen, R.S.M.

A t first sight, the phrase "John Paul II's new feminism" seems to be a contra-diction because feminism is usually thought of as an ideology while John Paul II, a Catholic, supports not an ideology but the teachings of a living divine person, Jesus Christ. Just as it is contradictory to have a Catholic secularism, Catholic Marxism, or Catholic Freudianism, so a Catholic feminism would seem to be a prima facie logical impossibility.

The Danish Protestant philosopher Søren Kierkegaard suggested resolv-ing a seeming contradiction between faith and reason into a paradox. In *Fear and Trembling* he said that "faith's paradox is this, that the single individual is higher than the universal . . . [and] determines his relation to the universal through his relation to the absolute, not his relation to the absolute through his relation to the universal."[1] An analogy from Kierkegaard's approach to paradox would be: when the individual universalizes feminism and Catholicism, they appear mutually exclusive. Universal forms of feminism often view organized religion, especially Catholicism and the Christian God, as enemies. Kierkegaard's paradox is limited, however, because it suggests that the single in-dividual is isolated and unable to communicate, while John Paul II's stance of faith is able to be well articulated.

New feminism, as John Paul II defines it, is clearly God centered; he wel-comes new feminists within the Catholic Church and missions them toward particular kinds of actions in contemporary culture. Since it first appeared in his 1995 encyclical *Evangelium vitae (The Gospel of Life)*, the expression "new feminism" has been used to describe a call and duty of Catholic women. In the

---

1. Stated through the pseudonymous author Johannes de Silentio in Søren Kierkegaard, *Fear and Trembling* (Great Britain: Penguin Books, 1985), Prolegomena II, pp. 97-98.

pope's words: "it depends on them [women] to promote a 'new feminism'" to transform culture.[2] Something revolutionary is happening here. Why is the pope asking Catholics to become new feminists and feminists to become new feminist Catholics? Could it be that he wants us to engage with this contradictory phrase in such a way that we discover something new through the difficult encounter?

Perhaps a hint of the pope's intentions may be discovered by rereading the final two sentences of the Lenten retreat he preached, while still Cardinal Karol Wojtyla, to the papal household of Pope Paul VI in March 1976, referring to the new advent for humanity and the church: "[This is] a time of great trial but also of great hope. For just such a time as this we have been given the sign: Christ, 'sign of contradiction' (Lk 2,34). And the woman clothed with the sun: 'A great sign in the heavens' (Rev 12,1)."[3] Could the phrases "John Paul II's new feminism" and "new feminist Catholic" be best understood as participating in the dynamic of a *sign of contradiction,* a sign to be opposed, rather than as a paradox or a simple contradiction?

Since we want to approach the topic of new feminism primarily from a philosophical perspective, we turn now to the anthropology of relation underlying the pope's new feminism and consider how a woman's identity either fosters or interferes with her relations with others. We will use three different kinds of sources for this philosophy of relation: Karol Wojtyla's writings as a philosopher, John Paul II's official teachings as pope, and church documents which hold a continuity of thought with the Holy Father's teachings. Drawing particularly upon *Evangelium vitae,* #99, several distinctions between new feminism and old feminism will be made. The analysis will be divided into four different categories of philosophical relation: (1) the soul/body relation, (2) interpersonal relation, (3) similarities in new and old feminism, and (4) differences in new and old feminism.

2. John Paul II, *Evangelium vitae,* in *Origins,* 24, no. 42 (April 6, 1995): 690-733, #99. In May 1997 Helen Alvaré, who works for the United States bishops conference, published an article entitled "The New Feminism" in *Liguorian Magazine,* and Mary Ann Glendon, the head of the Vatican delegation to the United Nations Conference on Women in Beijing, wrote an article entitled "The Pope's New Feminism" in *Crisis* (March 1997). Then in May 2001 a major Pontifical University in Rome sponsored an international conference entitled "Women and Cultures in the Perspective of a New Feminism." The conference was held at the Regina Apostolorum Athenaeum, and included such prominent Catholic participants as Professor Angela Ales Bello, dean of the Faculty of Philosophy at the Pontifical Lateran University, and Alicja Crzeskowiak, president of the Polish Senate. See Zenit.org News Agency, May 23, 2001.

3. Karol Wojtyla (Pope John Paul II), *Sign of Contradiction* (New York: Seabury Press, 1979), p. 206.

The Soul/Body Relation

Since the soul/body relation was the starting point for several philosophies of the person and of woman's identity proposed throughout the history of philosophy, it is a reasonable starting point for our analysis. In *The Acting Person* Wojtyla says he wants "to rethink anew the dynamic human reality in terms of the reality of the acting person."[4]

Aristotle had argued that the soul must always be understood as the act of a particular body. Saint Thomas concurred that the soul/body composite is actualized by the soul.[5] Thus the act of the soul has a certain kind of priority in understanding the human being. Wojtyla affirms: "It is to metaphysical analysis that we owe the knowledge of the human soul as the principle underlying the unity of the being and the life of a concrete person."[6]

New feminism draws upon these two fundamental components: hylomorphism and a dynamic reality of acting persons. The metaphysics of hylomorphism holds that the soul is the act of the body and that the person is a unity of soul and body.[7] The phenomenology of human experience holds that the human body must always be situated within the reality that a woman or a man is a person, and that an act reveals the person. For Wojtyla the soul itself is not identified as feminine or female, but rather as the soul of a woman who is a female human being. John Paul II only analogically describes a man as feminine when as a member of the church he represents the mystery of bride in relation to Christ, the bridegroom.[8] The pope reserves the nonanalogical use of femininity to women alone and of masculinity to men alone.

A particular person cannot be understood without reference to the single lived soul/body composite. A woman or man develops toward an actualized end or perfection. The composite human being needs to be understood within this dynamism of actuality and potentiality. Wojtyla uses Aristotle and Thomas's notions while infusing them with a new dynamism drawn from a variety of contemporary sources, including the total experience of women and men which is circumscribed by the way the person integrates or transcends the

4. Karol Wojtyla, *The Acting Person* (Dordrecht: D. Reidel, 1979), p. 203.

5. Thomas Aquinas, *Summa theologica* I, q.77, a.6.

6. Wojtyla, *The Acting Person*, p. 186.

7. Wojtyla, *The Acting Person*, p. 203: "[T]he traditional philosophy of Aristotle and Aquinas, which . . . discovers in [the human being] alongside of the *hylic* or material element also the element of *morphe* or form; hence the theory of *hylomorphism* and the analysis of the human being carried out within its frame."

8. John Paul II, *Mulieris dignitatem* (Boston: Daughters of St. Paul, 1988), #25.

self in particular acts.[9] Through human acts the person may integrate soul and body; through human acts the person may transcend limitations of space, time, and history. For Wojtyla the human person is a dynamic composite reality, capable of continuous actualization toward a more perfect identity as a man or woman. When one component of the soul/body relation is accentuated to the detriment of the other, a distortion in gender identity usually occurs and the real potentiality of a person becomes thwarted in the face of "pseudo-ends."

The first systematic distortion of the soul/body relation for woman's identity, often called "the unisex distinction," occurred in book 5 of Plato's *Republic*, where it was argued that the begetting or bearing of children had nothing to do with the nature of a man or woman. Plato argued that the nature of the human being was determined by the quality of a sexless soul alone.[10] Plato proposed in his utopia that men and women with the same kinds of natures do the same things and receive the same education. He added that there should be a slight compensation in time for women's general weakness and men's greater strength.[11] Socrates, Plato's spokesman in the *Republic*, was aware of social conditions in Greece which limited women's development. He argued that leaving women's potential undeveloped was not only unnatural, but also detrimental to the state.[12] Plato recognized the equal dignity of women and men, and he wanted to restructure society so that all women and men could reach their full potential of wisdom, goodness, and participation in society. Yet his proposal failed precisely because he did not have an understanding of the proper soul/body relation.[13]

This distortion was continued by the Cartesian mind/body distinction which asserted the superiority of the autonomous mind over the body. A new era of unisex theories entered Western philosophy, building on the foundation of Cartesian feminism. While trying to help women achieve a fuller actualization by rights to education and participation in civil government, the Cartesian

9. Wojtyla, *The Acting Person*, p. 256.

10. Plato, *Republic* 454e, in *The Collected Dialogues of Plato*, ed. Hamilton and Cairns (Princeton: Bollingen, 1969).

11. Plato, *Republic* 455e. "Then there is no pursuit of the administrators of a state that belongs to a woman because she is a woman or to a man because he is a man. But the natural capacities are distributed alike among both creatures, and women naturally share in all pursuits and men in all."

12. Plato, *Republic* 456c.

13. See Sr. Prudence Allen, R.S.M., *The Concept of Woman: The Aristotelian Revolution, 750 B.C.–A.D. 1250* (Grand Rapids and Cambridge, U.K.: Eerdmans, 1997), and *The Concept of Woman: The Early Humanist Reformation, 1250-1500* (Grand Rapids and Cambridge, U.K.: Eerdmans, 2002), for many versions of the Platonist and Neoplatonist argument about woman's identity.

feminists consistently appealed to a sexless reason as the core of a woman's identity. This unisex model suffered from the same problem as its ancestral Neoplatonic model, namely, of defending equality at the expense of real differentiation.

John Paul II consistently argues against this unisex error. At the beginning of his pontificate in 1979, he stated that men and women are fundamentally different ways of being persons. He reflected on the story of Adam: "Precisely the function of sex, which is, in a sense, a 'constituent part of the person' (not just an 'attribute of the person'), proves how deeply man, with all his spiritual solitude, with the uniqueness, never to be repeated, of his person, is constituted by the body as 'he' or 'she.'"[14] Nearly twenty years later, in his 1995 "Letter to Women," he continued to assert a real difference in sex and gender identity along with a principle of complementarity: "Woman complements man, just as man complements woman: men and women are complementary."[15] He does however accept the unisex principle of the fundamental equality of man and woman: "Womanhood expresses the 'human' just as much as manhood does, but in a different and complementary way."[16]

Another type of systematic distortion in the soul/body relation, called "the polarization distortion," occurred in the works of Aristotle. The Greek philosopher tried in book 1 of the *Politics* to correct some of the difficulties within the Platonic unisex theory. He erroneously emphasized a particular bodily configuration in women, concluding that the female was by nature inferior to the male. His particular assumption was that the female body was colder than the male's. Consequently her reasoning powers were weakened, ethical judgment impaired, ability to generate fertile seed blocked, and virtues mitigated in relation to man. Aristotle's sex and gender polarity theory was systematically transmitted and enhanced by later authors.[17] The error in this traditional gender polarity view was not so much that the body per se was overvalued as that a particular aspect of the bodily identity of woman was erroneously overvalued. This particular characteristic (her coldness, infertility, etc.) had deep-seated negative consequences for her soul (her weakness in reasoning, ethical judgment, and political life).

In late Renaissance philosophy a mirror image of this traditional polar-

---

14. John Paul II, audience of November 21, 1979, in *Original Unity of Man and Woman: Catechesis on the Book of Genesis* (Boston: St. Paul Editions, 1981), p. 79.

15. John Paul II, "Letter to Women," June 29, 1995, #7 in *The Genius of Women* (Washington, D.C.: NCCB/USCC, 1999), pp. 45-59.

16. John Paul II, "Letter to Women," #7.

17. See Allen, *The Concept of Woman,* vols. 1 and 2, for detailed accounts of this transmission.

ity view emerged. Woman was thought to be by nature superior to the male, because of the overvaluation of a particular aspect of her body. For example, Henry Cornelius Agrippa (1486-1535) argued for woman's natural superiority from her generation from the refined bone of man. Lucrezia Marinelli (1571-1653) argued that women's virtues were greater and vices less than men because of the greater balance within her bodily nature. In more recent times, some radical feminists defend the superiority of a woman's genes, anatomy, hormones, or generative capacities. Inversely, some male theorists argue that the male genes, anatomy, hormones, or generative capacities are naturally superior to the female.[18] All these polarity theories derive from an isolated emphasis on a bodily aspect, drawing a consequent imbalance with the soul/body relation.

John Paul II argues against all forms of traditional and reverse polarity by asserting unequivocally the fundamental equality of men and women in dignity and worth. He often invokes a *theological* defense of this equality. Two such examples are found in his apostolic letter *Mulieris dignitatem:* (1) *"both man and woman are human beings to an equal degree, both are created in God's image";* and (2) *"Man is a person, man and woman equally so,* since both were created in the image and likeness of the personal God."[19]

Karol Wojtyla also offers a *philosophical* defense of human dignity by an appeal to experience. In his essay "The Dignity of the Human Person," he says the natural dignity of the person "is also verified by the whole of humanity in its ongoing experience: in the experience of history, culture, technology, creativity, and production. The effects of human activity in various communities testify to this dignity."[20] He offers three arguments to demonstrate how collective human experience proves the principle of human dignity. The first is an argument by contrast with all other living things in nature. Because human beings continually transform nature, they experience themselves as higher than nature. The second is an argument from the essential properties of the human being, experienced by their effects in the world. The effects of human acts reveal that the human person has intellect and will, and these properties consti-

---

18. See Sr. Prudence Allen, R.S.M., "Sex Unity, Polarity, or Complementarity," in *Women and Men: Interdisciplinary Readings on Gender,* ed. Greta Hoffman Nemiroff (Canada: Fitzhenry and Whiteside, 1987), pp. 3-20.

19. John Paul II, *Mulieris dignitatem,* #6, emphasis John Paul's.

20. Karol Wojtyla, "On the Dignity of the Human Person (1976)," in his *Person and Community: Selected Essays* (New York and Paris: Peter Lang, 1993), p. 178. At the beginning of the personalist movement in France, Emmanual Mounier defended woman's dignity in an article entitled "La femme et aussi une personne" in *Esprit* (June 1936): 292-97. Karol Wojtyla, perhaps following Mounier's approach, defended woman and man as two ways of being a person.

tute "the whole natural basis of the dignity of the person."[21] The third is an argument from the end of human life. Here Wojtyla points to human experience that reveals that we do not simply live for things such as culture, technology, or work, but that these things are the means we use to live and accomplish our true purpose or call in life.

The appeal to human experience is an important foundation for new feminism. Experience draws upon the unity of body and soul through the operation of the senses and of consciousness. In *The Acting Person* we read: "An insight into the relation between the soul and the body may be reached only through the total experience of man," and "the soul-body relation is also intuitively given — in an implicit way — in the experience of man as a real being."[22]

Recognition of the simultaneous equal dignity and significant differentiation of woman and man's identity came from Christian philosophy. Hildegard of Bingen (1098-1179) was the first to attempt systematic philosophical arguments in support of this position. She made her anthropological foundation the body/soul relation by describing the effect of the humors and elements on human character.[23] More recently Saint Edith Stein (1891-1942) offered a phenomenological defense of this theory by considering the lived experience of the body in both women and men.[24] In *Love and Responsibility* Wojtyla, perhaps following Stein's intellectual lead, argued for the fundamental equal dignity of the sexes and that woman's body disposed her in a particular way to pay attention to another person.[25]

The continuous search for a foundation for integral gender complementarity is an important part of the relational philosophy of many Christian philosophers in the Western tradition. It involves seeking a proper balance in the soul/body relation. As the balance shifts, the complementarity is in danger of sliding into either a unisex or a polarity model. Some might argue that Hildegard placed too much emphasis on the body's influence on the soul, while others might argue that Stein placed too much emphasis on the soul's influence on the body. Even so, these theorists remained within the bounds of a complementarity model. Beyond the discussion of soul/body relation there exists the fundamental category of interpersonal relations.

21. Wojtyla, "On the Dignity," p. 178.

22. Wojtyla, *The Acting Person*, pp. 256 and 257.

23. See Prudence Allen, R.S.M., "Hildegard of Bingen's Philosophy of Sex Identity," *Thought: A Review of Culture and Idea* 64, no. 254 (September 1989): 231-41.

24. Edith Stein, *Essays on Woman* (Washington, D.C.: ICS, 1987), and Prudence Allen, "Sex and Gender Differentiation in Hildegard of Bingen and Edith Stein," *Communio* 20 (summer 1993): 389-414.

25. Karol Wojtyla, *Love and Responsibility* (San Francisco: Ignatius, 1993), p. 280.

Interpersonal Relation

John Paul II's philosophical anthropology draws upon two historical traditions in its consideration of interpersonal relations: classical Aristotelian and Thomistic metaphysics, and twentieth-century personalism. Aristotle situated philosophical relation in the category of accidents in his *Categories*.[26] The inheritance of Aristotelian logic posed a problem for medieval philosophy, which understood the divine persons in the Trinity as distinguished by essential, not accidental, relations. The natural question that occurred to medieval philosophers concerned whether the human person, created in the image of God, would also have essential, rather than accidental, relations.[27] Recently Rev. Norris Clarke, S.J., argued for a creative retrieval of Thomas Aquinas's theory in considering relations as essential for human identity and for all kinds of real substantial entities. He stated: "[E]xisting *in itself*, naturally flows over into being as relational, as turned *towards others* by its self-communicating action. *To be* fully is to be *substance-in-relation*."[28] The general principle of good naturally diffusing itself must be augmented when we consider the unique way in which persons communicate with other persons. There is an additional factor of free choice or of act communicating to act.

Drawing upon the metaphysical analysis of relations, the body is considered a potentiality in relation to the soul, as in Thomas Aquinas's definition of the soul as "the act of a body having life potentially."[29] When we turn to interpersonal relations — although powers of the soul, such as sight and hearing — may be characterized by potentiality as well as act "the soul by its very essence is an act."[30] Accordingly interpersonal relations may be characterized both by potentiality in relation to act and by act of one person in relation to act of another person.

While Pope John Paul II is careful to root personalism in Thomistic philosophy, he is most interested in its practical and ethical consequences developed in the twentieth century by a number of Catholic philosophers.[31] The

26. Aristotle, *Categories* 1b25. See Allen, *The Concept of Woman: The Aristotelian Revolution*, pp. 104-6 and 210.

27. See Jeffrey E. Brower, who recently traced this systematic debate in "Medieval Theories of Relations," in *The Stanford Encyclopedia of Philosophy*, ed. Edward N. Salta (fall 1999), URL = http://plato.stanford.edu/archives/fall 2001/entries/Brower.

28. W. Norris Clarke, S.J., *Person and Being* (Milwaukee: Marquette University Press, 1998), p. 14, emphasis Clarke's.

29. Aquinas, *Summa theologica* I, q.77, a.1. English translation from the Christian Classics edition (Westminster, Md., 1948).

30. Aquinas, *Summa theologica* I, q.77, a.1-2.

31. See the following sections in Wojtyla's *Person and Community:* "The Problem of the Theory of Morality," pp. 145-46, and "Thomistic Personalism," pp. 165-75.

Holy Father tells us in *Gift and Mystery:* "My formation within the cultural horizon of personalism also gave me a deeper awareness of how each individual is a unique person."[32]

Personalism emphasizes the importance of interpersonal relations. In *Crossing the Threshold of Hope,* John Paul II refers to the "personalistic truth about man, who becomes fully himself to the extent that he gives himself as a free gift to others."[33] The founders of personalism described this essential aspect of personal identity in varied yet similar ways. Gabriel Marcel, in the 1940 text *Du Refus à l'Invocation,* described availability *(disponibilité)* to give oneself to another as essential to the full exercise of personal freedom.[34] In a 1945 lecture, Jacques Maritain described personal love as "capable of giving and of *giving itself;* capable of receiving not only this or that gift bestowed by another, but even another self as a gift, another self which bestows itself." Maritain continued: "this brief consideration of love's own law brings us to the metaphysical problem of the person."[35] Wojtyla, in his first book, *Love and Responsibility* (1960), approaches the reciprocal acts of two persons: "The route from one 'I' to another leads through the free will, through a commitment of the will. . . . It is reciprocity which determines whether that 'we' comes into existence in love."[36]

The early founders of personalism distinguished between an *individual,* who was self-focused, self-absorbed, and unavailable to give the self to another

---

32. John Paul II, *Gift and Mystery: On the Fiftieth Anniversary of My Priestly Ordination* (New York: Doubleday, 1996), p. 94. The personalist movement began in France in 1934 when Jacques Maritain, Nikolay Berdyayev, Gabriel Marcel, and Emmanuel Mounier met together in Paris in a philosophy group and developed the "Personalist Manifesto." Mounier published an article in Cracow, Poland, on his new movement in France shortly before Wojtyla moved there to attend university. In 1942, in the midst of World War II, the first underground Polish translation of Mounier's "Personalist Manifesto" was distributed. In May 1946, shortly after the war ended, Mounier lectured at the Jagiellonian University in Cracow and published several articles in Polish journals; and in the summer of 1947, Wojtyla visited France. These historical details may be confirmed by the following sources: Janusz Zablocki, "The Reception of the Personalism of Mounier in Poland," *Dialectics and Humanism,* no. 3 (1978): 145-62, and George Huntston Williams, *The Mind of John Paul II* (New York: Seabury Press, 1981), pp. 91-90.

33. John Paul II, *Crossing the Threshold of Hope* (New York: Knopf, 1994), p. 209. See theme of self-gift developed in Martin Buber, *I and Thou* (New York: Scribner, 1970); Emmanuel Mounier, *Personalism,* translated from *Le personalisme* (1950) by Philip Mairet (Notre Dame, Ind.: University of Notre Dame Press, 1952); and Jacques Maritain, *The Person and the Common Good* (Notre Dame, Ind.: University of Notre Dame Press, 1985).

34. Gabriel Marcel, *Creative Fidelity* (New York: Noonday Press, 1969), chap. 2, "Belonging and Disposability," esp. pp. 50-57.

35. Maritain, p. 39.

36. Wojtyla, *Love and Responsibility,* p. 85.

and to receive the gift of another, and a *person* capable of self-gift and of availability to another. Emmanuel Mounier summarizes this distinction very well when he states that the person emerges by "continually purifying himself from the individual within him, . . . by making himself *available* (Gabriel Marcel) and thereby more transparent both to himself and to others."[37] Mounier identifies five "original actions" of the person: going out of oneself, understanding oneself from another's point of view, taking upon oneself the joys and troubles of another, generous self-giving to another, and creative fidelity to the other person.[38] Pope John Paul integrates these particular personal actions in developing new feminism.

Wojtyla describes the anthropological structure of essentially interpersonal actions in *The Acting Person*. In a chapter entitled "Intersubjectivity by Participation," he states that "participation is the factor that determines the personalistic value of all cooperation. The sort of cooperation — or, more precisely, of acting together with others — in which the element of participation is missing, deprives the actions of the person of their personalistic value."[39] Wojtyla vigorously rejects a utilitarianism which places a premium on the usefulness that a person has for another in contemporary culture. The characteristics of perceived uselessness, weakness, intellectual impairment, ugliness, or lack of health are used to support arguments for abortion or euthanasia, i.e., the ending of the lives of so-called "devalued" existents.

John Paul introduces "the personalistic norm" as the way in which two persons ought to relate to one another. In *Love and Responsibility* he states this norm in a *positive form:* the only proper attitude or action toward another person is love.[40] It may be restated: one ought always act toward a human being (a person) as an end worthy of love. One ought never reduce a human being (a person) to a means not worthy of love. In an early essay, "The Personal Structure of Self-Determination," he reflected on the personalistic dimension of this norm by saying it is precisely when one becomes a gift for others that one most fully becomes oneself. This "law of the gift," if it may be so designated, is inscribed deep within the dynamic structure of the person.[41]

---

37. Mounier, *Personalism,* p. 19, emphasis Mounier's.

38. Mounier, *Personalism,* pp. 20-22.

39. Wojtyla, *The Acting Person,* p. 269. See also Wojtyla, "Participation or Alienation?" in *Person and Community,* pp. 197-207.

40. Wojtyla, *Love and Responsibility,* pp. 41 and 67-68. See also Andrew Woznicki, *A Christian Humanism: Karol Wojtyla's Existential Personalism* (New Britain, Conn.: Mariel Publications, 1980), pp. 31-33, 41, and 67-68. He uses the term "personalistic norm" rather than "personalist norm."

41. Wojtyla, *Person and Community,* p. 194.

Immanuel Kant's second articulation of the categorical imperative introduced the personalistic norm in the *negative form:* "One should always treat another person as an end in himself or herself and never as a means."[42] In spite of his reservations about Kant's post-Enlightenment isolation of the human being and the purely rational basis for his categorical imperative, the pope stated: "Kant recognized this truth and expressed it in his famous second categorical imperative: *act in such a way that the person is always an end and never a means of your action.*"[43]

The passions which spring up within a person are an important aspect of human experience and of interpersonal relations. In *The Acting Person* Wojtyla considered the positive function of the passions in motivating a person toward an end and in showing the value of particular ends revealed by our acts. He describes the relation between emotivity, consciousness, and efficacy. Furthermore, he describes how too much emotionalization of consciousness can interfere with ability to think and to choose good ends. It leads to distorted thinking; it interferes with self-knowledge and with proper actualization of the person; and it harms interpersonal relations.[44] To clarify this interaction of passion, consciousness, thinking, and choice, let us take the example of abortion, and consider what particular passions might be operative. John Paul notes five: sorrow, fear, anger, pleasure, and desire.

A woman may choose to have an abortion out of *sorrow.* John Paul refers to a woman being abandoned and left alone in a state of pregnancy. "[She] alone pays and she pays *all alone!* How often is she abandoned with her pregnancy."[45] She may have been used, hurt, and discarded by someone who did not love her. She may be unable to care for her child because of poverty or other reasons. To mitigate a deep interior suffering, the woman may choose to believe erroneously that she is not killing a human being. Her emotions may lead her intellect to a distorted "truth" which makes it easier for her will to choose the abortion. In *On the Christian Meaning of Human Suffering,* the pope shows how Jesus Christ comes to meet a person in the heart of suffering just as he did when the woman caught in adultery was about to be stoned to

---

42. See Immanuel Kant, *Foundations of the Metaphysics of Morals* (Indianapolis: Bobbs-Merrill, 1978), sec. 2, #438-39, pp. 56-57. "The principle: Act with reference to every rational being (whether yourself or another) so that it is an end in itself is your maxim." See Wojtyla, *Love and Responsibility,* pp. 27-28 and 37.

43. Karol Wojtyla, "The Constitution of Culture through Human Praxis," in *Person and Community,* p. 267.

44. Wojtyla, *The Acting Person,* "The Emotionalization of Consciousness," pp. 50-56, and "Personal Integration and the Psyche," pp. 220-58.

45. John Paul II, *Mulieris dignitatem,* #14.

death (John 8:3-11). This encounter with the one who is the Truth reveals untruth and heals the sorrow. In *Evangelium vitae,* #99, John Paul addresses women who have had an abortion: "The wound in your heart may not yet have healed. Certainly what happened was wrong. But do not give in to discouragement and do not lose hope. Try rather to understand what happened and face it honestly."

Another motivation for an abortion may be the passion of *fear.* The pregnant woman may be afraid of all sorts of (real or imagined) future sufferings. These could include fear about giving birth to a handicapped child, fear of interruption of goals, fear of rejection because of the circumstances of the pregnancy, or fear of inability to care well for the child. It may be easier to destroy the cause of the fear if the woman distorts the truth about the act of abortion. Since a remedy for fear is daring, Pope John Paul II often encourages the bravery and heroism of women who chose to allow their developing child to be born.[46]

While *anger* may be appropriate as a response to an unjust aggressor experienced in a terrorist or criminal act, the pope argues that there can be no acceptable rationale for killing the innocent child even if the mother has a rightful anger at the man who fathered the infant.[47] Sometimes anger is not directed at a particular man. Women who defend a "pseudoright" to control their bodies may also begin to dominate the bodies of others, i.e., of the developing human being in their uterus or Third World women, through a misguided feminist ideology. Mary Ann Glendon noted the "colonialist" attitude embodied in the support for abortion by First World women at the Beijing UN conference.[48] This choice may also become the concrete expression of an attitude of supremacy, domination, or tyranny of the strong over the weak.[49]

In *Mulieris dignitatem,* #10, John Paul asks: "In the name of liberation from male 'domination,' women must not appropriate to themselves male characteristics contrary to their own feminine 'originality.'" He repeats this request to women in *Evangelium vitae,* #99, where he asks them to reject "the temptation of imitating models of 'male domination,'" which he views as a consequence of the rejection of

---

46. See John Paul II, *Evangelium vitae,* #86.

47. John Paul II, *Evangelium vitae,* #60.

48. Mary Ann Glendon notes how "an exaggerated individualism in which key relevant provisions of the Universal Declaration of Human Rights are slighted — for example, the obligation to provide 'special care and assistance' to motherhood. This selectivity thus marks another stop in the colonization of the broad and rich discourse of universal rights by an impoverished libertarian rights dialect" ("Vatican Stance: Women's Conference Final Document," in *Origins: Catholic Documentary News Service* 25, no. 15 [September 28, 1995]: 235).

49. John Paul II, *Evangelium vitae,* #23.

God.[50] From this attitude of opposition to God, "everything else becomes profoundly distorted. Nature itself, from being *mater* (mother), is now reduced to being 'matter,' and is subjected to every kind of manipulation."[51] When the justification for abortion is connected with the false claim that all that occurs is the termination of pregnancy and elimination of some tissue, the developing human being is reduced to matter to be dominated by the mother and manipulated by the most modern uses of technology.

Sometimes a defense of abortion may be based on a desire for the *pleasure* of the sexual act without any connection to a child who could result from the act. The pope describes this as a practice "rooted in a hedonistic mentality unwilling to accept responsibility in matters of sexuality, and [implying] . . . a self-centered concept of freedom which regards procreation as an obstacle to personal fulfilment," viewing a child "as an enemy to be avoided at all costs" and abortion as "the only possible decisive response to failed contraception."[52] As with most enemies, the one to be destroyed is described as a "thing" rather than a human being worthy of dignity and life. The distorted thinking and naming offers a pseudojustification of the killing in order to keep satisfying the passion for pleasure.

In *Love and Responsibility* Wojtyla said men more than women have a tendency to seek sensual pleasure in the sexual act, through their desire for a woman's body. Women more than men tend to use sexual relations out of a *desire* for nearness, affection, intimacy, and exclusivity.[53] This motivation is not primarily hedonistic, but rather utilitarian, because the woman uses the man to satisfy her emotional needs. If she becomes pregnant, she might consider an abortion, particularly if the man did not want a child and she is concerned about losing his affection or the relationship.

The desire for intimacy is in itself a very positive passion in the human person. It is ontologically a desire for authentic relationship and for genuine and lasting love. Wojtyla notes: "True love, the kind of love of others worthy of a human person, is that in which our sensory energies and desires are subordinated to a basic understanding of the true worth of the object of our love."[54]

50. See Wojtyla's early identification of a philosophical root of this problem in "The Constitution of Culture through Human Praxis," in *Person and Community*: "Nietzsche proclaimed the death of God. After God, the human being began to die. The image of the human being is gradually being erased from our culture, just as culture itself tends to disappear in an economic and political system where huge masses, bureaucracies, and gigantic machines predominate" (p. 275 n. 17).

51. John Paul II, *Evangelium vitae*, #22.

52. John Paul II, *Evangelium vitae*, #13.

53. Wojtyla, *Love and Responsibility*, pp. 109-14.

54. Wojtyla, "Thomistic Personalism," in *Person and Community*, p. 173.

Thus we need to consider what external and internal factors mitigate against a woman fulfilling this desire. Identifying these factors is one of the main goals of feminism. Now that the basic principles of the soul/body relation and interpersonal relation have been elaborated, as well as an example of how interpersonal relations may be affected in a situation of distorted thinking through an emotionalization of consciousness, we are in a better position to evaluate Pope John Paul II's new feminism. In the next two sections we will consider similarities in new feminism and old feminism and then differences between the two.

Similarities in New Feminism and Old Feminism

To begin this comparison of new and old feminism,[55] I would like to offer a "heuristic" description of feminism as an organized "response to perceived limitations to the freedom of women to develop their potential for full personal growth and perfection."[56] It aims at identifying factors which inhibit the flourishing of a woman's equal dignity with man, and it offers methods for transforming or removing those factors or obstacles.

The pope claims in *Evangelium vitae*, #99, that "new feminism acknowledge[s] and affirm[s] the true genius of women in every aspect of the life of society and overcome[s] all discrimination, violence and exploitation."[57] Similarities in new and old feminism will be found in the identification of kinds of discrimination, violence, and exploitation which limit women's full development. John Paul II's new feminism supports and updates many fundamental principles of feminism as it emerged from the fifteenth to the twentieth centuries. Even though these limitations pertain not exclusively to women, feminism reveals how they affect women in very specific ways.

Discrimination

Discrimination often interferes with women's access to education or participation in civil society. From the perspective of philosophical anthropology, dis-

---

55. In 1882 Hubertine Auclert was the first to begin the public use of the term "feminist" to describe her work for women's suffrage in her periodical *La Citoyenne*. The term "feminist" was adopted by a congress in Paris at the end of the nineteenth century, and it entered popular usage from that time on. See Karen Offen, "Defining Feminism: A Comparative Historical Approach," *Signs* 14, no. 1 (1988): 126.

56. See Sr. Prudence Allen, "Can Feminism Be a Humanism?" pp. 251-84 in this volume.

57. John Paul II, *Evangelium vitae*, #99.

crimination thwarts the development of the nature of a person. Discrimination in education keeps the higher faculty of the soul, the intellect, in an inferior stage of development. While the will, memory, imagination, and senses may operate interiorly to their full capacity, discrimination in work and politics may severely limit the options for choice and sharing of one's gifts with society and culture. Therefore, in addition to the fact that discrimination contravenes human rights and justice, it also harms the human person and society.

Wojtyla's role in the development of *Gaudium et spes,* the Vatican II document on the church in the modern world, is well documented.[58] Paragraph 29 argues that "discrimination in basic personal rights on the grounds of sex . . . must be curbed and eradicated as incompatible with God's design."[59] Identified later in the same paragraph is discrimination against "women who are denied the chance freely to choose a husband, or a state of life, or to have access to the same educational and cultural benefits as are available to men." Then in 1995 the Holy See's position paper for the UN Conference on Women emphasized the need to overcome these forms of discrimination: "Access to education, on all levels, is a focal point in the liberation and promotion of women. Education is the prerequisite for access to employment, to personal autonomy and to complete participation in economic, social and political life."[60]

In addition to noting discrimination in education and culture, John Paul addresses discrimination against women in work and especially those who have chosen to be married and raise a family. He writes in his "Letter to Women": "Much remains to be done to prevent discrimination against those who have chosen to be wives and mothers."[61] The Holy See specifically argued at the UN conference in Beijing that women have a right to work, a right to re-

58. See George Weigel, *Witness to Hope: The Biography of Pope John Paul II* (New York: Harper, 1999), pp. 158-80, and Rocco Buttiglione, *Karol Wojtyla: The Thought of the Man Who Became Pope John Paul II* (Grand Rapids and Cambridge, U.K.: Eerdmans, 1997), pp. 177-231.

59. *Gaudium et spes,* in *Vatican Council II: The Basic Sixteen Documents,* ed. Austin Flannery, O.P. (Northport, N.Y.: Costello Publishing, 1996), #29. This passage is also quoted in the foreword by Msgr. Dennis M. Schnur, to *Pope John Paul II on the Genius of Women* (Washington, D.C.: NCCB/USCC, 1997), p. 1.

60. *Holy See's Position Paper at the Beijing Conference on Women,* in *L'Osservatore Romano* 36 (September 6, 1995): #10. In the same document discrimination directed particularly toward women is explained as an attack on the principle of the equal dignity of all human beings: "Men and women enjoy the same identical dignity. . . . Without a clear understanding of the meaning of human dignity, discrimination will never be avoided. Women are — and have been historically — the first to suffer. In reality discriminatory practices against women, in all their forms, are none other than the expression of a lack of recognition of the equal dignity of women" (#1).

61. John Paul II, "Letter to Women," #4.

main at home to care for young children, and a right to both work and have children.[62]

The Holy Father's analysis of discrimination goes deeper than confronting external areas of injustice and specific inequalities. In his 1995 message for the world day of peace, he considers the deep effects on the personal identity of women who experienced discrimination from their early childhood: "If, from the very beginning, girls are looked down upon or regarded as inferior, their sense of dignity will be gravely impaired and their healthy development inevitably compromised. Discrimination in childhood will have lifelong effects and will prevent women from fully taking part in the life of society."[63]

Violence

Violence, which radically contravenes a woman's exercise of free will, is the second area in which the pope challenges new feminists to overcome. From the perspective of philosophical anthropology, the human person is wounded by violence in all its forms: verbal, visual, or physical. In a letter to Gertrude Mongella, secretary-general of the United Nations Fourth World Conference on Women, John Paul asks "women to do even more to save society from the deadly virus of degradation and violence which is today witnessing a dramatic increase."[64]

The pope has identified several ways women are particularly harmed by violence in his "Letter to Women": "Then too, when we look at one of the most sensitive aspects of the situation of women in the world, how can we not mention the long and degrading history, albeit often an underground history, of violence against women in the area of sexuality?"[65] He vigorously stated his condemnation of sexual violence against women and asked for political and legal action to defend women from this kind of violence. Violence reduces a woman from a person worthy of love to a thing to be dominated by the will of the man. While the exercise of her free will is inhibited, she still remains interiorly free but wounded.[66]

62. *Holy See's Position Paper,* 1.1 See also an earlier articulation of this in John Paul II's *Encyclical on Human Work:* "It will redound to the credit of society to make it possible for a mother — without inhibiting her freedom, without psychological or practical discrimination, and without penalizing her as compared with other women — to devote herself to taking care of her children and educating them in accordance with their needs, which vary with age" (#19).

63. John Paul II, *World Day of Peace Message,* January 1, 1995, in *The Genius of Women,* #8.

64. John Paul II, welcome to Gertrude Mongella (May 1995), in *The Genius of Women,* #5.

65. John Paul II, "Letter to Women," #5.

66. In the *Holy See's Position Paper at the Beijing Conference on Women,* particular forms of violence against women are even more specifically identified. Physical violence against

In his apostolic letter *On the Dignity and Vocation of Women,* the pope identifies the deeper root of violence against women as an effect of original sin which ruptures the fundamental equality in the original creation of man and woman. He notes further that "this threat is more serious for the woman, since domination takes the place of 'being a sincere gift' and therefore living 'for' the other; 'he shall rule over you.' This 'domination' . . . is especially to the disadvantage of the woman."[67] In *Evangelium vitae* he considers how the structure of a materialistic society fosters the domination of the strong over the weak. "[I]nterpersonal relations are seriously impoverished. The first to be harmed are women, children, the sick or suffering, and the elderly. The criterion of personal dignity . . . is replaced by the criterion of efficiency, functionality and usefulness."[68] Violence harms the potential soul/body development; it inflicts a wound into interpersonal relations. While both men and women are affected by this rupture of their fundamental equal dignity, both old and new feminists emphasize that women are "especially disadvantaged" and "seriously impoverished."

Exploitation

The third area John Paul II identifies as an obstacle in women's development is exploitation. In *Love and Responsibility* Wojtyla notes that both women and men have a tendency toward exploiting the other in an intimate relationship. A woman tends to use a man for sentiment, for satisfying her need to love and be loved; a man tends to use a woman for pleasure, to satisfy his desire for sexual pleasure. Calling them two forms of "subjective egoism," the feminine and masculine forms, he describes how a woman or a man can with effort become free from these potential avenues of exploiting a person of the opposite sex.[69]

women includes, it is explained, not only rape, war, genital mutilation, forced prostitution, and arranged marriages, but also forced contraception, sterilization, and abortion. See Mary Ann Glendon, "Vatican Delegation in Beijing," *Origins* 25, no. 13 (September 14, 1995): esp. #4, para. 7, p. 205.

67. John Paul II, *Mulieris dignitatem,* #10. In the same paragraph he also identifies the roots in original sin of discrimination: "These words of Genesis refer directly to marriage, but indirectly they concern the different spheres of social life: the situations in which the woman remains disadvantaged or discriminated against by the fact of being a woman. The revealed truth concerning the creation of the human being as male and female constitutes the principal argument against all the objectively injurious and unjust situations which contain and express the inheritance of the sin which all human beings bear within themselves."

68. John Paul II, *Evangelium vitae,* #23.

69. Wojtyla, *Love and Responsibility,* pp. 143-66.

Both old and new feminism have focused particularly on how an exploited woman is used as a means to a utilitarian or hedonistic goal rather than treated as an end in herself. She is reduced from someone worthy of love to a thing to be used and discarded when no longer useful. In the "Letter to Women" the pope states: "Nor can we fail, in the name of the respect due to the human person, to condemn the widespread hedonistic and commercial culture which encourages the systematic exploitation of sexuality and corrupts even very young girls into letting their bodies be used for profit."[70]

In *Evangelium vitae* the pope considers how an imbalance in the soul/body relation contributes to this distorted interpersonal relation. When the body "is reduced to pure materiality . . . to simply a complex of organs, functions and energies to be used according to the sole criteria of pleasure and efficiency," the sexual relation of a man and a woman is also "depersonalized and exploited."[71] The reduction of the body to a mechanical cluster of organs also leads to "procedures that exploit living human embryos and fetuses."[72]

To summarize: John Paul II's feminism in the areas of discrimination, violence, and exploitation builds on traditional feminism. In this sense it is not so much a new feminism as a *renewed feminism*. Systematic analyses of discrimination against women in education, work, and politics; of verbal and physical violence; and of exploitation in work and sexual activity have a long history. Some of this history will now be briefly recounted.

Historical Background of Feminism

Christine de Pizan (1363-1431), an early Renaissance feminist, explored obstacles against women's education, the violence of slander and physical violence against women, and the exploitation of widows. She systematically defended women against false generalizations, wrongful accusations, injustices of word and deed, and satirical bias. In her major works on this topic, *Epistre au Dieu d'Amours* (1399), *Querelle de la rose* (1402), and *Le livre de la cité des dames* (1405), she argued for a renewed relation of justice between men, women, and God; the moral value of faithful love between husband and wife; integral dia-

---

70. John Paul II, "Letter to Women," #5. In *Evangelium vitae* (#3) the pope directly quotes the passage from *Gaudium et spes* (#27) concerning the insult to human dignity evident in "slavery, prostitution, the selling of women and children, as well as disgraceful working conditions, where people are treated as mere instruments of gain rather than as free and responsible persons."

71. John Paul II, *Evangelium vitae*, #23.

72. John Paul II, *Evangelium vitae*, #63.

logue between women and men; the importance of virtue; and freedom from those factors which inhibit women and men from sustaining mature interpersonal relationships.[73] Marie le Jars de Gournay (1565-1645), a later Renaissance feminist, appealed to Plato in *Egalité des hommes et des femmes* to defend the topic of equal rights for women and men in political life; and in *Grief des dames* she argued against deprivation of goods and liberty that women experienced.[74]

The Cartesian feminists, Anna Maria van Schurman (1607-78), François Poullain de la Barre (1647-1723), and Mary Astell (1666-1731), argued systematically against discrimination in education on the basis of the same identity of mind in all human beings.[75] Mary Astell and other later Cartesian feminists, Marie Jean Antoine Marquis de Condorcet (1743-94), Olympe de Gouges (Marie Gouze) (1748-93), and Mary Wollstonecraft (1759-97), used the Cartesian principle of equality to argue forcefully for women's rights and the need to overcome discrimination against women's participation in politics.[76] These detailed feminist arguments all occurred before the nineteenth century. As noted, John Paul's reflections on these kinds of obstacles to women's development

73. Christine de Pizan, *Poems of Cupid, God of Love,* trans. and ed. Thelma S. Fenster and Mary Carpenter Erler (Leiden and New York: Brill, 1990); *La Querelle de la rose: Letters and Documents,* ed. Joseph L. Baird and John R. Kane, North Carolina Studies in the Romance Languages and Literature (Chapel Hill, 1978); and *The Book of the City of Ladies,* trans. Earl Jeffrey Edwards (New York: Persea Press, 1983). For a detailed analysis of the quality and logic of her arguments, see Allen, *The Concept of Woman: The Humanist Reformation,* chap. 7, pp. 537-658.

74. Marie le Jars de Gournay, *Egalité des hommes et des femmes* (1622) and *Grief des dames* (1626).

75. Anna Maria van Schurman, *De ingenii mulierbris ad doctrinum et meliores* (1641); François Poullain de la Barre, *De l'égalité des deux sexes* (1673) and *De l'education des dames pour la conduite de l'esprit dans les sciences et dan les moeurs. Entretiens* (1679); and Mary Astell, *A Serious Proposal to the Ladies for the Advancement of their True and Greatest Interest* (1694), and attributed to Astell, *An Essay in Defence of the Female Sex* (1696).

76. Marie Jean Antoine Marquis de Condorcet, "Lettres d'un Bourgeois de New-Haven sur l'unité de la législation," in *Recherches Historiques et Politiques sur Les Etats-Unis de L'Amérique septentrionale avec quatre Lettres d'un Bourgeois de New Haven sur L'uniteé de la législation* (Paris, 1788) and *Sur l'admission des femmes au droit de la Cité* (1798); Olympe de Gouges, "Les Droits de la Femme" (Paris, 1701), translated in Darline Gay Levy, ed., *Women in Revolutionary Paris, 1789-1795; Selected Documents with Notes and Commentary* (Urbana: University of Illinois Press, 1979); and Mary Wollstonecraft, *Thoughts on the Education of Daughters with Reflections on Female Conduct in the more Important Duties of Life* (London, 1787), *A Vindication of the Rights of Women* (1792), and *An Historical and Moral View of the Origin and Progress of the French Revolution and the Effect it has Produced in Europe* (1793-94). For a systematic analysis of these texts see Sr. Prudence Allen, "Descartes, The Concept of Woman and the French Revolution," in *Revolution, Violence, and Equality,* ed. Yaeger Hudson and Creighton Peden, Studies in Social and Political Theory, vol. 10, no. 3 (Lewiston, Queenston, and Lampeter: Edwin Mellen Press, 1990), pp. 61-78.

continue a long line of previous feminist arguments. More recently, "Marxist feminists," including Karl Marx himself, Friedrich Engels, Rosa Luxemburg, Marlene Dixon, and Shulamith Firestone, have focused on the systematic exploitation of women's work in such far-reaching areas as industry, housework, and prostitution.[77] While the pope appreciated Marx's philosophical critique of alienation, he also noted that Marx neglected "what is essential, [namely] how we relate to one another, even somehow despite the structures."[78] Secular humanist feminists, such as John Stuart Mill, Betty Friedan, and members of the National Organization for Women, have promoted equal rights and the need for equal pay for equal work; they also opened new opportunities for the kind of work women ought to be able to perform.[79] Phenomenological feminists like Saint Edith Stein and existential feminists like Simone de Beauvoir focused in the twentieth century on ways culture and the lived experience of the body form deep feminine self-understanding in women.[80]

In conclusion, this section on a comparison of similarities in old and new feminism has shown that John Paul's critique of discrimination, violence, and exploitation of women supports and updates many of the fundamental principles of old feminism. Differences between the two forms of feminism will be better seen in arguments about women's own responsibility to themselves and to society.

Differences between New and Old Feminism

It may seem that feminism only considers woman as a victim of cultural discrimination, violence, or exploitation. Feminism also elaborates woman's re-

---

77. Karl Marx, "Wages of Labor" and "Private Property and Communism," in *Early Writings* (New York, Toronto, and London: McGraw-Hill, 1964), pp. 80 and 153-54; Frederick Engels, *The Origin of the Family, Private Property, and the State* (New York: International Publishers, 1972); Rosa Luxemburg, *Selected Political Writings*, ed. Dick Howard (New York: Monthly Review Press, 1971); Marlene Dixon, *The Future of Women* (San Francisco: Synthesis Publications, 1980); and Shulamith Firestone, *The Dialectic of Sex* (New York: Bantam Books, 1971).

78. Wojtyla, "Participation or Alienation?" p. 206.

79. John Stuart Mill, *The Subjection of Women* (1869), in *Three Essays* (London: Oxford University Press, 1969); Betty Friedan, *The Feminine Mystique* (New York: Norton, 1963); and "National Organization for Women: Statement of Purpose (1966)," in *This Great Argument: The Rights of Women*, ed. Haminca Bosmajian and Haig Bosmajian (Menlo Park, Calif.: Addison-Wesley, 1972).

80. Stein, *Essays on Women*, is a translation of *Die Frau: Ihre Aufgabe nach Natur und Gnade* (Louvain: E. Nauwelaerts, 1959). Her public lectures on women began in 1928. Simone de Beauvoir, *The Second Sex* (New York: Vintage, 1953), is a translation of the 1949 *Le deuxième sex.*

sponsibility and duty to change both herself and society. Borrowing a theme from Aristotle's *Ethics* (1095a13-21), that everyone seeks happiness but differs about what it is and how it should be sought, one could say that all women want to be liberated but differ about what women's liberation is and how it ought to be brought about.

In 1995 the pope pointed out that what is needed is the "ultimate anthropological basis of the dignity of women, making it evident as part of God's plan for humanity."[81] The anthropological foundation precedes any ethical norms. This means that norms are derived from the ontological foundation of human identity and not from other sources such as reason by itself, passions, or usefulness.[82] By drawing upon a wider range of John Paul's works, we find concrete measures for this anthropological foundation to be used to evaluate different forms of feminism.

In *Love and Responsibility* Wojtyla notes that "duty always grows out of the contact of the will with some norm."[83] We have already introduced one norm, the personalistic norm emphasizing that a person should always be treated as an end in the self, a someone worthy of love. Wojtyla also claims that "The commandment to love is . . . a form of the personalistic norm."[84] Embedded within the personalistic norm are two other guides for action: one can be called "the principle of human dignity," and the other the "law of reciprocity," also known as "law of the gift" and "law of entrustment."

An act involves the exercise of both intellect and will; the intellect makes the judgment about the truth of something, and the will makes a choice that appears good based on the truth the intellect has grasped. In *Fides et ratio* Pope John Paul II defines a human being as "one who seeks the truth."[85] There is a relentless drive to discover the truth about oneself and about the meaning of life deep within every woman. A person can run away from the truth at first because of fears about the demands it might make; yet in the end, the deep long-

81. John Paul II, "Letter to Women," #6. He said later in the same section: "when one looks at the great process of women's liberation, the journey has been a difficult and complicated one, and at times, not without its share of mistakes. But it has been substantially a positive one, even if it is still unfinished. . . . This journey must go on" (referring back to his *World Day of Peace Message*, #4). This view was also noted by Mary Ann Glendon in her response as head of the Vatican delegation to the Beijing conference, "Vatican Stance," p. 234.

82. See Wojtyla's critique of reasoning itself (Kant), passions (Hume), or usefulness (Mill) as the basis for ethics in "On the Directive or Subservient Role of Reason in Ethics in the Philosophy of Thomas Aquinas, David Hume, and Immanuel Kant" and "Human Nature as the Basis of Ethical Formation," in *Person and Community*, pp. 57-72 and 95-99.

83. Wojtyla, *Love and Responsibility*, p. 120.

84. Wojtyla, *Love and Responsibility*, p. 121.

85. John Paul II, *Fides et ratio* (Boston: Daughters of St. Paul, 1998), #28.

ing for union with the truth — even with the one who "is the way, the life, and the truth" — propels the person to keep on a pilgrimage for a truth that is lasting and firm. The two pathways that are used in this search are faith and reason. Woman's duty consists initially in being faithful to this search for truth and then making choices that are based on a true good.

Principle of Human Life

The roots of this principle can be seen in the beginning of the often quoted passage from *Evangelium vitae*, #99: "In transforming culture so that it supports life, women occupy a place in thought and action which is unique and decisive. It depends on them to promote a 'new feminism.'" While the pope points to the need to have a proper respect for ecology, women hold a unique place in relation to supporting *human life*. This is why it is helpful to describe the duty and norm not simply as pro-life, but as pro-human life: "Through your commitment to life . . . you will become *promoters of a new way of looking at human life*" (emphasis mine).

The principle of human life has a wider reach as well: *The dignity of human life should be supported toward its full development for the common good.* The first factor of *human dignity* arises from the creation of the human being "in the image of God" with the faculties of intellect and will. The dignity is in the human being, as a unified soul/body being, and not simply in the higher faculties of intellect or will. The dignity of human life is supported for Christian feminists because Jesus Christ took on human nature. The duty contained in the principle of life itself is stated in *Evangelium vitae*, #81: "Society as a whole must respect, defend and promote the dignity of every human person, at every moment and in every condition of that person's life."

The second factor in the principle of human life, or *full development,* is also defended in *Evangelium vitae:* "The life which God bestows upon man is much more than mere existence in time. It is a drive towards fullness of life" (#34).[86] Again in #30 John Paul points to one's duty to work toward fulfillment.[87] This principle of the full development of human life is important not only in relation to the previous discussion of the obligation to confront discrimination, violence, and exploitation, but also in the further identification of

---

86. See also *Evangelium vitae,* #35: "[W]hether man or woman, . . . God . . . [is] the definitive goal and fulfilment of every person."

87. He states: "[T]he Gospel of life includes everything that human experience and reason tell us about the value of human life, accepting it, exalting it and bringing it to fulfilment."

woman's particular genius in supporting the full development of all persons within the sphere of her influence.

The third factor in the principle of human life, or *common good*, is a fundamental precept of personalism. We refer to the definition in the *Catechism of the Catholic Church*, #1906: "By common good is to be understood 'the sum total of social conditions which allow people, either as groups or as individuals, to reach their fulfilment more fully and more easily.' The common good concerns the life of all."[88] The duty associated with the common good is identified as the virtue of solidarity defined in *Sollicitudo rei socialis*, #38: "solidarity . . . is a firm and persevering determination to commit oneself to the common good; that is to say, to the good of all and of each individual because we are all really responsible for all."[89]

Measuring the old feminisms by the principle of human life, we find only one or two forms that agree with the new feminism of John Paul II. The Renaissance feminism of Christine de Pizan coheres most fully with new feminism. As a faithful Catholic, this fourteenth-century feminist considered it her duty to work for the full development of all women and men for the common good. While her efforts were oriented toward eradicating discrimination, violence, and exploitation of women, her goal and methods were consistent with Christian principles of social action, namely, with the virtue of solidarity.[90] The early Cartesian feminists, mostly Christian Protestants, also cohered with many aspects of new feminism in respect to the goal and methods of feminism. However, a difference in anthropological foundation, by following Descartes and placing the primary identity of woman in her sexless mind rather than in her soul/body unity, opened a fissure which eventually led to more recent Cartesian-type unisex views. The effects of this fissure is seen in Locke's view of a developing fetus or an elderly person with mental impairment as not a person because of the lack of evident continuity of consciousness.[91]

---

88. *Catechism of the Catholic Church.* The reference included within this passage is to *Gaudium et spes*, #26 and 74.

89. John Paul II, *Sollicitudo rei socialis*, in *Origins* 17, no. 38 (March 3, 1988): 643-60. See also Sister Prudence Allen, R.S.M., "Foundational Virtues for Community," *Etudes maritiennes/Maritain Studies*, no. 12 (1996): 133-49.

90. For a detailed analysis of this, see Allen, *The Concept of Woman: The Early Humanist Reformation*, chap. 7.

91. See John Locke, *An Essay concerning Human Understanding* (Indianapolis: Hackett, 1996): "[I]n this alone consists personal identity, i.e., the sameness of a rational being: and as far as this consciousness can be extended backwards to any past action or thought, so far reaches the identity of that person" (bk. 2, chap. 27, #9, p. 138).

Nineteenth- and twentieth-century Marxist feminism, radical feminism, and postmodern feminism are most strongly in conflict with new feminism because they reject the common good and support the development of only a portion of society: the working class, women, or the educated elite.[92] Our focus will not be the more radical forms of feminism, but moderate feminism derived from secular pragmatic humanism.[93] Secular humanism developed from post-Enlightenment thought as articulated by various humanist manifestos of the twentieth century.[94] It claims that all truths and laws are simply made by human beings and that human experience is the sole criterion for evaluating truth and moral values. Any threat to human autonomy and to the goal of living happily "without pain" in secular culture is aggressively attacked. God, as the source of objective truth and moral values and organized religion which supports objective truth and moral values, became identified as the enemy.[95] Differences between secular humanist feminism and new feminism can be sharpened by a consideration of abortion.

The National Organization for Women (NOW) claims that "In 1967 NOW became the first national [American] organization to call for the legalization of abortion and for the repeal of all anti-abortion laws."[96] It identifies Betty Friedan as one of its founders. Focusing on what it calls "abortion rights,"

92. A Marxist feminist argues that only the dignity of members of the working class should be supported. Karl Marx stated: "atheism as the annulment of God is the emergence of theoretical humanism, and communism as the annulment of private property is the vindication of real human life as man's property" ("Critique of Hegel's Dialectic," in *Early Writings*, p. 213). Shulamith Firestone argues for "freedom from the tyranny of reproduction and childbearing" and asserts that "[m]achines thus could act as the perfect equalizer, obliterating the class system based on exploitation of labor" (Firestone, pp. 225 and 201). A radical feminist supports only the full development of women while ignoring the development of men. A postmodernist feminist argues against human identity itself and acts to negate any forces in language or culture which try to maintain an identity for man or woman. Monique Wittig argues, for example, that gender must be destroyed and that women and men, "as classes and as categories of thought or language . . . have to disappear, politically, economically, ideologically" ("The Mark of Gender," *Feminist Issues*, Fall 1985, p. 6, and "The Straight Mind," *Feminist Issues*, Summer 1980, p. 108).

93. Pragmatism, as an erroneous theory of truth, has been well critiqued by John Paul II in *Fides et ratio*, #87-89. He applies its effects to feminism in the *Holy See's Position Paper*, #2: "Only the particular attention of the Conference to the inalienable dignity of each woman can avoid discrimination based on 'pragmatic' reasoning."

94. See Corliss Lamont, *The Philosophy of Humanism* (New York: Ungar, 1982), for the humanist manifestos of 1933 and 1973 (pp. 285-300).

95. See the analysis by Allen in "Can Feminism Be a Humanism?" in this volume.

96. See www.now.org/history/history.html. See also "National Organization for Women," pp. 190-91.

NOW makes the further claim: "An estimated one in two adult women in the U.S. will have an abortion, thereby exercising a basic human right to control their bodies."[97] Feminists in this tradition base their actions and words on falsehoods and choices for the lesser good. In *Mulieris dignitatem*, #40, the pope recalls that "the father of lies . . . wishes to devour 'the child.'"

What distortions of truth does secular humanist feminism put forward in its attempt to justify abortion? The pope identifies several falsehoods in his writings: (1) the developing human being, an embryo or fetus, is solely a part of the woman's body; (2) the developing human being is a cluster of tissue and organs; (3) an abortion is simply an interruption of pregnancy; and (4) a woman has a right to procure an abortion. Underneath each lie is an erroneous philosophical anthropology which, if accepted and acted upon by a particular woman, will end with the killing of a child.

Concerning the argument that the fetus is a part of the woman's body, he states in *Evangelium vitae*, #60: "Some people try to justify abortion by claiming that the result of conception, at least up to a certain number of days, cannot yet be considered a personal human life. But in fact, 'from the time that the ovum is fertilized, a life is begun which is neither that of the father nor the mother; it is rather the new life of a new human being with his own growth. It would never be made human if it where not human already.'"[98] Drawing upon evidence from contemporary science, the pope emphasizes the human genetic structure of the developing being. Leaving aside the religious arguments about the creation of an individual eternal soul by God at the moment of conception, he thereby defends the independent identity of the conceived human being, even while dependent upon the mother for its developing life.

With respect to the misleading description that abortion simply ends some process, i.e., an interruption or termination of pregnancy in the mother, John Paul states in #59 that this erroneous use of vocabulary hides the real nature of the act, which is murder of an innocent human being at the very beginning of his or her life. Joined to his explanation is an argument against the position that abortion is acceptable in situations of rape or incest where the pregnancy resulted from an aggressively unjust act. The implication of the old feminist argument is that just as the church allows killing in self-defense, so abortion in this case should be allowed. Here is John Paul's response from #58: "[In procured abortion] the one eliminated is a human being at the very beginning of life. No one more absolutely innocent could be imagined. In no way could this human being ever be considered an aggressor, much less an unjust

97. See www.now.org/issues/abortion/rights-rep.html.
98. John Paul II, *Evangelium vitae*, #60, including in it a passage from *Donum vitae* I.1.

aggressor!" Abortion also contradicts the more fundamental basic human right to life, and therefore it can only be a "pseudo-right or no right at all."[99]

Meaning of Law

The world is permeated by different levels of law: divine law (also eternal law), moral law (also natural law), and civil law (also positive law). According to Catholic thought, there ought to be a hierarchy of priority in an ascending order of civil law conforming to moral law conforming to divine law. Divine law is revealed through Scripture and ecclesiastical teachings; moral law may be discovered through reason but is rooted in human nature and not simply a rational principle;[100] and civil laws vary from one civil unit to another but should have as their point of reference the moral law.[101] When the pope states that there is no right to abortion, he is speaking of moral (or natural) and divine law, which state that there is a right to human life. Civil law which contravenes moral and divine law is not authentic law, just as laws in Germany in World War II supporting the genocide of Jewish people were not authentic laws. In other words, no law can make an act licit when it is intrinsically illicit.[102] John Paul II summarizes his claim in *Evangelium vitae*, #72: "Laws which authorize and promote abortion and euthanasia are therefore radically opposed not only to the good of the individual but also to the common good; as such they are completely lacking in authentic juridical validity." He emphasizes that a society with a duty to protect all persons' right to life that neglects this common good makes their civil law authorizing abortion or euthanasia cease "by that very fact to be a true, morally binding civil law."

At this point we must ask why moderate feminists think so differently about this question. A failure to comprehend the divine origins of law flows from secular pragmatic humanism, which considers any dependence upon outside authority as a loss of human autonomy. This view does not understand

---

99. In *Holy See's Position Paper*, #13, John Paul II states that "The Holy See continues to insist that no human right to abortion exists because it contradicts the human right to life. The human right to life is the basic human right: all others stem from it." The right to life is equally shared by all human beings. In *Evangelium vitae*, #58, the pope explicitly states that it is not the case that some human beings (mothers) have a greater right to life than other human beings (developing unborn children).

100. Karol Wojtyla, "The Human Person and Natural Law," in *Person and Community*, pp. 181-85.

101. John Paul II, *Evangelium vitae*, #70.

102. John Paul II, *Evangelium vitae*, #62.

that divine laws are life-giving and life-fulfilling, and that divine government exists to order all things toward the end, which is eternal union with God and the communion of saints.[103] The end of divine law is the fulfillment of personal life, and ipso facto the fulfillment of a woman's life. Tremendous benefits will come to a person who freely chooses to stay in the line of divine law. Moral law and civil law ought to help people achieve this through their freely chosen acts. When civil law does not conform to eternal law, when it promotes rejection of eternal law by distorted concepts, it actually interferes with a woman's ability to become the person she was created to be. The roots of French, British, and American law in the Enlightenment mentality of Kant, Rousseau, Hobbes, and Locke have their effects on old feminisms which spring from these roots.[104]

What is the intense driving force of so many old feminists to support abortion? The Holy Father in his "Letter to Women," #5, observes: "Before being something to blame on the woman, it [abortion] is a crime for which guilt needs to be attributed to men and to the complicity of the general social environment."[105] In addition to the rejection of divine law, acts of men, and often strong cultural pressures, women have to ask what their own motives are. In *Fides et ratio*, #1, John Paul reminds us that "[t]he admonition *Know yourself* was carved on the temple portal at Delphi, as testimony to a basic truth to be adopted as a minimal norm by those seeking to set themselves apart from the rest of creation as 'human beings,' that is, as those who 'know themselves.'"

The Personalistic Norm and Women's Genius

In this final part of our paper, we will consider the anthropological foundations of women's unique and decisive part in promoting new feminism. In *Mulieris dignitatem* the Holy Father connects women's genius with the principle of human identity and the personalistic norm: "unilateral progress can . . . lead to a gradual *loss of sensitivity for man, that is, for what is essentially human*. In this sense, our time in particular *awaits the manifestation* of that 'genius' which belongs to women, and which can ensure sensitivity for human beings in every

---

103. Aquinas, *Summa theologica* I, q.22.

104. See *Evangelium vitae*, #20-24, for an analysis of how the loss of God leads to relativism, secularism, materialism, hedonism, and utilitarianism. Also see #52-75 for his extensive elaboration of the development of different attitudes toward law, and the position of new feminism toward them.

105. This is repeated even more forcefully in the *Holy See's Position Paper*, #13: "Abortion is not a problem uniquely concerning women; it also involves men and society. . . . The irresponsibility of men, and often of society, is at the root of many abortions."

circumstance: because they are human! [*sic*] and because 'the greatest of these is love' (cf. 1 Cor 13:13)" (#30). Woman's part in culture and the basis for her unique genius are founded upon her openness to the life of another person and her capacity to treat other persons as worthy of love.

Complementarity is not simply a matter of biology or body; it has an ontological foundation. In the "Letter to Women," #7, the pope states that "Womanhood and manhood are complementary *not only from the physical and psychological points of view,* but also from the *ontological.*" He adds: "It is only through the duality of the 'masculine' and the 'feminine' that the 'human' finds full realization." In *The Acting Person* the underlying ontological foundation of complementarity is clearly stated: complementarity is a characteristic of all human persons; "mutual complementariness is in a way an intrinsic element in the very nature of participation, . . . that is, as the dynamic factor of the person, . . . [as] an attitude that allows man to find the fulfillment of himself in complementing others."[106] Thus woman's contribution to the common good, as an expression of woman's particular genius, complements man's contribution to the common good, as an expression of man's particular genius.[107]

Why does John Paul state that a woman seems to have, more than man, a unique openness to another person? Clearly he does not want to make the broad claim that women are better than men ethically or ontologically. What then is the origin of her "sensitivity for human beings in every circumstance" that he associates with women's genius? To answer these questions we will draw upon the fourfold identification of the roots of complementarity he identifies: "Women and men are the illustration of a *biological, individual, personal and spiritual complementarity.*"[108] This complementarity is always of a man and woman as two concrete human beings in relation and not as fractional parts of a man and a woman who in relation make up only a "single human being." For purposes of analysis it is possible to identify the four different aspects of the former kind of ontological complementarity.

The ontological logic of John Paul II's anthropology of complementarity can be summarized as follows: (1) relation is an essential aspect of substances or beings; (2) some beings are living substances; (3) persons are human beings ex-

---

106. Wojtyla, *The Acting Person,* p. 285.

107. John Paul II has begun to address various forms of men's genius in his apostolic exhortation on Saint Joseph, *Guardian of the Redeemer* (Boston: St. Paul Books and Media, 1989), and in discussions of pastoral charity. Some of these characteristics are summarized in Sr. Prudence Allen, R.S.M., "Freedom and the Fatherhood of Priests," *Homiletic and Pastoral Review* (January 2002): 18-27.

108. John Paul II, *Holy See's Position Paper* 1.1. See also Sr. Prudence Allen, "Integral Sex Complementarity and the Theology of Communion," *Communio* 17 (Winter 1990): 523-44.

pressing both availability and giving in relations with others; (4) participation is the way of human relation that leads to personal fulfillment; (5) complementarity is an intrinsic element in participation among human persons; and (6) men and women express four particular kinds of complementarity, i.e., biological, individual, personal, and spiritual.

Concerning the *biological* roots of women's genius, Pope John Paul indicates two ways woman's lived experience of the body predisposes her to be open to another person. Woman's lived experience from puberty to menopause of the biochemical changes occurring in her monthly cycles is "the origin of the maternal instinct" or the natural orientation of woman toward another human being.[109] Even if the woman never becomes pregnant, there is an interior maternal orientation toward conceiving and fostering the life of another human being. This interior access to the personalistic norm is not a biological determinism, but rather a psycho-emotive consciousness of a somato-vegetative aspect of her experience as a woman. A woman's body gives a different sort of preconditioned experience than does a man's body of the personalist orientation toward new life, if a woman chooses to access it.[110]

If a woman's experience expands beyond this awareness of her monthly preparations to receive new life to include the experiences of pregnancy, birth, and upbringing of a child, then she may strengthen the experiential foundation for her natural orientation toward another person. In an Angelus reflection of 1995, John Paul II notes: "Opening herself to motherhood, she feels the life in her womb unfolding and growing. This indescribable experience is a privilege of mothers, but all women have in some way an intuition of it, predisposed as they are to this miraculous gift."[111]

John Paul considers how a woman's lived experience of motherhood has the potential of leading a man, who is in some ways outside of the process, into discovering his own fatherhood. Since a man's datum of subjective and objective experience differs by virtue of his lived material identity as a male person, the woman has *to lead* a man into the experience of fatherhood in a unique way:

> The unique contact with the new human being developing within her gives rise to an attitude towards human beings — not only towards her own child, but every human being — which profoundly marks the woman's personality. It is commonly thought that *women* are more capable than men of paying attention *to another person*, and that motherhood develops this pre-

109. Wojtyla, *Love and Responsibility*, p. 280.
110. See Wojtyla, *The Acting Person*, pp. 88-95.
111. John Paul II, "The Vocation to Motherhood" (#1), in *The Genius of Women*, p. 25.

disposition even more. The man — even with all his sharing in parenthood — remains "outside" the process of pregnancy and the baby's birth; in many ways he has to *learn* his own *"fatherhood" from the mother.*[112]

This is the biological foundation for the "female genius" to which John Paul refers. In *Mulieris dignitatem* he confirms: "Motherhood implies from the beginning a special openness to the new person: and this is precisely the woman's 'part.'"[113]

The second root of woman's genius involves woman as an *individual*. In the nineteenth century the existentialist philosophers Nietzsche and Kierkegaard taught that through the exercise of free will a human being can become a self-defined individual. He or she can make the self into a unique individual self. Wojtyla notes a difference between a biological experience of something happening in the self and an experience of self-determination as an individual: "The first definition of self-determination in the experience of human action involves a sense of efficacy . . . : 'I act' means 'I am the efficient cause' of my action and of my self-actualization as a subject, which is not the case when something merely 'happens in me.'"[114]

Simone de Beauvoir developed the existentialist implications of a woman's capacity to become an individual. At the beginning of *The Second Sex* (1949), Beauvoir argued that biology is not destiny: "At the bottom, life is concerned only in the survival of the species as a whole; at the top, life seeks expression through particular individuals, while accomplishing also the survival of the group."[115] While there is a great value in the self-determination that makes one an individual through willed acts, individuality in the extreme becomes detrimental to interpersonal relations.[116]

The phenomenological feminist Saint Edith Stein in "Problems of Woman's Education" considered in some detail the difference between woman's biological nature as part of the human species and her individual nature as a

112. John Paul II, *Mulieris dignitatem*, #18.
113. John Paul II, *Mulieris dignitatem*, #18.
114. Wojtyla, "The Personal Structure of Self-Determination," in *Person and Community*, p. 189.
115. Beauvoir, *The Second Sex*, p. 16. See also Janine Langen, "Simone de Beauvoir: The Human Person as Co-existent," in *Images of the Human*, ed. Leonard Kennedy (Chicago: Loyola University Press, 1995), pp. 535-76.
116. Beauvoir, who based her existential analysis on the philosophy of Jean-Paul Sartre, argued that women had too long been defined by men or other forces outside the self. Wojtyla criticized the extreme individualism of this form of existentialism: "Sartre, whose analysis leads him to conclude that the subject is closed in relation to others," seems to contradict the view that people can open up to relation with others ("Participation or Alienation?" p. 203).

woman: "The species humanity, as well as the species femininity, is revealed differently in different individuals."[117] Stein gave much attention to the value of woman's choices to become a particular kind of individual open to others. She reflects on decisions about education, work, vocation, as well as her relation to her lived experience of the body. When considering education, she notes: "We saw a threefold goal prescribed by the nature of woman: the development of her humanity, her womanhood, and her individuality. These are not separate goals just as the nature of a particular human individual is not divided into three parts but is *one*: it is human nature of a specifically feminine and individual character."[118]

That women have access to a maternal instinct has recently been challenged by some feminists who argue that many women appear not to manifest such an instinct while many men do.[119] The pope argues only that it is possible for women to access the maternal instinct if they choose to because of the lived experience women have of their bodies. "Every woman can observe in herself the changes which occur in the relevant phase of the cycle. Apart from these there exist objective scientific methods known to biology and medicine, which help us to determine the moment of ovulation, i.e., the beginning of the fertile period."[120] John Paul does not deny that many women do not access the subjective source of the maternal instinct. He agrees that many women intentionally cut themselves off from this access by technological or psychological means.[121] While access to this root of woman's genius is a choice or decision, it cannot be reduced to "a feeling that comes and goes." It involves intellect and will, and it occurs on the level of individual human identity. The choice reveals a woman's relation to her own nature.

Is it true that women do have a choice to access a maternal instinct which orients them toward another human being? If it is true that artificial methods of birth control often interfere with this access, why do so many women argue

117. Stein, *Essays on Women*, p. 178.

118. See Stein, *Essays on Women*, p. 182; and Allen, "Sex and Gender Differentiation in Hildegard of Bingen"; Allen, "Edith Stein: The Human Person as Male and Female," in *Images of the Human*, pp. 397-432; and Allen, "The Passion of Edith Stein," *Fides Quaerens Intellectum* 1, no. 2 (Winter 2002): 201-50.

119. See Elisabeth Badinter, *Mother Love: Myth and Reality* (New York: Macmillan, 1980). After considering the examples of many women who appeared to have manifested no such maternal instinct, the author asks: "How then can one avoid concluding, even if it seems cruel, that mother love is only a feeling . . . [that] may exist or may not exist; appear and disappear; reveal itself as strong or weak . . . ?" (p. 327).

120. Wojtyla, *Love and Responsibility*, p. 280.

121. This recognition occurs in his discussion in "The Problem of Birth Control," in *Love and Responsibility*, pp. 278-88.

that use of technological methods of birth control are central to women's full development?[122] The answer lies in a different value of technology and its relation to the human person. Those who support artificial birth control as central to a woman's identity often claim that reproductive technologies are in themselves *value-free* but are good to the extent that women control them.[123] More accurately, the technology of birth control, as a form of domination or control of woman's or man's body, is not good because it inevitably leads to contraventions of the personalistic norm. Technology is never "value-free"; it always has a specific value depending upon the extent to which it treats a person as an end or as a means. Thus, when a woman decides about how to use technology in relation to her own reproductive capacities, she is defining herself as an individual woman.

Pope John Paul II suggests that one important source for woman's access to a personal liberation is through an intelligent awareness of the experience of her body.[124] It can be argued that technology, when used to dominate the self, may cut off woman's own unique access to the "feminine genius" or the orientation toward the person, by making her own nature inaccessible to herself. If technology leads to a loss of sensitivity to a woman's lived experience of the body, then women run the risk of losing the very foundation from which they have special access to the personalist norm. They risk giving away their "birthright."

The *personal* aspect of woman's identity participates in the personalist theme of self-gift to another and of receiving another. The historical development of this notion of personal identity was discussed above under "Interpersonal Relation." To be a person means for John Paul to be open and available to

122. See Joan Rothschild, "Afterward: Machina Ex Dea and Future Research," in *Machina Ex Dea: Feminist Perspectives on Technology*, ed. Rothschild (New York: Oxford University Press, 1983): "In no field are the technological changes likely to be far greater than in one basic to women's work: biological reproduction. Because control over reproduction is a fundamental condition for women's freedom, reproductive control is a recurrent theme of feminist research on reproductive technology" (pp. 219-20).

123. The following summary by Rothschild in her introduction to *Machina Ex Dea* illustrates the value-free claim about technology: "Such technology may not 'free' women at all if women do not control it or it is harmful to their health. But the existence of safe and effective technologies of birth control can provide women with a tool for control of their own reproduction, which is a necessary condition for liberation. Again we see technology operating as an independent variable" (p. xxiv). A similar kind of position is stated by Jalna Hamner, "Reproductive Technology," in *Machina Ex Dea*, pp. 195-96.

124. In a discussion of a proper method of birth control, Wojtyla states that "both [the man and the woman] should get to know about the female organism and make their decision dependent on a precise knowledge of its functions" (*Love and Responsibility*, p. 283).

receiving another person. In *Mulieris dignitatem,* the pope refers to Vatican II (*Gaudium et spes,* #24) to reiterate his acceptance of what distinguishes personal identity: "The human being is a person, a subject who decides for himself. At the same time, man 'cannot fully find himself except through a sincere gift of self.'"[125] In his own words, "This 'law of the gift'. . . is inscribed deep within the dynamic structure of the person."[126]

The emphasis upon act in interpersonal relations permeates the writings of Pope John Paul II about women. He distinguishes different levels of motherhood within a woman: "Motherhood *in the bio-physical sense* appears to be passive: the formation process of a new life 'takes place' in her, in her body, which is nevertheless profoundly involved in that process. At the same time, motherhood *in its personal-ethical sense* expresses a very important creativity on the part of the woman, upon whom the very humanity of the new human being mainly depends."[127] Creativity, in a personal-ethical sense, involves acts of intellect and will, of knowing and loving, by the mother.

A woman is capable of giving herself to another person if she chooses to act in accord with her nature which is predisposed toward giving herself to a child: "In this openness, in conceiving and giving birth to a child, the woman 'discovers herself through a sincere gift of self.'"[128] This is not a biological or even an individual aspect of woman's identity: "Motherhood *is linked to the personal structure of the woman and to the personal dimension of the gift.*"[129] If through the exercise of intellect and will a woman chooses to develop a personalistic attitude toward her child, she may nurture a capacity to lead other persons into a similar development of personal identity.

Several feminists have noted today that woman's ethical personality is marked by care or concern for other persons. At the same time as they rightfully seek to protect women from being expected to do everything to take care of others, they also often do not extend this attitude of care to the developing human being. They do not recognize the autonomous identity in the developing child, nor do they understand how it is woman's part to defend the weakest and most vulnerable members of society.[130] This discrepancy between wanting to align woman's identity with care or concern of others while at the same time refusing to care about the defenseless human being developing within a preg-

---

125. John Paul II, *Mulieris dignitatem,* #18.

126. Wojtyla, "The Personal Structure," p. 194.

127. John Paul II, *Mulieris dignitatem,* #19, emphasis John Paul's.

128. John Paul II, *Mulieris dignitatem,* #18.

129. John Paul II, *Mulieris dignitatem,* n. 18, emphasis John Paul's.

130. See Carol Gilligan, *In Another Voice* (Cambridge, Mass., and London: Harvard University Press, 1982).

nant woman may be interpreted as an "antigenius" mentality in some women.[131] The genius mentality of woman, in contrast, expresses an authentic capacity to be attentive to another person in every sphere and circumstance of her activity without falling into patterns of exploitation.

John Paul notes several areas in which the capacity of woman to receive another person and give herself to another person can transform the world. In his "Letter to Women" he says the greater presence of women in society will lead to a humanization of institutions organized "according to the criteria of efficiency and productivity."[132] He states further in an Angelus reflection (August 20, 1995), that the greater presence of businesswomen in executive positions in the economy is "giving it a new human inspiration and removing it from the recurring temptation of dull efficiency marked only by laws of profit."[133]

The genius of women is manifesting itself in politics, where they are both focusing on "basic areas of human life" and "on behalf of peace."[134] Woman's genius also extends throughout wide areas of society. John Paul notes "that women's contribution to the welfare and progress of society is incalculable . . . [and even more needed] to save society from the deadly virus of degradation and violence which is today witnessing a dramatic increase."[135] He asks that women's genius be "more fully expressed in the life of society as a whole," and that "the widest possible space [be] open to women in all areas of culture, economics, [and] politics."[136] These brief considerations raise a hope that John Paul's new feminism opens a wider radius of women's participation in society.

The final aspect of woman's identity is *spiritual*. The spiritual aspect of a person's identity consists in the orientation of the eternal soul toward God, both with respect to its origins and its final end. In Christian understanding it also includes the belief in the resurrection of the body at the end of time, so that the person has a distinct identity as a particular woman or man. The spiritual aspect is not simply eternal life of a sexless soul nor an undifferentiated nonmaterial force. It consists in the highest operations of intellect and will and the transformation and integration of the human person who develops the self

---

131. While John Paul II does not use the word "antigenius," it is possible to use it in the context to characterize women who act directly against what he describes as woman's genius.

132. John Paul II, "Letter to Women," #4.

133. John Paul II, *The Genius of Women*, p. 32 (#1).

134. John Paul II, *Mulieris dignitatem*, #1 and 2, p. 34.

135. John Paul II, "Welcome to Gertrude Mongella, Secretary General of the Fourth World Conference on Women in May 1995 at the Vatican," in *The Genius of Women*, p. 41, #5.

136. John Paul II, "Letter to Women," #10, in *The Genius of Women*, p. 54, and also "The Feminine Genius" (Angelus reflection of July 23, 1995), in *The Genius of Women*, p. 27, #1.

through consciously willed acts. This self-formation occurs in cooperation with grace.

The pope's new feminism proclaims Jesus Christ as a sign which will be opposed, a sign of contradiction. In *Evangelium vitae,* #29, he states: "In Christ, the Gospel of life is definitively proclaimed and fully given." Jesus Christ, true God and true man, guides humanity spiritually toward the perfection of new feminism. Jesus Christ reveals us to ourselves.[137]

In his *Sign of Contradiction* the pope describes two common responses to Jesus Christ as *the* sign: direct opposition and indirect opposition. *Direct opposition* is a more extreme response; it is an undisguised rejection of the truth as proclaimed by Jesus Christ. Direct opposition may be found in Mary Daly, who describes herself as "post-Christian" and argues that Jesus Christ as true man and God could never be the savior of woman.[138] Direct opposition may also be found in Simone de Beauvoir, who developed feminism from a consistent atheistic position throughout her life.[139] Both Daly and Beauvoir were baptized Roman Catholics, turned against their faith, and promoted feminism directly opposed to the teachings of Jesus Christ.

An *indirect opposition* to the sign of contradiction seeks to "reshape" the full truth of the person of Jesus Christ to fit secular assumptions of modern civilization while "paying him lip-service."[140] Indirect opposition to John Paul's new feminism occurs in feminists who seek to reshape and secularize moral and social teachings while remaining Catholic in name. Others, such as belong to NOW, are simply silent about God, privatizing religious beliefs. Still others indirectly oppose Jesus Christ by saying they are following him while acting

---

137. Cf. Council Vatican II, *Gaudium et spes,* #22.

138. Mary Daly, *Beyond God the Father: Toward a Philosophy of Women's Liberation* (Boston: Beacon Press, 1973) and *Gyn/ecology: The Metaphysics of Radical Feminism* (Boston: Beacon Press, 1978).

139. In her early work, *The Ethics of Ambiguity* (New York: Philosophical Library, 1948), Beauvoir describes God in Sartre's words as "an impossible synthesis of the for-itself and the in-itself" (p. 14). In her foundational feminist text, *The Second Sex* (New York: Knopf, 1957), she ridicules Christianity and distorts its relation to woman's identity and its teachings against abortion. And at the end of her interview, *Adieux: A Farewell to Sartre* (London: Penguin Books, 1984), she agrees that to not believe in God is the way to cure human beings of their alienation (p. 445). The denial of the existence of God then leads to the denial of the nature of man and of woman as is seen in her claim in the following interview at the end of her life: "[T]here is no human nature, and thus no feminine nature. It is not something given." Also: "the embryo, as long as it is not yet considered human, as long as it is not a being with human relationships with its mother or its father, it's nothing, one can eliminate the embryo" (Margaret A. Simmons, "Two Interviews with Simone de Beauvoir [1982]," *Hypatia* 3, no. 3 [Winter 1989]: 18-19).

140. Wojtyla, *Sign of Contradiction,* p. 199.

contrary to the content and witness of his teachings: they call themselves Catholics or Christians, but they choose contraceptives.[141] The acts reveal the person, and opposition to John Paul's new feminism, through willed acts, participates in the same dynamic as that of direct or indirect opposition to Jesus Christ.

Many new feminists embrace the core of John Paul's spiritual understanding of woman's identity. When a woman accepts that *"God entrusts the human being to her in a special way,"*[142] she can discover the commandment of love, the new law of reciprocity, and her particular part in acting in accordance with the teachings and model of Jesus Christ. She can in an intimate and personal way fulfill her personal destiny of movement toward union with God by choosing to live in conformity with the personalistic norm and the commandment of love. The divine source of this aspect of woman's identity reinforces the claim that woman's particular attention to the person is not simply the result of biological determinism or even of her own willed acts. The pope notes that *"A woman is strong because of her awareness of this entrusting, strong because of the fact that God 'entrusts the human being to her,' always and in every way, even in the situations of social discrimination in which she may find herself."*[143]

A second spiritual aspect of woman's identity is found in her attraction to the *commandment of love* and *law of reciprocity*. The ultimate source of this norm is not some rational principle but the teachings of Jesus Christ, who revealed the will of the Father during his time on earth. In *Evangelium vitae* John Paul traces the historical development of the law of the Old and New Covenant which "has entrusted the life of every individual to his or her fellow human beings, brothers and sisters, according to the law of reciprocity in giving and receiving, or self giving and of the acceptance of others."[144] Jesus Christ, in the witness of his life on earth, "showed what heights and depths this law of reci-

---

141. See, for example, the open letter in the *New York Times*, October 23, 2000, from 3,000 who signed themselves as "Roman Catholic Voters" and argued "Support programs that make contraceptives, including emergency contraception, easily available to women here and in poor countries." Complete text may be found at Catholic Speak Out, www.quixote.org/cso or cso@quixote.org

142. John Paul II, *Mulieris dignitatem*, #30.

143. John Paul II, *Mulieris dignitatem*, #30.

144. John Paul II, *Evangelium vitae*, #76. John Paul II states in *Dives et misericordia* (Boston: Daughters of St. Paul, 1980) that "the original anthropomorphic aspect" of the word used in the Old Testament for mercy "*(rahamim)* in its very root, *denotes the love of a mother* (*rehem* = mother's womb). From the deep and original bond — indeed the unity — that links a mother to her child there springs a particular relationship to the child, a particular love . . . it constitutes an interior necessity: an exigency of the heart. It is, as it were, a 'feminine' variation of the masculine fidelity to self expressed by *hesed*" (n. 52).

procity can reach." Now through the Holy Spirit, "Christ gives new content and meaning to the law of reciprocity, to our being entrusted to one another."[145]

A third aspect of spiritual identity focuses on the *fulfillment of a woman's identity*. In *Mulieris dignitatem* the particular relationship of the law of reciprocity to woman's identity is specified: "*the dignity of women is measured by the order of love*, which is essentially the order of justice and charity."[146] He affirms the foundation of the commandment of love: "Love is an ontological and ethical requirement of the person. The person must be loved, since love alone corresponds to what the person is."[147] Acts of love may be done by the personal choice of will and intellect, but they also have their inspiration and source in the Holy Spirit which prompts a person to imitate Jesus Christ. Only by entering into a full relation with others by acting according to the commandment of love and the law of reciprocity will a woman (or man) find fulfillment and perfection: "This ontological affirmation also indicates the ethical dimension of a person's vocation. *Woman can only find herself by giving love to others*."[148]

In *Fides et ratio*, which describes the complementary roles of faith and reason in the search for fulfillment, John Paul notes the inner momentum that drives a person toward the ultimate goal: "From all that I have said to this point it emerges that men and women are on a journey of discovery which is humanly unstoppable — a search for the truth and a search for a person to whom they might entrust themselves. Christian faith comes to meet them, offering the concrete possibility of reaching the goal which they seek."[149]

John Paul II often uses the notion of a journey to an ultimate destination to describe our life on earth. Likening this journey to a pilgrimage, the pope characterizes Mary as our pilgrim guide. Because she completed the pilgrimage in her own life as a woman, she is able to guide others today. Mary, the great sign in heaven, continues to serve as a metaphor for the church and for the body of the faithful in the church. Indeed, Mary becomes the vibrant source of the new feminism to which John Paul is appealing in his new evangelization.

145. John Paul II, *Evangelium vitae*, #76.

146. John Paul II, *Mulieris dignitatem*, #29, emphasis John Paul's.

147. John Paul II, *Mulieris dignitatem*, #29.

148. John Paul II, *Mulieris dignitatem*, #30. The pope has recently recognized four Christian women whose lives expressed the genius of Christian feminism. Saint Therese of Lisieux, named doctor of the church, revealed how the strengthened will could support a vigorous contemplative love at the heart of the church; Saint Edith Stein revealed how a sharpened intellect could support a martyr's gift of life in love; Mother Teresa of Calcutta revealed how an increase of love for the poorest of the poor could transform countries around the world, and Blessed Gianna revealed how an increase of love for just one unborn child could witness to a mother's gift of life.

149. John Paul II, *Fides et ratio*, #33.

Mary, Jesus' mother, is a great sign from heaven because she is "the one who accepted 'Life' in the name of all and for the sake of all . . . she is thus most closely and personally associated with the Gospel of Life."[150] The pope emphasizes Mary's interpersonal dialogue at the annunciation: "*She is truly the Mother of God, because motherhood concerns the whole person,* not just the body, nor even just human 'nature.' . . . [T]hrough her response of faith Mary exercises her free will and thus fully shares with her personal and feminine 'I' in the event of the Incarnation. . . . This event is clearly *interpersonal in character:* it is a dialogue."[151]

Mary was not only engaged in an interpersonal dialogue with God, she also leads us in an interpersonal way. The second part of the encyclical *Mother of the Redeemer,* entitled "The Mother of God at the Center of the Pilgrim Church," reveals that Mary is our pilgrim guide because she walked the path of women's genius on earth before we do. John Paul II describes her this way: "Mary became not only the 'nursing mother' of the Son of Man but also the 'associate of unique nobility' of the Messiah and Redeemer. As I have already said, she advanced in her pilgrimage of faith, and in this *pilgrimage* to the foot of the Cross there was simultaneously accomplished her maternal *cooperation* with the Savior's whole mission through her actions and sufferings."[152]

With "burning charity" Mary seeks to restore supernatural life to all men and women. Mary is the great sign from heaven because she embodies personally and spiritually the pathway for pilgrims. May the fruits of a new feminism truly transform our culture to support the full dignity of human life.[153]

---

150. John Paul II, *Evangelium vitae,* #102.

151. John Paul II, *Mulieris dignitatem,* #4 and 5.

152. John Paul II, *Redemptoris mater* (Boston: Daughters of St. Paul, 1987), #39.

153. With gratitude for suggestions for revision of earlier drafts of this paper by the students and faculty at the University of Notre Dame; St. John Vianney Theological Seminary; and by Mother Mary Quentin Sheridan, R.S.M., superior general of the Religious Sisters of Mercy of Alma; Sr. Rita Rae Schneider, R.S.M., Ph.D.; Sr. Mary Judith O'Brien, R.S.M., J.D., J.C.D.; and Kevin Rickert, Ph.D.

Woman's Threefold Vocation according to Edith Stein

Sibylle von Streng Translated by Sr. Allison Braus, O.C.D.

Edith Stein's thought most certainly finds its place in our approach to woman with the reality of her dynamic essence. This is true on two accounts. The first and most essential is that Stein's entire life is a demonstration of the person as a being in the process of becoming, as drawn toward a goal, as called to fulfillment in a concrete setting within the confines of external life circumstances and particularly within the specific limitations of his or her constitution. Stein's biography portrays a being in the process of becoming *(fieri)* who, while manifestly faithful to herself, experiences numerous "conversions," or who is even revealed to herself as she explores the paths her mind and concrete life situations propose. The biographical element is thus primary. Given her talents and choices, her writings accompany her through life and are a reflection of her life. In Stein's writings we encounter, on a theoretical level, both the constancy and the movement characteristic of her experience. Constancy is found in her interests and essential motives: the search for truth, a consistently centralized interest in the person, a tendency toward conceptualization, a concern for integrating both the concrete and reflection. Movement is mainly perceived in the topics on which she writes. Stein's works at first claim a direct relation to the phenomenological studies initiated by Husserl. She shows particular interest in the questions they enfold concerning the person and the basic distinction between psychology and the phenomenology of the person.[1] After her

---

1. For the development of these topics, see Stein's treatise on empathy (Edith Stein, *Zum Problem der Einfühlung, Verlaggesellschaft* [reprint, Munich: Gerhard Kaffke, 1980]), in English, *On the Problem of Empathy,* vol. 3 of *The Collected Works,* trans. Waltraut Stein (Washington, D.C.: ICS Publications, 1989). See also *Beiträge zur philosophischen Begründung der Psychologie und der Geisteswissenschaften,* in English, *Philosophy of Psychology and the Humanities,* trans. Mary Catherine Baseheart and Marianne Sawicki, ed. Marianne Sawicki (Washington, D.C.:

conversion to Catholicism and her studies of Thomism, Stein takes up her research on the person in greater depth, elaborating an ontology (exposed in
extenso in *Endliches und Ewiges Sein*),[2] which she then uses as the basis for a
new concept of anthropology. Her research also leads her to practical philosophy (concerning the role and education of women) and to mysticism.[3] The
changes in her work clearly seem to be dictated by her biographical situation.
Also worth noting is that the content of Stein's philosophy testifies in itself to
this active discovery of truth, and as we shall see, her research is particularly
beneficial to her anthropology. From the first to the last of her works, the person remains central to her reflection.

What is to be said of this anthropology and, in particular, of the anthropology of woman? The method Stein proposes for accessing the person is that
of Husserl's phenomenology. "If we wish to know what man is, we must place
ourselves, in the most vivid way possible, in the situation in which we experience man; that is to say, that which we experience within ourselves and that
which we experience in our encounter with other humans."[4] The return to the
thing in itself, in this case man and woman, takes place in a mental act called intuition. Our approach to the person and to the woman will be an intuitive one.
In the following pages we propose, first of all, a glance at Stein's anthropology
of woman. This analysis will be followed by a description of woman's threefold
vocation in the order of grace based on an article Stein presented in 1932.[5]
Finally, we shall approach the contemporary woman on a daily basis, and particularly the contemporary conditions in which she seeks personal fulfillment.

ICS Publications, 2000). Contributions of the original German text appeared in *Jahrbuch für
Philosophie und phänomenologische Forschung*, vol. 5 (Halle an der Saale, 1922).

2. Edith Stein, *Endliches und Ewiges Sein* (Louvain: Nauwelaerts, 1950). The English
translation of this work is *Finite and Eternal Being: An Attempt at an Assent to the Meaning of
Being*, trans. Kurt F. Reinhardt (Washington, D.C.: ICS Publications, 2002).

3. See, for example, Edith Stein, *Ganzheitliches Leben* (Freiburg, Basel, and Vienna:
Herder Verlag, 1990) and *Verborgenes Leben* (Druten: De Maas & Waler; Freiburg: Herder
Verlag; Basel and Vienna, 1987).

4. Edith Stein, *Der Aufbau der menschlichen Person* (Freiburg, Basel, and Vienna: Herder
Verlag, 1994), p. 51. This work is the sixteenth volume of the edition in print by Herder and
Nauwelaerts of Edith Stein's collected works *(Werke)*.

5. "Beruf des Mannes und der Frau nach Natur — Gnadenordnung," in English, "The
Separate Vocations of Man and Woman according to Nature and Grace." This text first appeared
in the periodical *Die christliche Frau* (Cologne, 1932). It was reprinted in the fifth volume of the
collected works *(Werke)* as "Die Frau, ihre Aufgabe nach Natur und Gnade," in English, *Essays
on Woman*, trans. Freda Mary Oben, 2nd ed. (Washington, D.C.: ICS Publications, 1996), pp. 59-
85. This volume is composed of texts on woman: conferences, unfinished manuscripts, articles,
etc., which we will refer to throughout this article.

This will enable us to determine to what extent Steinian anthropology may contribute to contemporary debate.

An "Essentialist" Anthropology of the Person and of the Woman

Stein defends the thesis that body, soul, and spirit are neither the products of thought nor mere concepts, but are real, concrete components of the human person. Man is a complex concretion participating in different areas of reality, in different regions of being: the material, the psychic, and the spiritual. How then are we to consider the unity of the person? How is this heterogeneous entity held together? Experience leads us to an intuitive sense of man's unified nature, encompassing the human person's living body and spiritual soul. "What we are confronted with in experience is *this* man: the body we perceive reveals the spirit within it."[6] What really distinguishes each of us from other human bodies and establishes our unity is that we perceive our own corporal self, that we are free and personal subjects, that "man is a physical and psychic being, but within him, the body and soul have a personal form *(personale Gestalt)*. This means that an 'I' dwells within it."[7] Experience thus brings to light the existence of a corporeal and personal *I*.

A Specific Difference

From an ontological perspective, the Steinian view is strongly essentialist and thus, in the case at hand, each man participates in the general essence (or essentiality) of the human being as well as in a particular essence: "this man."[8] In addition to these two entities (essence "humanity" and essence "person"), experience presents us with a very particular distinction between sexes. The human species exists in two forms, the masculine and the feminine, which seem each to correspond to a type.[9] There arises the question: In which region of be-

---

6. Stein, *Aufbau der menschlichen Person*, p. 127.

7. Stein, *Aufbau der menschlichen Person*, p. 120.

8. These essences are not to be confused with concepts. Essences exist on their own, independent of the human mind. They can be discovered but not created by this latter. This is precisely why we can qualify Stein's thought as essentialist.

9. Types are by definition variable. Childhood, for example, is a type, adulthood another, and every individual, in the process of his development, passes from one to the other. Species, on the other hand, is stable and does not vary. The difference between type and species is explained in "Problems of Women's Education," in *Essays on Woman*, p. 173.

ing does the apparent type difference between man and woman originate? On a physical level a woman's participation in the feminine type may be easily grasped, since her body differs from that of a man. Is our inquiry to cease here, or should it be pursued with regard for the psyche or even for the personal mind? Here the question is significant: Do woman and man differ on a spiritual level? Since Stein persistently affirms that these different spheres overlap, we may conclude that the femininity of a woman's body involves her entire being. Should a feminine mind exist, moreover, this would lead us to deduce that the substantial form of the feminine world, and thus also its finality, can be understood in a way which is feminine. The spheres (material, psychic, spiritual) which constitute woman would then be influenced by this femininity.

Let us attempt to define what we mean by "feminine type": "Even if we intend to disregard individualities, is there then *one* type of woman? . . . Can the complete multiplicity which we meet with in life be reduced to a single unity, and can this unity be distinguished from man's soul?"[10] To answer her question, Stein analyzes some of literature's outstanding female characters: Goethe's Iphigenie, Ibsen's Nora, and Undset's Inguun. Do the three literary types presented — the heroic saint, the darling doll, and the child of nature — share some common core? "These three women share one common characteristic: a longing to give love and to receive love, and in this respect a yearning to be raised above a narrow, day-to-day existence into the realm of a higher being."[11] The feminine soul may be characterized by an aspiration to personal love in mutual giving. In other words, where Stein proposes other ways of considering the feminine soul, she comes to the same conclusion: matters of the heart are central to the concerns and aspirations of the feminine soul. (Let us specify, along with Stein, that it is the feminine soul in general we are concerned with here, and not every woman's soul.) Woman then is naturally drawn to persons while, as experience proves, man's desires are more readily directed toward exterior efficiency, leading him to a concentration on objective action.[12]

We should also keep in mind that "in both instances the structure of the human soul is fundamentally the same. The soul is housed in a body on whose

10. Stein, "Spirituality of the Christian Woman," in *Essays on Woman*, p. 88. Various papal documents such as John Paul II's "Letter to Women," *Origins* 25, no. 9 (July 27, 1995) make the same observation: "[I]n giving themselves to others each day, women fulfill their deepest vocation. Perhaps more than men, women acknowledge the person, because they see persons with their hearts" (p. 143, #12). See also John Paul II, *Apostolic Letter Mulieris Dignitatem: On the Dignity and Vocation of Women* (Boston: St. Paul, 1988), #18, henceforth cited *Mulieris dignitatem.*

11. Stein, "Spirituality," p. 93.

12. Stein, "Spirituality," p. 94.

vigor and health its own vigor and health depend — even if not exclusively nor simply. On the other hand, the body receives its nature *as body* — life, motion, form, gestalt, and spiritual significance — through the soul."[13] Every soul exists within a body, and Stein affirms that the soul-body relationship is lived more intimately in a woman than in a man: "Woman's soul is present and lives more intensely in all parts of the body, and it is inwardly affected by that which happens to the body; whereas, with men, the body has more pronouncedly the character of an instrument which serves them in their work and which is accompanied by a certain detachment."[14]

We can in fact speak of a feminine *Eigenart*,[15] of a "typically" feminine soul which experience reveals as sensitive to the personal, to harmony, to the global, etc. This conclusion brings Stein to define the difference between man and woman not as a type difference which would thus be variable, but as a specific difference. Even if we consider it obvious that the physical difference between man and woman is specific, the question remains open on the psychic and mental levels.[16] Stein is clear on this point:

> I am convinced that the species *humanity* embraces the double species *man* and *woman;* that the essence of the complete *human* being is characterized by this duality; and that the entire structure of the essence demonstrates the specific character. There is a difference, not only in body structure and in particular physiological functions, but also in the entire corporeal life. The relationship of soul and body is different in man and woman; the relationship of soul to body differs in their psychic life as well as that of the spiritual faculties to each other.[17]

The feminine model of the soul is nonetheless lived in multiple manners by concrete women; the variety of literary figures Stein chooses exemplifies this view by showing that while each woman embodies the feminine soul, she does so in her own way. The author goes on to specify that there are women who are impregnated with femininity to a greater or lesser degree, and she even states that there are men who more fully participate in the feminine soul type than certain women.[18] Stein justifies this flexibility within a framework as appar-

13. Stein, "Spirituality," p. 94.

14. Stein, "Spirituality," p. 95.

15. The expression *persönliche Eigenart,* used by Stein, has been translated as "personal distinctiveness" throughout the present article.

16. Here we have the very problem today's gender studies have attempted to bring out.

17. Stein, "Problems of Women's Education," p. 187.

18. This is continually brought out in modern philosophical studies on woman. See, for example, S. de Beauvoir, S. Lilar, P. Allen, gender studies, etc.

ently rigid as species, through ontology and through personalism. On an ontological level she draws upon the distinction between nature (concrete reality) and essence (ideal reality, telos):[19] "So could the nature of woman, how she is suited to her destiny, admit of modification without woman's essence being annulled thereby."[20] Here too the person's individuality is preponderant. It is the person's responsibility to give character to each of his or her acts, to include them in his or her own personal distinctiveness, be it closer to the essence woman or to the essence man.

Having already stated that every person participates in the general essence "humanity" and in the particular essence corresponding to his or her person, we shall complete Stein's essentialist anthropology by adding that every woman participates in the general and specific essence "femininity" (Frauentum), just as every man participates in his masculine essence.

This claim concerning essences at different levels may seem to contradict the idea of personal becoming that we are attempting to bring out: "We are trying to attain insight into the innermost recesses of our being; we see that it is not a completed being but rather a being in the state of becoming."[21] Upon closer analysis, however, due to the interpenetration of more-or-less general essences in Stein's ontology, Endliches und Ewiges Sein, we find that there is no contradiction. On one hand the person (like all other living beings) is a being in the process of becoming, and on the other hand the person participates in the general essence of humanity as well as in his or her own particular essence. How are these views to be reconciled? In this: that humanity consists precisely in being this form and in simultaneously tending toward it; this may be said of its particular essence and of the essence "man" or "woman."[22] In other words, each person's humanity is both a starting point and an aim to be attained.

> It is possible, to be sure, to derive a universal *meaning* from being human, a meaning which is realized in all three concepts of Aristotle, and a meaning which neither comes to be nor passes away. But the being human of this particular human being is actual and actuating [*wirksam*] in this person.

19. In a commentary of Saint Thomas, Stein draws upon his distinction between nature and essence. The nature of a thing designates what is produced in the creative act, and thus actually exists in the world. Essence, on the other hand, designates the thing as it really and necessarily is; it represents the goal of a thing's adequate becoming. See Stein, "Problems of Women's Education," pp. 180-81.

20. Stein, "Problems of Women's Education," p. 278.

21. Stein, "Spirituality," p. 88.

22. For Aristotle the end is the cause of movement. Anything that moves is not only drawn to its end but is also set in motion by it. Stein, Finite and Eternal Being, p. 225.

This person shares it with no other human being. It is not, prior to the person's own being, but steps into existence [*tritt ins Dasein*] together with the person. It determines *what* this particular human being is at any particular time, and this changing what expresses a more or less extensive approximation to the end.[23]

Humanity is both present in reality and a goal to reach. In order to participate in what he truly is, man must unceasingly conform to his archetype, to his own essence, to his *eidos*.[24]

The Unity of Substantial Form:
The Spiritual and Personal Soul

In her ontology as well as in her anthropology, Stein perceives concomitant entities: ontological essences on the one hand, different spheres of reality on the other. How is their coexistence to be understood? To answer this, Stein employs the principle of substantial form, encountered in her studies of Thomistic philosophy. For the person, for example, it would be erroneous to affirm the predominance of either spirit or matter. Reality shows that, on the contrary, body, soul, and spirit are inextricably, yet ordinately, intertwined. The human being is an ordered cosmos due to the preeminence of substantial form, which regulates it according to a very strict and pure law, integrating every level of being.[25] "Substantial form is the principle which constitutes all human individuals. This principle is a unified whole, even if it presupposes an array of substances as conditions of its existence."[26] In a way Stein refuses to allow inferior forms to be

23. Stein, *Finite and Eternal Being*, p. 226.

24. This realization is however imperfect on several levels. For one, man is a complete whole. (Like the child, man does not have absolute access to all the possibilities of his essence.) In addition, man is imperfect and even if he came to the perfect realization of *his* humanity, he would not arrive at the realization of humanity, but only at that of his individual being. "Even the individual human being is incapable of unfolding in its life all the possibilities which have their ground or foundation in its essence or nature (in the sense of the individual essence or nature). The individual human being's power is so limited that he or she has to pay for the highest accomplishments in one field by shortcomings or deficiencies in other fields. We may therefore assume that the perfection of the individual human being in the state of glory will not only free each human being from the impurities of its corrupt nature but also unfold its as yet unfulfilled possibilities." Stein, *Finite and Eternal Being*, p. 507.

25. All of life is regulated by this very strict and pure law, as described by Stein in an admirable passage of *Finite and Eternal Being*, p. 113: "Once I begin to realize this, my heart rejoices in anticipation of the light of glory in whose sheen this coherence of meaning will be fully unveiled to me."

26. Stein, *Aufbau der menschlichen Person*, p. 128.

dissolved in the superior form: "All matter *(Stoff)* continually submits to its formal principle." The unity of substantial form must be understood as follows: one form is superior to the others and governs the whole, ruling over it and determining its finality. "There is unity insofar as the assemblage is itself lawful, whereby there is a superior order and an inferior one. The dominant form determining the *telos* is one and can be understood as the substantial form proper even if the concrete substance is not determined by it alone."[27] Furthermore, "there is in living beings *(Lebenwesen)* a manifold of material elements held together, permeated, and molded into an organic whole by a superior, living form — a whole which is proportioned in accordance with the structural law of that superior form."[28]

An individual's unity is then based on the unity of substantial form. All things can be reduced to a principle of substantial form which makes up their unity and presides over their development. What is this superior form for man? According to Stein, it is the personal and spiritual soul. By "soul" we mean a life principle attached to the body, and by "spiritual" we mean endowed with spirit, and in our present case, personal spirit. We have said substantial form is present as a given and as a telos. The finality of this state of becoming is in fact supplied by the form, its essence. Thus the spiritual and personal soul constitutes the finality of man's development. If this soul's own movement is a sort of development, it is precisely because its finality is already present, already given.[29]

On a general level we have come to see the spiritual and personal soul as the substantial form of the person. The same thing must be asserted on the level of particulars: this person's spiritual soul is his or her substantial form. What then is this spiritual soul on a particular level? Stein also refers to it as the core of the person, for it is the center of gravity for the physical and psychic person. The author continues to affirm that the human being lives as a person to the extent that he or she is a psychic body. Every level of being preserves its own function and, far from being effaced, is integrated and elevated into superior reality,

27. Stein, *Aufbau der menschlichen Person,* p. 163.

28. Stein, *Finite and Eternal Being,* p. 268.

29. See, for example, Stein, *Philosophy of Psychology,* p. 231. Stein insists upon the distinction between *Entwicklung* and *Entfaltung,* which are both most often translated by the English word "development," with the original German following in parentheses when necessary. *Entwicklung* denotes an active process during which the person passes through various states. It is therefore used to describe psychic development, including the emergence of new aptitudes. *Entfaltung* does not have the same meaning, because all the properties are, in this case, already present from the beginning. The process it describes is like the opening of a flower: nothing new appears, but what was already present manifests itself. It is therefore used for the hidden qualities of the soul, which are always present and given in the person but may be hidden or manifest.

which, in this instance, is the personal spirit. In this way the body receives the mark of the person in a very particular manner. Every human person is the bearer of individual properties (all different manifestations of the personal core) that leave their personal mark on the entire being and therefore also on the living body.

Personal Distinctiveness

In her endeavor to reach the core of personal particularity, or what we shall call personal distinctiveness *(persönliche Eigenart)*, Stein's purpose is to foreground the person's individuality rather than the psychophysical individual's character.[30] With psychic character we are still far from individuality founded in the unity of qualities. Stein explains this elsewhere in opposition to intellectual qualities, stating that "there are properties which pertain to personality more closely than the intellectual."[31] In his or her most inner self, the person is heart and will: "While the function of the understanding does not issue from the interior, from the depths of the ego, those depths do awaken in affective and dispositional life."[32] The affective activity and the activity of the will express the person's relationship to values, or rather this relationship's manner of being. "How you pick up values and how you behave toward them, how you enjoy

30. Ineffable individuality is a property of spiritual beings alone, while the psyche is a set of stable properties which a subject can certainly share with another. Although they are not insignificant for the subject's individuality, these qualities do not form his individuality in the strict sense (as in personal core or distinctiveness). The psyche, by definition, is rooted in the living body. It is thus an individual as far as identity is concerned, just like material things (which are always examples of types). The psyche is however more than just a material thing. What distinguishes the two is the psyche's ability to develop in accordance with "internal necessity" (organism). This development always takes place on the basis of typical properties and according to a developmental process which is also typical. The psyche then, even if it cannot be determined in an exact manner, can be understood and explained in a general manner. This individuality may be compared to "a crossroads of general laws"; it is a sort of complex unit which, although elusive, is nonetheless understandable based on general types. For this reason one can deduce a posteriori an adult's character from a remembrance of the child he once was. One cannot, however, clearly assert that a given child will become a given adult. For a more in-depth study of Stein's philosophy of person, see *Einführung in die Philosophie* (Freiburg: Herder; Basel; Vienna, 1991), vol. 12 of her collected works *(Werke)*, pp. 153-61, as well as *Philosophy of Psychology*, pp. 226-38, and "Die ontische Struktur der Person und ihre erkenntnistheoretische Problematik," in *Collected Works*, vol. 6, *Welt und Person, Beitrag zum christlichen Wahrheitsstreben* (Louvain: Nauwelaerts, 1962).

31. Stein, *Philosophy of Psychology*, p. 227.

32. Stein, *Philosophy of Psychology*, p. 227.

things, how you make yourself happy, how you grieve and how you suffer: that all depends on the quality of the soul."[33] This manner of being is personal distinctiveness, individuality in its most basic sense. It leaves its mark on every one of the subject's real acts, throughout his or her psychic life. It is in this way that the expert can identify the personal touch or style of a painter or poet, and thus proceed to put it into words. He will, however, never be able to define this style. Individuality proper, understood as the unique quality, is ineffable, absolutely untouchable: "The entire character of the person, his or her natural dispositions as a whole, colored by psychic individuality, can be destroyed. The soul can be torn away from the natural foundation on which it rose, and yet, it preserves its individuality. This individuality is *intangibilis*. Whatever enters the soul, and whatever leaves it is in a way impregnated by this individuality. Even grace is received by each soul in its own particular way."[34]

This individuality exists only in the spiritual sphere, but it is present in the *objective* spiritual sphere as much as in the *subjective* spiritual sphere. A person's genuine achievements bear the stamp of his or her individuality, and although it is in a way which differs from that of the personal subject, such achievements come from the spirit. Like the personal subject, a personal achievement has an individual quale. Stein gives the example of a landscape, not considered as a piece of nature, but as "a unity of a specific character."[35] It is a fact that the mountain scene celebrated by the poet or reproduced by the painter is not merely a sample of nature, but is an object, highly spiritualized by the artist as well as by the viewer.

An analysis of *psychic* individuation (complexity of type) has presented us with various traits shared by several individuals. This individuation finds its source in the psyche's properties and in their development in psychic life. Individuality proper, however, finds root in the person's core. The person's soul is formed of lasting qualities which invest it from within.[36] (This is not true of the character or of the psyche.)[37] It is therefore the manner in which one lives psy-

---

33. Stein, *Philosophy of Psychology*, p. 228.

34. Stein, "Die ontische Struktur der Person," p. 153.

35. Stein, *Philosophy of Psychology*, p. 307

36. The various texts that deal with personal style reflect Stein's thought in its purest form. They portray her personal touch and a genuine expression of herself. She is in no way constrained by learned notions, and the fullness of her intuition shines through, allowing us to perceive her personal distinctiveness. Stein's ontology is expressed within the established structure of Thomistic philosophy (or at least that which was known to her), and comes across as narrow. Here, in her analysis of the person, the framework is mobile, so that without negating the essentialism of her ontology her personalism rectifies its stiffness.

37. Stein, *Philosophy of Psychology*, p. 230.

chic traits which manifests individuality in the proper sense, or personal individuality.

Woman's Threefold Vocation in the State of Grace

Stein's reflections in a 1932 text lead the reader into a vast discussion concerning the state of woman and her part in the original state, in the state of sin, and in the realm of grace.[38] A few preliminary considerations can elucidate the matter for us. Genesis points mainly to the unity of the human vocation. In the beginning, woman's vocation is not explicitly distinct from that of man. Woman is called to assist man in the threefold task God gives him: to be in God's image, to multiply, and to be master of the earth. In the account of the first sin, however, a differentiation of tasks is revealed. After sin, woman is punished in her maternity and man in his work. What this means, according to Stein, is that even before sin the responsibility for descendants was allotted to woman in particular, while it was especially man's responsibility to be master of the earth. As long as harmony presided between woman and man, they assisted one another in each of these tasks. It is only when conflict arises between man and woman subsequent to sin that the responsibility of each is specified. Sin alters the unity within the couple: in addition to an uneasiness consecutive to sin, the relation between man and woman is transformed into a relation of submission and obedience and their respective vocations become specialized due to a lack of cooperation.

Authenticity of Life

The author encourages us to suppose that our vocation can be carried on in the state of grace. What then becomes of the woman in this new situation? In accordance with the renowned expression of Edith Stein, that "no woman is only woman,"[39] one must affirm that every woman is a human being: both a woman and a personal, individual being. She thus shares with all human beings the essence "human being" and with all women the essence "woman." In addition, every concrete woman is eminently personal, and this means that her own particular features leave their personal mark on all her authentic acts.

In addition, we have considered the human being as perpetually in the

---

38. Stein, "Separate Vocations," in *Essays on Woman*, pp. 59-85.
39. Edith Stein, "The Ethos of Women's Professions," in *Essays on Woman*, p. 49.

process of becoming, as developing his own qualities and bringing *(Entfaltung)* his most intimate individual being to maturity through his personal acts. We also know that this state of becoming is set in motion by the end it seeks to attain, and that this end is established by the essences in which all human beings participate. Every human person thus participates in the essence humanity and at the same time contributes to its realization through his or her personal state of becoming. Woman as such participates in the general essence woman which she enriches through her feminine state of becoming. One might object that this affirmation limits the woman's personal freedom. If she tends by nature toward the achievement of a part of her essence humanity on one hand and of her essence woman on the other hand, is she not condemned to a type of feminine life? Could we not go so far as to say that the individual would, in the end, be destined to express the general?[40]

Stein's profound personalism allows us to cast aside this objection. We have already spoken of the core of the person, of the person's quale, personal and intangible distinctiveness. For Stein it is this distinctiveness, and not the general essences of being human or being woman, which is most determinative in the realization of the person. To express this she makes use of the concept of authentic life.[41] The authenticity of personal life is based on both types and individuality. One might, at first, be tempted to assemble type and inauthenticity on one hand, personal distinctiveness and authenticity on the other. It is in fact the case that behavior which has a personal touch is often considered genuine, while standard or typical reactions seem more imposed than freely chosen. This tendency is however an oversimplification of reality. According to such a hypothesis, social and communal life as a whole, which necessitates the sharing of typical traits, would be directly qualified as inauthentic.[42]

It is nonetheless true that personal distinctiveness confers upon every — even typical — life an authentic character. This distinctiveness marks every one of the subject's genuine acts in the manner of a signature or seal, making it an authentically personal act. We recognize the author of a given word, of a given act, by its stamp of authenticity, just as we can attribute a given work to its artist when we recognize a specific personal trait. There are, however, in personal acts, certain components which do not have their source in the soul's core. The

40. Stein makes a distinction between inferior, living nature and human nature. The first finds its fullness in the expression of species. The human person's aim is mainly personal: its center and its end dwell within it.

41. "Authenticity" is a term Stein holds dear and is already present in her first writings *(On the Problem of Empathy)*. Her entire life expresses a constant concern for authenticity.

42. In her treatise on empathy, Stein shows that knowledge and even interpersonal relations are always based on something established.

act is not immanent to the soul, it participates in the external world. From this we can conclude that it is impossible to conceive an individual entirely cut off from the outside world. In the concrete, this means that my psychophysical body presents a number of typical traits, either in my morphology, my functions, my sensibility, my "type" of intelligence, etc. The aim of a so-called authentic life is to live these qualities according to one's own personal distinctiveness, in which case the person's core is expressed without confusion. What is to be said then of authenticity? In approaching this question, Stein makes use of Scheler's analysis of the "contagion" of sentiment *(Gefühlsansteckung)*.[43] Given the fact that a person's standpoints can have a contagious effect, another person can ascribe to them without truly integrating them into his or her life — almost blindly. If this were the case, they would not really be *personal* standpoints, and might not even originate in the person.[44]

This can be illustrated by two cases. One can imagine, on one hand, a person whose entire character and development lie within the bounds of the ordinary or typical, manifesting nothing of the personal. This would be an extreme instance of the average man. Inversely, there is the case of "an integrally individual person, in whom there is nothing typical,"[45] which can only be simulated, for every person represents a type, even if it is in his or her own manner. At most, this person would be someone with a very strong personality, overshadowing yet not eliminating every trace of type. The will enables us to combat the dangers of inauthenticity. The person can, to a certain extent, determine his or her environment and thus also the influences against which he or she must struggle. This personal freedom can be extended to the interior world: the per-

43. See Stein, *On the Problem*, p. 23, and *Philosophy of Psychology*, pp. 175-91. In these works she refers to M. Scheler, *Sympathiegefühle* (Max Scheler, *Die Idole der Selbsterkenntnis in Gesammelte Werke* III, *Vom Umsturz der Werte* [Bern: Franke Verlag; Munich, 1972]). Stein's view of the "contagion" of sentiment complies with Scheler's theory on all but one point. While Scheler considers that a condition for the subject's "contagion" is his awareness of the other's experience, for Stein the subject can be "contaminated" without even realizing it (*On the Problem*, p. 24).

44. See Stein, *On the Problem of Empathy*, and *Philosophy of Psychology*, pp. 175-91. In spite of this, one should not too hastily conclude that there is no standpoint. There is one, but it is tainted with inauthenticity. Like authentic sentiment, inauthentic sentiment leads to the formation of personal properties, which then bear the traits of the inauthenticity (or authenticity) of one's sentiment. What then is to be said of the personal core? Should there be a person who, for a variety of reasons, is not grounded in his personal core, he or she would lead a life devoid of anything belonging to the individual proper; here the person would merely exemplify a type. Less serious in respect to authenticity is the case of the person whose original constitution is unable to develop because of exterior circumstances.

45. Stein, *Einführung in die Philosophie*, p. 154.

son "has the freedom to nip in the bud any stirrings of the soul that are induced within her."[46] The person can also retreat from the influence of another's personal distinctiveness. One's freedom to influence another person's development is limited by that person's resistance to such influence.

Authenticity as the Fullness (Entfaltung) of Personal Distinctiveness

Let us now apply the above considerations to the theme which interests us here: woman. The person as such contains within himself or herself a personal and spiritual core. The development (Entfaltung) of this center is the aim of the person's psychophysical existence.[47] The unfolding (Entfaltung) of the how (Sosein) necessarily passes by way of corporal and physical development which itself belongs to types. As we have seen, the human being is a concretization of different elements which overlap without effacing one another. "The spiritual and the body-soul being of the human being are not externally juxtaposed, but one."[48] The personality or personal distinctiveness, as personal and related to the higher life, must then also permeate the corporal and physical life without annihilating it. The Sosein of a specific woman is meant to express itself and to authentically develop within the framework of her essence woman and her essence humanity. In the last analysis it is the duty of the personal and strictly individual soul to take charge of the development of the body and the psyche. In doing so the soul shows forth (Entfaltung) its most intimate and ineffable core: its manner of being. It belongs to the human being to "spiritualize" his body, just as his relationship to the spirit (for example, to God) implies his materiality.[49] It is in this sense that Stein speaks of the threefold formative power of the soul,[50] meant to bring general essences to their fullness and to bring out per-

---

46. Stein, *Philosophy of Psychology*, p. 268.

47. The case of pure spirits (angels) is less complex, for they are exclusively spiritual beings. An angel's life consists in the development (Entfaltung) of its essence, its personal core. Angels do not have souls, understood as the living center of being, and because of this, "The meaning of their being is no other than the unfolding (Entfaltung) of what they are . . . in a life of pure self-giving to God: in knowledge, love, and service" (Stein, *Finite and Eternal Being*, p. 506).

48. Stein, *Finite and Eternal Being*, p. 506.

49. Man's corporal constitution is the basis for one of the ways of grace: the sacramental way. An analysis of this is to be found in Stein's "Die ontische Struktur des Person." The sacraments seek to reestablish the original relationship between body and soul.

50. Stein, *Finite and Eternal Being*, p. 462.

sonal distinctiveness. The soul's dynamic force is one, even if its action has a triple orientation: development of the body, of the soul, and of the spiritual life.

Above all, woman is a person and must thus give priority to the development *(Entfaltung)* of her *Sosein*, of her own personal distinctiveness. She is also rooted in a psychic body, and therefore can only achieve fulfillment through life in the body and soul — in other words, through her development as a human being and as a feminine being. The authenticity of her life must thus come about through the active assumption of all that she is. Personal distinctiveness cannot efface a concrete woman's humanity and femininity without damaging her authentic development *(Entfaltung)*. Personal distinctiveness must, on the contrary, pass through and penetrate the woman's entire being.

The particular human being is in relation to humanity as body parts relate to the body as a whole. It is every human's duty to incarnate the "general nature of man" in order to be a member of the whole of humanity. Humanity must therefore be understood in two ways: it signifies the general essence of man as well as the living whole formed by human beings throughout the history of the world.[51] A twofold relation corresponds to this double meaning: that of "the individual human being to 'humanity.' The individual human being is an embodiment of the universal, and this human being is a member of the whole."[52] Only those who are "well advanced in their development"[53] are capable of an intuitive grasp of this humanity which, we shall recall, is real and not conceptual. An intuitive understanding such as this is accompanied by a sense of duty. Seeing himself as the part of a whole, man feels indebted to "perfected humanity"[54] for his personal contribution. Everyone and therefore every woman has the duty to participate in humanity's realization, for "it is of the very essence of humankind that every individual as well as the entire human family are to become what, according to their nature, they are destined to be in a process of temporal unfolding *(Entfaltung)*, and that this unfolding depends on the cooperation of each individual as well as on the common effort

51. "The species *humanity* is realized perfectly only in the course of world history in which the great individual, humanity, becomes concrete." Stein, "Problems of Women's Education," p. 189.

52. Stein, *Finite and Eternal Being*, p. 509.

53. This awareness takes place within a state of interiority by which the subject is present to himself. In a commentary on Saint Teresa of Ávila's *Interior Castle*, Stein describes the different stages of the person's interiority. See *Welt und Person; Seelenburg*, vol. 6, *Werke*, pp. 39-69. Elsewhere, she specifies: "Our conscience does not provide us with a completed image of what we should be," which would serve as a guideline for behavior. It is rather in concrete life situations, in our encounters with specific people, that this image takes shape for us *(Aufbau der menschlichen Person*, p. 120).

54. Stein, "Problems of Women's Education," p. 192.

of all."[55] It is clear in light of these considerations that each person is called to realize the general essence of humanity through his or her own contribution, that is, by penetrating and enriching this essence with his or her own distinctiveness.

Aside from the pure entity of perfected humanity *(vollendete Menschentum)*, Stein also speaks of perfected womanhood *(vollendete Frauentum)*.[56] We have seen that womanhood is characterized by a specific relationship amongst the soul's aptitudes in which the heart enfolds and directs the will (with the risk of losing the sense of reality). It is the duty of women to bring this feminine world to its fullness in a movement which is an integral part of the realization of humanity. Women are called to realize humanity in their womanhood, for the masculine world cannot do so on its own. "Moreover, the fact that Adam needed as a *complement* a female companion and that Adam and Eve were destined to generate a *race* [*Geschlecht*] of human beings, seems to indicate that Adam did not in and by himself embody the fullness of humanity, but that this fullness was to be realized in and through the entire human family."[57]

Humanity and the feminine world are fully realized in a similar manner, by means of the personal life of each woman. Her responsibility to live an authentic life, faithful to her personal distinctiveness, is an integral part of her vocation to be human (to be in God's image) and to be woman, as well as an enrichment for these vocations. What then does today's woman have to offer for the realization of humanity? What are the life conditions (social, economic, cultural, etc.) which allow her to actively contribute to this realization? Such are the fundamental questions which deserve to be voiced and considered in an effort to meet the challenge of the "new feminism."

The Contemporary Woman in Her Daily Life

States of Life

With Stein we have stressed the fact that a woman's humanity and femininity can only find completion through her fulfillment in real life. By developing in a way which is in keeping with her *Eigenart* and her own essence, woman (as well as man) can truly contribute to the realization of humanity as well as to her species. In compliance with what her Catholic faith proposes, Stein suggests

55. Stein, *Finite and Eternal Being*, p. 526.
56. Stein, "Problems of Women's Education," p. 195.
57. Stein, *Finite and Eternal Being*, p. 525.

that there are three states of life for women: wife and mother, consecrated celibacy in the religious life, and celibacy "in the world."[58]

To each state there corresponds, for Stein, a genuine vocation, as each person is called *(berufen)* to the state which best suits him. A general attitude of soul is what predisposes one to a specific state in life, and for every vocation there is a corresponding attitude of the soul or a personal predisposition.[59] Nursing, for example, requires a willingness to serve, just as circumspection and determination are required of an entrepreneur.[60] Upon this base Stein proposes an analysis of the "natural" state of life found in marriage and motherhood, and the supernatural state of celibacy, whether consecrated in religious life or not, along with their corresponding attitudes of soul. She also invites us to reflect on "other natural vocations of the woman": professional vocations. As we shall see in what follows, her approach to professions as genuine vocations clearly tends toward ideal situations and is unfortunately more often relative to aspirations than to reality.

Regarding states in life, let us keep in mind that if we hold it to be true that there is an attitude of soul which corresponds to each state or, on a larger scale, to each vocation, then young people must be taught to discern within themselves the predispositions to their own vocation. We may happily note that this view is extensively published today in certain educational settings, for the professional orientation of young people. The legitimate concern for personal fulfillment in professional life is being discussed and thus also the importance of serious reflection prior to choosing what type of education is to be pursued. Why then is the discussion not broadened to include the fundamental choice of

58. Stein proposes these three states throughout the collection of articles, conferences, and various works assembled in *Essays on Woman*. As an example we can cite "The Ethos of Women's Professions," a conference given on September 3, 1930, for the Catholic Academic Association in Salzburg. Here she confronts the three states of life (marriage, celibacy, and consecrated life) with the concrete life conditions of her time. Emphasis is placed on the difficulties confronted by married women with children who seek to harmoniously combine work and family life. See *Essays on Woman*, pp. 43-57. Stein uses even greater concision when defining the aims of Christian education for girls. The education of the Christian woman must "lead her to that which makes her capable of either fulfilling her duties as wife and mother in the natural and supernatural sense or of consecrating all her powers to the kingdom of God in a God-dedicated virginity. (Marriage and the religious life should not be set up as alternatives. Signs indicate that our time needs people who will lead a God-dedicated life 'in the world'; this is certainly not to say, however, that conventual life is 'outmoded.')" Stein, "Spirituality," pp. 101-2. See also "Problems of Women's Education," p. 156.

59. Stein, "Ethos," pp. 43-44.

60. Stein, "Ethos," p. 44. It is important to specify here that in certain cases vocation can be opposed to natural inclination. Stein, "Problems of Women's Education," p. 204.

a state of life? While the professional decision is subject to reflection and consideration, we must unfortunately observe that personal orientation in marriage or celibacy is too often left to the chance of circumstance.[61]

In contemporary debate on woman, just as in women's contemporary life, the question of her fulfillment, her realization, and in a way her happiness is frequently brought up. How can women in our society find fulfillment in the three states mentioned above? Let us take for example what Stein refers to as the "natural" state, that of marriage. Does a mother who remains at home in the service of her family not renounce personal fulfillment? Is she not compromising herself in a world which holds in higher esteem the wholesome and constructive qualities of "active life"? Can a woman really be involved both at home and in her profession, confronting both worlds without betraying either of them? Then there are those who freely choose celibacy; if motherhood is absent from their lives, is the essential feminine experience not also missing?

The regulation of a woman's life clearly presents its own particularities. Women are aware that they can become mothers. They also know they either can or must work. Thus, based on experience, personal fulfillment can be regarded in a specifically feminine way. How can today's young women be prepared for the free and conscious construction of their lives? The diverse aspirations we have recognized in the adult woman lead us to see the necessity of an appropriate preparation for young women. To enable them to freely choose a state of life, they should be informed of their different options.[62] They should also be made aware of the typically feminine difficulty involved in seeking compatibility between work and motherhood.

Stein speaks of the attitudes of soul which predispose persons to a personal vocation. We know these attitudes are partially innate. Her concept of a threefold human vocation, mentioned above, is enlightening for women of her time and ours: humans are to be in God's image, to multiply, and to be masters of the earth. The three vocations are initially meant for both man and woman, although there is a natural allotment of responsibilities between them. We have also seen that every person is primarily responsible for the development

61. In *The Christian State of Life*, trans. Sister Mary Francis McCarthy (San Francisco: Ignatius, 1986), pp. 73-74, Adrienne von Speyr points out the necessity of serious reflection which, assisted by God's grace, can enable persons to discern their vocation to a state of life. For von Speyr, each state of life reflects trinitarian love: marriage accentuates charity among human persons, celibacy places emphasis on man's filial love of God. This is also the perspective presented by John Paul II in *Mulieris dignitatem:* both marriage and celibacy realize woman's vocation (as well as man's) to be an unconditional gift to God or to the spouse.

62. Von Speyr (p. 56) describes one of today's common tendencies to indefinitely delay the decision for a state of life, thus undergoing life instead of freely choosing it.

(Entfaltung) of his or her personal distinctiveness. We have yet to analyze the authentic accomplishment of women's vocations in the state of grace — lived subsequent to sin and to God's grace — and to see how men and women are called to fulfill these three initial vocations in a freely chosen state of life and in a way which is absolutely personal.

The Fallen State

In her analysis of the feminine soul, Stein enumerates characteristics of the woman which seem to befit her vocation to motherhood. Her sense of personal being, for example, provides her with a natural disposition for education. But just as sin accentuates division between man and woman in their respective duties, it also affects their particular vocations. The relationship of man and woman to their offspring is degraded, for instance, not to speak of relations within the couple itself. Stein describes at length the primordial vocation to fatherhood,[63] bestowed on man in addition to his personal and particular vocation. The deterioration which came into play with sin has considerable effects on paternal responsibility: man experiences an "inclination to shirk his paternal duties."[64] Similarly, woman suffers from an exacerbated maternal sentiment and an inclination to cling to her children at any cost. She is tempted to view her child as her property, in an attachment which is detrimental to his or her freedom. After the fall, woman tends toward the unilateral development of her aptitudes. She concentrates her efforts on affectivity, without regard for the initial harmony amongst the faculties of sentiment, understanding, and will. For man, on the other hand, the great temptation lies in an inclination to invest his energy in the faculties of understanding and will, to the detriment of personal entities.[65]

It is worth calling to mind here, that "the root of the evil lies again in her (or his) perverted relationship to God."[66] If man and woman do not live up to their respective vocations, it is mainly because they have sinned against God by not fulfilling their primary vocation: to be in God's image. The archetype of every human being is to be found in God, just as the archetype of every human community is in the Trinity.[67] Humanity is thus set in motion: "We who are 'on

---

63. Stein, "Separate Vocations," pp. 72-73.

64. Stein, "Separate Vocations," p. 73.

65. This degeneracy is already predicted by Genesis, which announces man's dominion over woman as well as woman's concupiscence (Gen. 3:16).

66. Stein, "Separate Vocations," p. 75.

67. In *Mulieris dignitatem,* John Paul II extensively develops the themes of man's creation in God's image and of the unity of God and man through communion. See esp. #6-8.

our way' in our pilgrimage to the heavenly Jerusalem experience in ourselves the conflict between corrupt nature and grace which, like a growing plant, can grow and bloom, triumphing over all pestilence."[68]

Once sin has been committed, nature's original condition — which precedes that of grace — is degenerate. Only the redemptive act, by which the order of grace is established, leads the way to triumphant glory. Christ, the new Adam, becomes a part of history through the virgin Mary and, ever present in the church, redeems corrupt nature. Although "the redemptive act did not restore corrupted nature with one stroke,"[69] man is thus renewed in his divine vocation. This state of grace introduced into the world provides humanity with the means to combat sin and tend toward life with God. "We have indicated how the nature and original vocation of man and woman may be sought after and restored; only as God's children can this be attained."[70]

Restoring the Original Condition through Education

Throughout her conferences on woman, Stein extensively develops the idea of the correction of the state of sin by grace. She points out deviations peculiar to man as well as those which characterize woman, and proposes concrete means to counter these evils. Her experience of teaching in a boarding school for young women allows her to consider at length the type of education most suitable to the feminine soul.[71] To avoid the unilateral development of a woman's emotional life, without the exercise of reason and willpower to complement it, she might be given access, for example, to the studies of language and grammar. These somewhat difficult subjects can be of much benefit to a woman, teaching her to think clearly and keenly and, even more importantly, enabling her to curb a typically feminine weakness, for "mental clarity is often dulled by her emotions, desires and libidinal drives."[72] This advice is valid beyond the school setting. Within the framework of married life, it is the husband's responsibility to make sure that his wife does not "lapse into a life of mere sensuality."[73]

68. Stein, "Separate Vocations," p. 76.
69. Stein, "Separate Vocations," p. 76.
70. Stein, "Separate Vocations," p. 75.
71. In 1923, having attempted in vain to present a thesis, Stein began a career as a teacher at Saint Madeleine of Spire Boarding School for Young Women, run by Dominican sisters. She remained there until 1931, and during this time she became familiar with Thomistic philosophy and began more systematic research on the role of the woman.
72. Stein, "Separate Vocations," p. 218.
73. Stein, "Separate Vocations," p. 77.

Should he fail to do so, he would bear the consequences of laxity in her higher life. Such negligence can lead to possessiveness toward children, and the absence of receptivity in their upbringing. The husband would gain much from including his wife in his own intellectual activity and in seeking her counsel. He will find that she can give him "invaluable advice"[74] because of her ability to see man as a whole and to seek his fulfillment. This assertion perfectly coincides with that of John Paul II, according to whom women "see persons with their hearts."[75] We have now seen the practical applications of this plan to "restore" the original condition. Above all, it is an effort to reestablish man's relationship to God and to woman, as well as all human relations. It is the wife's duty to guide her husband and her children in their faith, for "a quality unique to woman is her singular sensitivity to moral values and an abhorrence for all which is low and mean. . . . Allied closely to this sensitivity for moral values is her yearning for the divine and for her own personal union with the Lord, her readiness and desire to be completely fulfilled and guided by his love."[76] For these reasons woman is particularly suited for the religious and moral education of children.

According to Stein in "Grundlagen der Frauenbildung"[77] and "Probleme der Frauenbildung,"[78] education is meant to form. What is it to form? The present soul (that of the student, of the child, of the person), which must be fashioned in order to become what it must be for its own personal character, is indelible, intangible. In light of the above, it appears useful to proceed to educate young people not only in order to instruct them or to insure their intellectual development, but also always keeping in mind the formation of the soul, which, in the end, results in the formation of the person. "Education is not an external possession of learning but rather the *gestalt* which the human personality assumes under the influence of manifold external forces."[79] In the Christian view adopted by Stein, the soul is in pursuit of an ultimate goal: the resto-

74. Stein, "Separate Vocations," p. 78.

75. John Paul II, "Letter to Women," p. 143, #12.

76. Stein, "Separate Vocations," p. 78. This receptivity is also brought out by John Paul II, who uses the Gospel as evidence: "Christ speaks to women about the things of God and they understand them; there is a true resonance of mind and heart, a response of faith." *Mulieris dignitatem*, #15.

77. This is a conference Stein gave on November 8, 1930, at Bendorf on the Rhine before the education committee of the Catholic Association of German Women. See "Fundamental Principles of Women's Education," in *Essays on Woman*, pp. 129-45.

78. This text was written as the basis for a course Stein gave in 1932 at the Deutsche Institut für Wissenschaftliche Pädagogik, where she was active until her dismissal in 1933, due to her Jewish origin. See Stein, "Problems of Women's Education," pp. 147-235.

79. Stein, "Fundamental Principles," p. 130.

ration of filial love toward God and a yearning for eternal life.[80] Within a lifetime this restoration takes place through the life choices one is called to freely make. Education is essential in providing youth with an awareness of the existence of these choices, and in enabling them to choose in full consciousness, thus freely.

In an article on education, Stein attempts to define what she refers to as "perfected femininity" *(Idee des vollendeten Frauentums)*. This goal to be attained will assist her in defining the means by which educators can prepare the feminine soul to enter into its fullness. If we understand Stein, the ideal feminine soul is a thing of impressive beauty and excellence:

> The soul of woman must therefore be *expansive* and open to all human beings; it must be *quiet* so that no small weak flame will be extinguished by stormy winds; *warm* so as not to benumb fragile buds; *clear,* so that no vermin will settle in dark corners and recesses; *self-contained,* so that no invasions from without can imperil the inner life; *empty of itself,* in order that extraneous life may have room in it; finally, *mistress of itself* and also of its body, so that the entire person is readily at the disposal of every call.[81]

The Free and Conscious Choice of a State of Life — Natural Vocation and Supernatural Vocation

This ideal feminine soul must be concretely realized in personal life, through the person's fulfillment within a freely chosen state of life. In the order of nature, the feminine being finds purpose in her union with man. This evidently does not mean that woman exists entirely for man's sake, for every creature has its own purpose, "and that is its particular way of being an image of the divine being."[82] Because this union is closely allied to procreation, it can be concluded that the tendency toward union leads the woman, in a free decision, to an attachment to man, and that together the two found a family. This is one of woman's concrete vocations, and it is therefore suitable for educators to prepare young women, by example and formation, for this state of life. "The fruit of an

---

80. On May 22, 2000, at a congress held in Rome entitled "A New Feminism for the New Millennium," Jo Croissant expressed an idea similar to this. She stated, in sum, that today's woman can promote a new feminism through the rediscovery of her role as a "daughter of God."

81. Stein, "Fundamental Principles," pp. 132-33. The pages which follow in the text are a development and commentary of this quotation.

82. Stein, "Problems of Women's Education," p. 196. See also John Paul II, *Mulieris dignitatem,* esp. #6.

ideal educational program, i.e., a relevant one, should be that each girl would be fit for both marriage and celibacy."[83]

Practically speaking, how is a young woman to be prepared to choose family life, to make a personal commitment as spouse and mother? On the other hand, how is she to be presented with an adequate image of celibacy and religious life? In an effort to respond to these questions, Stein undertakes an analysis of educational structures: family, school, state, the church, and "other formative factors" such as literature and art.[84] Let us first specify that education begins in the family. This latter is the first formative agent and plays a decisive role in the child's life.[85] A girl experiences family life through her development within the warmth and receptivity of her home. Here the mother's presence is essential: "nothing can replace the girl's growing up near a mother who embodies authentic womanhood."[86] How relevant to our time is Stein's remark! Examples of authentic womanhood, consisting in an attitude of soul, or rather of the entire person, which "sees to the heart" of man, are rarely exalted in our day. Contact with real women in their material, personal, and spiritual selves is paramount for young women. By being there in a way which is implied by her daily concerns for education, the home, and economic resources, a mother provides her children, and especially her daughters, with this training.

Other possible vocations are also to be considered: celibacy and religious life. When dealing with preparation for this state of life, Stein comes to the question of boarding schools for young girls, and in particular boarding schools of a religious character. There is an advantage to the fact that such schools are set up in a way that resembles family life (to begin with, the superior is called "mother"), thus providing boarding students with a type of security as well as a spirit of collegiality and solidarity. What is more, life in schools of this sort offers its pupils access to religious life on a daily basis. The girls come to see that here virginity is lived positively, as something chosen, a gift from God, an indestructible bond to Christ. This experience may then prove decisive in the student's future life choices. "Children who witness such a truly dedicated and God-filled life will not be able to evade its persuasive power."[87] Based on this experience, they will be given the means either to properly evaluate the ideal and beauty of virginity or to respond positively to God's call in favor of celibacy.

83. Stein, "Problems of Women's Education," p. 204.

84. See Stein, "Problems of Women's Education," pp. 206-27.

85. Michel Schooyans develops this point in the last section of his work *La face cachée de l'ONU* (Paris: Le Sarment, 2000), pp. 187-226.

86. Stein, "Problems of Women's Education," p. 221.

87. Stein, "Problems of Women's Education," p. 228.

It seems truly essential today to introduce young people to persons in all states of life. Only in this way will they be able to freely and serenely consider their alternatives once they reach adulthood. An education in a religious establishment is not always a possibility, nor is it desirable in every case. It does however remain important for young people to be exposed to those who testify to a life entirely devoted to the service of Christ.

In such circumstances celibacy can be seen as a gift, which is freely chosen, and thus recalls marriage. Marriage too proceeds from the spouses' mutual gift, and as we have seen, is the form of life which corresponds to the human being's natural vocation. Celibacy consecrated to God results "not only from a free *choice* on the part of man, but also from a special *grace* on the part of God, who calls a particular person to live celibacy."[88] It is not the human being's natural vocation, but is a supernatural vocation. The call to celibacy nonetheless remains a personal vocation in which God's call and God's grace are addressed to an individual person. In the model of celibate life, the human being, the woman in this case, realizes her femininity in a way which differs from that of marriage. We have brought out some of woman's essential and specific characteristics, one of which is her desire to give and to receive love. We have likewise exposed the ideal feminine soul as described by Stein. In consecrated celibate life a woman freely offers herself to God and receives Christ as her spouse. Motherhood is also a fundamental aspect of consecrated life. Woman, naturally drawn to all that is personal, experiences a type of maternity in religious or consecrated life: spiritual motherhood.[89] Whether she chooses an apostolic life (in the world or in a religious order) or a contemplative life, she devotes herself to persons in need, either caring for them directly or through prayer. The perfection of woman's essence comes about through the unfolding *(Entfaltung)* of personal distinctiveness in concrete women. This unfolding takes place in particular vocations, in freely chosen states of life: marriage, celibacy, and religious life. In each state the anthropological structure as taught by faith is profoundly respected and nurtured: the human being is created in God's image; he cannot live alone but is called to a mutual or interpersonal relationship; he is a free and rational being who finds his realization, his fulfillment, in loving communion, in the gift of self.

We have seen the usefulness and importance of exposing young people to genuine witnesses, present in different states of life. We have however not yet spoken of the examples provided us by the Catholic faith, which illustrate to perfection the goals of accomplished humanity and femininity: Christ and the

---

88. John Paul II, *Mulieris dignitatem*, #20.
89. See John Paul II, *Mulieris dignitatem*, #21.

blessed virgin Mary. The latter should, in the final analysis, be the paradigm of all feminine formation. The figure of Mary indicates that woman's vocation may be realized both in maternity and in consecrated virginity. While woman's natural vocation implies marriage and biological maternity, there exists for her another way: the "supernatural vocation," in which she freely chooses to be the bride of Christ. In this condition she also acquires spiritual motherhood. Woman's vocation is thus necessarily expressed in a variety of ways. Very particular vocations exist because each person has his or her own distinctiveness, which can be considerably removed from the type to which he or she belongs. Stein gives the example of Teresa of Ávila, whose activity may be clearly distinguished from that of traditional feminine vocations. This very diversity, Stein tells us, enriches the essence of "perfected femininity": "It is not possible to generalize about individuality as one might generalize concerning the image of perfected humanity or perfected womanhood. But we must understand clearly that these two general categories do not constitute fully the goal of girls' education. Rather, this goal can be reached only in the concrete wholeness of an individual person."[90] The diversity of religious orders is representative of the multiplicity of personality types. Numerous orders, both apostolic and contemplative, have come forth throughout the history of the church. Still today, new types of consecrated life appear, thus responding to the aspirations of Christians who desire to follow Christ in a radical manner, in accordance with their personal calling.

The ultimate aim of all life being the eternal order, it is necessary to consider the conditions of our time in order to better define adequate goals. Stein is fully conscious of the fact that every time has its corresponding way of life and its specific concerns. She takes particular care to warn her contemporaries of the dangers of biologism and materialism, prevalent at the time. Biologism considers "humanity and the relationship of the sexes merely on a biological basis," and materialism completely denies "woman's unique nature and particular destiny, which disclaims an organic cooperation of the sexes and organic social patterns but seeks rather to consider all individuals as similar atoms in a mechanistically ordered structure."[91] Stein says the only bulwark capable of countering these harmful currents is the Catholic faith, laying the ground for metaphysics, social theory, and education as well as the praxis which corresponds to them. Today's world faces these same challenges. Biologism and materialism are still at work to the detriment of the man-woman relationship as well as to the family in general, which has not ceased to lose ground. On one

90. Stein, "Problems of Women's Education," p. 202.
91. Stein, "Problems of Women's Education," p. 206.

hand there is the deplorable dissolution of the family unit, subsequent to a lost consciousness of the meaning of the family. On the other hand there is a low economic, cultural, and social esteem for the family, which merely accelerates its dismemberment. Regarding woman, one can only regret an apparent asymmetry between her successful ascendance in professional life and the vanishing sense of her place within the family. Rather than promoting the unity of the person through the integration of his or her private and public activities, society continually separates the two poles (for both man and woman), making it difficult to accord cumulated activity in both spheres.

Considering that every person is called to a state of life and to a particular vocation related to certain attitudes of the soul, and that the goal of education is to form the soul in view of its personal fulfillment, we must assert that it is urgent to promote an awareness of women's vocations. The value of the maternal and familial experience needs to be reaffirmed. In a desire to show women that professional life is a way to fulfillment, Western culture forgets and sometimes even denigrates the beauty of motherhood and life in the home. In addition to this, the birthrate in wealthy countries has dropped significantly and households no longer include more than two generations. As a result, the everyday life of youth has undergone a sweeping change. Today's young people often have no contact with the family entity.

The Professional Vocation

Let us now look to the woman "in the world," who either desires to take part in the working world or is obliged to do so. Stein, extraordinarily modern for her time, tells us "there is no profession which cannot be practiced by a woman."[92] It is nonetheless important to distinguish between occupation and vocation proper. Although it is true in principle that one's dispositions may enable one to exercise a number of professions, a profession whose practice is incompatible with a woman's (or man's) inclinations and natural gifts is undesirable. Stein finds it unfortunate that "today, almost on an average, people are in 'vocations' to which they are not called by nature; one can almost consider it a stroke of luck when it is otherwise."[93]

In the best of cases, therefore, and whenever possible, professional choice is made within the framework of vocation, within the movement toward "becoming what one is meant to be." Achieving this goal calls for both woman-

92. Stein, "Ethos," p. 49.
93. Stein, "Separate Vocations," p. 82.

hood and selfhood. As this latter surpasses subjection to type classification, Stein concentrates on womanhood to give direction to her research: In what professions can feminine being develop? Woman is traditionally involved in education, in caring for the sick and for children; in our day she also cares for the elderly. In these areas there is in fact a call for maternal care, for an attentiveness to the person as a whole. In such professions the woman who aspires to "give of herself in love" and to receive love can find enrichment in her contact with youth or with the sick, while at the same time enriching their lives through her affection and her attention. Today fields open to women are greater in number, and although at first glance certain occupations may seem unrelated to what is characteristically feminine, they nonetheless have a lot to gain from the presence of women. Stein is primarily concerned here with all occupations which involve bringing people together. They are areas which allow all feminine virtues to unfold. "One can even say that the development *(Entfaltung)* of the feminine nature can become a blessed counterbalance precisely here where everyone is in danger of becoming mechanized and losing his humanity."[94] Stein's perspective reveals woman as a being close to the concrete and to the person, sensitive to the totality of things, while the masculine figure is described as having a greater inclination toward abstract knowledge. But all that is abstract relates in the end to concrete, living reality. In this, woman benefits man by offering her point of view. "Thus the participation of women in the most diverse professional disciplines could be a blessing for the entire society, private or public, precisely if the specifically feminine ethos would be preserved."[95]

Let us now consider a woman's work from the standpoint of her own fulfillment. We have said that woman's soul carries within it the same aptitudes as man's. Both man and woman must tend to the development and full realization of their aptitudes. If the home setting does not allow a woman to engage in the development of her natural dispositions, an exterior activity is then necessary, and it is "reasonable" to take all possible measures to bring about her involvement in some such activity.[96] Stein's purpose here is then to encourage the harmonious development of both private and professional life. This is the ideal situation, and is an unfortunate distance from reality. Stein's claim can however be applied to present experience. "Let us begin by calmly comparing the actual life of women as it generally is today with our requirements. Many of the best women are almost overwhelmed by the double burden of family duties and

94. Stein, "Ethos," p. 50.
95. Stein, "Ethos," pp. 50-51. See also *Mulieris dignitatem,* #30, in which John Paul II calls women to bring forth their own "genius" in order to awaken in man a sense of the personal.
96. Stein, "Separate Vocations," p. 80.

professional life — or often simply of only gainful employment. Always on the go, they are harassed, nervous, and irritable. Where are they to get the needed inner peace and cheerfulness in order to offer stability, support, and guidance to others?"[97] This passage brings out some of the obstacles to woman's personal development. First of all, there is the enormous amount of energy required in reconciling family and professional life.[98] In our time as well, women experience this type of overextension. An example of this is the simultaneous occurrence of "emergency" situations: an urgent business appointment on one hand, a sick child on the other. In reality it is not always possible to meet all demands. A second obstacle to woman's development (also relevant to man) lies in a choice of employment which is insufficiently considerate of her personal inclinations. Such a choice is not conducive to the development (Entfaltung) of personal distinctiveness and arises when the insufficiency of a single salary obliges her to seek employment. It is common knowledge that the contemporary world is faced with new challenges, obliging women to work in order to survive. The fragility of the family bond and a lack of recognition for the woman at home are examples of such circumstances which relegate selection of a fulfilling profession to a secondary factor. What results for woman by no means contributes to her well-being. Aside from these cases, "we would consider the group of women, by no means negligible, who choose a profession suitable to their ability and inclination. Among them may be found quite a few who discover, after their initial gratification, that their expectations are unfulfilled and they long to be elsewhere. Frequently, this is due to their having taken pains to fill their post 'just like a man.'"[99]

An important distinction comes into play here: while many women find themselves having to work for economic reasons, others can freely choose to either work or remain at home.[100] In the first instance, a single salary being insufficient, the woman is drawn to exercise a lucrative activity. This is nothing new, but there is a generalization of this phenomenon in certain countries due to a growing number of single-parent families — due largely to divorce — which is nonetheless noteworthy. It is an established fact that "divorce is costly, and

97. Stein, "Ethos," p. 54.

98. Let us recall Stein's theory that a vital force is the basis for all physical and psychic development as well as for all personal actions. There is only a limited quantity of vital energy available, and all energy "burned" reduces the amount of exploitable energy. For this reason a permanent replenishment is necessary. The most detailed exposure of this theory can be read in *Philosophy of Psychology*, pp. 1-116.

99. Stein, "Ethos," p. 55.

100. We should note here that Stein only mentions the first case in her writings, and be reminded that her own mother was a widow responsible for insuring her family's subsistence.

raises expenditures in the areas of transportation, housing and alimentation, for example."[101] In such cases woman rarely has the leisure to choose a fulfilling profession, which corresponds to her vocation; necessity plays the primary role. In the second instance mentioned above, various situations come into play. The ideal case is a woman, conscious of the personal advantage of a professional activity in accordance with her "personal distinctiveness," who chooses a position adapted to her personal organization of time. When harmoniously exercised, her occupation can be beneficial for the professional milieu, for the family, and for the woman herself. The limitations of such an arrangement surface when the family is in some way negatively affected by this professional activity, either by the stress it causes or by the absence of the mother or spouse. For the woman forced to work out of necessity, who is very often content with whatever occupation she can find,[102] the ideal of professional fulfillment Stein describes is not even a question. The only way to find some type of fulfillment in this case is to exercise the profession in an "authentic" manner: the woman must remain herself; she must remain woman, contributing to what is human within her own limitations.

We have yet to mention the cases — numerous in certain countries and in certain milieux — of women who, more or less consciously, take up professions due to social pressure. This pressure, which can arise from different sources, contributes to a devalorization of work in the home. There is, as a consequence in part of the feminism of the sixties and seventies, a social image to consider. This feminism turned its back on the traditional image of the housewife, denouncing it as an example of man's exploitation of woman.[103] The church in particular was accused of consigning women to traditional roles. The intellectual world thus took a stand in support of a new image, an image of free and fulfilled womanhood, but an image modeled after that of men. The fulfilling environment for womankind thus slowly shifted from the home to the workplace. This type of feminism thrived in privileged settings, the only settings ca-

101. Schooyans, p. 212. The author concludes that "the undivided family has greater resources at its disposal for savings and the establishment of a home, for cultural investment and especially for the health and education of children."

102. Stein deplores the existence of such situations. They can be compared to unaccomplished states of life. She gives the examples of women who, although meant for marriage, never marry, thinking in particular of women having lost a fiancé or future husband in battle. In these situations an occupation directed toward the person can allow a woman to make use of her attentiveness toward others.

103. These ideas have their source in the work by Simone de Beauvoir, *Le deuxième sexe* (Paris: Gallimard, 1949). In English the work is entitled *The Second Sex*, trans. H. M. Parshley (New York: Vintage, 1989).

pable of applying its theories, and today we perceive their underlying dogmatism: the accomplished woman conveyed by the media is the "working woman," the woman who is very active professionally, and not the woman who devotes all her time to her family. Here, too, women are not truly free to find personal fulfillment in the settings which correspond to them. In a certain sense, instead of allowing women to find their way, an ideal fulfillment is imposed upon them. Only an authentically personal attitude (in the Steinian perspective developed above) can curb this pressure and allow the woman to remain faithful to herself, to her personal distinctiveness, and to her vocation by freely choosing her lifestyle and (if applicable) her professional activity. If society holds itself to be a personally fulfilling environment, it must provide everyone with the possibility for self-discovery. It must found the place in which one can develop with fidelity to oneself. In addition, this new female archetype has made woman a full-fledged contributor to the economy, as Michel Schooyans accurately observes: "Genuine free choice hardly exists for women." Social pressure has a tendency to make them feel guilty if they do not exercise a paying profession and if they do not contribute through their work to fiscal returns, social security, mutual funds and other unemployment funds."[104] Once again, this description is valid only in a specific type of society, but within that framework it truly corresponds to reality.

Here we see again the necessity of promoting a formation and a consciousness among the youth of reality and its conflicts. In schools, psychological and pedagogical services expend energy in an effort to guide young people toward professional life. It is also becoming common practice to introduce them to sexuality; yet it is rather unfortunate that no effort is being made to awaken within them an awareness of the family entity or even of motherhood and fatherhood. It is particularly important that young girls be informed of the conflict which may arise within them should they be able or obliged to take on the duties (and joys) of both motherhood and professional life. Only the consciousness of set values, which are just and real, which sustain the person, can effectively prepare them for life. This formation is all the more imperative when considering that Western countries rarely allow for contact between different generations. A household rarely includes more than two generations, and families are only becoming smaller. In such circumstances it is not unusual for young people, and particularly young women, to have practically no experience in matters relative to childhood or education. A mother's fulfillment in the home is simply not addressed. In addition, the separation of generations adds to a woman's household responsibilities. She often suffers from solitude and no

---

104. Schooyans, p. 196.

longer profits from the diversity of tasks made possible by the cohabitation of three generations.

Certain studies have evaluated the wealth that a family represents for a country, and in particular the contribution of a family mother to the formation of human capital. Although this fact may seem obvious, it is completely ignored by society and contemporary culture. According to Gary Becker, "a mother's work is responsible for at least 30% of a nation's gross internal product, a contribution entirely absent from national budgets."[105] This contribution in the home is often brought up in defense of a salary for such women, as compensation for their work and a way to give it value. Although this initiative is praiseworthy, it has its negative aspect: it is likely to be detrimental to motherly devotion, leading in a way to its decline. There is a risk that work in the home, motivated by love for children and family, would be reduced to a series of calculated exchanges. Perhaps a compromise should be established which would really allow women to choose freely, on both economic and social grounds. Part-time employment, which continues to gain ground, merits acknowledgment here, for it often allows women to establish a certain equilibrium between personal fulfillment, family commitment, and economic factors. Beyond these concrete means, mentalities must evolve toward a greater recognition of the family, of motherhood, of fatherhood, of childhood, and thus of life. John Paul II is consistent in pointing out this necessity: "It is the woman who 'pays' directly for this shared generation, which literally absorbs the energies of her body and soul. It is therefore necessary that *the man* be fully aware that in their shared parenthood he owes *a special debt to the woman.* No program of 'equal rights' between women and men is valid unless it takes this fact fully into account."[106]

Let us also note that throughout life, and particularly throughout the life of a woman, priorities evolve as situations are modified. Life always requires reevaluation, and this stresses its dynamic character and the dynamic character of the choices it implies. To devote oneself entirely to one's children in the years preceding their schooling does not preclude a woman from returning to the professional sphere later. Certain professions do however admit such interruptions more easily than others.

Stein presents us with a portrait of the women of her time in their struggle to find fulfillment in their work. In it we find many similarities with today's situations: the economic necessity to work; the danger of losing one's individual or feminine identity in an inadequate professional activity; overexertion ensuing from the accumulation of domestic and professional tasks; etc. Today the

105. Cited by Schooyans, p. 217.
106. John Paul II, *Mulieris dignitatem*, #18.

list could go on to include, among others, one of the difficulties mentioned above: the denigration of work in the home, which can exert a certain pressure upon women. Mentalities have changed so radically that what was average one hundred years ago is now unacceptable. In Western countries it is not unusual for women to work merely in order to gain social recognition. There is a danger that this be to their own detriment, leading them to follow inauthentic motives in conflict with their personal individuality. A further difficulty may be illustrated by a woman who wishes to "cultivate her natural dispositions" in an activity "outside of the home," but who cannot do so either for want of the proper infrastructure, such as child care, or for economic reasons.[107]

Are we not then encouraged to promote a society that takes into consideration woman's profound aspirations, facilitating their fulfillment through the development of adequate infrastructures? Are we not also called to stimulate thought concerning woman's specific worth and dignity? The promotion of a new anthropology of woman that places her at man's side or engaged in dialogue with him would confirm their equal dignity, their specific qualities, and the value of their cooperation. The feminism of the sixties and seventies aimed at leveling differences and proposed a model of femininity based on masculinity.[108] In order to restore justice, we must, on the contrary, promote an understanding of womankind that accentuates its significance, or to use the words of John Paul II, its own *genius*.[109] We must seek to bring out the importance of interpersonal communion which is "a call and a task."[110] "In the name of liberation from male 'domination,' women must not appropriate to themselves male characteristics contrary to their own feminine 'originality.'"[111] On the contrary, "a wholesome collaboration of the sexes in professional life will be possible only if both achieve a calm and objective awareness of their nature and draw practical conclusions from it."[112]

Conclusions

Throughout our analysis we have attempted to approach woman as a threefold yet unified entity: she is a human being, a feminine being, and a personal, indi-

---

107. Some countries do provide quality services of variable efficiency in these areas.

108. This confusion had already made its way into the mentalities of Stein's time. She often denounces its perverse effects. See, for example, "Ethos," p. 55.

109. John Paul II, "Letter to Women," p. 141, #9.

110. John Paul II, *Mulieris dignitatem*, #7.

111. John Paul II, *Mulieris dignitatem*, #10.

112. Stein, "Ethos," p. 57.

vidual being. Although, through a mental process, we have considered these aspects separately, we must hold to the claim that the human individual's nature is actually one: it is *human nature* in its specific masculine (or feminine) expression and in its individual expression. What is said of woman in her state of nature can also be applied to her state of becoming. In both cases we must assert fundamental unity. "We saw a threefold goal prescribed by the nature of woman: the development *(Entfaltung)* of her humanity, her womanhood, and her individuality. These are not separate goals, just as the nature of a particular human individual is not divided into three parts but is one: it is human nature of a specifically feminine and individual character."[113] The *process of development* in the human soul is both one and threefold.

The process by which woman achieves her fullness concerns her entire person and all her activities. It is her responsibility to contribute to the fulfillment of the essences "humanity" and "woman," and she can only seek to accomplish this through the actions of her personal life. By being herself she authentically and adequately participates in the realization of the essences she both incarnates and brings to life. In so doing, the accomplished essences are imbibed with her personal distinctiveness. In other terms, she realizes humanity and feminine being in her own way, and this is her personal vocation. For this reason we can state that her personal fulfillment, which is the very meaning of her being, is simultaneous to her specific human fulfillment. Through authentic action, in conformity with her personal distinctiveness, the particular woman (just as man) is doing exactly what she is called to do: to adequately realize the essence "humanity."

In accordance with Edith Stein, we can say that every woman is called to impress upon her surroundings something specifically her own. In order to do so, she must work at her own fulfillment that, as *Mulieris dignitatem* indicates, can only be attained in the gift of self. This personal touch is an enrichment for her family, for her community, for her professional setting, and for any community she should come to know. Its purity and authenticity will be proportionate to the woman's realization in accordance with her personal essence. Although anthropological and contextual limitations render the ideal unattainable, it must be unfailingly sought. The woman's personal effort toward realization will not only benefit those around her, but will also have its effects on the feminine world, and even on all of humanity. Everyone is called to contribute.

Stein's analysis, although strongly essentialist, can be a true encouragement for women in their daily life, offering them a harmonious and unifying

---

113. Stein, "Problems of Women's Education," p. 192.

outlook on their various activities. It is the outlook of authentic personal realization, of the development *(Entfaltung)* of personal distinctiveness, necessarily beneficial to all. Concretely speaking, for the woman who fulfills her vocation within the framework of marriage, this analysis opens the way to a threefold realization of the self as wife, mother, and personal subject, possessing unique qualities to be developed as far as possibility will allow. The woman who develops these qualities through teaching, through household or intellectual work, in athletic, cultural, or spiritual activities will benefit all those around her: to the husband will be given a serene wife, to the children a well-disposed mother, and to the woman herself the joy of having worked for her vocation and of developing in truth, that is, for the good of all. The goal of the formation and the becoming is to deploy within each one, in the purest and most perfect manner possible, his or her individual and specific humanity. "In order to develop to the highest level the humanity specific to husband and children, woman requires the attitude of selfless service."[114] This is the aim of education and the process of becoming.

114. Stein, "Spirituality," p. 110.

PART II

THEOLOGICAL ANTHROPOLOGY

The New Feminism: Biblical Foundations and Some Lines of Development

Fr. Francis Martin

The term "new feminism" is well enough known not to need explanation.[1] It can be said that it represents a definitive shift from a consideration of women's rights to reflection on the very nature of woman herself. Only from this second vantage point will it be possible to articulate the new humanism required by this change of perspective. By integrating what is true in the efforts of the rights-oriented feminism into the question "Who is a woman?" we will arrive at a genuine development of doctrine in the area of Christian anthropology.[2]

Basing ourselves on the reflections of John Paul II regarding the various states of human existence, and expanding them for our purposes here, we can say that humanity knows three fundamental states: that of innocence (prehistory); that of sinfulness (history as we know it); and that of transformation, when all that is truly human is transformed by the immediate self-gift of the Trinity offered to every human being and even to material creation itself. The

---

1. The expression has achieved notoriety because of the use made of it by Pope John Paul II in his recent writings. The most salient papal text in this regard is found in *Evangelium vitae*, #99: "In transforming culture so that it supports life, women occupy a place, in thought and action, which is unique and decisive. It depends on them to promote a 'new feminism' which rejects the temptation of imitating models of 'male domination,' in order to acknowledge and affirm the true genius of women in every aspect of the life of society, and overcome all discrimination, violence and exploitation." For other expressions of this notion in the writings of John Paul II, see the whole of the paragraph cited; also *Mulieris dignitatem*, #4, 5, 18, 20, 30; "Letter to Women," #9; *Laborem exercens*, #19.4; also Paul VI, *Vatican II, Closing Speech*, December 7-8, 1965.

2. This study relies upon an earlier work and develops it in several directions. Portions of that earlier work are used here with the permission of the editor. See Francis Martin, "The New Feminism: A New Humanism?" *Josephinum Journal of Theology* 8, no. 1 (2000): 5-26.

second state itself must be considered in two different historical realizations: the time before Christ when the spark of hope was kept alive in and through Israel, and that after Christ, the state of restored humanity or recapitulation. This last-named state is an anticipated realization of the state of transformation which will be the healing of our present condition of "diminished existence" in and through the sublation of the state of innocence effected by the cross of Christ.[3]

In studying biblical anthropology, therefore, we must look at the basic teaching on the nature of man as presented in the first two chapters of Genesis, and the account of the diminished existence that is ours as a result of sin. But we must also listen to the description of a humanity in the state of recapitulation if we are to understand the reality of man and woman. This study will thus have three parts. Part One will consider the teaching of Genesis, humanity as created by God and its present diminished existence. Part Two will reflect on humanity, man and woman, in the state of restored existence, and this is presented in Ephesians 5:21-33. Part Three will offer some brief philosophical considerations on the new feminism based on the two previous parts.

Part One: Basic Teaching on Man and Woman as Found in Genesis 1–3

The Image of God

There are five passages in the Old Testament which use the term "image" when describing man and his relationship to God. Three are found in the early chapters of Genesis, and the other two (Sir. 17:3 and Wis. 2:23) clearly depend upon the Genesis teaching. I will give here a literal translation of the three Genesis texts, leaving the words 'ādām and "Elohim" without a translation. "And Elohim said: 'Let us make 'ādām in our image, as our likeness, that they may rule over the fish of the sea, and the birds of the heavens, and the tame beasts, and all the earth, and all the creeping things creeping on the earth.' And Elohim created the 'ādām in his image: in the image of Elohim he created him, male and female he created them" (Gen. 1:26-27).

---

3. A customary Christian view which divides history into the periods of Israel, the church, and heaven is summed up in this phrase of Saint Ambrose: "Primum igitur umbra praecessit, secuta est imago, erit veritas. Umbra in lege, imago vero in evangelio, veritas in caelestibus" (*On Psalm 43*, Corpus Scriptorum Ecclesiasticorum Latinorum, 64:204). The division I am referring to here is also found in, and forms one of the basic structures of, Karol Wojtyla (John Paul II), *The Theology of the Body: Human Love in the Divine Plan*, trans. L'Osservatore Romano (Boston: Pauline Books and Media, 1997).

The next text is found after the Yahwist account of creation, the sin of the first couple, and the murder of Abel. It introduces the second *toledot,* or generation section.[4] By once again insisting that *'ādām* is still the image of God despite all the sin introduced into history, the redactor is making his point that sin cannot completely efface the primary resemblance and relation that *'ādām* has to God. "This is the list of the generations of *'ādām:* On the day when Elohim created *'ādām* he made him in the image of Elohim; male and female he created them, and he blessed them and called their name *'ādām* on the day they were created. And *'ādām* lived one hundred and thirty years and he begot in his likeness, as his image, and he called his name Seth" (Gen. 5:1-3).

The last of the texts that speaks of the image of God follows the account of the flood, that ultimate punishment for the universal corruption of mankind. Once again, even after this disaster brought on by human sin, the image quality remains and is the source of the dignity of *'ādām,* still the object of God's special care: "He who sheds the blood of the *'ādām,* by *'ādām* his blood will be shed. For in the image of Elohim he made the *'ādām.* But you, be fruitful, be many, swarm on the earth and be many (or rule) on it" (Gen. 9:6-7).

Two points emerge from these texts. The first is that only *'ādām* is the image of God, and the second is that *'ādām* is male and female. We will look briefly at these points since they form the basis of the search to articulate the genius of woman.[5]

Paramount in the ancient Near East is the notion that the image makes present the power of what is imaged. This is the reason why all images of YHWH are forbidden to Israel: YHWH will be present and reveal himself and his power according to his own good will and pleasure; to try to manipulate this is an abomination.[6] On the contrary, for the pagan world the multiplication of

4. For a discussion of these ten divisions of the book of Genesis, see Gordon J. Wenham, *Genesis 1–15,* ed. David A. Hubbard and Glenn W. Barker, Word Biblical Commentary 1 (Waco: Word, 1987), p. xxii.

5. I am summing up here work I developed more at length in "Male and Female He Created Them: A Summary of the Teaching of Genesis Chapter One," *Communio* 20 (1993): 240-65. For more information see Wenham, *Genesis 1–15,* and Claus Westermann, *Genesis,* vol. I/1, Biblischer Kommentar: Altes Testament (Neukirchen-Vluyn, 1974), pp. 147-55, where there are sizable bibliographies. The most complete survey of recent thinking is found in the balanced study of Gunnlaugur A. Jønsson, *The Image of God: Genesis 1:26-28 in a Century of Old Testament Research,* Coniectanea Biblica, Old Testament Series 26 (Almqvist and Wiksell International, 1988). See also Phyllis Bird, "Male and Female He Created Them: Gen 1:27b in the Context of the P Account of Creation," *Harvard Theological Review* 74 (1981): 129-59.

6. This is the original significance of the commandment "You shall not make an image *(pesel)* for yourself" (Exod. 20:4; Deut. 5:8). For an excellent discussion of the denial of images

images of the gods was an exercise of piety. In the same way, a king could multiply his presence and authority, it was thought, by setting up images of himself. The presence of both terms "image" and "likeness" on the statue of a king, set up to assert his authority over a region,[7] confirms the suggestion frequently made that the basic notion mediated by the declaration of the divine intention in Genesis 1:26 is that 'ādām is to be God's vice-regent, the embodiment of his authority here on earth.

Against this background it is most likely that the expression of God's intention in the Priestly tradition asserts that 'ādām is the royal representative of God himself, embodying and exercising God's own authority in regard to the earth and all that lives on it. This certainly is the line of thought developed by Psalm 8, which continues the royal terminology in its meditation on Genesis 1: "You have crowned him with glory and honor, you have made him rule over the works of your hands, you have put everything under his feet" (Ps. 8:6-7).[8] However, while the notion of royal representative correctly locates the basic category of thought, or the basic semantic shape of the term, it does not exhaust all the implications of the statement of God's purpose as the Priestly author intends it.

In addition to the fact that Elohim must make 'ādām capable of ruling,[9] he also addresses him directly. The presence of the Sabbath at the end of the Priestly text points to still another facet of 'ādām: his vocation to worship while the mention of God's special care in protecting the blood of 'ādām (Gen. 9:6) also points to a unique dignity. In trying to elaborate a biblical understanding of man as the image of God, we must take all three texts into account.

We find two opinions that seek to express the reality of image in terms that sum up the position in Genesis 1:26-28 and the other Genesis texts. The first is what I have been calling "royal representative" and what Jønsson calls the "functional interpretation." With the notable exceptions of Claus Westermann and James Barr, this opinion, with differing nuances, is held by nearly all Old Testament scholars.[10] The second opinion, whose most strenuous proponent

---

of YHWH to Israel, see Gerhard von Rad, *Old Testament Theology,* vol. 1, trans. D. M. G. Stalker (New York: Harper and Brothers, 1962), pp. 212-19.

7. A. R. Millard and P. Bordreuil, "A Statue from Syria with Assyrian and Aramaic Inscriptions," *Biblical Archaeologist* 45 (1982): 135-41.

8. For a study of this psalm, see Luis Alonso Schökel, *Treinta Salmos: Poesía y Oración, Estudios de Antiguo Testamento,* vol. 2 (Madrid: Ediciones Cristianidad, 1981), pp. 63-78.

9. By reading the verb form as an indirect volition, the phrase is saying: "Let us make 'ādām . . . that they might rule." That is, "Let us make them capable of representing us ('in our image') so that they may rule." Had the author wished to express the notion that being the image of God consisted totally in having rule, he could have used another grammatical form (a "converted perfect"): "and then they will rule. . . ." We will return to this point.

10. See the summary of opinions in Jønsson, pp. 219-25.

was Karl Barth, and which is sustained by Westermann and others, is that the image of God is to be found in the divinely conferred capacity to relate to God.[11] It is possible to integrate these latter two by considering what in human-kind makes it apt to be God's representative and how the other image state-ments develop the relational dimension of image while retaining the basic se-mantic field of *selem* (image). We will return to this.

Male and Female

By using the Hebrew terms *zākār* and *nĕqēbah,* which accent the physical char-acteristics of male and female, the author of Genesis 1 is telling us two things. First, that physicality enters into the imaging of God: bodily, therefore histori-cal, existence is the sphere in which God is imaged, that is, made present. Sec-ond, that this is accomplished by *'ādām* as male and female. This is particularly clear if we pay close attention to the wording of the first two texts given above: "And Elohim created the *'ādām* in his image: in the image of Elohim he created him, male and female he created them" (1:26-27); and "On the day when Elohim created *'ādām* he made him in the image of Elohim; male and female he created them, and he blessed them and called their name *'ādām* on the day they were created" (5:1-2).

The key to understanding these texts lies in appreciating what is conveyed in the term *'ādām.* Of the forty-seven instances of the word in the book of Gen-esis, forty-six occur in the "world history" found in the first eleven chapters, and even there they are concentrated around the decisive events of world his-tory: creation, sin, the flood, and the tower of Babel.[12] In the first three chap-ters, where humanity is considered in its constitution and its state of dimin-ished existence, *'ādām* covers a semantic field that includes "humanity," "humankind," and an individual person most often referred to as "the man," though the word is beginning to take on the characteristics of a personal name (4:25). None of the above English equivalents mediates exactly what the He-brew term conveys. In the translation of the two principal texts above, we can see an oscillation between the singular: "he created him, male and female he created them" (1:26-27); "he made him in the image of Elohim; male and female he created them . . . blessed them . . . called their name *'ādām* . . . they were cre-

<hr>

11. For an account of this opinion and its relation to the "point of contact" dispute with E. Brunner, see Jönsson, pp. 65-76.

12. For a complete study of this term, see Claus Westermann, "Adam," in *Theological Lex-icon of the Old Testament 1,* ed. Ernst Jenni and Claus Westermann (Peabody, Mass.: Hendrickson, 1997), pp. 31-42.

ated" (5:1-2).[13] This oscillation and the insistence that male and female are made in the image of God and *together* receive the name '*ādām* force us to say that the sacred text is teaching that '*ādām* as the image of God exists as male and female. That is, male and female are different realizations of the one reality of image as royal representative capable of being addressed by God, and of imitating and worshiping him. Furthermore, part of this image reality is realized in obedience to the command: "Be fruitful, be many, fill the earth and subjugate it." This contradicts, as we shall see, the notion that gender is irrelevant in considering the essence of human nature. The traditional understanding of a human being as the image of God, which accents his resemblance to the Word of God incarnate and/or his spiritual endowments, has actually been deepened and opened from within itself from the modern sensitivity to the fact that '*ādām* as male and female shows us the constitutively relational nature of the human person.

One Flesh: Chapters 2 and 3 of Genesis

The teaching on man and woman in the second and third chapters of Genesis may, for our purposes, be gathered around three points: first, the relation between God and '*ādām;* second, the relation between man and woman; and third, the damaged state of those relations in our present diminished existence.

God and Adam

After the "structural" presentation of creation in Genesis 1, we are immediately placed in the historical perspective of Genesis 2 and 3 with the remark in 2:5 that the reason there was as yet neither green plant nor field shrub is because "YHWH God had not sent any rain on the earth and there was no '*ādām* to cultivate the soil (*'ādāmâ*)." Culture depends upon both divine and human activity. Then "YHWH God fashioned the '*ādām* with dust from the soil (*'ādāmâ*) and breathed into his nostrils the breath of life, and the *ādām* became a soul alive." This text states three things: first, that man is formed directly by God; second, that he is a mysterious unity of matter and breath; and third, that in common with other creatures he is a "soul alive" and yet achieves this status in a

---

13. This second text is framed by two uses of '*ādām* which refer to an individual, though viewed as joined to his posterity. See the study by Jean de Fraine, *Adam and the Family of Man,* trans. Daniel Raible C.PP.S. (New York: Alba House, 1965).

unique way: being endowed with the very breath of God.[14] Thus the more humanistic tradition with which we are dealing here, rather than having recourse to the abstract notion of "image," portrays *'ādām* as endowed with the vital quality of God, his breath.

But there is more. The *'ādām* who is taken by YHWH Elohim and settled in the garden, as Israel was taken and settled in the land, is given a command, a sort of covenant. He is invited to a higher level of relation with God: that of trust and obedience. That is, he is offered a covenant, a command from God through which he may express his response to all that God has done for him and can move from a self-contained existence to one that is more profoundly relational.

A Helper Matching Him

Despite the fact that he can somehow share the life of God and relate to him in personal trust, YHWH God sees that *'ādām's* being alone is "not good." (A daring statement considering the use of the word "good" in the previous account.) It is at this point that God deliberates with himself, "Let me make," and describes the object of his intention as "a helper matching him." Grammatically the words do not reveal the gender of this "helper," but they evoke the notion that the helper (the word is most often used of God as helper)[15] is destined to overcome the solitude of *'ādām* by "matching" him. YHWH God has a mysterious "sleep" come upon *'ādām,* as upon Abraham at the moment of the covenant promise (Gen. 15:12), and taking a rib, extracts from *'ādām* something hid-

---

14. Note that being a "soul alive" is not what distinguishes *'ādām* from the rest of creation; the same is said in 2:19 of all the animals named by the man, and is used in 9:10; 1:20, 21, 24 of various living things. What makes the man unique is that he has been given life-breath directly by God; there is something of God in him. Places in the book of Job reflect the same notion of being formed from earth and possessing the spirit/breath of God. Thus Elihu says to Job: "For the spirit *(rûaḥ)* of God has made me, the breath of the Almighty *(nišmat šadday)* gives me life. . . . Behold I am like yourself with respect to God, I too, have been pinched from clay" (Job 33:4, 6; see also 34:14-15). In the same vein, the book of Wisdom describes the miserable lot of the potter who makes clay gods: "His heart is ashes, his hope meaner than dirt, and his life more ignoble than clay, because he knew not the one who fashioned him and infused him with an active soul and breathed into him a vital spirit" (Wis. 15:10-11). The translation is taken from David Winston, *The Wisdom of Solomon,* Anchor Bible 43 (New York, 1979), p. 285.

15. Nineteen of the twenty-one instances of the noun refer to divine help. See Jean-Louis Ska, "'Je vais lui fair un allié qui soit son homologue' (Gen 2,18). A propos du terme *'ezer-'aide,'*" *Biblica* 65 (1984): 233-38. Marie de Merode, "'Une aide qui lui corresponde.' L'exégèse de Gen 2,18-24 dans les récits de l'Ancien Testament, du judaïsme et du Nouveau Testament," *Revue Théologique de Louvain* 8 (1977): 329-52.

den within him, as it were, and builds it up "into a woman." Then, like the friend of the bridegroom, he leads her to *'ādām*.[16] For the first time *'ādām* speaks:

> This one, at last
> is bone from my bone and flesh from my flesh;
> this one shall be called woman,
> for from man was
> this one taken.

The helper is someone who matches *'ādām* but is not a replica. She is woman *(iššâ)* because she is taken from, yet differs from, man *(iš)*. Communion is between likes who are yet unlike. In naming her, *'ādām* himself assumes a new name: her presence "matching him" is a revelation of who both of them are in relationship. The poetic and theological genius who articulates this deep reality about humanity sees its paradigmatic realization in the marriage relationship which he portrays in terms of a covenant. The words "bone" and "flesh" allude to the conditions presupposed or effected by a covenant proposed in these terms. To cite but one example: when the tribes of Israel approach David at Hebron to ask him to accept the kingship, they describe themselves as "your bone and your flesh" (2 Sam. 5:1; see also 19:13). It is precisely because of this unique covenant that "a man leaves his father and his mother and cleaves to his wife and they become one flesh." The degree of alienation from our own physicality which we modern Westerners experience makes it almost impossible to understand the "one flesh" relationship spoken of here. By marrying, a man assumes as his primary relationship that which he has to his wife, with whom he makes one new family (one of the meanings of "flesh" in Hebrew). In that covenant relationship — sealed, fostered, and deepened through spiritual, psychic, emotional, and physical intercourse — the two human beings create a third reality: a communion of persons which has as its fruit new human life.[17] The expression of this free and unveiled communication is found in the concluding line of Genesis 2: "They were both naked, the man and his wife, and they felt no shame with one another."

16. Rabbi Abin, commenting on this verse, said: "Happy the citizen for whom the king acts as the bridegroom's friend." *Genesis Rabbah* 18.3. The question of whether to translate the phrase here as "to *'ādām*" or "to the *'ādām*" involves a discussion of whether one considers the Masoretic interpreters to be treating the word as a proper or common noun. I will treat some of the theological implications of this question later. For the philological aspect, see Umberto Cassuto, *A Commentary on the Book of Genesis*, pt. 1, *From Adam to Noah* (Jerusalem: Magnes Press, Hebrew University, 1961), pp. 166-67.

17. For a more complete discussion of this issue, see the discussion later in this article.

Diminished Existence

The disobedience of *'ādām* ("Is it that *you* have eaten of the tree which *I* told *you* not to eat?") brings in its train the two most primal effects of sin: shame — they knew they were naked; and fear — they heard his voice and hid (3:7-8, 11). Then, in the only instance in the Bible in which God himself directly adjudicates punishment, the serpent, the woman, and the man are addressed. The serpent is cursed, and in a mysterious passage, victory is promised to the seed of *the woman.*[18] The woman is promised "labor" in bringing forth children — her glory becomes also her pain — and then the new conditions of the relationship between herself and the man are described: "Your urge will be towards your husband and he will dominate you." The two sides of this now warped and adversarial relationship are described in terms of domination and connivance in domination. In the man/woman relationship (the paradigm of all human relating) we are shown the depth of the wound inflicted by sin. The lie of power and the lie of helplessness feed off each other and have produced such a situation that even two millennia of Christianity have made little more than a beginning in unmasking and overcoming the bondage brought by sin into the history of human relating.

Not only is the relation man/woman, husband/wife paradigmatic of all human relating, but its degree of integrity or disintegration affects all of human life and human society. This is true not only because the relation of parents to each other has a preponderant effect on the humanity of their children, but also because the interior poise or lack of it that derives from this fundamental relationship of man and woman has its repercussions in all of a person's ability to realize the goal of human life in reciprocal relations of generosity and receptivity. The wound caused in us by the disruption of our relation to God has resulted, as Genesis teaches, in shame, fear, and death. These three produce an adversarial relation between man and woman, who cannot be human without each other, but who strive for self-realization and self-protection by domination by the man and by the woman's self-denying acceptance of this in her willingness to trade freedom for security. The following text from *Mulieris dignitatem*, #10, expresses the effects, particularly upon the woman, of this disruption:

> Therefore when we read in the biblical description the words addressed to the woman: "Your desire shall be for your husband, and he shall rule over

---

18. This is one of six texts in the OT which attribute seed to a woman: Gen. 3:15; 4:25; 16:10; 24:60; Lev. 22:13; Isa. 54:3. Additional texts which merit attention are: Num. 5:28; 1 Sam. 2:20; Ruth 4:12; Gen. 19:32, 34; 38:9.

you" (Gen 3:16), we discover a break and a constant threat precisely in regard to this "unity of the two" which corresponds to the dignity of the image and likeness of God in both of them. But this threat is more serious for the woman, since domination takes the place of "being a sincere gift" and therefore living "for" the other: "he shall rule over you." This "domination" indicates the disturbance and loss of the stability of that fundamental equality which the man and the woman possess in the "unity of the two": and this is especially to the disadvantage of the woman, whereas only the equality resulting from their dignity as persons can give to their mutual relationship the character of an authentic "communio personarum." While the violation of this equality, which is both a gift and a right deriving from God the Creator, involves an element to the disadvantage of the woman, at the same time it also diminishes the true dignity of the man.

The man is not cursed, but through him the universe ("the ground") is cursed and becomes recalcitrant. The man's efforts to implement the commission given to him by God now become "labor." And finally, there is death — the place where there is no praise of God. Death means being cut off from shared life. Having been formed from dust and endowed with the very breath of God, 'ādām must now live under the weight of an illusory need to dominate and with the threat of being cut off from life, passing his days in futility.

Much more could be said about the depth of the rupture that has taken place in human relations. The daily tales from everywhere in the world, the enforced sterilizations, the battered women and homeless men all confirm it. Specifically about man/woman relations, we should consider the ways woman has been particularly victimized in the relation of domination and dominated. There is, however, a wounding of the man in this twisted relationship that has not been sufficiently appreciated. By forcing a sort of alienation to exist between himself and woman, man has returned to a state not of productive solitude, but of frustrated fear and loneliness: "It is not good for man to be alone." By seeking to extort what can only be given freely, man condemns himself to the counterfeit of the only thing that can give meaning to his life. In the struggle for existence in this world, the man exerts a kind of dominative power not only on the material universe but also in his relations. This too leads to frustration since, as John Paul II often says, joining two principles: "A human being, whether male or female, is a person, and therefore, 'the only creature on earth which God willed for its own sake'; and at the same time this unique and unrepeatable creature 'cannot fully find himself except through a sincere gift of self.'"[19]

---

19. John Paul II, *Mulieris dignitatem*, #10, citing *Gaudium et spes*, #24.

In this sense fatherhood, in the full sense of the term, is more difficult to achieve than motherhood because it involves an imitation of God the Father which can only take place through identification with Jesus. To quote "Adam," the character in Karol Wojtyla's play *The Radiation of Fatherhood:* "After a long time I came to understand that you do not want me to be a father unless I become a child. That is why your Son came into the world. He is entirely Yours."[20] The inability to surrender and thus become a source of life is the deepest wound in the man, and that is why, though the woman is the more oppressed, the man is often weaker.[21] The very tangible and human fact of the disruption of human relating is the measure of the power of the redemption brought to humanity by Jesus Christ.

Part Two: The Letter to the Ephesians

A Brief Commentary on Ephesians 5:21-33

For the convenience of the reader I will present a literal translation of the verses as they are discussed. Not every aspect of this rich passage will be treated here. Rather I will restrict my remarks to those aspects which can elucidate our concern here with a Christian anthropology.

Verse 21
Subordinating yourselves to one another in the fear of Christ;

Verse 21 acts as a sort of "hinge" verse, concluding a list of five participles with imperatival force which make more precise what it means to be "filled with the Spirit" (5:18), pointing out aspects of community life in the Spirit.[22] This last recommendation then leads to a particular aspect of community life, namely, life in a Christian family. It calls for mutual self-subordination in the fear of Christ. Since both of the key terms will figure largely in the rest of the passage, and because they are part of a very specific anthropology, we will discuss them briefly.

20. Karol Wojtyla, *The Radiation of Fatherhood,* in *The Collected Plays and Writings on Theatre* (Berkeley: University of California Press, 1987), pp. 335-64, at p. 339.

21. See Walter Ong, *Fighting for Life* (Amherst: University of Massachusetts Press, 1981).

22. Eph. 5:21 as found in the context of the preceding verses: "And do not get drunk with wine — that is dissolute — rather be filled with (the) Spirit, *addressing* one another with spiritual psalms and hymns and songs; *singing* and *praising* with your heart to the Lord; *giving thanks* always in the name of our Lord Jesus Christ to our God and Father; *subordinating* yourselves to one another in the fear of Christ" (Eph. 5:18-21).

The participle *hypotassomenoi* is a middle form of the verb *hypotassein*, and has the notion of "to subordinate oneself." It is found in four of the six New Testament passages that contain domestic codes.[23] Even within the New Testament the middle form of the verb has a rather large range of meanings, but they can be reduced to a general sense of voluntary self-subordination to the divine order, whether of the providential order of the state (Rom. 13:1-10; 1 Pet. 2:13-17), the human institution of slavery (1 Pet. 2:18-20; Titus 2:9), young people to their elders (1 Pet. 5:5), the community to its leaders (1 Cor. 16:16), and perhaps women to the established order in the community (1 Cor. 11:3; 14:34). It is also used of Jesus' relation to his parents (Luke 2:51) and of his self-subordination to the Father after the last enemy (death) has been destroyed (1 Cor. 15:28).

Given the fact that *hypotassesthai* is, with the one exception of *phobētai* in Ephesians 5:33, the only verb used in the New Testament exhortations to wives, and that this verb, with two exceptions,[24] is *never* found in extant Greco-Roman and Hellenistic Jewish literature that discusses wife/husband relationship, we are entitled to see in the New Testament usage evidence of a conscious Christian choice to find a suitable word and fill it with a content proper to Christian marriage. Such a procedure is found for *agapē, ekklēsia, kerygma, syneidēsis,* and many other words.

In fact, all of Christian theological predication can be judged as true or false only by taking the words in their total context, in the sentence, and even more broadly, in the context of the New Testament. Thus, for instance, the statement "Christ is alive now" is true when the transposed or analogical meaning of the word "alive" is understood. But this can only be achieved in the light of faith.[25] The exhortation to mutual self-subordination, of which the wife's self-subordination to her husband is a particular instance, is part of a much larger Christian teaching on the role of humility and love in all relationships.[26] Mutual relationships are so described, among other places, in Philippians 2:1-4:

23. It is found in Eph. 5:21, 24; Col. 3:18; Titus 2:5; 1 Pet. 3:1. The other two texts alleged as domestic codes, 1 Tim. 2:8-15 and 6:1-10, do not contain any specific verbs describing the relation between husbands and wives and, in any case, are not "codes" in any usual sense of the term.

24. These are Plutarch, *Moralia* 142E, and Ps.-Callisthenes, *Life of Alexander the Great* 1.22.4 (Alexander tells his mother, who has been offended by Philip: "It is fitting [*trepon*] for a wife to subordinate herself to her husband").

25. I owe this remark to Msgr. Robert Sokolowski, in a private communication.

26. "The findings as a whole suggest that the term *hypotassesthai* played a general catechetical-type role in primitive Christian exhortation" (Gerhard Delling, "*tassō*, etc.," in *Theological Dictionary of the New Testament*, vol. 8, ed. Gerhard Kittel and Gerhard Friedrich [Grand Rapids: Eerdmans, 1972], p. 45).

"So if there is any encouragement in Christ, any incentive of love, any participation in the Spirit, any affection and sympathy, complete my joy by being of the same mind, having the same love, being in full accord and of one mind. Do nothing from selfishness or conceit, but in humility count others better than yourselves. Let each of you look not only to his own interests, but also to the interests of others."

In the light of the overall context, commentators define the meaning of *hypotassomenoi* here and in similar New Testament passages as "a voluntary attitude of giving in, of cooperating, assuming responsibility and carrying a burden."[27] And note that "The implication is that *the one 'subjecting' himself does so through an act of his sovereign will and that he could equally elected to have done otherwise*."[28] It should be noted once again that verse 21 with its call to *mutual* self-subordination sets the tone for the rest of the exhortation.

The second phrase that merits some attention is "the fear of Christ." This is echoed in the last line of this section (v. 33) to form an inclusion: "as for the wife, let her fear her husband." The notion is that our mutual subordination and our communion with each other are supernatural realities effected by the death of Christ. Just as "fear of the Lord" is the beginning and perfection of wisdom — the very soul of the reverence, obedience, trust, and awe within a covenant relation with God — so is "fear of Christ" the specification of all these faith attitudes now directed to Christ, who has become the source of the new covenant. It is noteworthy that a similar use of the term "fear" occurs in the First Letter of Peter, where as Leonhard Goppelt points out, the term refers to an attitude of reverence before God in the living out of human relations, "in responsibility before God and in view of God's judgment."[29] The final exhortation to wives that they "fear" their husbands must be seen in the same light and reflects a similar combination of affection and responsibility before God as can

---

27. Markus Barth, *Ephesians 4–6*, Anchor Bible 34A (New York: Doubleday, 1974), p. 710.

28. J. W. Bowman, "The Gospel and the Christian Family: An Exposition of Ephesians 5:22 to 6:9," *Interpretation* 1 (1947): 436-49.

29. Leonhard Goppelt, *A Commentary on 1 Peter*, ed. Ferdinand Hahn, trans. John E. Alsup (Grand Rapids: Eerdmans, 1993), p. 244. "Likewise, women subordinate yourselves to your husbands so that, even if some are disobedient to the word, through the behaviour of their wives, without a word, they may be won over, as they see your pure behaviour (conducted) in fear" (1 Pet. 3:1-2). "Do not be afraid of them and do not be troubled, rather, sanctify the Lord in your hearts, ready at all times to give account to anyone who asks you to answer for the hope that is in you. (Do this) however, with gentleness and fear as those who have a good conscience, so that in regard to that for which you are slandered they will be shamed — those who discredit your good manner of life in Christ. For it is better that — if God so wills it — you suffer as those who conduct themselves rightly and not as those who do evil" (1 Pet. 3:14-17). See also 1 Pet. 1:17; 2:18.

already be found in Leviticus 19:3, "Let a man fear his mother and father" (note the word order).[30]

Verses 22-23
22a wives to your husbands
22b as to the Lord
23a because a husband is head of his wife
23b just as Christ is head of the church:
23c he is the savior of the body.

With these verses the advice to the community is applied to the household. There seems to be a subtle softening even of the Christian use of *ypotassesthai* in verse 22a, since the verb is not repeated from verse 21. This also serves to indicate that what is being said here is part of the mutual self-subordination of verse 21. The self-subordination of wives to their husbands is given its proper context with the phrase "as to the Lord" (v. 22b). It will require the rest of the context to give us a more exact understanding of the full meaning of these words, but the general sense is clear. The foundation of the woman's attitude is found in her faith: her acts of love and self-giving are such that they look to the Lord and terminate in him.[31]

The description of the husband as the "head" of his wife in verse 23a is contextualized by giving the relation between Christ and the church ("just as"/ *hōs kai*) as the exemplar of the husband/wife relationship. That is, the headship of the husband participates in the headship of Christ precisely under this aspect: Christ is "the savior of the body." The significance of this phrase will be apparent in the consideration of verse 25. The fact that the term "head" is applied to the husband and not to the wife, and that the verb "to subordinate oneself" is applied to the wife and not to the husband, leads to the legitimate ques-

---

30. The Old Testament background sets the context here for the meaning of the term "fear" both in 1 Peter and Ephesians and elsewhere in the New Testament (*ex. gr.* Phil. 2:12). The fact that the term is occasionally found in some Neo-Pythagorean texts, which lack the monotheistic orientation toward God, does not mean that the meaning is the same. See David Balch, "Neopythagorean Moralists and the New Testament Household Codes," in *Aufstieg und Niedergang der römischen Welt*, Teil II, Band 26, ed. H. Temporini and W. Haase (Berlin and New York: Walter de Gruyter, 1982-88), pp. 380-411, at p. 397.

31. Note, for instance, how slaves are urged to serve with an attitude of faith, knowing the one they are serving and who it is who will reward them. They are told to obey "as to Christ . . . serving with your inner intention with good will as to the Lord, not to men" (Eph. 6:5-8; see also Col. 3:23). The point of convergence in using the expression for wives is not that they are the same as slaves, but that their faith vision of their very different place in the church and in their marriage is equally governed by the reality and accessibility of Christ.

tion as to whether there does not still linger in this text a remnant of the Hellenistic notion of the superiority of the man. I will touch on this in Part Three, but it might be remarked here that there is an equal possibility that we moderns, after more than two centuries of cultivating dominative power, may perhaps read into this text our own lingering pagan notion that human relations are determined by the structures of domination and coercion.

Verse 24

24a But just as the church subordinates itself to Christ,
24b so, too, wives to their husbands in everything.

With the exception of verse 33c, these are the last words addressed to the wives. The remaining 75 percent of the text is addressed to husbands. Just as Christ's self-giving act of love ("he is the Savior of the body") is held up as the way in which the husband is to be "head" of his wife, so now the loving self-subordination of the church to Christ is held up to the wife as the exemplar of her relation to her husband, "as to the Lord." We should note that once again the verb *hypotassesthai* is not present in the second part of the sentence, with the result that the noun "wife" is never the direct subject of this verb in the whole passage. Just as the first omission places the wife's self-subordination within the context of the life of the eschatological community, so this omission serves to place her relation to her husband within the context of the church's relation to Christ, which thus serves as model and source of her relation to her husband. Thus the expression "in everything" *(en panti)* is not a juridical norm but is measured by the confidence the husband inspires in her by the quality of his love. Thus the relation is not command/obedience, but generosity/receptivity. The rest of the passage seeks to portray the extent of the generosity to which the husband is *obliged* (see v. 28a below).

25a Husbands, love your wives
25b just as Christ loved the church
25c and gave himself over for her

Just as *hypotassesthai* characterizes the attitude of the wife in most of the exhortations to Christian households (Col. 3:18; 1 Pet. 3:1; 1 Tim. 2:11; Titus 2:4), so *agapan* explicitly (Col. 3:19) or equivalently (1 Pet. 3:7; Titus 2:6) describes the virtue most needed in the husband. The Ephesians passage, however, goes much further in making explicit what is left implicit in the other texts, namely, that this verb must be given its full Christian significance and be a genuine share in the love that God has shown to us in Christ. The specifically Christian love enjoined upon the husband is expressed not only in the characteristic verb *agapan,* but also in the analogical appeal to the act of Christ expressed in the rhythm "loved . . . gave himself over," which takes up the fundamental principle of Christian activity in Ephesians 5:2 (echoing Gal. 2:20), in which Paul tells us that he lives now by faith in the Son of God: "who loved me and gave himself over for me." The term *paradidonai,* "give/hand over," had become by this time a means of evoking the whole passion process.[32] The husband, therefore, is called to love his wife in the power of the act of love in which Christ died and lives forever. The Ephesians text thus initiates a genuine *imitatio Christi* whose basic principle is one of participation in the present reality and activity of Christ.[33] This principle, that *agapan* always involves some share in the cross of Christ, is the source of that restoration, that recapitulation, by which we are enabled to complete our understanding of a revealed anthropology.

> *28a Even so husbands are obliged to love their own wives*
> *28b as their own bodies.*
> *28c He who loves his own wife loves himself.*
> *29a No one ever hated his own flesh;*
> *29b rather, he provides and cares for it*
> *29c just as Christ [does] for the church,*
> *30 because we are members of his body.*

A new dimension of the instruction, linking it with the previous presentation of Christ's love ("even so"), begins with the first and only mention of obligation in the whole passage: husbands are "obliged" *(opheilousin)* to love their own wives as their own bodies. This obligation is rooted in God's love for us manifested in Christ, as 1 John 4:11 expresses it: "Beloved, if God so loved us, we ought *(opheilomen)* to love one another." Also 1 John 3:16: "In this we have come to know love: he laid down his life for us. And we ought *(opheilomen)* to lay down our lives for the brothers." And the same foundation is found in the command in Ephesians 5:1-2, which always lies in the background of this discussion: "Be, then, imitators of God, as beloved children, and walk in love just as Christ loved us, and gave himself over for us, an offering and sacrifice to God unto a fragrant odor." Another way of expressing the debt or obligation incumbent on

---

32. See, for instance, Rom. 4:23-25: "It was not written for his sake alone that it was reckoned to him, but also for our sake to whom it is going to be [also] reckoned, we who believe in him who raised Jesus our Lord from the dead, who was handed over for our transgressions and raised for our justification."

33. I have discussed this New Testament notion in "Historical Criticism and New Testament Teaching on the Imitation of Christ," *Anthropotes* 6 (1990): 261-87.

all Christians is found in Romans 13:8: "Owe [*opheilete*] nothing to anyone, except to love one another; for the one who loves has fulfilled the law [i.e., has more than satisfied all his obligations]."

We may ask why the norm for this love of husband for wife is not only given as that of the love of Christ for the church, but is also presented as "love for their own [*heauton*] bodies." I believe that behind these lines stands an Old Testament anthropology that looked upon unity between human beings as grounded on the fact that they share "flesh" *(baśar)*. The concept moved in concentric circles. Humanity as a whole can be called "all flesh," and this outer circle becomes progressively more dense until the immediate family is considered to be sharing the same flesh. Thus the laws against incest in Leviticus 18 begin with the enigmatic phrase (literally): "No one shall approach any flesh of his body/flesh *(baśar)* to uncover nakedness (i.e., have sexual relations). I am YHWH." This is further specified by specific instances of what "flesh of his body/flesh" may mean. For example, "You shall not uncover the nakedness of your father, that is, the nakedness of your mother; she is your mother, you shall not uncover her nakedness" (18:6). "You shall not uncover the nakedness of the wife of your father, she is your father's nakedness" (18:7). "You shall not uncover the nakedness of your mother's sister because she is your mother's flesh" (18:13). It is clear from this that there are degrees of what we would call consanguinity which the Hebrews considered "con-fleshness." The source of this is marriage. That is why when a man marries a woman they become "one flesh." From their total union there arises a "new flesh," and those born to them are one flesh with them and with each other. In this sense a man's wife is his flesh: their commitment has given rise to a new entity. The notion that a wife is the "flesh" of her husband is found in the first-century *Life of Adam and Eve* 3: in response to Eve's plea that Adam kill her in order to placate God, Adam says, "How is it possible that I should let loose my hand against my flesh?"[34] We also read in Sirach 25:26: "If she [an erring wife] walks not by your side, cut her away from your flesh with a bill of divorce."[35] In addition, members of the same family are described as being "flesh" of each other. Judah dissuaded his brothers from killing Joseph "for he is our flesh," and Isaiah 58:7, after urging kindness in general to those in need, adds, "and do not turn your back on your own flesh."

A development of this notion is found in the phrase (literally) "bone of my bone and flesh of my flesh" and similar expressions which, as we have seen, indi-

---

34. James H. Charlesworth, ed., *The Old Testament Pseudepigrapha*, vol. 2 (New York: Doubleday, 1985), p. 258.

35. For this verse see Patrick W. Skehan and Alexander A. Di Lella, *The Wisdom of Ben Sira*, Anchor Bible 39 (New York: Doubleday, 1987), *in loc.*

cate the familial bonds, either very close or at least among Israelites, which form the basis for a covenant.[36] Both expressions, "one flesh" and "bone of my bones and flesh of my flesh," occur in Genesis 2:23-24, texts alluded to in the Ephesians passage we are considering. When we add to this the fact that there is no current word for "body" in Hebrew, we realize that the substitution in Greek of the word *sōma* (body) where *sarx* (flesh) might be expected would occasion no surprise. Paul, in fact, when he loosely cites Genesis 2:24 in 1 Corinthians 6:16, speaks of "one body": "Do you not know that anyone who joins himself to a prostitute becomes one body [with her]? For it says, 'the two will become one flesh.'"

The lines in the passage we are studying now are based on just this type of thinking and reflect, I think, the fundamental source of Paul's description of the church as the body of Christ. All our author has done here is render more explicit the equation body/flesh = bride, which Paul had already exploited in 2 Corinthians 11:2-3: "I feel a divine jealousy for you, for I betrothed you to Christ to present you as a pure bride to her one husband. But I am afraid that as the serpent deceived Eve by his cunning, your thoughts will be led astray from a sincere and pure devotion to Christ." Time does not allow us to develop this line of thought here, but it is important to consider some of its anthropological implications for the new feminism.[37]

If it is true that the wife is the "body" of her husband, the opposite is also true. This second and correlative principle is not developed, I think, for two reasons. First, the author's perspective is not merely the relation between man and woman, or even that of Adam and Eve, but rather the restored relation between man and woman that is now revealed and made accessible in Christ's relation to the church. Secondly, speaking of the woman as the "body" or "flesh" of the husband allows for a greater development of the notion of "head" which does not mean "more elevated" or "superior" but rather "the one who takes the initiative in love." An initiative that does not meet with response is no initiative at all, and thus we are confronted with what I will discuss shortly as "asymmetrical reciprocity." The notion of "body," therefore, evokes the image of intimacy and reciprocity, not that of inferiority or instrument. This latter notion is read into the text from our post-Cartesian mind-set. Part of this notion is already caught in the medieval expression that woman is or represents the "humanity" of Christ.[38]

36. For a complete treatment of this point, see Maurice Gilbert, "'Une Seule Chair' (Gen 2,24)," *Nouvelle Revue Théologique* 100 (1978): 66-89.

37. For an initial development of what I hope to treat at greater length in another study, see Paulus Andriessen, "The New Eve, Body of the New Adam," in *The Birth of the Church* (New York: Alba House, 1968).

38. One could consult the study by Caroline Walker Bynum, "'. . . And Woman His Humanity': Female Imagery in the Religious Writing of the Later Middle Ages," in *Gender and Reli-*

31a For this reason,
31b a man will leave his father and mother
31c and be joined to his wife
31d and the two will become one flesh.
31c This mystery is great:
32a for my part, I am speaking
32b in reference to Christ and the church.

Without any indication that he is citing a biblical text, probably because he considers it too well known, the author, with slight variations from our present Septuagint text, begins with "For this reason." The reason in the text is that, as the Lord God *(Kyrios ho Theos)* leads the woman to *'ādām*, *'ādām* exclaims, "This now is bone of my bones and flesh of my flesh; she shall be called woman because from her man *(andros)* she was taken." In the Ephesians text the reason referred to is that Christ provides and cares for his own flesh, the church, because we are members of his body. This is going to be the basis for the comparison.

The Genesis text continues to speak of a man leaving father and mother, which is an aspect ignored by Paul, who puts the accent on the man being joined to his wife so that the two become one flesh. The physical union between Christ and the church is precisely the great mystery, as the author explicitly says, and it is precisely that union which forms the model for husband and wife and is itself the living source of the love that binds them together. As Pierre Benoit expresses it: "In this union (between Christ and the Church), which is the model for human marriage, and which is not endowed with any less physical realism, the 'mystery' of the Genesis text is fully realized and definitively clarified."[39]

We may ask why the author, after citing the Genesis text with the intention of applying it primarily to the union between Christ and the church, calls it a "mystery." Some commentators point to the fact that *raz* and *sod*, the Semitic terms that lie behind the New Testament *mystērion*, can sometimes mean the secret meaning of a text, and they apply that meaning here.[40] But the author's point is that the *mystērion* is an aspect of God's plan now revealed. He is insisting on the analogical relation between the union of husband and wife, who become one flesh, and the union of Christ and the church, who form one

---

gion: On the Complexity of Symbols, ed. Caroline Walker Bynum, Stevan Harrel, and Paula Richman (Boston: Beacon Press, 1986).

39. Pierre Benoit, "Corps, Tête et Plérôme dans les Épîtres de la Captivité," in *Exégèse et Théologie 2* (Paris: Cerf, 1960), pp. 107-53, cite at p. 135.

40. This is the position of Raymond Brown in his fine study, *The Semitic Background of the Term "Mystery" in the New Testament* (Philadelphia: Fortress, 1968), p. 65.

flesh. The "mystery" is not primarily in the text but in the realities it is mediating to us. As Augustine said: "In ipso facto, non solum in dicto, mysterium requirere debemus."[41]

With the creation of the new man by Christ's act on the cross, it becomes apparent, as Heinrich Schlier expresses it, that "In Adam as the original (ursprünglichen) man, the creation of God, the future Christ is already hidden, but really present. Christ is the revealed, original man ... in the creation is already hidden the redemption provided in Christ."[42] Adam, as Paul tells us, was the "type" (typos) of the one to come (Rom. 5:14), who is the "second man (anthrōpos), the one from heaven" (1 Cor. 15:47). While these texts place the accent on Jesus Christ as the individual man who recapitulates the reality of the "first man," our Ephesians text reminds us that, as we now see Christ, the "second man," we understand that creation itself is a prophecy of redemption. This means that in the corporate reality of man and woman as Genesis describes it, the unity of Christ and the church is already present in a proleptic symbol. The great mystery, therefore, is in the *fact* of Christ's physical union with the church. Thus every union of husband and wife, as they are themselves members of the body of Christ, is a share and a symbol of what is still ineffably mysterious because it is so abundantly real. We will draw consequences from this revelation shortly.

> 33a But still, let each of you individually
> 33b love his own wife as himself,
> 33c as for the wife, let her fear her husband.

The exhortation is now concluded, with the husband mentioned first this time. The initial word, *plēn*, may be used, as here, to round off a discussion. A final practical word is offered to each party: the husband should "love" and the wife should "fear." The injunction to the husband is based on Leviticus 19:18, a text already invoked in rabbinic teaching about marriage. We can read in the Babylonian Talmud the following statement: "Our rabbis taught: Concerning a man who loves his wife as himself, who honours her more than himself. . . . Scripture says, 'And you shall know that your tent is in peace.'"[43] But even the Levitical text has been sublated in a way not unlike the Johannine texts in which Jesus tells us to love each other as he loves us (John 15:12; etc.).

---

41. *On Psalm 68*, in *Patrologia Latina*, 36:858. For a number of patristic texts on this same theme, see Henri de Lubac, *Catholicism: Christ and the Common Destiny of Man*, trans. Lancelot Sheppard and Sister Elizabeth Englund (San Francisco: Ignatius, 1988), pp. 165-70.

42. Heinrich Schlier, *Der Brief an der Epheser. Ein Kommentar* (Düsseldorf: Patmos Verlag, 1958), p. 278. Translation is basically that of Barth, p. 643 n. 141.

43. *b. Yebamot* 62b.

We would expect that just as the key word, *agapan,* used repeatedly in regard to the husband, is echoed in this summary, so too the word *hypotassesthai* would be used in the final address to the wife. Once again, however, as we have seen, the author avoids making the wife the explicit subject of this verb and reverts instead to his general admonition in 5:21, "subordinating yourselves to each other in the fear of Christ." In the Christian life a fear that is not founded upon love is a monstrosity. The meaning of this phrase must be discovered within the love relation established by Christ among all his members and in a special way between husband and wife. In this sense we may invoke the famous phrase of Augustine, *amanti loquor.*

Part Three: Principles in the Definition of Woman

Having considered the principal biblical texts which mediate to us a revealed anthropology of man and woman, we are ready to institute what will really be a beginning of some philosophical reflections on this revelation in order to render it more intelligible. I will consider only two principles here: identity and difference, and relation of asymmetrical reciprocity.

Identity and Difference

The early chapters of Genesis usually employ the term "the man," *hā'ādām,* with the article, thus blurring the distinction between the word as a personal name and as a common noun. In fact, the Septuagint uses *anthrōpos* to translate *'ādām* throughout Genesis 1 and the first part of chapter 2, first using *ho adam* (with the article) at 2:16 and as a personal name at 2:19 to designate *adam* in the act of naming the animals. This fluidity in the Hebrew text, echoed in its own way by the Greek text, manifests a mentality that sees each human being as the complete embodiment of humanity, realizing humanity and summing it up. This is particularly true of those who are looked upon as the origin of a tribe or a people: thus Israel is the name of a person and the name of the people

44. See H. Wheeler Robinson, *Corporate Personality in Ancient Israel,* ed. John Reumann, Facet Books, Biblical Series 11 (Philadelphia: Fortress, 1964), and his critics, J. R. Porter, "The Legal Aspects of the Concept of 'Corporate Personality' in the Old Testament," *Vetus Testamentum* 15 (1965): 361-80; J. W. Rogerson, "The Hebrew Conception of Corporate Personality: A Re-Examination," *Journal of Theological Studies* 21 (1970): 1-16. For a balanced approach see Jean de Fraine, *Adam and the Family of Man,* trans. Daniel Raible, C.PP.S. (New York: Alba House, 1965).

who originated with him. The usual name given to such a perception is "corporate personality," first coined in this sense by H. Wheeler Robinson and subsequently criticized and perfected by others.[44]

This grammatical consideration, however, and the mentality it manifests, is overshadowed by the manner in which the Priestly tradition, twice, as we have seen, explicitly describes *'ādām* as "male and female," using terms which accent their physical differences, and links this with the image of God. Division into male and female, however, cannot mean the creation of two beings, only one of which is fully human. On the other hand, it is not necessary, in fact is impossible in the light of the biblical texts just considered, to make of gender something secondary to being human, something to be assigned along a sliding scale according to predisposition or preference. The philosophical insight that enables us to retain both these truths is "dual unity," which may perhaps be better expressed as "identity and difference."[45]

The term "dual unity" has been made popular through the work of Hans Urs von Balthasar, who attributes the term to A. Frank-Duquesne.[46] A dual unity may be defined as "two distinct but inseparable realities, each fulfilling the other and both ordained to an ultimate unity that we cannot as yet imagine . . . two entia in a single *esse*, one existence in two lives, but by no means two different fragments of a whole, to be fitted together like a puzzle."[47] There are three ways of considering man as a dual unity: body and soul, man and woman, individual and community. It is important to note, however, that man and woman are a unique kind of dual unity since *all* of humanity exists differently in each of them, not merely an aspect, as is the case with soul/body or individual/community. It is for this reason that the expression "identity and difference" is more apt.

No one human being exhausts the reality of humanity: there is always the "other" who cannot be reduced to what I am. Man and woman together make up humanity, and they are not only "distinct but inseparable realities" but are also ordained to an ultimate unity that is not that of parts going to make up a whole, but rather two modes of existing as human that are irreducible to one another — they are identical and different — as they make a third reality, a

45. I owe this latter phrase to an unpublished study by Angelo Scola, "Il Disegno de Dio sulla Persona, sul Matrimonio e sulla Famiglia. Riflessione Sintetica" (paper given at the Settimana Internazionale di Studio, Rome, August 22-27, 1999, and published by Pontificio Istituto Giovanni Paolo II per Studi su Matrimonio e Famiglia).

46. A. Frank-Duquesne, *Création et Procréation* (Paris: Ed. de Minuit, 1951); Hans Urs von Balthasar, *Theo-Drama: Theological Dramatic Theory*, vol. 2, *Dramatis Personae: Man in God* (San Francisco: Ignatius, 1992), esp. pp. 365-82.

47. Frank-Duquesne, pp. 42-46, cited by Balthasar, pp. 365-66.

communion of persons. This understanding reverses a way of thinking about human nature that is latent in nearly every cultural expression known to us, namely, that the man is the norm and the woman is the normed. Identity and difference, on the other hand, means that man and woman are reciprocal norms for each other. Being, that is, human being, is not divided: it is asserted as existing in two transcendentally related modes that cannot be reduced to each other.

Relationship: Asymmetrical Reciprocity

As we have seen, the Priestly tradition in Genesis 1 is a descriptive narrative that presents the structure of creation as it is intended by God. The Yahwist presentation, on the other hand, is an existential poetic narrative that is searching in history for the origins of human existence as we know it. Thus, rather than speak of the image of God, *'ādām* is portrayed as the direct object of God's action, formed from the earth and sharing in God's breath, and elevated by an invitation to obedience and trust through a covenant. The woman is taken from *'ādām* to match him and be the embodiment of God's help to him. Because of her, *'ādām* has someone to "face" him, to be a covenant partner with him, and together they form one flesh in unveiled communication.

Relationship

At this point we must return to our previous consideration of the image of God and enter briefly into a discussion regarding human personhood.[48] The classical definition of person, given by Boethius and modified somewhat in the course of history, asserted basically that a person is "an individual substance of a rational nature."[49] Modern philosophical and theological thought has advanced the understanding of person, and thus would understand these terms in a more existential manner than how they were formerly understood. When "substance" is seen in the light of creation, it becomes obvious that it is what it

48. For a more complete account of what I present here schematically, see W. Norris Clarke, "Person, Being, and St. Thomas," *Communio* 19 (1992): 601-18; Clarke, *Person and Being* (Milwaukee, 1993); David Schindler, "Norris Clarke on Person, Being, and St. Thomas," *Communio* 20, no. 3 (1993): 580-92; and Clarke, "A Response to David Schindler's Comments," *Communio* 20, no. 3 (1993): 593-98.

49. For a discussion of this definition and its history, see Max Müller et al., "Person," in *Sacramentum Mundi: An Encyclopedia of Theology,* ed. Karl Rahner (New York: Herder and Herder, 1969), pp. 404-19.

is by its relation to God, that it subsists as what it is, and that it expresses what it is by relation to other beings. Thus W. Norris Clarke proposes a triadic structure of being: "being *from* another, being *in* oneself, and being *toward* others."[50] Given the dynamic structure of all being, it is true to say that the *individuum,* the *concretum,* seen in the light of its reality as created, is constituted by relation: to God, to itself, and to other beings. This last relation, to other beings, is what Maritain calls "the basic generosity of existence,"[51] in which every being at its own level does impart something of itself: *bonum est diffusivum sui.*

Similarly, when we reflect on what "rational" means, we see that the unique and incommunicable reality of a person is also constituted by relation; it is *from* God, it relates *in* itself and to itself, and it is a being *toward* others. What is unique in the instance of person is that this threefold relation is actualized in the personal activity of freedom by which the relation becomes *relationship.* Thus the particular property of a "rational" substance is that it is constituted by relation in such a way that this is given properly human existence in the free acts by which the person realizes himself or herself. In scholastic terms relation is, in a unique way, an intrinsic mode, or a "proper accident" of the relational substance, and this is realized in *act.* In the case of the person, this act is a spiritual act, one of freedom. This philosophical elaboration is expressed biblically by saying that *'ādām* is the image of God, and can find himself only in a relationship of mutual self-giving love. In order to understand, however, how this relationship transpires between man and woman who are both identical and different, we must look at the foundation of reciprocity, namely, generosity and receptivity.

Receptivity[52]

Martin Heidegger has accused Aristotle of introducing into Western thought the identification of *archē* and *aitia,* thus effecting a notion of cause as being always prior and always dominant. This may or not be historically accurate, but the notion is certainly to be found in modernity, which, in this as in many areas, has reduced Greek thought to but one aspect of its original abundance. With such a notion of cause, the only correlate can be passivity. Thus "cause" signifies

50. Clarke, "Response," p. 596.

51. Jacques Maritain, *Existence and the Existent* (New York: Doubleday, 1957), p. 90.

52. In this section I am indebted to the work of Kenneth Schmitz, especially "Created Receptivity and the Philosophy of the Concrete," *Thomist* 61, no. 3 (1997): 339-71, and "Neither with Nor without Foundations," *Review of Metaphysics* 42 (1988): 3-25. This section also utilizes material found in my study, *The Feminist Question: Feminist Theology in the Light of Christian Tradition* (Grand Rapids: Eerdmans, 1994), esp. chap. 6, used with permission of the publisher.

power, and that upon which the cause exercises an influence is patient of that power.

There are two aspects of causality that must be restored to our consideration: "generosity" and "person." Both are part of the biblical understanding of causality, which looks to God as the source and model of what it means to cause. To cause is to communicate actuality in some form. God, the First Cause, communicates being itself to his creatures, not in an act of "domination" but in an act of supreme generosity, and creation is not "passive," it is receptive. Created causality shares in its own way the nature of God's causality. This can be seen in the manner in which one being communicates something of itself to another, in the way the act of knowing consists in receiving what the known is sharing of itself, and most especially in the interaction of persons. It is important to note that it is proper to spiritual activity that something be shared without loss to the one sharing, and that this is received in such a way that there is an increase in being without mutuation.

While there is generosity and receptivity on every level of being, and indeed there is generosity and receptivity in the very act of creation, since God cocreates the receptivity with the creature, it still remains true that what is proper to human interaction is precisely that communication which is being achieved through the mutual causality of freedom: "My argument is that receptivity is a principle of personal being at the concrete level. Far from being a principle that is neither act nor potency, I mean by it an *integral mode* constituted of both act and potency."[53] This will become clearer when we look at the other aspect of human relating, especially man/woman relating, namely, asymmetry.

Asymmetry

Asymmetry adds the note of difference to the notion of receptivity and the reciprocal "causality" realized in the relation of generosity/receptivity. Not only are man and woman, husband and wife, related in such a way that their reciprocal giving and receiving finds its initiative in the man's love and a particular perfection in the woman's love, but their equal contributions are different, they are "asymmetrical."[54] Asymmetry, in our context, refers first and foremost to the fact that "sexual difference, in a significant and immediate way, testifies that the other always remains 'other' for me."[55] When the irreducible "otherness" of

---

53. Schmitz, "Created Receptivity," p. 349.

54. I am indebted in these few lines to the direction indicated by Angelo Scola, "The Nuptial Mystery at the Heart of the Church," *Communio* 25 (1998): 630-62, esp. pp. 643-49.

55. Scola, *art. laud.*, p. 645.

the other is taken seriously, then we find a way out of the impasse created by still one more exaggeration of Greek thought. The ancients' self-referential mode of thought was twisted by the Enlightenment so that knowledge of another person is reduced from the abundance and mystery of the other's personal existence to an interior event within the knower. The one aspect of existence for which Kantian epistemology cannot take any account is precisely human interaction, beginning with a simple conversation.

When causality is appreciated in its multiple realizations, and when difference does not automatically imply a relation of "superiority/inferiority," then it is clear that two realities can cause equally, though in an asymmetrical manner: soil and seed in the production of a plant, object and knower in the act of knowing. Applied to our consideration here of a new humanism, we can see that human interactive causality, made up of mutual generosity and receptivity, is a unique instance of reciprocal asymmetry. We can see that what has often been lacking in Christian thought, even if at times the lack has been overcome in practice, is an understanding of that mode of being and acting which is irreducibly *personal*. The new feminism, beginning with the Genesis teaching on man and woman, and seeking to elaborate this through the concepts of dual unity, identity and difference, receptivity and asymmetry, has begun to form the basis for a genuine development of doctrine, a new humanism that sheds the light of faith on what it means to have an integral humanity expressed in the life of the church.

The paradigmatic realization of this new humanism is found in the spousal relationship in which, to use the concepts of John Paul II, two subjectivities relate to each other as two unique persons who cannot be reduced to "another self," but who rather form, in a mysterious manner, a "bi-subjectivity."[56] Time does not allow me to develop this concept here. The most striking manifestation of reciprocal asymmetry is to be found in the conception of a child. Not only on the personal level is the conjugal act an asymmetrical realization of love between equals, but the conception itself, as the science of genetics tells us, is an instance of the same equal causality. This biological fact, sublated[57] throughout the whole of the human person, male or female, allows

56. See, for instance, the Wednesday audiences of August 25 and September 1, 1982, in Wojtyla, pp. 314-21.

57. The following is a good description of theological sublation. It is given by Bernard Lonergan, who says he is here following Rahner, not Hegel: "What sublates goes beyond what is sublated, introduces something new and distinct, yet so far from interfering with the sublated or destroying it, on the contrary needs it, includes it, preserves all its proper features and properties, and carries them forward to a fuller realization within a richer context" (Bernard Lonergan, *Method in Theology* [New York: Herder and Herder, 1972], p. 241).

us to move from the medieval notion that in conception the man was *agens quod inducit formam* and the woman was *patiens quod offert materiam,* to an understanding that in the procreation of a new human life the depth of the mystery of human intersubjectivity finds a human fruit.

The Cross: The Way to Restored Relationships

The marriage relationship is the most interhuman realization of asymmetrical reciprocity. The husband's role is one of generosity, he is to "communicate actuality" by laying down his life. The wife receives this communication and thus gives it actual existence. A gift not received is not a gift at all. By placing husband and wife in the context of mutual generosity and receptivity, it becomes clear that the only priority in such a relation is the priority of love. In the teaching of Ephesians, as we have seen, the husband is "head" because, in some mysterious way, his loving initiative enables the woman to assume her role as embodying in a particular and preeminent way the vocation of every human being who "cannot find himself except through a sincere gift of self."[58] Commenting on the notion of headship, Pope John Paul II states how the principle of "receptivity" is actually realized through the love of the husband. "That good which he who loves creates, through his love, in the one that is loved, is like a test of that same love and its measure. Giving himself in the most disinterested way, he who loves does so only within the limits of this measure and this control."[59]

When we return once again to the example of Christ as head of his bride the church, we see that this relationship is initiated by the fact that Jesus Christ is head as "Savior of the body," and that the husband is to imitate that act by which Christ "loved the church and gave himself over for her." The answer and healing for the domination, violence, and oppression that are never far from any human relationship are to be found in the act of love in which Jesus Christ died. The Gospels are replete with Jesus' teaching on noncoercive relating.[60] He unmasks the lie of domination and the lie of helplessness by calling us to live out our imaging of God. It is thus that in marriage, the paradigm of all human relating, there is to be realized that form of love which heals and sublates, that is, recapitulates, God's original intention by giving it an actual historical existence. That love is a share in Christ's gift of himself on the cross. It is identical in each person and yet different. It is asymmetrical, being both generous and re-

---

58. *Gaudium et Spes,* #24.
59. General audience of September 1, 1982, in Wojtyla, p. 319.
60. It is sufficient to read the Beatitudes to see this heart of his teaching.

ceptive. In this movement of love, woman has a priority in that, by her very be-ing, her receptivity to another involves her in a creative generosity that norms the very meaning of love. This is, to use John Paul II's phrase, the "genius of woman." In the reciprocal relationship between man and wife, the exemplar and source of other relationships, there is one love that restores us to humanity. It is the love within the Trinity as this is breathed out into us by Jesus Christ when he "handed over the Spirit" and the church was born from his side.

Feminist Experience and Faith Experience

Michele M. Schumacher

> *Christianity, it seems to me, has often short-changed people when it comes to developing their own religious awareness. Particularly is this true of Christianity in its Protestant form. To be religious — through the fact that Christianity has had a highly developed myth and structure of doctrine — has become a case of believing this system to be objectively true. (Dare I say that there may be something peculiarly male about this striving for distance and objectivity, rather than looking to one's own experience and possibility of receptivity?)[1]*

If Christianity has indeed suffered a loss of subjective meaning under patriarchal influence, as the post-Christian feminist Daphne Hampson claims, under feminism it has, at the opposite extreme, suffered a loss of objective content. What most strikes Hampson about feminist theology — not unlike modern theology in general — "is how profoundly secular it is." It has, quite simply, progressed toward something other than theology properly understood: discourse *(logos)* about God *(Theos)*. "It is as though theology has lost its moorings. In the case of feminist theology, what seems to have replaced talk of God is largely talk of women's experience. It is not even women's experience of God: it is simply women's experience."[2]

This challenges us, in the context of a new feminism, to specifically ad-

---

1. Daphne Hampson, *Theology and Feminism* (Cambridge, Mass., and Oxford: Blackwell, 1990), p. 172.

2. Hampson, p. 170. As examples she cites the "theologies" of Elisabeth Schüssler Fiorenza, Rosemary Ruether, Mary Daly, Catherine Keller, and Sallie McFague.

dress the *experience of faith* — including, most especially, that of women — whereby is meant the experience of a living relationship and the appropriation of a lasting heritage.[3] More specifically I wish to recommend an approach admitting a continuity between the objective and the subjective dimensions of faith, such that the former (experiences *of God*) give rise to the latter (*experiences* of God). As explained by Jean Mouroux,

> the rhythm of religious experience is made up of an act of awareness and a positing which are interconnected — an awareness of the given relationship, which comes from creation itself, from God's pure generosity towards us and within us, but which is no more than a preliminary sketch of the reality, because it is an appeal to our liberty; and a positing of this relationship, which is personally accepted with gratitude and then willed, and hence renewed, deepened, and transposed to a different level — for it raises us from the ontological level to the spiritual level, and leads to our communion, not as a merely natural being but as a personal being, with God.[4]

As differing from the "old" brand of feminist theology, the *primary* question of a new feminist theology is not how our human or feminine experiences might affect our conception of the Godhead — if the Godhead is considered at all — nor how a critique of "the androcentric bias of religion and theology" might affect theology's methods and procedures.[5] While these remain interesting and important questions, at the forefront of our investigation is instead *the question of the relationship between experience and faith,* and thus that, more fundamentally, of the meaning of faith itself, both as object and act, as gift and response.[6] As such, it is not a guise by which patriarchal "order" is maintained through the subjection of unsuspecting women, an attempt to bring them into conformity with an "objectified" masculine standard. Indeed, a new feminism must never be understood as an attempt to deny the oppression of women under patriarchy, nor to heavy-handedly assert the church's power over them. It is not submission that is sought, but the "obedience of faith," to borrow a phrase from the Second Vatican Council.[7] This requires, of course, that faith itself be properly interpreted. Faith

---

3. That is to say, the individual's experience of faith is understood as lying within the context of the community of faith, as we shall see.

4. Jean Mouroux, *The Christian Experience: An Introduction to a Theology,* trans. George Lamb (New York: Sheed and Ward, 1954), pp. 18-19.

5. Catherine Mowry LaCugna, ed., *Freeing Theology: The Essentials of Theology in Feminist Perspective* (San Francisco: Harper Collins, 1993), pp. 1-2.

6. Hence the question, as we shall see, of the proper subject-object relation within an authentically Christian epistemology of faith.

7. Council Vatican II, Dogmatic Constitution on Divine Revelation, *Dei verbum,* #5.

is not, I insist, a refusal to understand or question; nor is it, at the opposite extreme, a purely intellectual assent or a simple desire to comprehend something of the mystery of God and the cosmos. It is, rather, a giving of the self to the one who has first given himself, even unto death, to each human person and to all humankind. Far from severing the faithful from the community of the church, which is often judged by feminists as corrupted by patriarchal thinking, a new feminism challenges women and men to live so deeply their personal experience of faith as to thereby enliven the shared faith of the community. This is the challenge to live what is believed by personally committing oneself to the church's Bridegroom, who, as revelator of the Father by the Spirit, is in the final analysis both the object and the subject of the church's faith.

Beginning with an exposition of the largely subjective role of experience within traditional feminist theology and an exposition of feminist epistemological models constructed in reaction to the extreme objectivism many feminist thinkers attribute to patriarchal thought, I will argue for an authentic experience of faith as characteristic of a new feminist theology. This experience of faith will be presented in terms of a biblical epistemology "wedding" the believing subject with the object of his faith: the divine subject who gives himself, in an act of love, as an "object" to be known and loved. Similar to the impossibility of the believer being separated from the object of his faith in a new feminist theology is, I will argue, the impossibility of the individual believer being divorced from the community of faith. I will conclude by offering a positive challenge for new feminist theologians to avoid the dangers of both patriarchy and traditional feminism by developing an attitude of faith which is personal and ecclesial, concrete and universal, objective and committed.

Experience in Feminist Theology

In terms of the development of experience within contemporary theological reflection — a development that parallels the rise of modernity[8] — feminist theology has arrived only recently on the scene, dating back to Valerie Saiving Goldstein's 1960 article arguing for women's particular contribution in religious studies due to their unique (what she calls "feminine") experiences.[9] Twenty years later, Goldstein's analysis is taken up and developed by Judith Plaskow,

8. On this see Angelo Bertuletti, "Il concetto di 'esperienza,'" in *L'Evidenza e la Fede*, ed. Giuseppe Colombo (Milan: Glossa, 1988), pp. 112-81.

9. Valerie Saiving, "The Human Situation: A Feminine View," *Journal of Religion* 40 (1960): 110-12; reprinted under her married name, Goldstein, in *Womanspirit Rising: A Feminist Reader in Religion*, ed. Carol P. Christ and Judith Plaskow (San Francisco: Harper and Row, 1979), pp. 25-42.

who critiques the theologies of Reinhold Niebuhr and Paul Tillich for highlighting and developing "certain aspects of human experience" in their theologies while others, i.e., those of women, "are regarded as secondary or ignored." "The effect of this tendency, which is not incidental but springs from the very definitions of sin and grace, is to identify human with male experience. This identification," Plaskow concludes, "not only impoverishes theology but leads it to support prevailing definitions of femininity."[10] In the meantime, American feminist theologians of such influence and stature as Mary Daly, Rosemary Radford Ruether, and Elisabeth Schüssler Fiorenza began critiquing not merely theologies purporting to speak from the universal human situation while reflecting a uniquely male perspective, but also the very tradition and core symbolism of Christianity — indeed, even Scripture itself — as reflecting and reinforcing an oppressive patriarchal social structure. Daly went so far as to argue that this was irredeemably the case and declared herself "post-Christian."[11] Her influence is so powerful that a "serious Christian response," as Carol Christ sees it, "will have to show that the core symbolism of Father and Son does not have the effect of reinforcing and legitimating male power and female submission, or it will have to transform Christian imagery at its very core."[12]

For these authors it was not enough to assert that theology — at least to the extent that it claims to reflect a universal human situation — should consult women's experience, but that it should critically (even "suspiciously")[13] regard its own sources which, far from being purely objective, are "themselves codified collective human experience,"[14] and *male* experience at that! Hence, while Ruether and Fiorenza point to the "androcentric bias" of male *interpreters* of Scripture and tradition who judge maleness as normative, they also recognize the same bias in the Bible itself: it is "authored by men, written in androcentric language, reflective of religious male experience, selected and transmitted by male religious leadership."[15]

10. Judith Plaskow, *Sex, Sin, and Grace: Women's Experience in the Theologies of Reinhold Niebuhr and Paul Tillich* (Washington, D.C.: University Press of America, 1980), p. 4.

11. See Daly's preface to the second and subsequent editions of *Beyond God the Father: Toward a Philosophy of Women's Liberation* (Boston: Beacon Press, 1973).

12. Carol Christ, "The New Feminist Theology: A Review of the Literature," *Religious Studies Review* 3 (1977): 203-12, cited at p. 205. See also Elisabeth Schüssler Fiorenza, "The Will to Choose or to Reject: Continuing Our Critical Work," in *Feminist Interpretation of the Bible*, ed. Letty M. Russell (Philadelphia: Westminister, 1985), pp. 125-36, esp. p. 130.

13. See Elisabeth Schlüssler Fiorenza, *In Memory of Her: Feminist Theological Reconstruction of Christian Origins* (New York: Crossroad, 1984).

14. Rosemary Radford Ruether, *Sexism and God-Talk* (Boston: Beacon Press, 1983), p. 12.

15. Fiorenza, "Will to Choose," p. 130; cf. Rosemary Radford Ruether, "Feminist Interpretation: A Method of Correlation," in *Feminist Interpretation of the Bible*, pp. 111-24.

The very fact that feminists are able to point to these biases is, Ruether claims, evidence of a "grace," i.e., the "infusion of liberating empowerment from beyond the patriarchal cultural context, which allows them (women) to critique and stand out against these androcentric interpretations of who and what they are."[16] Hence these "enlightened" women (and men) claim for themselves the authority to judge Scripture and tradition in accord with what Ruether refers to as the "critical principle of feminist theology": "Whatever denies, diminishes, or distorts the full humanity of women is, therefore, appraised as not redemptive. . . . What does promote the full humanity of women is of the Holy, it does reflect true relation to the divine, it is the true nature of things, the authentic message of redemption and the mission of redemptive community."[17]

While it remains ambiguous what kinds of women's experiences ought to be consulted in theological discourse,[18] when it comes to critiquing the sources there is implied a very particular, "critical" experience: that "experience which arises when women become critically aware of these falsifying and alienating experiences imposed upon them as women in a male dominated culture."[19] As an experience of what they term "grace," it necessarily entails a radically new sense of "conversion" as well: "that through which women get in touch with, name, and judge their experiences of sexism in patriarchal society."[20] Similarly, Elizabeth Johnson speaks of a twofold dialectic which "can be suitably described in the classic language of conversion": (1) the experience of oppression which is interpreted as such (i.e., as oppressive) and thus wrong; and (2) the confirmation of women's "beauty and power as active subjects of history."[21]

In this very particular use of the "classic" terms of grace and conversion there is substantially reformulated the proposition argued by traditional (and

---

16. Ruether, "Feminist Interpretation," p. 114. Similarly, within the intersubjective theology of Thandeka, "[g]race is the liberation of the self from the confines of conceptual schemes, socially constructed identities, public policies, and private strategies that have reduced the expanse of the self to the submissive/combative strategies of a tributary. These human-imposed restrictions of the self are sin" ("The Self between Feminist Theory and Theology," in *Horizons in Feminist Theology: Identity, Traditions, and Norms,* ed. Rebecca S. Chopp and Sheila Greeve Davaney [Minneapolis: Fortress, 1997], p. 96). See also Anne Carr, *Transforming Grace: Christian Tradition and Women's Experience* (San Francisco: Harper and Row, 1988).

17. Ruether, "Feminist Interpretation," p. 115.

18. See Carr, *Transforming Grace*, pp. 118-23; Carr, "The New Vision of Feminist Theology," in *Freeing Theology*, pp. 22-23; Ruether, "Feminist Interpretation," pp. 113-14.

19. Ruether, "Feminist Interpretation," p. 113.

20. Ruether, "Feminist Interpretation," p. 114.

21. Elizabeth A. Johnson, *She Who Is: The Mystery of God in Feminist Theological Discourse* (New York: Crossroad, 1992), pp. 62-63; cf. Carr, *Transforming Grace*; Plaskow, p. 179.

thus male!) theologians throughout the church's history and integrated, more recently, into the innovative theological model of Bernard Lonergan, for example. Theology, it has been presumed, at least in its "mediating phase," as Lonergan refers to it, is to be performed from a converted stance. While Lonergan understands this conversion as intellectual and moral as well as religious, the assumption has always been — as expressed by Saint Anselm's *fides quaerens intellectum* — that the theologian does not merely reflect upon an object which is given as a proposition for faith, but has actually been "converted" to this faith, which is to say that he or she has *appropriated* it by means of a willing self-surrender. Even Friedrich Schleiermacher — the Protestant "father of modern theology" who is often faulted by orthodox theologians for attempting to derive the contents of the Christian faith from what he calls religious consciousness — approached theology from within the Augustinian-Franciscan tradition, according to which it was seen as a "practical knowledge, based on a participation of the knowing subject in the spiritual realities, a touching and tasting *(tactus*[22] and *gustus)* of that with which it deals."[23] So too, Catholic theologians as explicitly opposed in their methodologies as Karl Rahner and Hans Urs von Balthasar share the opinion that theology must be informed by faith:[24] the theologian is necessarily a believer speaking *from* faith and not merely *about* faith.

Admittedly, the cognitive aspect of faith largely overshadowed its presen-

---

22. I have taken the liberty to change an obvious error. In the text, one finds instead *haptus.*

23. Paul Tillich, *Systematic Theology,* vol. 1 (Chicago: University of Chicago Press, 1951), p. 40. Tillich, writing in 1951, claimed that "No present-day theology should avoid a discussion of Schleiermacher's experiential method, whether in agreement or disagreement." In Tillich's day "the crucial question of theology" was "whether or not, or to what degree," the detachment of neoorthodox theology from Schleiermacher's method was justifiable. For Tillich this detachment is warranted not by a psychological interpretation of Schleiermacher's famous definition of religion as the "feeling of absolute dependence" (by which he meant "ultimate concern about the ground and meaning of our being"), but by the deriving of faith from consciousness: "The event on which Christianity is based (he called it 'Jesus of Nazareth') is not derived from experience; it is *given* in history. Experience is not the source from which the contents of systematic theology are taken but the medium through which they are existentially received" (pp. 41, 42).

24. The debate between these very influential theologians concerns, more specifically, the manner in which faith shapes experience. Opposed, in Balthasar's sense, to his own insistence that the experience of faith proceeds from the concrete encounter with Christ, Rahner's correlation method is bringing into dialogue the transcendental and existential structures of human existence, on the one hand, with the content of faith, on the other, in an effort to demonstrate the continuity between an experience of grace and its explicit symbolic thematization in a move from the implicit to the explicit. On this method see Francis Schüssler Fiorenza, *Foundational Theology: Jesus and the Church* (New York: Crossroad, 1985).

tation as a personal surrender in Catholic teaching throughout the four centuries which followed the Protestant Reformation.[25] An inevitable consequence of the church's effort to counterbalance both Luther's notion of faith as confidence and modernism's conception of faith as a religious sentiment, this largely conceptual vision of faith was appropriately transformed by the Second Vatican Council's presentation of the same as a salvific relationship between the human person and the triune God. Faith, *De verbum* teaches, is both gift *and* assent, obedient surrender *and* receptive acceptance.[26] This continuity between the two aspects of faith (the subjective and the objective) is of particular significance for the feminist standpoint: conscious of what they consider the oppressive (i.e., patriarchal) nature of the traditional sources of faith and thus of theology — namely, Scripture and tradition — feminists simply refuse to appropriate them, at least until the biblical texts have been "liberated" of patriarchal themes and perspectives through a process of correlation bringing women's critical experience to bear upon them. A sort of dialogue ensues between this experience and the texts, with the former assuming the predominant "voice": it (women's critical experience) establishes the normative principle by which the biblical text can be judged.[27] While Ruether is explicit about her use

---

25. The ambivalence during the period of the Protestant Reformation between the subjective consciousness of salvation *(sola experientia)* and its objective principle *(solus Christus; sola Scriptura)* constitutes, according to Angelo Bertuletti, an important element in the anthropological turn of modernity and anticipates the conflict between this turn and the comprehension of faith. The problem of the mediating character of subjectivity — the question concerning the possibility and guarantee of an objective coincidence of thought and reality — emerges in the modern debate between rationalism and empiricism, which is presented by Bertuletti in terms of two poles of experience: the experience of reason *as reason* (in which case experience represents a problem for reason: rationalism) and experience *as experiment* (in which case experience is presented as a principle of reason: empiricism). The present theological appeal to experience is thus, Bertuletti argues, a legacy of theology's dialogical and antithetical relation to modern rationality throughout the course of its historical development. See "Il concetto di 'esperienza.'"

26. See the treatment of Henri de Lubac, *La Révélation divine* (Paris: Cerf, 1983). From a feminist perspective, see Mary Catherine Hilkert, "Experience and Tradition: Can the Center Hold?" in *Freeing Theology,* pp. 59-82. The Council's vision is prevalent in the encyclical by John Paul II on the splendor of truth, *Veritatis splendor,* August 6, 1993: "It is very urgent to rediscover and to set forth once more the authentic reality of the Christian faith, which is not simply a set of propositions to be accepted with intellectual assent. Rather, faith is a lived knowledge of Christ, a living remembrance of his commandments, and a truth to be lived out. . . . It is an encounter, a dialogue, a communion of love and of life between the believer and Jesus Christ" (#88).

27. See Francis Martin, *The Feminist Question: Feminist Theology in the Light of Christian Tradition* (Grand Rapids: Eerdmans, 1994), pp. 203, 210-11.

of the correlation method — as are Anne Carr[28] and Letty Russell,[29] who adopts Ruether's approach — Fiorenza openly rejects it for reason of the method's presumption that a correlation *does* in fact exist between what Ruether refers to as "the feminist critical principle" of the "affirmation and promotion of the full humanity of women" and "that critical principle by which biblical thought critiques itself and renews its vision as the authentic Word of God over against corrupting and sinful deformations," namely, the prophetic-messianic tradition, which is not to be confused with "a particular body of texts, which then would be understood as standing as a canon within the canon."[30] Certainly Scripture does contain certain "liberating paradigms and resources" for Fiorenza. These are to be discovered, however, not in virtue of a presupposed correlation between the critical principles of feminism and those of the Bible. Rather, she maintains that "the historical experience of women-church with the Bible" permits this discovery. In other words, the "locus or place of divine revelation and grace is . . . not the Bible or the tradition of a patriarchal church but the *ekklēsia* of women and the lives of women who live the 'option for our women selves.'"[31]

Not only has Fiorenza thus redefined for herself and other like-minded feminists the community of faith, she has also challenged the meaning and authority of faith itself. If, more specifically, what is and what is not the authentic Word of God is determined by a critical principle *apart from the Bible,* then, as George Stroup rightly notes, "the Bible no longer has the freedom to speak either good news or judgment to the reader. . . . [T]he principle itself becomes the primary authority for Christian faith and the Bible becomes a witness to the critical principle rather than a witness to the God revealed in Jesus Christ."[32] The objection with this feminist approach concerns — it bears repeating — the meaning of Christian conversion; for if personal or even common experience becomes the measure of the Word of God, then it is "very easy," as Elizabeth

28. Carr, *Transforming Grace,* pp. 116ff.

29. See Letty Russell, "Authority and the Challenge of Feminist Interpretation," in *Feminist Interpretation of the Bible,* pp. 137-46.

30. Ruether, "Feminist Interpretation," p. 117. Francis Martin — despite Fiorenza's explicit claim to the contrary — recognizes the use of the correlation method in her attempt "to establish a commonality between women's present experience of oppression and the reconstructed history of the social situations in which the biblical texts originated" (Martin, *The Feminist Question,* p. 218). At the same time, he criticizes her use of the method, as well as that of Ruether and Carr, for establishing as a foundation and norm a very particular interpretation of women's experience.

31. Fiorenza, "Will to Choose," pp. 132, 128.

32. George Stroup, "Between Echo and Narcissus: The Role of the Bible in Feminist Theology," *Interpretation: A Journal of Bible and Theology* 42 (January 1988): 19-32, cited at p. 31.

Achtemeier notes, "to ignore or discard anything in the biblical word that is unpleasant or that calls us and our lifestyles into question." Achtemeier insists that "there is a 'givenness' to the canon. It has been assembled and handed down to us; it contains words that stand over against us and judge us; and we have to come to grips with it."[33] She concludes that while the church has determined the canon, the canon has also determined the church.

Ironically, in presenting their experience as the tribunal by which is judged both Scripture and tradition, *feminists adopt a strategy similar to that which they attribute to patriarchy:* the delicate balance between the objective and subjective aspects of faith — that which is known and that whereby it is known — is tipped, this time with the load weighing heavily in the direction of subjective experience. The difficulty with the traditional feminist approach lies not merely in this biased tipping of the scale, that is to say, in the undue emphasis in a theology of revelation upon the knowing subject over and above the object known or, more correctly, upon the modification of the knowing subject by the object known.[34] While this specific manner of altering the "object" of faith is certainly already objectionable, feminist theology takes this alteration further still. If, more specifically, the danger in much traditional theology is, as feminists claim, that the image of God is falsely objectified to fit a masculine ideal — the projecting of the male self upon the Godhead — in much feminist theology God is either "re-created" in the image of women[35] or simply ignored. In the latter case, God — as noted by Hampson above — is no longer explicitly addressed: not even as "she"!

33. Elizabeth Achtemeier, "The Impossible Possibility: Evaluating the Feminist Approach to Bible and Theology," *Interpretation: A Journal of Bible and Theology* 42 (January 1988): 45-57, cited at p. 51.

34. In the theology of Schleiermacher, for example, Francis Martin observes a "dichotomy between a direct apprehension of God and a subsequent articulation of this in terms of a religious tradition" (*The Feminist Question*, p. 171). It is "not merely the modification of the subject that is known," Martin argues, "but God who is known. He is incomprehensible but not indeterminate" (p. 194).

35. This is particularly apparent in the popular reference to goddess worship in what has been coined "thealogy." "The primary source, the continuing referent, for thealogical inspiration is one's Self, understood as the consciously reflective Self in communication with others" (Emily Erwin Culpepper, "Contemporary Goddess Thealogy," in *Shaping New Vision: Gender and Values in American Culture*, ed. Clarissa Atkinson, Constance Buchanan, and Margaret Miles, Harvard Women's Studies in Religion Series, no. 5 [Ann Arbor: UMI Research Press, 1987], pp. 51-71, cited at p. 52). Culpepper refers to the works of Carol Christ, Helen Diner, Elizabeth Gould Davis, Mary Daly, Merlin Stone, Z. Budapest, and Starhawk, to name but a few. See also Elizabeth E. Green, "Thoughts about Sexual Difference and Theology: The Italian Debate," *Concilium* (1996/1): 124-31, esp. p. 126.

Experiential Knowing: A Subject-Object Commingling

The feminist critique of the church's faith as corrupted by patriarchy, as bearing a masculine bias which serves to oppress women, has ironically fallen prey to the same problematic. That is to say, in an attempt to denounce one ideology — a patriarchal church — feminism has created another: the *ekklēsia* of women. In so doing it has not only challenged the mediating role of the church in communicating revelation; it has, in this extreme instance, actually driven a wedge between the believing subject and the object of his faith. For the feminist theologian this continuity is not easily ascertained, as we have seen, and certainly not to be taken for granted. On the contrary, the subject is alerted to suspiciously regard what is presented by a "male-dominated" church as faithworthy. It is, of course, important to mark the distinction between believing the church and believing *in* the church.[36] In proposing a new community of faith, feminists do not necessarily seek, however, to thereby give clearer expression to the object of their faith. Indeed, the relation between this new community and an object of faith (if any) is ambiguous at best.[37]

This move obviously calls into question the idea of faith as receptive. Granted, receptivity is hardly an honorable concept in a modern intellectual environment that has equated it with passivity, even to the extent that it is perceived as infringing upon human freedom.[38] As such, feminism can hardly be faulted for its refusal to appropriate it as characteristic of women. In contrast, however, to the derogatory notion of receptivity understood as *passive passivity* — where something is simply undergone or suffered — a new feminism challenges us to

36. "In the Apostles' Creed we profess 'one Holy church' (*Credo . . . Ecclesiam*), and not to believe *in* the church, so as not to confuse God with his works and to attribute clearly to God's goodness *all* the gifts he has bestowed on his Church" (*Catechism of the Catholic Church*, #750).

37. In traditional (nonfeminist) theology, it is the object of faith which (at least in theory, if one wishes to seriously entertain the feminist critique) creates the community of faith. In feminist theology this relationship is arguably reversed.

38. "Similarly, flight from receptivity in modern theologies of Christian love parallels a general fear of receptivity in a modern age when for Sartrean man 'to receive is incompatible with being free,' and for 'protean man' everywhere there is a 'suspicion of counterfeit nurturance.' But such fears are the result of an experience and an interpretation of receptivity which is oppressive, deceiving in its illusory offer of meaning and happiness, destructive in its enforced passivity. It is not only women but all persons who can sense that certain forms of receptivity, of passivity and submission, are not appropriate for the human person and never truly constitutive of Christian love" (Margaret A. Farley, "New Patterns of Relationship: Beginnings of a Moral Revolution," *Theological Studies* 36, no. 4 [December 1975]: 627-46, cited at pp. 636-37). See also Francis Martin's treatment of receptivity in his contribution to this volume, "The New Feminism: Biblical Foundations and Some Lines of Development," esp. pp. 164-65.

reappraise the value of receptivity as *spiritual (or active) passivity,* so named because the powers of the human spirit are active: this experience is characterized by "an element of expectation and appeal, of acceptance and consent."[39]

While Jean Mouroux describes the authentically free person as open to the richness of the world, to others, and to God, this openness is more properly understood in terms of the communion toward which it is directed, a communion that characterizes experience itself. As defined by Mouroux, "there is experience when the person is aware of himself in relationship to the world, himself, or God. More precisely, experience is the act through which the person becomes aware of himself in relation to the world, himself, or God."[40] Here the boundaries between the experiencing subject and the experienced object are not easily distinguishable, for as Mouroux points out in this passage, one knows oneself — grasps oneself as a knowing subject and thus as a person — in the very act whereby an object is known. Self-knowledge is, in other words, mediated knowledge. The blurring of the subject-object boundary is, however, even more accented when the object of one's knowledge and experience is in fact a *subject,* that is to say, a person. The latter is really only known when — and to the extent that — he reveals himself, when he "unmasks" himself, becoming naked, as it were, before the knowing subject to whom he thereby gives himself.[41]

The opening of the self in experience is therefore only potentially receptive, which is to say that it is dependent upon an object — in this case a subject who "opens" himself in an act of self-donation. This is particularly apparent in the analogy of the intimate and mutual "knowledge" of spouses who are given to one another in love.[42] In the act of their mutual self-surrender in the sexual embrace, the man, William May explains, gives himself in a receiving sort of way, whereas the woman receives the man in a giving sort of way.[43] What is noteworthy in this analogy is not that women might be considered in terms of receptive giving and men in terms of active giving, nor that epistemological models might

39. Mouroux, p. 12.

40. Mouroux, pp. 10-11.

41. Kenneth Schmitz describes the vulnerability that accompanies the giving of any gift, not to mention one as precious as the person himself. "For when it is refused, a gift, so to speak, bends back upon the giver, leaving him exposed and wounded. . . . But there is risk to the receiver as well, who is made vulnerable by the initiative of the giver." More specifically, "In reception the receiver opens himself up to the intention of the giver and to the significance of the gift." See Kenneth L. Schmitz, *The Gift: Creation* (Milwaukee: Marquette University Press, 1982), p. 49.

42. "Adam *knew* Eve his wife, and she conceived and bore Cain, saying: 'I have begotten a man with the help of the Lord'" (Gen. 4:1).

43. See William E. May, *Marriage: The Rock on Which the Family Is Built* (San Francisco: Ignatius, 1995), pp. 48-49.

be drawn from this analogy which would attribute a different mode of thinking to women than to men. Rather, the *mutual conditioning of gift and reception,* which is particularly apparent in this vivid example, points to the mutual conditioning *of object and subject* within what I esteem an authentic epistemological model. Drawing from the analogy of marital love in the sexual embrace, we are perhaps better able to comprehend what is meant by an intimate knowledge of another person, that is to say, knowledge gained in virtue of a mutual self-gift: the knowing subject willingly gives himself as a "receptacle" for the subject who willingly reveals himself. Anything less would be, as it were, a violation of the gift: not just any gift, but a gift which is the person himself. The receptivity here in question supposes a self-gift "matching" that of him who gives himself to be known. The knowing subject ought to so give of himself as to thereby receive the other's self-gift. Authentic knowledge of persons thus supposes a *communion* comparable to that of the one-flesh union of man and wife: the man receives the woman he loves in the very act of giving himself to her; the woman gives herself to the man she loves in the very act of receiving him into herself.

This sort of *knowledge by communion,* whereby the "other" who is known is lovingly received and honored as he or she is *in truth,* is the very opposite of that which many feminists attribute to rational (Enlightenment) and "patriarchal" epistemologies: the manipulation, overpowering, dominating, or subjecting of the object known (who may in fact be a subject) to oneself and one's own interests.[44] In contrast to the abstract, autonomous knower of Cartesian rationalism and Baconian empiricism, feminist authors insist upon the engaged knower, which is to say that knowledge, as they perceive it, is never simply "neutral." Not only does this mean that praxis should be joined to theory,[45] but also

---

44. Caroline Whitbeck, for example, contrasts the self-other *relation* of feminist thought with the self-other *opposition* typifying male thought. See Whitbeck, "A Different Reality: Feminist Ontology," in *Beyond Domination: New Perspectives on Women and Philosophy,* ed. Carol C. Gould (Rowman and Allanheld, 1984), pp. 64-88. See also Evelyn Fox Keller, *Reflections on Gender and Science* (New Haven: Yale University Press, 1984); Sandra Harding, *The Science Question in Feminism* (Ithaca, N.Y.: Cornell University Press, 1986); Susan Bordo, *The Flight to Objectivity: Essays on Cartesianism and Culture* (New York: State University of New York Press, 1987).

45. See, for example, Mary M. Solberg, *Compelling Knowledge: A Feminist Proposal for an Epistemology of the Cross* (Albany: State University of New York Press, 1997); Pamela Dickey Young, *Feminist Theology/Christian Theology: In Search of Method* (Minneapolis: Fortress, 1990); Grace M. Jantzen, *Power, Gender, and Christian Mysticism* (Cambridge: Cambridge University Press, 1995); Marcella Althaus-Reid, "The Indecency of Her Teaching: Notes for a *Cuceb* Teaching of Feminist Theology in Europe," in *Feminist Theology in Different Contexts,* ed. Elisabeth Schüssler Fiorenza and M. Shawn Copeland (London: SCM Press, 1996) (*Concilium* 1996/1), pp. 133-40. Similarly, Elizabeth Schüssler Fiorenza argues that an important assumption of liberation theology is that "all theology, knowingly or not, is by definition always engaged for or

that knowledge is not universal according to the male standard.[46] Emphasizing
the passivity and manipulability of the objects of knowledge, "malestream"
epistemology, as Rebecca Chopp calls it,[47] tends to distort and immobilize human subjects "when they occupy the place of the 'objects' studied." Women, for
example, "too often live as self-fulfilling prophecies, adhering to the restricted
options constructed for them by experts who," Lorraine Code explains, "claim
to know them better than they could hope to know themselves."[48] In this is particularly apparent the ideological tendencies of this patriarchal epistemology
which oppresses those who do not "meet the mold." Created by a certain group
of privileged white men to reflect their own limited manner of thinking, it has
also, the argument continues, been created *for* them: to serve their ideology. It
is, more specifically, in the interest of this select group of men "to perpetuate
the 'natural' recognition that women, and persons of colour, are irrational,
weak in the mind, too dependent, and incapable of abstract thought."[49] Far
from universal and objective, knowledge is thus, many feminists maintain, historical, related to power and interests, and thus open to change and transformation.[50] Current scientific practices, for example, are so influenced by patriarchy that they actually perpetuate "androcentric values."

---

against the oppressed" (*Bread Not Stone: The Challenge of Feminist Biblical Interpretation*
[Boston: Beacon Press, 1984], p. 45).

46. Hence the need, as E. A. Grosz expresses it, to openly admit the *"masculinity of
knowledges"* so as "to clear a space within the 'universal' and to reclaim women's places in it"
(Grosz, "The In(ter)vention of Feminist Knowledges," in *Crossing Boundaries: Feminisms and
the Critique of Knowledges,* ed. Barbara Caine, E. A. Grosz, and Marie Lepervanche [Boston and
London: Allen and Unwin, 1988], pp. 92-104, cited at p. 97). Similarly, Susan Bordo argues that
"Feminism, in exposing the *gendered* nature of Western thought, has contributed significantly
to intellectually dismantling the Enlightenment mythology of abstract, universal man and its
epistemological corollary of an abstract, universal reason. There is no 'view from nowhere,'
feminists have insisted; all thought is socially located" (Bordo, "Feminist Skepticism and the
'Maleness' of Philosophy," in *Women and Reason,* ed. Elizabeth D. Harvey and Kathleen
Okruhlik [Ann Arbor: University of Michigan Press, 1992], pp. 143-162, cited at p. 159).

47. Rebecca Chopp, "Eve's Knowing: Feminist Theology's Resistance to Malestream
Epistemological Frameworks," *Concilium* (1996): 116-23, p. 117.

48. Lorraine Code, "The Unicorn in the Garden," in *Women and Reason,* pp. 263-82, cited
at pp. 263-65.

49. Chopp, p. 117. See also Lesley J. Rogers, "Biology, the Popular Weapon: Sex Differences in Cognitive Function," in *Feminisms and the Critique of Knowledges,* pp. 43-51.

50. Susan Hekman ("The Feminization of Epistemology: Gender and the Social Sciences,"
in *Feminism and Epistemology: Approaches to Research in Women and Politics,* ed. Maria J. Falco
[New York and London: Haworth Press, 1987], pp. 65-83) notes a striking similarity in the social
sciences between feminism and antifoundationalism in their common attack upon the rationalist epistemology of the Enlightenment, particularly with regard to the dualisms on which that
epistemology rests (rational/irrational; subject/object), dualisms which are regarded by feminists

From this it is hardly surprising that many feminists refuse analogies which describe women's thinking in terms of their bodily structures.[51] Such reasoning — which arguably demonstrates the fallacy of patriarchy's "superrational" logic — tends to marginalize women in a world of clichés, denying them equal opportunities for education, work, etc. On the other hand, many feminists argue that women have somehow managed to escape the object-subject dualism characterizing Enlightenment thought. Theirs is a more unified or integral knowing based not so much, of course, on a different, specifically feminine "essence"[52] as on certain experiences common to women, especially women living under patriarchy: the experiences, for example, of reproduction;[53] of raising children or of being raised to be a mother;[54] of performing tasks which require a certain attentiveness to the sensual, concrete, and rela-

---

as derivative of the fundamental male/female dualism. The problem, as Hekman conceives it, lies not merely in what she objects to as essentialism, but also in the misconception of knowledge according to the rationalist mode. Like antifoundationalists, she argues that "human understanding involves the 'fusing of horizons,' that is, the merging of the perspectives of knower and known that repudiates the opposition on which Enlightenment epistemology is based" (p. 70). Knowledge is not, she insists, "abstract, absolute and divorced from emotion, intuition and feeling. Rather it is relational, contextual and grounded in particular historical societies" (p. 72). For a good summary of the various feminist positions, see chap. 9 of Elaine Graham, *Making the Difference: Gender, Personhood, and Theology* (Minneapolis: Fortress, 1996), pp. 192-213.

51. A similar move is made in arguing from biology to archetype. See the critique of Yvonne Pelle-Douel, *Être femme* (Paris: Editions du Seuil, 1967), esp. p. 38.

52. To be sure, certain — especially French — feminists do make the connection between the distinctiveness of women's thought patterns and their unique psychosomatic structures. See Elaine Marks and Isabelle de Courtivron, *New French Feminism* (New York: Schocken Books, 1981). Some feminists point out that attribution of a relational mode of thinking to women comes "dangerously" close to arguing for an essential feminine nature. See, for example, Sally Alsford, "Women's Nature and the Feminization of Theology," in *Is There a Future for Feminist Theology?* ed. Deborah F. Sawyer and Diane M. Collier (Sheffield: Sheffield Academic Press, 1999), pp. 126-38; Susan Parsons, "The Dilemma of Difference: A Feminist Theological Exploration," *Feminist Theology* 14 (January 1997): 51-72. See also the objection of Elisabeth Schüssler-Fiorenza, "G*d at Work in Our Midst: From a Politics of Identity to a Politics of Struggle," *Feminist Theology* 14 (1997): 203-10.

53. See Mary O'Brien, *The Politics of Reproduction* (London and New York: Routledge and Kegan Paul, 1981).

54. See Nancy Chodorow, *The Reproduction of Mothering: Psychoanalysis and the Sociology of Gender* (Berkeley and Los Angeles: University of California Press, 1978); Dorothy Dinnerstein, *The Mermaid and the Minotaur* (New York: Harper and Row, 1977); Jane Flax, "The Conflict between Nurturance and Autonomy in Mother-Daughter Relationships and within Feminism," *Feminist Studies* 4 (1978): 171-92; Luise Eichenbaum and Susie Orbach, "The Construction of Femininity," in *Women's Spirituality: Resources for Christian Development*, ed. Joann Wolski Conn (New York and Mahwah, N.J.: Paulist, 1986), pp. 128-49; Sara Ruddick, "Maternal Thinking," *Feminist Studies* 6 (1980): 342-67.

tional;[55] or of living under oppression and struggling against the prevailing order.[56]

Although some feminists caution against using experience as the basis for a feminist epistemology[57] — especially one which would substitute itself for rationalist epistemologies more commonly attributed to men — many insist on the importance, for both men and women, of a more experimental epistemology than patriarchy has been able or willing to offer. The models are varied, but the common idea of bringing into unison the subject and object in the intellectual enterprise is constant. Hence we have what Sara Ruddick calls "maternal thinking," what Susan Bordo refers to as "sympathetic thinking" with reference to the medieval notion of "participating consciousness," what Evelyn Fox Keller has termed "dynamic objectivity," what Carol Gilligan and Nel Noddings refer to as "care" thinking, and what Nona Lyons has called the thinking of the "connected self," an idea similar to that of Nancy Chodorow, who attributes to girls a sense of "empathy" whereby they perceive themselves as continuous with the external object-world.[58]

The crucial point in this argument is not that women think differently than men, nor even that feminism has advanced a powerful critique of modern notions of rationality, especially as targeting the "three fatal separations" noted by David Tracy: thought separated from feeling and experience, content separated from form, and theory separated from practice.[59] More importantly for

---

55. See Nancy Harstock, "The Feminist Standpoint: Developing a Ground for a Specifically Feminist Historical Materialism," in *Discovering Reality and Feminist Perspectives on Epistemology, Metaphysics, and Methodology and Philosophy of Science,* ed. Sandra Harding and Merrill B. Hintikka (Dordrecht, Boston, and London: D. Reidel, 1983), pp. 157-80; Hilary Rose, "Hand, Brain and Heart: A Feminist Epistemology for the Natural Sciences," *Signs* 9 (1983): 73-90.

56. See Jean Baker Miller, *Toward a New Psychology of Women* (Boston: Beacon Press, 1976); Alison Jaggar, *Feminist Politics and Human Nature* (Totowa, N.J.: Rowman and Allanheld, 1983).

57. See, for example, Judith Grant, "I Feel Therefore I Am: A Critique of Female Experience as the Basis for a Feminist Epistemology," in *Feminism and Epistemology,* pp. 99-114; Sheila Greeve Davaney, "The Limits of the Appeal to Women's Experience," in *Shaping New Vision,* pp. 31-49.

58. Ruddick, "Maternal Thinking"; Bordo, *The Flight to Objectivity;* Keller, *Reflections on Gender and Science;* Carol Gilligan, *In a Different Voice: Psychological Theory and Women's Development* (Cambridge, Mass., and London: Harvard University Press, 1982); Gilligan, ed., *Mapping the Moral Domain* (Cambridge, Mass., and London: Harvard University Press, 1988); Nel Noddings, *Caring: Feminine Approach to Ethics* (Berkeley: University of California Press, 1984); Nona Plessner Lyons, "Two Perspectives: On Self, Relationships, and Morality," in *Mapping the Moral Domain,* pp. 21-48; Chodorow, esp. p. 167.

59. David Tracy, "Concilium Round Table: The Impact of Feminist Theologies on Roman Catholic Theology," in *Feminist Theology in Different Contexts,* pp. 90-97, cited at p. 91.

our purposes is the fact that feminist thought has, at least in a limited way, advocated the reunification of subject and object in epistemological models. To the extent that it has, it concurs with what I will present as necessary to an authentic epistemology of faith.

Knowledge of God as an Experience of Faith

If the importance of preserving the subjectivity of a person who is the object of another's knowing is evident in the foregoing, it is more apparent still in our *knowledge of God by faith*. This supposes, of course, that what is known by faith is not simply a doctrine but a person, not simply a word *from* God but the very Word *of* God (cf. John 1:14) who reveals the Father in giving himself as "bread of life for the world" (John 6:35). "In giving us his Son, his only Word (for he possesses no other), he [the Father] spoke everything to us at once in this sole Word — and he has no more to say . . . because what he spoke before to the prophets in parts, he has now spoken all at once by giving us the All Who is His Son. Any person questioning God or desiring some vision or revelation," continues Saint John of the Cross, "would be guilty not only of foolish behavior but also of offending him, by not fixing his eyes entirely upon Christ and by living with the desire for some other novelty."[60] Faith too must therefore be understood as something more than a creedal statement or a list of propositions for belief when these are not understood as directly implicating the believer, even to the extent that he or she be willing to witness *(martyrion)* unto death. Radical as martyrdom might appear, in certain circumstances it may be the only adequate expression of faithfulness: it is a logical consequence of the gift of self implied in our profession of faith. This profession, which is made with the heart as well as the lips, is a response to God's faithfulness, a gift of self to the God who gives nothing less than his own self, and this to the bitter end. "Faith is never a mere intellectual assent," explains the Orthodox theologian Paul Evdokimov,

> but a fidelity of the person to the Person. When I love and give myself totally, I do something entirely different from submitting myself. I listen to the voice of my own depth; all worlds converge into it and speak to me — and the question of "submission" no longer applies. Christ does not submit Himself to the Law; He fulfills it. By accomplishing it, He transforms it. . . .

60. John of the Cross, *The Ascent of Mount Carmel* 2, 22; cited by the *Catechism of the Catholic Church*, #65.

by pronouncing my *fiat,* I identify with the beloved being. The divine will becomes mine, and wells up from my own will; "The life I live is not my life; but the life which Christ lives in me" (Gal 2:20). What God demands of man is the fulfillment of the Father's will as if it were our own will. This is the meaning of the words: "you must be perfect as your heavenly Father is perfect" (Mt 5:40).[61]

Significant to this understanding of faith is not only the fact that the cognitive aspect must be united to the volitional one,[62] but also that *both* these subjective aspects of faith are dependent upon an objective one. Our faith in God and our *faith*fulness to God is never a human initiative but a response to his abiding presence within us. This, explains Edward Malatesta in reference to Johannine theology, is, in turn, "not a reward given for our obedience; it is rather a source of this obedience. Because He first takes the initiative to enter into personal communion with us, we are drawn to reply and to continue to reply through fidelity to His work with loving devotion to His person."[63] "If man — like everything — is created in the Word, it follows," Hans Urs von Balthasar reasons, "that the word-dimension is part of man's being, not only the interpersonal word, but also the answer to the Word who was in the beginning. . . . In Jesus Christ this word is addressed to us articulately and in a way we simply cannot avoid hearing, and it also liberates us and empowers us to give answer."[64] Our ability to recognize God's Word is — like the word of Scripture and the Word expressed in Scripture — God's gift: the gift of faith. It follows that one *cannot clearly distinguish faith as God's gift from faith as our response,* God's coming to us from our coming to God. Certainly the scholastic distinction between objective and subjective redemption remains useful for pointing out both the giftedness of faith and the necessity of our response to and reception of God's gifts by faith.[65] Human and divine action are, however, so united in any act of faith as to remain indistinguishable, humanly speaking. A sound epistemology of faith thus implies a commingling of divine and hu-

61. Paul Evdokimov, *Woman and the Salvation of the World: A Christian Anthropology on the Charisms of Women,* trans. Anthony P. Gythiel (Crestwood, N.Y.: St. Vladimir's Seminary Press, 1994), p. 51.

62. See Jean Borella, *The Sense of the Supernatural,* trans. G. John Champoux (Edinburgh: T. & T. Clark, 1998), chap. 1.

63. Edward Malatesta, *Interiority and Covenant,* Analecta Biblica Investigationes Scientificae in Res Biblicas, no. 69 (Rome: Pontifical Biblical Institute, 1978), p. 274.

64. Hans Urs von Balthasar, *Theo-Drama: Theological Dramatic Theory,* vol. 2, *Dramatic Personae: Man in God,* trans. Graham Harrison (San Francisco: Ignatius, 1990), p. 73.

65. "To all who received him, who believed in his name, he gave the power to become children of God" (John 1:12).

man persons: the participation of the human being in God's own engagement in human history.[66]

Even in the Old Testament, to *know* that Yahweh is God is to *experience* his divinity present in both his words and actions and to acknowledge it.[67] The God who has manifested his saving power to the patriarchs is known "for all time" and "for all generations" as "the God of your fathers, the God of Abraham, the God of Isaac, and the God of Jacob" (Exod. 3:15). To proclaim his name is to tell of his greatness (cf. Deut. 32:3), to recall what he *did* (created you, made you, established you, v. 6), to acknowledge what he *does* (adopts, protects, v. 10), and to foretell what he *will do* (avenge blood, v. 43). All three dimensions of time (past, present, future) are implied by the divine name "I AM" (Exod. 3:14; cf. Rev. 1:8, 17; 4:8; etc.). If, then, Israel is told to remember the saving deeds of the Lord — such as the great Passover (Deut. 16:3) — and not to forget these in times of prosperity (cf. Deut. 4:9; 6:12; 8:11; etc.), this recollection, this acknowledgment and this act of faith, are in view of her (Israel's) response: her faith in Yahweh is expressed as *faithfulness* to the covenant the Lord initiates on her behalf.[68] Because, more specifically, Yahweh made of Israel a people in bringing her out of Egypt,[69] she in turn is commanded to acknowledge him as her one and only God (Deut. 5:6-8). This is the first and most important commandment, from which the others proceed as a commentary of what it means

66. This is, for example, the central insight of Hans Urs von Balthasar's five-volume work *Theo-Drama: Theological Dramatic Theory* (San Francisco: Ignatius, 1973-98).

67. John McKenzie notes the following examples: "Know therefore this day, and lay it to your heart, that the LORD is God in heaven above and on the earth beneath; there is no other" (Deut. 4:39); "Know then in your heart that, as a man disciplines his son, the LORD your God disciplines you" (8:5); "'You are my witnesses,' says the LORD, / 'and my servant whom I have chosen, / that you may know and believe me / and understand that I am He. / Before me no god was formed, / nor shall there be any after me'" (Isa. 43:10); etc. McKenzie, *Dictionary of the Bible* (New York: Collier Books and Macmillan Publishing Company, 1965), p. 486.

68. "You have seen all that the LORD did before your eyes in the land of Egypt, to Pharaoh and to all his servants and to all his land, the great trials which your eyes saw, the signs, and those great wonders; but to this day the LORD has not given you a mind to understand, or eyes to see, or ears to hear. I have led you forty years in the wilderness; your clothes have not worn out upon you, and your sandals have not worn off your feet. . . . You stand this day all of you before the LORD your God . . . that you may enter into the sworn covenant of the LORD your God, which the LORD your God makes with you this day; that he may establish you this day as his people, and that he may be your God, as he promised you, and as he swore to your fathers" (Deut. 29:2-5, 10a, 12-13).

69. Yahweh said, "I will be your God; you will be my people." Henceforth they are *his* people (Deut. 29:13; Lev. 7:27), *thy* people Israel (Deut. 21:8; 26:15-18), *your* people (i.e., the people of the Lord) (Exod. 4:21), *my* people (as proclaimed by the Lord: Exod. 3:10; 5:1; 6:7, 26; 7:16; 8:1; 9:1; etc.).

to have this privileged relationship with Yahweh, of what it means to have invested one's faith in the Faithful One of Israel.

Israel's faith in Yahweh is thus expressed as obedience *(fidelity)* to his commandments (cf. Num. 15:40), but more than this it requires — and this is the purpose of the commandments themselves — her transformation in his likeness. To be God's "holy people" means to be *like* the Holy One of Israel, to be assimilated to him.[70] To follow Yahweh by faith into the desert is but a preparation for following in his ways: *being faithful as he is faithful.*[71] As Yahweh, for example, has acted mercifully on Israel's behalf, she is to act mercifully toward the orphan and the widow, the stranger and the slave.[72] To be faithful to the Law is to internalize it — that it abide in one's heart and in one's soul — wherefrom it gives rise to actions like those of Yahweh.[73] In all that one thinks and does, this Law should have a determining influence, even to the point of being "incarnated" in one's very self. "For this law which I enjoin on you today is not beyond your strength or beyond your reach. It is not in heaven, so that you need to wonder, 'Who will go up to heaven for us and bring it down to us, so that we may hear it and keep it?' . . . No, the word is very near to you, it is in your mouth and in your heart for your observance" (Deut. 30:11-12, 14).

If already in the Old Testament the people of Yahweh experience his power and presence through the "possession" of his word within their hearts, in the New Testament the Christian is actually given "the mind of Christ" (1 Cor. 2:16)[74] in whom this "word" (Law) is fulfilled (Matt. 5:17); for in him "all the promises of God find their Yes" (2 Cor. 1:20). "What person knows a man's thoughts except the spirit of the man which is in him? So also no one compre-

---

70. "Be holy, for I am holy" (Lev. 11:44; 19:2; 20:7; 1 Pet. 1:16; cf. Matt. 5:48); "For you are a people holy to the LORD" (Deut. 7:6; 14:2, 21; 28:9).

71. "Remember how Yahweh your God led you for 40 years in the wilderness, to humble you, to test you and know your inmost heart — whether you would keep his commandments or not. He humbled you, he made you feel hunger, he fed you with manna which neither you nor your fathers had known, to make you understand that man does not live on bread alone but that man lives on everything that comes from the mouth of Yahweh. The clothes on your back did not wear out and your feet were not swollen all those forty years. Learn from this that Yahweh your *God was training you as a man trains his child* and keep the commandments of Yahweh your God, and so follow his ways and reverence him" (Deut. 8:2-6).

72. See, for example, Deut. 10:12-20; Exod. 22:21; 23:9; Deut. 15:12-15; 24:6-22; Lev. 25:35-55.

73. This is the meaning of the command, for example, to "fasten these words on your hand as a sign and on your forehead as a circlet" (Deut. 11:18): on the hand they guard over one's action, on the forehead they guard over one's thoughts, knowledge, and plans.

74. McKenzie (p. 487) recognizes in the phrase "mind of God" "more His intention and will than His knowledge in the intellectual sense." Cf. Rom. 11:34: "For who has known the mind of the Lord, / or who has been his counselor?" and 1 Cor. 2:16: "For who has known the mind of the Lord so as to instruct him?"

hends the thoughts of God except the Spirit of God." We have received this Spirit, "that we might understand the gifts bestowed on us by God" (1 Cor. 2:11, 12b). Balthasar recognizes in the one "mind" of Christ, as it is here presented by Paul, "both the objective meaning [*Sinn*] of his figure (which in turn is God's mind/meaning) and the subjective spirit which governs Christ, i.e., the Holy Spirit, who although divine, is given to the believer so that he may understand."[75] This "Spirit of truth" who reveals the meaning of revelation is himself known to the disciples by his abiding presence within them (John 14:17). *To know God* is, from a biblical perspective, *to possess his Spirit,* but in such a way as *to be assimilated to him* by the power of this same Spirit: "And we all, with unveiled face, beholding the glory of the Lord, are being changed into his likeness from one degree of glory to another; for this comes from the Lord who is the Spirit" (2 Cor. 3:18). As a result of the divine indwelling, faith and charity become a way of life, a permanent disposition for the Christian. His knowledge of God grows with his love of God: God's own love poured forth into his heart (Rom. 5:5; cf. 2 Cor. 1:22) and "made perfect in him" (1 John 2:5; cf. 4:12). The one who loves is thus, from a Johannine perspective, "born of God and knows God." He, on the other hand, "who does not love does not know God; for God is love" (4:7-8). "So we *know and believe* the love God has for us. God is love, and he who *abides in love* abides in God, and God abides in him" (4:16).

To "know" God, biblically speaking, is thus much more than a theoretical knowledge of his existence. The distinction, common to Western philosophy, between the appetitive and intellectual powers is unknown to Hebrew thought,[76] with the result that *knowledge,* from a scriptural perspective, is *more experiential* than that to which we are perhaps accustomed. The New Testament tradition, borrowing from Greek thought and culture, does distinguish between that knowledge which, for example, concerns certain indisputable facts of our profession of faith (the Greek verb *oida,*[77] corresponding to the French

75. Hans Urs von Balthasar, *Does Jesus Know Us — Do We Know Him?* trans. Graham Harrison (San Francisco: Ignatius, 1983), p. 96. "In that sense," Balthasar continues, "the believer 'has' him."

76. This is particularly evident in that the heart is used to refer to the mind or intellect as well as to the will. It is used to express emotions (1 Sam. 2:1; Gen. 45:26; Ps. 40:13), to scheme (Prov. 6:18; 16:9), to discern (1 Kings 3:12), to desire (Deut. 15:9). Similarly in the New Testament: "For from within, out of the *heart* of man, come evil thoughts" (Mark 7:21; cf. Luke 6:45); "Each one must do as he has made up his mind" *(kardia)* (2 Cor. 9:7); "Settle it therefore in your minds *(kardia),* not to meditate beforehand how to answer" (Luke 21:14); "having the eyes of your *hearts* enlightened" (Eph. 1:18). "A man is what his heart is, and heart is used to designate the character," summarizes McKenzie (p. 344).

77. "Know, understand, perceive (. . . Eph. 5:5) experience, learn, know how; be acquainted with, recognize, acknowledge; remember (1 Cor. 1:16); pay proper respect to (1 Thess.

verb *savoir,* the Spanish *saber,* the German *wissen*) and that which concerns our life of faith (*ginōskein,*[78] corresponding to the French verb *connaître,* the Spanish *conocer,* the German *kennen*). The Hebrew influence nonetheless prevailed in New Testament thought, with the result that "to know God" *implies a "living union"* with him. Particularly in the perfect tense (as, for example, in 1 John 2:3, 12, 14: "to have known God"), it means "to have God" or *to have "community with God."* God cannot be appropriated, Balthasar explains, for he is "personified handing-over, and one 'knows' him and 'possesses' him only when one is oneself expropriated and handed over."[79]

The simultaneity of "appropriation" of God and expropriation of self accounts for the "exchangeable formulae" of Paul, who mentions both that "Christ [is] in me" or "in us" (Gal. 2:19f.; 4:9; Rom. 8:9-11; 2 Cor. 4:16; 13:2-5) and that we are, or live, or are found "in Christ" (Rom. 8:1; Gal. 3:2b; Phil. 3:9; etc.). The latter expression refers to the cause; the former to the effect; "but 'Christ in us' expresses," Balthasar argues, "the essential result of his mission." Christ has left Paul "intact as a conscious subject," but "he has also expropriated him in order to *personalize* him."[80] Similar to these expressions is the "mystical genitive" conveyed by the Pauline formula "faith of Christ Jesus" (Gal. 2:16, 20; 3:22; Eph. 3:12; Phil. 3:9; Rom. 3:22, 26) which, Balthasar argues, is not simply an objective genitive by which is meant faith whose "object" is Christ. This, Balthasar argues, is evident in that Paul is careful to employ the formula (in the dative) "faith in Christ Jesus" (Gal. 3:25; 5:6; Col. 1:15; 1 Tim. 1:14; 3:13: 3:15). Nor should it be interpreted simply as a subjective genitive by which it would be understood as Christ's own act of faith. Rather, the mystical sense assigned to this phrase by Balthasar and the authors he cites conveys the meaning of "faith *within* the reality of Christ, faith that as such shares in the fullness of the truth, the love, the action, the suffering, and the Resurrection of Christ and in all the

---

5:12)." Hence: "I write to you, not because you do not know *(oidate)* the truth, but because you know *(oidate)* it, and know *(oidate)* that no lie is of the truth" (1 John 2:21); "You know *(oidate)* that he appeared to take away sins, and in him there is no sin" (3:5); etc. See Barclay Newman, Jr., *A Concise Greek-English Dictionary of the New Testament* (London: United Bible Societies, 1971), p. 123.

78. "Know, have knowledge of (of sexual relations, Matt. 1:25; Luke 1:34); find out, learn, understand; perceive, discern; to have knowledge; acknowledge, recognize; *impv.* be very certain, remember." Hence, for example: "I write to you, fathers, because you know *(egnōkate)* him who is from the beginning . . ." (1 John 2:13, 14); "So we know *(egnōkamen)* and believe the love God has for us" (1 John 4:16). Newman, p. 37.

79. Hans Urs von Balthasar, *The Glory of the Lord: A Theological Aesthetics,* vol. 7, *Theology: The New Covenant,* trans. Brian McNeil, ed. John Riches (San Francisco: Ignatius, 1989), p. 400.

80. Hans Urs von Balthasar, *Theo-Drama: Theological Dramatic Theory,* vol. 3, *Dramatis Personae: Persons in Christ,* trans. Graham Harrison (San Francisco: Ignatius, 1992), p. 247.

other aspects of his reality and indeed is made possible by them."[81] The *en* of the formula "in Christ" thus "becomes *syn,* a participation in Christ's dying and rising and in his work *(synergoi)."*[82]

So it is with our knowledge of God. The effect, or consequence, of his abiding within us, this knowledge is more properly *his knowledge of us* than our knowledge of him: "if one loves God, one is known by him" (1 Cor. 8:3).[83] This, then, is a *mutual knowledge* foreshadowing the glory awaiting the faithful: "I shall understand fully, even as I have been fully understood" (1 Cor. 13:12b). Here Paul equates final knowledge of God with "being known by God; in the sense of John's immanence-formulas, the unmediated indwelling of mutual, loving insight."[84] Comparable to the mutual knowledge of the Son and the Father,[85] the mutual knowledge of the believer and God is in fact a *participation* in the knowledge that the divine persons have of one another: "No one knows the Son except the Father, and no one knows the Father except the Son and any one to whom the Son chooses to reveal him" (Matt. 11:27; Luke 10:22).[86]

Simply stated, that faith which has God as its object is a supernatural participation in God's own knowledge.[87] As such, it supposes that the believer has given himself without reserve so as to be filled with God's own Spirit who knows and loves within him. "To know as one is known," explains McKenzie, "is to accept God with the same totality with which God accepts the believer. The perfection of knowledge and the perfection of love merge into one; to

81. Hans Urs von Balthasar, *"Fides Christi:* An Essay on the Consciousness of Christ," trans. Edward T. Oakes, in *Spouse of the Word,* vol. 2 of *Explorations in Theology* (San Francisco: Ignatius, 1991), pp. 43-79 (cited at p. 58). Similar to the Pauline teaching is that of John the Evangelist, who "does not speak from the position of the human person who is required to give himself because he has been loved beforehand by God in Christ (Gal. 2:20); he speaks from the position of God himself, who is love that flows out to men in his Son: Man is required to fit himself into the rhythm of this movement" (Balthasar, *Glory,* 7:454).

82. Balthasar, *Theo-Drama,* 3:247.

83. Similarly, "you have come to know God, or rather to be known by God" (Gal. 4:9).

84. Balthasar, *Does Jesus Know Us?* p. 55.

85. "I am the good shepherd; I know my own and my own know me, as the Father knows me and I know the Father" (John 10:14-15).

86. Similarly, "I have given them the words which thou gavest me, and they have received them and know in truth that I came from thee; and they have believed that thou didst send me" (John 17:8). "Now the ultimate inner mystery of the Godhead, the mutual indwelling of the divine hypostases (an indwelling in which knowledge and love are no longer distinguishable), is revealed," Balthasar argues, "in the mutual unity of Jesus and men. From now on this divine unity — far beyond the mere Creator-creature relationship we find in the Psalms — will be the measure of and the ontological basis for the loving mutuality of knowing and being known" (*Does Jesus Know Us?* p. 52).

87. See *Summa theologica* II-II, q.45, a.1. Also see again 1 Cor. 2:11-12.

know fully one must choose without reservation."[88] In the final analysis, the believer's knowledge of God — like his love of God — is God's own knowledge[89] as shared through participation: knowledge which is given to the believer to the extent that he or she has made "room" within himself or herself for this divine gift. Analogical to the incarnation of the Word in the Virgin's womb is the reception of God's Word in the believer whereby he or she is transformed according to the likeness of God in whose image he or she was created. "God became man so that man might become God,"[90] Augustine fittingly proclaims. Similarly, Gregory of Nyssa explains that Jesus is born within believers, advancing "by different ways in those who receive him in wisdom, in age, and in grace. He is not the same in every person, but is present according to the measure of the person receiving him."[91] Through faith the experience of the self expands, Balthasar explains, "to an experience that encompasses both oneself and the other — oneself and the burgeoning Word of God, which at first seems to be growing in the self until in this growth it becomes evident that it is rather the other way around and that it is the self that is contained in the Word of God."[92]

Sensus Fidei and *Sensus Fidelium*: The Communal Experience of Faith

The convergence of the objective and subjective dimensions of faith in a relationship of *mutual immanence between the Word and the Christian* — in the simultaneous growth of the Word in the believer and of the believer in the Word — gives rise to what has traditionally been referred to as *sensus fidei*, the (subjective) "sense" of faith whereby the Christian may be said to "intuit" what is and what is not of the (objective) faith. An experiential type of knowledge characteristic of lovers, this may also be described as knowledge by affinity[93] or,

---

88. McKenzie, p. 487.

89. Or love, as the case may be, although the two remain inseparable.

90. "Factus est Deus homo ut homo fieret Deus" (Augustine of Hippo, *Sermo* 128, *Patrologia Latina* [hereafter *PL*], 39, col. 1997).

91. Third Homily in his *Commentary on the Song of Songs*, trans. Casimir McCambley (Brookline, Mass.: Hellenic College Press, 1987), pp. 86-87 (*Patrologia Graeca*, 44:828D).

92. Hans Urs von Balthasar, *The Glory of the Lord: A Theological Aesthetics*, vol. 1, *Seeing the Form*, trans. Erasmo Leiva-Merikakis, ed. Joseph Fessio and John Riches (San Francisco: Ignatius, 1982), p. 339.

93. In this type of knowledge "the heart precedes the intelligence," Jean-Pierre Torrell explains, whereby it is "infinitely richer and more precious" than that knowledge which is achieved by general ideas (Torrell, "Dimension ecclésiale de l'expérience chrétienne," *Freiburger Zeitschrift für Philosophie und Theologie* 28 [1981]: 3-35, cited at p. 18; see also p. 20).

more properly, by connaturality, for the faith of the one possessing it is informed by charity and governed by the gifts of the Holy Spirit. Hence the more intense the spiritual life of the believer, the sharper and more penetrating is his sense of faith.

Similar to this intuitive knowledge of faith but different in a very significant way, so as to be complementary, is *sensus fidelium:* what Jean-Pierre Torrell refers to as "the statistic expression (that is to say exteriorly manifest and thus somehow verifiable and measurable) of the theological experience of the believing community."[94] This important distinction between the individual's sense of faith and that which is predicated to the ecclesial community as a whole *(sensu fidei totius populi)* manifests, once again, a certain convergence between the subjective and objective dimensions of this faith. This convergence is complemented by a relationship of *mutual immanence between the church and her members.* The individual's faith is, more specifically, incited by that of the community that actually introduces her members into her "own" faith. This, on the other hand, is so internalized by the individual that he too can call it his own. In this sense the individual's faith *is* the church's faith,[95] which does not deny that he or she really does have something to contribute to it. The church's faith is, as it were, "enriched" by the particular faith experiences of each of her members. These provide additional "perspective,"[96] a sort of commentary on the faith by which it is understandable and visible for the world. There is thus a certain gain in the depth or insight of the faith without there being an increase in its "content."

The individual who has received from the vast treasury of the community's experience of faith is himself therefore really capable of contributing to it.[97] The same disposition — which is none other than faith — whereby he or she is receptive of the faith of Christ and his church is that by which he also me-

---

94. Torrell, p. 23.

95. On this see Avery Dulles, "The Ecclesial Dimension of Faith," *Communio* 22 (Fall 1995): 418-32.

96. Helpful for our purpose here is the distinction made by Father Francis Martin between *aspect* and *profile* as, respectively, that which can and that which cannot be shared in a common experience. "If God reveals himself to me in some similar way, or if I suffer in some similar way, there can be an overlap of aspect in our experiences, even though there can never be an overlap of profile." See Martin, *The Feminist Question*, p. 193.

97. Of course, my own experiences are differently received and communicated by the church than are those of Abraham, Moses, and the prophets, for example; different too from those of the virgin Mary and the apostles. Their experiences actually form part of the deposit of revelation which is "closed" with the death of the last apostle. Nonetheless, there is a real sense in which the believer's experience of faith is never private, but rather a communal "affair," which is to say that we always believe in communion with others.

diates this faith, offering it along with his or her own experiences of faith to others. "Simultaneously saved and savior," to borrow an expression from Saint Clement of Alexandria,[98] the person who has been expropriated for love of God is "open" to receive but also to give of his or her newfound wealth of grace. He or she does not horde the gifts he or she has been given but communicates them further in an act of generosity likened unto that of him from whom he has received them. Faith is "kept" only when it is given away; for, as the beautiful prayer of Saint Francis teaches, it is in giving that we receive. And to this we might add that it is in receiving that we are enabled to give; for Christian love is Christ's own love poured into our hearts, and our faith in him is in fact the faith that he himself gives us: a divine *habitus*.

In this sense it is true to say both that the church "creates" her members and that they, in turn, "create" the church, for both acts are accomplished under the influence and by the power of the same Spirit. It is into the church's faith that the individual is baptized, but this same faith is enriched and nourished by the individual's partaking thereof, by his or her adhering and sustaining of ecclesial faith. The community of believers who has "an anointing that comes from the holy one" (cf. 1 John 2:20 and 27) such that it "cannot err in matters of belief,"[99] the church does not merely hand on the faith she has received from the Lord; she lives it. The content of her faith which she presents to the world as believable — as worthy of faith — is that to which she has, in her members, given assent first of all. As Francis Martin puts it, "what is appropriated personally is possessed communally."[100] The so-called subjective faith of the individual believer is therefore not merely a response to the "objective" gift of revelation, it also contributes to and strengthens the objective character of this faith. The believer's "Yes" — his or her assent or accord *(Zustimmung)* to the content of the church's faith — is itself a witness to its authenticity and an invitation to others to join the community's reception of the risen Lord and his teaching. This assent is thus, more properly, a sharing in the church's consent to the Lord

98. "Ex uno et per unum et servantur et servant" (*Stromatum* 6.2; *Patrologia Graeca*, 9:414).

99. Second Vatican Council, Dogmatic Constitution on the Church, *Lumen gentium*, #12. "This characteristic is shown," the document continues, "in the supernatural appreciation of the faith of the whole people *(mediante supernaturali sensu fidei totius populi)*, when, 'from the bishops to the last of the faithful' they manifest a universal consent in matters of faith and morals. By this appreciation of the faith, aroused and sustained by the Spirit of truth, the People of God, guided by the sacred teaching authority *(magisterium)*, and obeying it, receives not the mere word of men, but truly the word of God (cf. 1 Th 2:13), the faith once for all delivered to the saints (cf. Jude 3)."

100. Martin, *The Feminist Question*, p. 3.

whereby she gives herself to him to realize his will: fiat. Because more specifically the church's faith is both her assent to the Lord and his teaching (the subjective act) as well as that which she thereby proposes as true and worthy of faith (the objective content), to be baptized into her faith is not merely a response to or an affirmation of what she judges "believable." It is more certainly a sharing in the church's own faithfulness, in her giving of herself to the Lord who has given himself to her as a bridegroom.

The believer is thus doubly receptive in faith: receptive with respect to the Lord and his teaching, of course, but also with respect to the church's faith. To grant this is not to strengthen what feminists present as a patriarchal ploy to control the minds and wills of unsuspecting women in the name of ecclesial authority. If, in fact, the believer may be said to be receptive of the church's faith, this means not only that he or she believes what the church believes, but also that he or she *believes in virtue of the church's faith:* it is she — the church, especially the church in Mary, as we shall see — who believes first of all and completely, so completely, in fact, that she thereby "opens up" a "space" into which her members are given share.[101]

Within this space we are, as it were, carried to maturity in Christ whereby we are holy according to the holiness of God and "perfect as our heavenly Father is perfect" (Matt. 5:48), which requires that we, like Mary-church, are filled with the "fulness of him who fills all in all" (Eph. 1:23). This, in turn, requires that we, too, perfectly receive him: that his wildly vulnerable gift of himself — even as a Lamb ready for the slaughter — be met, from our side, with an "equally" vulnerable openness and docility. Of course, generosity that is "prepared" to suffer the consequences of rejection does not give according to merit. The divine gift is, in other words, always total and complete. Nonetheless, it can only be *received according to* the extent of *our receptivity.* In fact, full Christian maturity supposes that our receptivity is complete, that there is no "holding back," no reservation preventing us from sharing in the holiness of the church which began with the incarnation of the Word in Mary's womb. Like the Word, we too are, as it were, carried and nourished in the "womb" of the church's faith — the faith of the communion of saints and especially of Mary — until we, like these saints, reach full "stature" in Christ (cf. Eph. 4:13); until Christ is fully formed in us (cf. Gal. 4:19), as he is in them.

101. "For in the faith of Mary, first at the Annunciation and then fully at the foot of the Cross, an *interior space* was reopened within humanity which the eternal Father can fill 'with every spiritual blessing.' It is the space of the new and eternal Covenant and it continues to exist in the Church, which in Christ is 'a kind of sacrament or sign of intimate union with God, and of the unity of all mankind.'" (John Paul II, encyclical letter on the mother of the Redeemer, *Redemptoris mater,* March 25, 1987, #28).

This is not to say that the church's assent takes the place of our own; for, as we have seen, there is a true converging of the individual's faith with that of the community in what might be considered a relationship of mutual immanence. The faith of each really strengthens the other without denying that the church's faith is more fundamental than the individual's: except, of course, in the case of the faith of the virgin mother of God, in whom the biblical figure of Daughter Zion is fulfilled. Because, as Saint Thomas teaches,[102] Mary's assent was sought on behalf of all humanity, she, the new Eve, is also the first "cell" of the church. In her is complete the convergence of the individual and the church, for in her the "measure" of Christ's total gift of self is met by an "equal" measure of total receptivity. The Virgin's fiat — "Behold the handmaid of the Lord"[103] — fully "corresponds" to the oblation of divine love: "a body you have prepared for me . . . 'Lo, I have come to do your will, O God'" (Heb. 10:5, 7). The Spirit's action of forming the body of Christ within her womb is thus "matched" by that of preparing her heart to receive him. Birth from God converges with birth from God's people. The gift of herself "enabling" God to fill her with himself,[104] Mary's faith is simultaneously maternal self-giving and bridal (covenantal) consent: she, Saint Augustine teaches, conceives Christ in her faith before she conceives him in her womb.[105] "By faith she believes; by faith she conceives."[106]

In the Virgin's faith is thereby manifest not only that faith has a concrete dimension whereby "words" become visible in actions, but also that one never believes for oneself alone. As Christ shares his Sonship with us, Mary shares her own maternal partaking in the divine communion, her own experience of faith. There is, Balthasar teaches, "a fluid transition from [the Marian] archetypal ex-

102. Aquinas, *Summa theologica* III, q. 30, a.1.

103. "The words 'Behold, I am the handmaid of the Lord' express the fact that from the outset she accepted and understood her own motherhood as a total *gift of self,* a gift of her person to the service of the saving plans of the Most High" (John Paul II, *Redemptoris mater,* #39).

104. "The mystery of the Incarnation was accomplished when Mary uttered her fiat . . . which made possible, as far as it depended upon the divine plan, the granting of her Son's desire" (John Paul II, *Redemptoris mater,* #13).

105. "Christum prius mente quam ventre concipiens" (*Sermo* 215.4: "In redditione symboli," *PL,* 38:1074). "Angelus nuntiat, virgo audit, credit, et concipit. Fides in mente. Christus in ventre. Virgo concepti miramini: virgo peperit, plus miramini: post partum, virgo permansit" (*Sermo* 25, *In Natali Domini* 13, *PL,* 38:1019). ". . . plus est Mariae, discipulam fuisse Christi, quam matrem fuisse Christi. Plus est felicius discipulam fuisse Christi, quam matrem fuisse Christi. . . . Plus mente custodivit veritatem, quam utero carnem. Veritas Christus, caro Christus. Veritas Christus in mente Mariae, caro Christus in ventre Mariae" (*Sermo* 25.7: *PL,* 46:937-38).

106. Augustine of Hippo: "fide credidit, fide concepit" (*Sermo* 25.7: *PL,* 46:937).

perience to imitative experience."[107] This is to say not only that Mary's faith "'*precedes*' the apostolic *witness* of the Church, and ever remains in the Church's heart, hidden like a special heritage of God's revelation," as Pope John Paul II is careful to note, but also that "those who from generation to generation among the different peoples and nations of the earth accept with faith the mystery of Christ . . . *seek in her faith support for their own*." Hence Mary's faith "continues to become the faith of the pilgrim People of God: the faith of individuals and communities."[108] It follows that the final criteria for determining the authenticity of Christian experience is, as Balthasar explains, not to be found in what one has "personally experienced and suffered, but far beyond this, in the extent to which he has made room in himself for the archetypal Christian experiences, among which Mary's experience of motherhood holds an important place."[109]

Toward a New Feminist Experience

If the feminist critique of patriarchy is true — that there is no "pristine" knowledge which, within the context of patriarchy, is not influenced by the goal of furthering the interests of men — then women can hardly escape the trap of thinking like men or of creating alternative epistemological models designed to promote their own interests rather than those of men. In either case they remain victims of patriarchy: whether as blinded "fools" deluded by patriarchal philosophy or as those initiated into the new "gnosticism" of feminism whereby their eyes are opened to patriarchy's malicious tactics. The central question of theological concern within this context is thus whether feminist epistemological models might operate from an ideology that is less offensive to — and possibly even favorable toward — the Christian faith than are patriarchal models. Indeed, the feminist critique of the church's faith as corrupted by patriarchy, as bearing a masculine bias which serves to oppress women, is not a peripheral matter for theologians. It is directed to the very heart of our identity as Christians by challenging what and who we believe, how we believe and why we believe. Depending on how these questions are answered, not only may theology disappear as a science, but the Christian, as such, may disappear with his or her God.

This challenges us to reassess the value of a properly Christian experience. In contrast to the experience at the base of the old brand of feminism — the *ex-*

---

107. Balthasar, *Glory of the Lord*, 1:340.
108. John Paul II, *Redemptoris mater*, #27, #28, emphasis John Paul's.
109. Balthasar, *Glory of the Lord*, 1:341.

perience of oppression under patriarchy requiring the consciousness thereof and thus the "grace" of liberation therefrom — is the *experience of faith* of the new feminism. Unlike the first experience, which, at least in the first instance, is distinguished by pure or *passive passivity* — the experience of being powerless under the oppressive reign of the "patriarchs" — the second experience is more properly "spousal," characterized as it is by "docile initiative and active surrender."[110] In this sense it is more properly described as spiritual or *active passivity*, because the powers of the human spirit are here active.[111] An authentic experience of salvation is thus not simply an awaking, or coming to consciousness, with regard to one's experience of oppression. Neither is it an experience of independence from man and his "god," nor a license to reincarnate God by separating "her" from the community of faith and creating in its stead a new community which better fits the feminist image of freedom: the "*ekklēsia* of women," for example. In such a case, our "savior" is less than human: "she" is a creation of our desire for deliverance in the manner in which we ourselves conceive it.[112] If Israel failed to recognize her Messiah because he did not match her hope for salvation, how much more have we failed to recognize him in the call to repentance as implied by the gift of redemption?[113] Far less (or that which amounts to the same) is religious experience an experience of the self projected upon God. Indeed, to the extent that feminism challenges us to call into question our sometimes too narrow conception of God, it ought to be lauded. Our God, it must be granted, deigned to dwell within the womb of the Virgin from whence he came to dwell among us. He willingly confines himself to the tabernacles of our churches and our hearts, but he simply cannot be confined to our imaginations! "If experience . . . even in a worldly sense is not a *state* but an *event* (and the very form of the word points to this with the prefix *ex-*), it follows that it is not man's entry *(Einfahren)* into himself, into his best and highest possibilities, which can become an experience *(Erfahrung)*, but, rather, it is his act of entering into the Son of God, Christ Jesus, who is naturally inaccessible to him, which becomes

110. Georges Chantraine, "Woman as Deprived of the Spirit: An Aspect of Luther's Thought on Woman," *Communio* (Fall 1983): 240-55 (cited at p. 241).

111. See above, n. 39.

112. Freedom from patriarchy, for example. Daphne Hampson argues, for example: "Many a woman — in a way in which this has not on the whole been true of men — has had to turn her back upon the religion within which she grew up. It simply became impossible. For any woman apprised of what the history of women has been, the question of theodicy raised by the previous conception of God has made that conception of God unthinkable. That God, moreover, was most clearly not made in her image, and became superfluous as she came to herself and acquired a feminist consciousness" (Hampson, p. 173).

113. On this see John Paul II, encyclical letter on the Holy Spirit, *Dominium et vivificantem*, May 30, 1986.

the experience that alone can claim for itself his undivided obedience."[114] Rather than the specific experience of freedom *from* oppression, Christian experience is — it bears repeating — *primarily and properly* the experience of freedom *for* self-realization within the mystery of Christ: the freedom to receive, without constraint, the fullness of grace in the person of Christ and thus according to the "measure" of his superabundant generosity — "no greater love is there than this . . ." (John 15:13). This is the experience not only nor primarily of liberation from the structures of sin controlling one as a victim; it is also and especially that of the liberation from sin as it controls one qua sinner; for "we know that our old self was crucified with him so that the sinful body might be destroyed, and we might no longer be enslaved to sin" (Rom. 6:6). Such is the experience of a living relationship which is itself liberating, a relationship which so challenges the beloved that he cannot do otherwise than entirely engage himself as a "slave of righteousness" (Rom. 6:18). This, in short, is the experience of faith: an entering into the movement of Christ's life so as to become a witness, with him and in him, to the Father. It is not "evidence" that is in the forefront of this action; for witnessing, in the biblical sense of the term, is never an "impersonal marshaling of facts" but "a personal attestation."[115]

To return then to Daphne Hampson's observations mentioned above,[116] if Christianity has indeed tended to regard faith as submission — even "blind" submission — to a structured system of "belief" as contrasted with feminist theology, which overlooks the properly objective character of faith altogether, then a new feminist theology ought to combine the best of both while avoiding their proper weaknesses. What is sought, more specifically, is a balance between the objective and subjective aspects of faith, *a subject-object commingling*. Emphasis here is upon the knowledge that one person has of another, a mutual knowledge based upon each one's gift to the other. As such it is an "understanding" knowledge of Christ and his teaching which supposes a unison of mind and heart and even a unison of minds and hearts. What is judged true is sought and achieved in a commitment of the person to a Person: the Word of God incarnate in Christ Jesus. The objective gift of revelation is thus complemented and "achieved" by the subjective gift of faith whereby the former is received and effective, one gift meeting and accomplishing another.

Such a commingling of the personal-subjective and the personal-objective dimensions of faith may be *an important contribution of a new feminism.*

---

114. Balthasar, *Glory of the Lord,* 1:222.

115. McKenzie, p. 935. McKenzie explains that the modern distinction between the witness of fact and of truth does not exist in the Bible. "Whether to fact or to truth in our sense, the witness consists in the commitment of a person to the truth which he attests" (p. 935).

116. See nn. 1 and 2 above.

Hampson notes, for example, the ethical importance in feminist thought of attentiveness to human persons and argues that this may have important implications for the manner in which we approach "receptivity to the presence of God in our world."[117] Hampson's argument bears surprising similarity to Pope John Paul II's recognition of the human being as entrusted by God "in a special way" to woman.[118] In the first instance, this "entrusting" refers to her physical maternity in virtue of which her femininity is manifest: woman is revealed as the one in whom human life is conceived and developed. The pope speaks of the unique contact between a mother and her child as giving rise to an attentiveness toward all human persons. This, in turn, constitutes what he refers to as the particular "genius" of women: the ensuring of a "sensitivity for human beings in every circumstance."[119] "It is commonly thought that *women* are more capable than men of paying attention *to another person,* and that motherhood develops this predisposition even more. The man — even with all his sharing parenthood — always remains 'outside' the process of pregnancy and the baby's birth; in many ways he has to *learn* his own *'fatherhood' from the mother.*"[120] Because, moreover, motherhood and fatherhood also have a profoundly spiritual dimension — being "not only 'of flesh and blood'" but implying an earnest "*'listening to the word of the living God'* and a readiness to 'safe-guard' this Word, which is 'the word of eternal life' (cf. John 6:68)"[121] — we might ask *whether spiritual maternity might be instructive with regard to spiritual paternity.* Such seems to be the implication when, commenting on the important Gospel scene of Martha's act of faith in Christ, "Yes, Lord; I believe that you are the Christ, the Son of God, he who is coming into the world,"[122] John Paul II writes: "Christ speaks to women about the things of God, and they understand them; there is a true resonance of mind and heart, a response of faith. Jesus expresses appreciation and admiration for this distinctly 'feminine' response, as in the case of the Canaanite woman (cf. Mt 15:28). Sometimes he presents this lively faith, filled with love, as an example. *He teaches,* therefore, taking as *his starting-point this feminine response of mind and heart.*"[123] This presentation of faith knowledge as feminine is not, it seems to me,

---

117. Hampson, p. 173.

118. John Paul II, *Mulieris dignitatem,* #30, emphasis John Paul's. See Michele M. Schumacher, "The Prophetic Vocation of Women and the Order of Love," *Logos* 2, no. 2 (Spring 1999): 147-92.

119. John Paul II, *Mulieris dignitatem,* #30; cf. #18.

120. John Paul II, *Mulieris dignitatem,* #18, emphasis John Paul's.

121. John Paul II, *Mulieris dignitatem,* #19, emphasis John Paul's.

122. John 11:27. *"This conversation with Martha,"* writes the pope, *"is one of the most important of the Gospels"* (*Mulieris dignitatem,* #15, emphasis John Paul's).

123. John Paul II, *Mulieris dignitatem,* #15, emphasis John Paul's.

a simple projecting of woman's bodily structure upon her mind and heart, an attributing to her of spiritual receptivity in virtue of her bodily receptivity.[124] If, however, this particular attitude of faith is observed in the women of the Gospels, for instance, then we might ask whether a particularly feminine attentiveness to persons may foster among women an attentiveness to the word of God incarnate in Christ Jesus and an attitude of faith which is first of all personal, concrete, and committed before it is objective, abstract, and intellectual. In other words, a properly feminine sensitivity to human persons may in fact sensitize women to the divine person of Christ, who is also the fullness of God's revelation. This sensitivity to God's Word revealed in Christ may, on the other hand, further sensitize women to human persons, especially the poor and needy with whom Christ identifies most particularly (cf. Matt. 25:40; Acts 9:4). To receive the One is to receive the others; to be a bride of Christ is to be a mother of souls, to nurture the faith of others within the "womb" of one's own. As the church, present in her saints, carries us within herself until we are brought to the fullness of life — our full stature in Christ — we too are called to carry others, to be "mothers" in *the* mother. Simultaneously saved and saviors, recipients of grace and mediators of grace, we, like mother church, give in virtue of a gift received and receive in virtue of a receptivity that is given. Gift meets gift: revelation invoking faith; faith receiving revelation; love encouraging and invoking love.

The primary concern of new feminist theologians — not unlike that of the Christian in general — is thus to so give of oneself as to make "room" therein for the divine "Other." This personal reception of the divine guest is, in turn, never for oneself alone, which is to say not only that the subjective understanding of Christ's suffering and death "for me" (cf. Gal. 2:20) is balanced by the more objective interpretation of the same "for all,"[125] but also that one so perfectly receives the Lord as to share his love for each of his members. The experience of faith thus bypasses the dangers of extreme objectivism and extreme subjectivism, characteristic of patriarchy and feminism respectively. As a gift of the Holy Spirit, authentic faith is both that which *is* received and that *whereby* it is received; a living heritage and personal assent; the deposit of revelation within the church and the obedient surrender whereby this deposit is appropriated, that is to say, accepted as one's own. More fundamental still, it is a response of the person to the Person, a personal witness to the Lord who gives himself to the one he also prepares to receive him.

---

124. Feminists are right, it seems to me, to insist upon the logical error of arguing from biology to archetype. See above, n. 51.

125. For example: "Christ loved the church and gave himself up for her" (Eph. 5:25); cf. Matt. 26:28; Mark 14:24; Luke 22:19-20; Rom. 5:8.

The Unity of the Two: Toward a New Feminist Sacramentality of the Body

Michele M. Schumacher

Nowhere is the problem of the relationship between nature and vocation, between "is" and "ought," so strongly posed — it seems to me — as in the feminist challenge to an all-male priesthood. The idea of women being "refused" holy orders for reason of their inaptitude to image Christ, who as supreme high priest offers himself to the church for the world's redemption, is perceived as a grave injustice — as "sacramental sex discrimination"[1] — and even as an explicit contradiction to the equality implied in man and woman's equal imaging of God in reason of their common rational nature.[2] As Elizabeth Johnson, firmly founded in New Testament theology, notes, man and woman share the vocation to be "christomorphic": "The image of Christ does not lie in sexual similarity to the human man Jesus, but in coherence with the narrative shape of his compassionate, liberating life in the world, through the power of the Spirit."[3]

To deny this would of course amount to denying women salvation, at least in the manner in which it has been perceived more or less consistently

---

With special thanks to Mary Shivanandan and my husband Bernard for their critical comments and suggestions.

1. Susan A. Ross, "God's Embodiment and Women," in *Freeing Theology: The Essentials of Theology in Feminist Perspective,* ed. Catherine Mowry LaCugna (San Francisco: Harper Collins, 1993), pp. 185-209, cited at p. 206.

2. See, for example, Rosemary Radford Ruether, *Sexism and God-Talk: Toward a Feminist Theology,* 2nd ed. (Boston: Beacon Press, 1993), p. 126. On man and woman's equal imaging of God, see John Paul II, apostolic letter, "On the Dignity and Vocation of Women," *Mulieris dignitatem,* August 15, 1988, #6.

3. Elizabeth Johnson, "The Maleness of Christ," *Concilium* (December 1991): 108-16, cited at p. 114. She makes reference here to Gal. 3:27-28; 2 Cor. 3:18; Rom. 8:29.

throughout much of the church's history: conformity to Christ by the gift of his grace in virtue of which one acts *as* Christ acts, not in an imitative manner, but by participating in the life of his Spirit, by acting under the inspiration, and in the power of, this same Spirit.[4] Such is the *admirabile commercium* proclaimed by the church fathers, that "marvelous exchange" whereby the eternal Word takes on our humanity and communicates to us his divinity (cf. 2 Pet. 1:4). In him we are a new creation: "For as many of you as were baptized into Christ have put on Christ. There is neither Jew nor Greek, there is neither slave nor free, there is neither male nor female; for you are all one in Christ Jesus" (Gal. 3:27-28).

With reflection upon this passage, let the obvious be made still more explicit: women do not, in virtue of our salvific conformity to Christ, bear the image of his masculinity! As feminists rightly remind us, there is no human perfection to be gained thereby. Nor is it to be obtained in the sacrament of orders whereby one is configured to Christ as an "instrument for his Church,"[5] since it is Christ himself who "acts and effects salvation through the ordained minister" regardless of the degree of the latter's holiness or lack thereof. "As for the proud minister," Augustine warns, "he is to be ranked with the devil. Christ's gift is not thereby profaned: what flows through him keeps its purity, and what passes through him remains clear and reaches the fertile earth. . . . The spiritual power of the sacrament is indeed comparable to light: those to be enlightened receive it in its purity, and if it should pass through defiled beings, it is not itself defiled."[6] Indeed, spiritual conformity to Christ is obviously not the prerogative of his ministers, but most feminist theologians are not to be appeased with a "lower" place in the church in exchange for a "higher" place in heaven. Concretely they deny the theological significance of the masculinity of priests by denying, as we shall see, the theological significance of the masculinity of Christ. In an effort to defend, against these objections, the sacramental meaning of Christ's maleness, I will begin by exposing the sacramental meaning of the human body in general, especially as it points to the relational

---

4. "The Doctors of the Church tell us that the mysteries of Christ's life are at the same time most excellent models of virtue for us to imitate and also sources of divine grace for us by reason of the merits and intercession of the Redeemer. They live on in their effect in us, since each of them is, according to its nature and in its own way, the cause of our salvation" (Pius XII, encyclical letter, *Mediator Dei*, November 20, 1947; English translation from *The Christian Faith in the Doctrinal Documents of the Catholic Church*, ed. J. Neuner and J. Dupuis [New York: Alba House, 1982], p. 378 [#1333]).

5. See the *Catechism of the Catholic Church*, #1581.

6. Augustine, *In Johannis evangelium* 5.15, in *Patrologia Latina*, 35:1422; cited in the *Catechism of the Catholic Church*, #1584. See also #1128.

meaning of human existence and the concrete vocation of the human person to realize himself or herself by becoming a gift for the others. This will enable us to examine more concretely the relational significance of Christ's own masculine humanity and its implications for a theology of salvation that grants a real place to human freedom. The connection, which follows from this argument for an all-male priesthood based upon the sacramental significance of Christ's masculinity, will invite an examination of the connection between the image of the bride and the baptismal priesthood of the faithful, which includes men as well as women. From there we will address the sacramental significance of the female body-person, and we will conclude by reexamining the sacramental significance of the human body as relational in its masculinity and femininity.

The Feminist Denial of the Sacramental Significance of Christ's Masculinity

To begin our investigation into the sacramental significance of the masculinity of Christ, we do well to seriously consider the feminist critique. Elizabeth Johnson, for example, argues that the church's insistence that Christ's maleness is essential to his identity and salvific mission is a de facto denial to women of "the fullness of their Christian identity as images of Christ."[7] Similarly, Rosemary Radford Ruether recognizes in the church's refusal to grant the "right"[8] of ordination to women — while simultaneously insisting upon their equal rights in the public domain — a reversal of what she attributes to classic Christianity: a contradiction between its anthropology of creation and its Christology. More specifically, she interprets the patristic vision of women as considering them unequal to men by nature[9] but equal in the realm of grace and salvation, which is to say that Christ has annulled this inequality. "How do we seem to have de-

---

7. Elizabeth Johnson, "Redeeming the Name of Christ," in *Freeing Theology,* pp. 115-37, cited at p. 119.

8. "No one has a *right* to receive the sacrament of Holy Orders. Indeed no one claims this office for himself; he is called to it by God. Anyone who thinks he recognizes the signs of God's call to the ordained ministry must humbly submit his desire to the authority of the Church, who has the responsibility and right to call someone to receive orders. Like every grace this sacrament can be *received* only as an unmerited gift" (*Catechism of the Catholic Church,* #1578).

9. That is to say, there was not attributed to them the same capacity to bear the image of God as was attributed to men. Ruether's specific interpretation has been called into question by David Vincent Meconi, "*Grata Sacris Angelis:* Gender and the *Imago Dei* in Augustine's *De Trinitate* XII," *American Catholic Philosophical Quarterly* 74 (2000): 47-62.

veloped to a reversed view in modern Catholic teaching, in which women become equal in nature or creation (secular society), but unequal in grace (in
Christ and in the Church)?"[10] For Ruether the church's defense of an all-male
priesthood in reason of its sacramental significance amounts, in other words, to
a de facto separation between the created, or natural, order and the supernatural order, or the order of grace. She thereby accuses the church of promoting in
practice the very contrary of what it teaches in theory.

Indeed, such a separation — if we were willing to grant it — would contradict the traditional understanding of sacraments whereby the natural and
visible is believed to bear within itself the supernatural, or graced. As a "sign
and instrument" of grace, it reveals and communicates grace. Hence the sacrament of orders, for example, "not only confers the grace proper to this particular function and state of life; it also confers an indelible character which con-
forms the sacred ministers to Christ the Priest, and enables them lawfully to
perform the acts of religion by which men are sanctified and God duly glorified
according to the divine ordinance."[11] As differing from the other six sacraments, then, the sacrament of orders confers grace whose sanctifying effect is
destined not primarily for the recipient himself, but for the church in whose
service he is thereby instituted: that he might, in virtue of this sacrament, perform the sacred rites (the other sacraments) "by which men are sanctified." If,
then, he is rightly said to be "configured" to Christ "by a special grace of the
Holy Spirit," this is — it bears repeating — "so that he may serve as Christ's instrument for his Church."[12] Clearly, then, it is not sanctifying grace that is being
refused women in denying them admission to the altar. What, then, are we to
make of Johnson's and Ruether's remarks?

Denied by these feminist theologians is of course the idea that the male
body is a more appropriate vehicle for conveying the sacramental meaning of
the ordained priesthood than is the female body, or even that it has any sacramental significance (i.e., sign value) at all.[13] In this sense it is ironically their
own argumentation that, it seems to me, leads to the nature-grace separation
that Ruether attributes to the church's defense of an all-male priesthood. By
denying, more specifically, the possibility that the human body, precisely as

10. Rosemary Radford Ruether, "Women's Difference and Equal Rights in the Church,"
Concilium (December 1991/6): 11-18, cited at p. 14.

11. Pius XII, *Mediator Dei*, #1733; AAS 39 (1947), pp. 521-95; English translation from *The
Christian Faith in the Doctrinal Documents of the Catholic Church*, p. 504.

12. *Cathechism of the Catholic Church*, #1581.

13. The sign value of the male priest might be compared, for example, to that of bread for
the Eucharist as an appropriate sign of the nurturing qualities of this sacrament or water for
baptism as an appropriate sign of the cleansing qualities of the sacrament.

sexual (in this case masculine), might bear real spiritual or sacramental significance, they thereby call into question the possible supernatural meaning of the natural realm, the sacramental value of creation. On the other hand, we must agree with Daphne Hampson's reasoning that "If it is to be held that both women and men find salvation in Christ, then it must be simply 'humanity' [and not masculinity] which is of significance as having been taken on."[14] The patristic witness to the full humanity of Christ — *quod non est assumptum, non est sanctum* (what is not assumed is not sanctified) — should not, in other words, be understood as denying sanctifying grace to women whose femininity he did not assume. The question "Can a male savior save women?" is thus rightfully dismissed by Ruether not because, as she argues, the maleness of Christ has "no ultimate [theological] significance," but because, as she also notes, "his ability to speak as liberator does not reside in his maleness." Nor does it reside, however, as she proposes, "in the fact that he has renounced this system of domination and seeks to embody in his person the new humanity of service and mutual empowerment."[15] This argumentation minimizes, it seems to me, the significance of the divine power at work in Christ's humanity, and thus also the validity of the mystical doctrine of salvation, according to which — as we shall see — human nature is redeemed by its assumption of the divine person of the Word. Neither, however, is it sufficient to dismiss the power of human persons to refuse the gift of salvation, which is to say that an adequate doctrine of salvation requires that the liberty of human persons be seriously addressed.[16] Indeed, as Ruether puts it, "We need to think in terms of a dynamic, rather than a static, relationship between redeemer and redeemed." By this she means that "Christ, as redemptive person and Word of God, is not to be encapsulated 'once-for-all' in the historical Jesus." While I disagree with any such minimizing of the significance of Christ's historical existence, I do agree with her conclusion that the Christian community "continues Christ's identity,"[17] that is to say (in *my* sense), by the power of his Spirit within its members.

For Ruether this continuation of Christ's "identity" serves as an additional argument as to why Christ's masculinity is not significant for his salvific

14. Daphne Hampson, *Theology and Feminism* (Cambridge, Mass., and Oxford: Blackwell, 1990), p. 55.

15. Ruether, *Sexism and God-Talk*, p. 137. "Can a Male Savior Save Women?" is the title of the fifth chapter of this book.

16. Hence Saint Thomas argues, for example, that Christ's merit is *sufficient* but not *efficacious* for all due to the intervention of the free will of the human person and of God's justice which requires that his grace be willingly received. See *De veritate* q.29, a.7, ad. 4.

17. Ruether, *Sexism and God-Talk*, p. 138.

mission, and thus also why an all-male priesthood has no real significance.[18] Ironically, however, this very argument may, as I will argue, actually sustain the contrary: the position that Christ's masculinity really *is* theologically meaning-ful.

The Sacramental Meaning of the Human Body: A Relational Value

Before actually demonstrating the significance of Christ's masculinity for his salvific mission, it is perhaps worth mentioning the sacramental significance of the human body in general and thus also of sexual differentiation. Of course, it must be granted, as does Pope John Paul II, that the human person "brings into the world his particular likeness to God, with which he transcends and domi-nates also his 'visibility' in the world, his corporeality, his masculinity or femi-ninity, his nakedness." The human body, on the other hand, is presented by the pope as a "primordial sacrament." "The sacrament, as a visible sign, is consti-tuted with man, as a body, by means of his visible masculinity and femininity. The body, and it alone, is capable of making visible what is invisible: the spiri-tual and the divine. It was created to transfer into the visible reality of the world the mystery hidden since time immemorial in God, and thus be a sign of it."[19] In the first instance, the body reveals something of God by making visible the person — precisely as a constitutive part of the human being[20] — created in God's image. Because, moreover, the human body is sexually differentiated, masculinity and femininity may actually be regarded as bespeaking something of God. Hence masculine and feminine traits are, the pope notes, both analogi-cally attributed to God by sacred Scripture.[21] Beyond this equality in the ana-logical realm, especially in that which concerns the imaging of God by the hu-man person, is the communal dimension of sexuality. "The fact that man 'created as man and woman' is the image of God means not only that each of them individually is like God, as a rational and free being. It also means that man and woman, created as a 'unity of the two' in their common humanity, are called to live in a communion of love, and in this way to mirror in the world the

18. Christ is also encountered, she argues, *"in the form of our sister"* (Ruether, *Sexism and God-Talk*, p. 137).

19. John Paul II, general audience of February 20, 1980. English translation from *The Theology of the Body: Human Love in the Divine Plan* (Boston: Daughters of St. Paul, 1997), p. 76.

20. On this, see John Paul II, general audience of November 21, 1979 (*Theology of the Body*, p. 49)

21. On this, see John Paul II, *Mulieris dignitatem*, #8.

communion of love that is in God, through which the Three Persons love each other in the intimate mystery of the one divine life."[22] Especially in the "one flesh" union of marriage whereby a man and a woman know each other and themselves as bodies and as persons, they "confirm and renew the existence of man [that is to say, man and woman] as the image of God."[23] This they do not only by transmitting this image through procreation, but also by their mutual self-gift expressed in and through the body. Helping each of them "to find themselves in communion of persons," the body is "the constituent element of their union" as husband and wife.[24] Each comes to a greater self-knowledge and a greater self-realization through their one-flesh union.[25] The choice implied by this union, however, "presupposes a mature consciousness of the body," a consciousness of the "unifying significance of the body in its masculinity and femininity."[26]

Hence, despite the feminist accusation of biological reductionism and even biological determinism in the theological anthropology of the pope,[27] his

22. John Paul II, *Mulieris dignitatem*, #7.

23. John Paul II, general audience of March 12, 1980. *Theology of the Body*, p. 83.

24. John Paul II, general audience of November 21, 1979. *Theology of the Body*, p. 50.

25. In the consummation of marriage there is obtained, according to John Paul II, both an objective knowledge of the body — an objectivity which lies "hidden in the somatic potentialities of the man and of the woman" — as well as a subjective knowledge: "the pure subjectivity of the gift — that is, mutual self-fulfillment in the gift" (John Paul II, general audience of March 12, 1980; in *Theology of the Body*, p. 81).

26. *Theology of the Body*, p. 50. "Sexual differentiation," writes Mary Rousseau, "is, in some way, what makes human *communio* possible" ("John Paul II's Letter on the Dignity and Vocation of Women: The Call to Communio," *Communio* 16 [summer 1989]: 212-32, cited at p. 222).

27. Patrick Snyder argues, for example: "We are in agreement with John Paul II when he affirms that the person is incarnated in a body. Can, however, the body, or to utilize the vocabulary of the pontiff, its determination, really and irreducibly confer upon the person a specific nature and vocation which would be defined by the simple observation of its biological reproduction?" (*La femme selon Jean-Paul II. Lectures des fondements anthropologiques et théologiques et des applications pratiques de son enseignement* [Québec: Fides, 1999], p. 228). To my knowledge the pope never uses the vocabulary subscribed to him by Snyder (i.e., "determination"); nor does he refer to the person in reproductive terms, unless, that is to say, Snyder were to incorrectly attribute to him an understanding of motherhood as reduced to its reproductive function. As if to respond to the first accusation, Mary Aquin O'Neill writes: "Setting himself against any naturalistic or deterministic answer to that query [namely, what 'makes' a person male or female?], John Paul II draws from the wellspring of Genesis the saving truth that being male or female is a matter of knowledge" ("The Mystery of Being Human Together," in *Freeing Theology*, pp. 139-60, cited at p. 154). Mary Ann Glendon, Vatican representative to the UN Fourth World Conference on Women (September 4-15, 1995) in Beijing, explains that while the Holy See "excludes dubious interpretations based on world views which assert that sexual identity can be

presentation of the "nuptial meaning"[28] of the body — its capacity to express self-giving love — ensures the self-determination of the human subject as implied by his or her consciousness and freedom.[29] It is this consciousness, in other words, which allows the human person to make of himself or herself a gift for the other. When, for example, it is said in Genesis 4:1 that Adam "knew" his wife, this knowledge, the pope comments, in no way detracts from the original and fundamental self-awareness implied in his act of naming the animals. By this act he differentiates himself from other living beings and affirms himself as a person. In knowing Eve he has still greater self-consciousness: he discovers thereby the meaning of his own body, as intrinsically related to the woman.[30] "If Eve was taken out of Adam," reasons Hans Urs von Balthasar, "then Adam had Eve within him without knowing it. Of course, God created her and breathed his breath into her; but God took the material for her out of Adam's living flesh infused with the Spirit. There was something feminine in him, which he recognizes when God brings him the woman. And the Creator gives the man the power to be creative in this creaturely womb. But the woman is taken from the man; the substance from which she is made is masculine. She knows the man from the beginning. She is, together with him, feminine in relation to God, but she also has the actively responding power with him."[31] If, even on the physiological level, the female body is never only a receptacle for sperm, as Margaret Farley rightfully insists,[32] there is all the more reason to recognize

---

adapted indefinitely to suit new and different patterns," it likewise "dissociates itself from the biological determinist notion that all the roles and relations of the two sexes are fixed in a single static pattern" ("Vatican Stance: Women's Conference Final Document," *Origins. CNS Documentary Service* 25, no. 15 [September 28, 1995]: 236).

28. See, for example, general audience of January 9 and 16, 1980 (*Theology of the Body,* pp. 60-66).

29. In his commentary on Gen. 2:23, for example, the pope argues that consciousness of this meaning is actually "deeper" than the somatic structure of the human being as male and female. "In any case," he continues, "this structure is presented right from the beginning with a deep consciousness of human corporality and sexuality, and that establishes an inalienable norm for the understanding of man on the theological plane" (general audience of November 14, 1979; *Theology of the Body,* p. 48). Similarly, he argues that the text of Gen. 2:25 "expressly requires that the reflections on the theology of the body should be connected with the dimension of man's personal subjectivity. It is within the latter that consciousness of the meaning of the body develops" (general audience of December 12, 1979; *Theology of the Body,* p. 52).

30. See John Paul II, general audience of March 12, 1980 (*Theology of the Body,* p. 80).

31. Hans Urs von Balthasar, *A Theological Anthropology* (New York: Sheed and Ward, 1967), pp. 312-13.

32. "Knowledge about the ovum, and the necessity of two entities (sperm and ovum) meeting in order to form a new reality, forever ruled out the analogy of the earth receiving a

in the mutual "knowledge" of the marital union the coinciding of activity and receptivity: the man giving himself in a receiving sort of way; the woman receiving the man in a giving sort of way;[33] the man creating in woman's womb; the woman giving man "the fully formed child that the seed can only indicate." As his "helpmate," she "does all the work, which he only, as it were, proposes and stimulates."[34]

In the mutual self-giving of spouses there is, according to the pope, "a common and reciprocal discovery, just as the existence of man, whom 'God created male and female,' is common and reciprocal from the beginning." Contrary, therefore, to "a one-sidedly 'naturalistic' mentality" whereby the "knowledge" of Genesis 4:1[35] would be interpreted as "a passive acceptance of one's own determination by the body and by sex," there is implied a self-determination empowered by knowledge.[36]

Not unlike the intention of Maria Teresa Porcile Santiso to construct a theological anthropology on the basis of the person and interpersonal relations rather than on sexuality and biology,[37] Pope John Paul II's purpose is to present a theological anthropology in which the human person is revealed in relations enabled by the body. As "a mass of potentialities" and "a potential of relations,"[38] the human body is presented by the pontiff as that whereby the person enters into relation with the world and with others. Far from *reducing the human person* — or more particularly, the woman — to the body understood as

---

seed which was whole in itself and only in need of nourishment to grow. Suddenly enwombing took on a different meaning, and inseeding had to be conceptualized in a different way. Even the passivity of the waiting womb had to be reinterpreted in the face of discoveries of its active role in aiding the passage of the sperm" (Margaret A. Farley, "New Patterns of Relationship: Beginnings of a Moral Revolution," *Theological Studies* 36, no. 4 [December 1975]: 627-46, cited at p. 637).

33. See William E. May, *Marriage: The Rock on Which the Family Is Built* (San Francisco: Ignatius, 1995), pp. 48-49.

34. Balthasar, *A Theological Anthropology*, p. 313.

35. "Adam knew Eve his wife, and she conceived and bore Cain. . . ."

36. General audience of March 12, 1980 (*Theology of the Body*, p. 80).

37. See Maria Teresa Porcile Santiso, *La Femme, espace de salut. Mission de la femme dans l'Église. Une perspective anthropologique* (Paris: Cerf, 1999), p. 141. She proposes thereby to avoid what she considers an error characteristic of a traditional theology of woman: the arguing from biology to archetype. See p. 69.

38. See Marie Hendrickx, "Un autre féminisme?" *Nouvelle revue théologique* 112 (1990): 67-79, cited at pp. 70-71. Hendrickx refers to the human being as "a being who necessarily bears within himself a project of relations." Similar is the perspective of John D. Zizioulas, for whom the body is "the mode by which man *is* as a *presence* through his ekstasis towards communion" ("Human Capacity and Human Incapacity: A Theological Exploration of Personhood," *Scottish Journal of Theology* 28 [1975]: 401-47, cited at p. 423).

merely a natural or biological fact, the sacramental perspective of John Paul II actually *elevates the human body* to the level of the person, that is to say, recognizing it as a constitutive part of the human person. As such, his approach is at odds with a reductionist view of the human body characteristic of contemporary Western culture:

> [T]he body is no longer perceived as a properly personal reality, a sign and place of relation with others, with God and with the world. It is reduced to pure materiality: it is simply a complex of organs, functions and energies to be used according to the sole criteria of pleasure and efficiency. Consequently, sexuality too is depersonalized and exploited: From being the sign, place and language of love, that is, of the gift of self and acceptance of another in all the other's richness as a person, it increasingly becomes the occasion and instrument for self-assertion and the selfish satisfaction of personal desires and instincts.[39]

It is thus difficult to understand how Patrick Snyder might recognize in the biological dimension of women the "dogmatic reference" of the papal conception of the nature and vocation of women.[40] If there were a dogmatic reference to be found in the pope's theological anthropology of women, it would in fact be, it seems to me, the very *contrary* of what Snyder suggests. Actually seeking to overcome the reductionism of our age, John Paul II argues for *"a deeper understanding of the truth about the human person"* as "a subject who decides for himself." As such, he or she necessarily strives toward self-realization that is, however, only achieved "through a sincere gift of self."[41] This truth, which accords with the "fundamental biblical truth about the creation of the human being — man and woman — in the image and likeness of God," not only constitutes the

39. John Paul II, encyclical letter on the gospel of life, *Evangelium vitae*, March 25, 1995, #23. The reference is to contemporary cultural perspective in general.

40. Snyder, p. 222. This follows for Snyder as a consequence of the pope's reference in *Mulieris dignitatem*, #18, to scientific analysis as confirming a natural disposition in women to maternity, although Snyder completely disregards the pope's comments following immediately thereafter: "What the different branches of science have to say on this subject is important and useful, provided that it is not limited to an exclusively bio-physiological interpretation of women and of motherhood. Such a *'restricted' picture* would go hand in hand with a materialistic concept of the human being and of the world. In such a case, what is truly essential would unfortunately be lost. Motherhood as a *human* fact and phenomenon is fully explained on the basis of the truth about the person" (emphasis John Paul's). His point here is comparable to that of Virginia Held, *Feminist Morality: Transforming Culture, Society, and Politics* (Chicago: University of Chicago Press, 1993).

41. John Paul II, *Mulieris dignitatem*, #18; cf. Vatican Council II, Pastoral Constitution on the Church, *Gaudium et spes*, #24, emphasis John Paul's. See also *Mulieris dignitatem*, #7.

very "definition" of the person;[42] it also "sum[s] up," according to John Paul, "the *whole of Christian anthropology.*"[43]

If it were thus maintained that the body is a sacrament of the person, it ought, then, to express the gifted nature of the person, a giftedness that John Paul presents as the source of his or her personal dignity and vocation.[44] Indeed, this point is the very heart of the pope's theology of the body and "the *indispensable point of departure*"[45] of his meditation on the dignity and vocation of women. Hence the question of whether the male body assumed by Christ is likewise sacramentally significant in communicating the giftedness of his person and what consequences might follow for women who obviously do not bear the image of his masculinity.

The Sacramental Meaning of Christ's Masculinity: A Relational Significance

In response to this essential question of whether Christ's maleness is theologically meaningful, we might turn again to John Paul's theology of the body where, with reference to Ephesians 5, he notes a continuity between marriage described as "an integral part" and "the central point of the 'sacrament of creation'"[46] and the sacrament of redemption: the sacrament of Christ's love for the church. The analogy of spousal love, which the pope recognizes as moving "simultaneously in two directions,"[47] indicates both "the identity of the mystery hidden in God from all eternity" and the "continuity of its actuation": the unity in God's plan of creation and redemption, of the first Adam and the second. "This redemptive gift of himself 'for' the Church also contains — accord-

---

42. John Paul II, *Mulieris dignitatem*, #7.

43. John Paul II, encyclical letter "On the Holy Spirit in the Life of the Church and the World," *Dominum et vivificantem*, May 18, 1986, #59; emphasis John Paul's.

44. As the source of his or her *dignity*, this giftedness expresses the fact that the person *is* himself or herself a gift: "*Man* — whether man or woman — *is the only being among the creatures* of the visible world *that God the Creator 'has willed for its own sake';* that creature is thus a person." As the source of his *vocation*, it expresses that fact that "man is called to exist 'for' others, to become a gift" (John Paul II, *Mulieris dignitatem*, #7).

45. John Paul II, *Mulieris dignitatem*, #7.

46. John Paul II, general audience of October 6, 1982 (*Theology of the Body*, p. 335; emphasis John Paul's).

47. John Paul II, *Mulieris dignitatem*, #23. "The covenant proper to spouses 'explains' the spousal character of the union of Christ with the Church, and in its turn this union, as a 'great sacrament,' determines the sacramentality of marriage as a holy covenant between the two spouses, man and woman" (#23).

ing to Pauline thought — Christ's gift of himself to the Church, in the image of the nuptial relationship that unites husband and wife in marriage. In this way, the sacrament of redemption again takes on, in a certain sense, the figure and form of the primordial sacrament [that is to say, the original unity of man and woman in the natural sacrament of marriage]."[48] On the other hand, the original unity of man and woman in the sacrament of creation is "introduced into this 'great mystery' of Christ and of the Church."[49] This follows as a consequence of the fact that Adam, as the Council taught, "was a type of him who was to come, Christ the Lord, Christ the new Adam." Thus preceding the first Adam in the order of the Creator's intention, the Second nonetheless follows him in time and in nature, which is to say that he willingly subjects himself to the "laws" and meaning of this nature. *Assuming* and not simply *absorbing* Adam's nature into himself, he thereby assumes its original, or "natural," sacramental meaning. At the same time, he raises this nature "to a dignity beyond compare,"[50] by which it is invested with a new, more profound sacramental meaning: a properly theological signification.

With regard to the original, or natural, meaning of Christ's masculinity, Mary Aquin O'Neill notes the consequences of John Paul's theology of the body for Christology: "If what the pope says about human self-knowledge and self-giving is true, and if an assertion of Jesus' true humanity requires that this reciprocity of being apply to him as well, he must have received his knowledge of himself as a man, as male, as masculine, from women."[51] Wishing to point us beyond both an "androgynous Christology" — in which Christ would be presented as "complete in himself, embracing the possibilities of female as well as male being" — and a docetic one which would deny the reality of his human body, O'Neill maintains a "'hermeneutic' of the conjugal"[52] according to which neither sex is, without the other, able to represent the fullness of humanity. With specific reference to the role of Mary in the life and mission of Christ, she argues that "No human life, not even that of Jesus, can embrace both sides of the human experience at the same time. One cannot be both male and female, nurturer and nurtured, actor and audience, the one to undergo suffering and the one to feel the suffering of the other all at the same time. The androcentric

48. General audience of October 13, 1982 (*Theology of the Body*, p. 337).

49. John Paul II, *Mulieris dignitatem*, #26.

50. Vatican Council II, *Gaudium et spes*, #22.

51. O'Neill, p. 155. Masculinity and femininity are, according to the pope, "two complementary dimensions of self-consciousness and self-determination and, at the same time, two complementary ways of being conscious of the meaning of the body" (John Paul II, general audience of November 21, 1979; *Theology of the Body*, p. 48).

52. O'Neill, p. 154.

bias in theology has repeatedly cast the spotlight on the one who acts but has left in the shadows the one who taught him so to act."[53] No human life, not even that of Christ, can reveal the whole nature of humanity, for man — precisely as human — is always "other" than woman, his "counterimage." With her he is "always in communion," Balthasar explains, without ever really "reaching" her thereby. For "the human 'I' is always searching for the 'thou,' and actually finds it ('This at last . . .'), without ever being able to take possession of it in its otherness."[54]

Because human nature is so constituted, Christ's masculinity is a necessary consequence of his real incarnation, a consequence which is so significant in fact that — as Daphne Hampson points out — regardless of how he is depicted by various artists and of how he is represented in different cultures — "yellow Christs and brown Christs, Christs who are serene and Christs in agony, Christs who are stylized and Christ in the image of the people who depicted him" — he remains the image of a man, i.e., male.[55] When, however, his maleness is adequately portrayed in terms of its relational meaning, it is hard to understand how Hampson can conclude, as she does, that anyone who "deeply cares that there should be good and equal relations between men and women" should be unwilling to grant to any one human being "the kind of status which Christians give to Christ."[56]

While Hampson criticizes what she esteems a useless effort of feminist theologians to seek a manner to represent women "in a religion where the Godhead is conceived in male terms,"[57] she also denounces as futile the "conservative" attempt to discover alternative ways for women to be symbolized in Christianity. Hampson does not specify the form these attempts have taken, but O'Neill cites, for her part, the obvious Marian symbol.[58] Because women "may

53. O'Neill, p. 156.

54. Hans Urs von Balthasar, *Theo-Drama: Theological Dramatic Theory,* vol. 2, *Dramatis Personae: Man in God* (San Francisco: Ignatius, 1990), p. 366. Balthasar specifies that the same is true of woman in relation to man.

55. Hampson, p. 77. She notes the uproar caused by the placing of a female figure, "Christa," on the cross in the Anglican cathedral of St. John the Divine in New York. "As could have been the case of no male figure, the Christa for many people represented a distortion of Christianity" (p. 77). In straightforward terms, "it would be difficult to argue that the fact that this religion has had at its centre a male figure has been of little significance" (p. 78).

56. Hampson, p. 76.

57. Hampson, p. 76.

58. Hampson (p. 73) also notes in a different context and with regard to feminists that there is a recent "fixation" upon Mary. "That this should be the case is perhaps a good indication of the need that Christian women feel to find themselves represented symbolically in their religion."

not image Christ in a sacramental way," a patriarchal church encourages them, she argues, to be like Mary, "whose dignity, it is said, lies in her motherhood."[59] Although O'Neill also insists upon the significance of Mary's place in the lives of men,[60] she interprets this significance as justifying the presence of women "at the altar."[61] She remains, however, ambiguous regarding the actual "role" of women at the altar, which is to say that it is not clear whether she recognizes them as acting in *persona Christi*. She does, however, admit an injustice in women being "saved in and through the ministrations of men" while "men are not saved in and through the ministrations of women. Attempts to reconcile such contradictory theological assertions end up recommending a notion of priesthood that discounts embodiment or that subtly implies the superiority of male embodiment because it enables the man to represent Christ and therefore God."[62] This apparently contradicts — at least from my perspective, as we shall see — her insistence upon the relational meaning of the human body-person. I do, however, agree with her insistence upon the feminine presence of Mary as essential to the life and revelation of Christ.

> Although embodiment as male or female represents limitations, loving in-
> teraction with the other can open up undreamed of possibilities. Jesus, as
> far as we know, begot no children, yet he gives life and love with his body
> through the Eucharist. Mary gave birth and fed with her body, yet she re-
> mains a virgin. Only the two figures together can reveal the radical saving
> truth about being male and female, virgin yet procreative, lover and life
> giver in the new age ushered in by the coming of the promised one. Only a
> hermeneutic of the two figures, male and female . . . , can allow for the dis-
> covery of the common and reciprocal story of salvation.[63]

O'Neill thus points to a sort of organic unity between the natural significance of "being human together" and the supernatural significance of the same.

59. O'Neill, p. 153.

60. "Mary is as much a model for men as Jesus is for women. But one without the other will result in a truncated theological anthropology" (O'Neill, p. 156).

61. See O'Neill, p. 157. In this passage she also challenges the celibacy of the priestly minister whose sacramental significance is implicated, it seems to me, in the same marital symbolism evoked by the priesthood in general, which is to say that it would be difficult to recognize in a married priest the image of Christ as bridegroom of the church, his one and only bride.

62. O'Neill, p. 153.

63. O'Neill, pp. 155-56. Similarly, John Paul II argues that as an adequate hermeneutic of "the human" requires an appropriate reference to the feminine, analogically it is so in the economy of salvation: there cannot be omitted from the mystery of Christ "the mystery of 'woman': virgin-mother-spouse" (*Mulieris dignitatem*, #22).

This unity is in fact already built into the nature of the sacramental economy, for the sacred symbols already communicate on a natural level something of their supernatural meaning. Hence baptism, to cite one, must be performed with water that signifies cleansing, rather than with oil, for example, which lacks this natural signification. It is not without precedence, then, that John Paul II recognizes within "the dual aspect of man's somatic constitution ('This at last is bone of my bone and flesh of my flesh') . . . an inalienable norm for the understanding of man on the theological plane."[64] With regard, more specifically, to the analogy of spousal love in the letter to the Ephesians mentioned above, Angelo Scola argues that the union of Christ and the church actually precedes that of man and woman, which is to say that the latter union is actually derived from the former, as any end of a thing may be said to determine its origin. "Dual unity finds its definitive archetype in the marriage between the Crucified and Risen Lord and his Body which is the Church."[65]

It is not surprising, then, that John Paul refers to the Eucharist as *"the Sacrament of the Bridegroom and of the Bride,"*[66] for it is that whereby Christ — really united to his body and bride, the church — realizes and makes present the redemptive act whereby she is created. "For it was from the side of Christ as he slept the sleep of death upon the cross that there came forth 'the wondrous sacrament of the whole Church,'" as the Second Vatican Council taught, following the fathers of the church.[67] The Genesis account of the creation of woman from the side of man is thus "the primordial prophecy . . . of the Church who receives her being from Christ."[68] So too Balthasar recognizes in the profound mutuality of man and woman in the natural order a foreshadowing of the mystery of Christ and the church.

> If the Church comes from Christ and, hence in everything which makes it the Church, lives from his substance, then the Son of God has this "feminine" element in him at the deepest level, not because he is a creature, but because he is the Son of the Father. He knows simultaneously what it means

---

64. General audience of November 14, 1979; *Theology of the Body,* p. 48.

65. Angelo Scola, "The Dignity and Mission of Women: The Anthropological and Theological Foundations," *Communio* 25 (spring 1998): 42-56, cited at p. 53.

66. John Paul II, *Mulieris dignitatem,* #26.

67. Council Vatican II, *Sacrosanctum concilium,* #5.

68. Monica Migliorino Miller, *Sexuality and Authority in the Catholic Church* (Ann Arbor: UMI Dissertation Services, 1993), p. 122. This original version differs from the 1995 version published by Associated University Presses (London and Toronto) and the University of Scranton Press.

to be God and to be begotten of the Father. In this double relationship he becomes the origin of the Church. The Church comes from within him through the power of the triune God, but also through his "first-born" love of the Father, which makes room for innumerable other children of God. What he gives is wholly his own, and, thus, he recognizes himself in us, as the Father also recognizes him in us. And we recognize ourselves in him, since we are his "other" (his "feminine completion") only through the communication of his substance.[69]

In this passage he touches upon what John Paul refers to as the "order of love": the communication — and thus the giving and receiving — of divine life and love within the Trinity that becomes a "law" for human fulfillment by the power of the Holy Spirit, "the personal hypostasis of love" through whom this love *which is of God, communicates itself to creatures.*[70] The divine "order of love" is definitively introduced into creation through the eucharistic union of Christ and the church, the sacrifice of the cross giving "definitive prominence to the spousal meaning of God's love." The presentation of Christ in Ephesians 5 as the divine "bridegroom" of the church expresses, according to the pope, the fact that God, who in Christ has loved us "to the end" (John 13:1), has likewise loved us "first" (cf. 1 John 4:19). His unfathomable gift of himself becomes the *measure* (cf. John 15:13) *and* the *source* of all human love, for the bride actually "lives his life" and "shares in his threefold mission." This she does precisely as the beloved one, as one who has first "received" the Bridegroom's gift of love — the gift of himself — and who, in virtue of his gift, has responded with her own self-gift.[71]

From within this perspective, salvation is not simply a matter of the divine nature of Christ permeating the human with life and holiness: what has traditionally been known as the mystical doctrine of redemption with its emphasis upon the divine condescension, the *descending mediation* of the Word.[72] Indeed, beyond the Augustinian image of the mystical marriage between God and man in the person of Christ, who proceeds from the Virgin's womb as from

69. Balthasar, *A Theological Anthropology,* p. 313.

70. John Paul II, *Mulieris dignitatem,* #29, emphasis John Paul's.

71. John Paul II, *Mulieris dignitatem,* #26. See also Michele M. Schumacher, "The Prophetic Vocation of Women and the Order of Love," *Logos* 2, no. 2 (Spring 1999): 147-92, esp. pp. 150-53.

72. Saint Cyrill argued, for example, that the body of Christ is united to life itself and in this way becomes a dispenser of life. Other examples may be found in the works of Saint Irenaeus (ca. 130–ca. 200), Saint Athanasius (ca. 296-373), and Pope Leo I. See Aloys Grillmeier, *Christ in Christian Tradition: From the Apostolic Age to Chalcedon (451),* trans. J. S. Bowden (New York: Sheed and Ward, 1965).

a wedding chamber,[73] is the Pauline image of Christ as bridegroom of the church. Here the emphasis is on that "marvelous exchange" whereby the Son of God becomes man so that human persons might, by divine adoption, become sons and daughters of God.[74] The mediating role attributed to Christ is, therefore, not simply on the level of natures (divine and human) — as might be suggested by the important formula of Gregory of Nazianzus, *quod non est assumptum, non est sanctum,*[75] or that of Pope Leo I referring to Christ's humanity as the instrument *(organon)* of his divinity[76] — but his personal self-donation: his completely unreserved gift of himself to the Father and, in virtue of the same, to those to whom the Father sends him (John 14:31).[77] The filial love of Christ is thus revealed as a bridal love for the church and for each individual destined to salvation in the church.[78] Hence the exhortation of Paul to the Ephesians: "Husbands, love your wives, as Christ loved the church and gave himself up for her, that he might sanctify her, having cleansed her by the washing of water with the word, that he might present the church to himself in splendor, without spot or wrinkle or any such thing, that she might be holy and without blemish" (5:25-27). Significant in this passage is not only the descending mediation effected by the eternal Word in his salvific incarnation and *kenosis* unto death (his assimilation of himself to humanity), but also the ascending mediation of his return to the Father along with his body-bride: his assimilation of humanity to himself. This in turn supposes that this bride "without blemish" is not just passively assimilated to the Lord, but that she becomes like him in the act of becoming one *with* him, that is to say, in her bridal gift of self, in her self-surrender to the Beloved.

73. "Verbum enim sponus, et sponsa caro humana; et utrumque unus Filius Dei, et idem filius hominis: ubi factus est caput Ecclesiae, ille uterus virginis Mariae thalamus ejus, inde processit tanquam sponsus de thalamo suo. . . ." Augustine, *In Johannis evangelium* 8.2.4; *Homélies sur l'Évangile de Saint Jean,* Bibliothèque Augustiniene 71 (Paris: Desclée de Brouwer, 1969), pp. 474-76; *Patrologia Latina,* 35:1452.

74. See Irenaeus, *Adversus haereses* 3.19.1; Sources chrétiennes 211, 374.

75. "What is not assumed is not sanctified."

76. Building upon this insight, Saint Thomas argues that as the instrument of his divinity, Christ's humanity is both sanctified and sanctifying. See *Summa theologica* III, q.34, 1. 1, ad. 3. See also a.3; q.48, a.1; and I-II, q.114, a.6.

77. To be sure, grace is communicated to Christ's members by the personal actions of their head, as Saint Thomas teaches (*Summa theologica* III, q.8, a.5, ad. 1) and not simply by the human nature he shares with all humanity. Of course, it must be granted that Christ's every action followed upon the hypostatic union (see q.3, a.11), in virtue of which his human actions are universally salvific. See III, q.7, a.1, ad. 3; q.8, a.1, ad. 1; q.43, a.2; q.48, a.6.

78. This is not to deny that God wills the salvation of all men. See 1 Tim. 2:4 and Vatican Council II, *Lumen gentium,* II, 16.

As relationally significant, the masculinity of Christ reveals not only the giftedness of his person but also the giftedness of the church and of each of her members who really give themselves to Christ, as we shall see.

Christ's Masculinity as Revelatory of the Bride's Gift of Self

This second form of Christ's mediation alluded to above — Christ's assimilation of humanity to himself[79] — is effected by his Spirit, who "comes *at the price of* Christ's 'departure,'"[80] that is to say, in virtue of his salvific passion. "The cross of Christ on Calvary stands *beside the path* of that *admirabile commercium,* of that *wonderful self-communication of God to man,* which also includes *the call* to man to share in the divine life by giving himself, and with himself the whole visible world, to God, and like an adopted son to become a sharer in the truth and love which is in God and proceeds from God."[81] Salvation is thus a matter of God's gift and our response, of our entering into the trinitarian communion by the very means that characterize it: the *mutual self-giving of persons.*

The corporal unity between Christ and the church — as portrayed in eucharistic imagery of patristic writers and explicitly expressed in the passage of Ephesians we have been considering[82] — is thus a dynamic one, which is to say that it does not suppress the person-to-person communion implied in an authentic "dialogue of salvation." It is thus true to say, for example, that the church as the "body of Christ" originates not only in Christ's sleep of death on the cross, but also in the corporal union of Christ and Mary: in the Son's partaking, as it were, of the mother's flesh in virtue of God's initiating love and of her own maternal self-giving, her virginal fiat.

I am therefore in perfect agreement with Ruether when she argues for a dynamic relationship between "redeemer and redeemed" — even to the extent that the Christian community might be regarded as continuing Christ's identity. The image of a "continued Incarnation,"[83] of Christ living on in his church,

---

79. This is traditionally known as subjective redemption in that it concerns the personal application of Christ's infinite merits.

80. John Paul II, *Dominum et vivificantem,* #14, emphasis John Paul's.

81. John Paul II, encyclical letter on the mercy of God, *Dives in misericordia,* November 13, 1980, #7, emphasis John Paul's.

82. "For no man ever hates his own flesh, but nourishes and cherishes it, as Christ does the church, because we are members of his body. 'For this reason a man shall leave his father and mother and be joined to his wife, and the two shall become one flesh'" (Eph. 5:29-31).

83. The image is from Charles Journet. See, for example, *L'Eglise du Verbe Incarné* II: *Sa Structure interne et son unité catholique* (Paris: Desclée de Brouwer, 1951), p. 581.

suggests, of course, that the eternal Word assumed a human body so as to assume *all* human flesh: female as well as male. On this point feminists and traditional Catholic theologians agree. Uniting himself with humanity in a "one flesh" union by his incarnation — and thereby also "in a certain way" with every human person[84] — he aims thereby to take all of humanity with himself in his "passover" to the Father (cf. John 3:13-15).[85]

This union — to strengthen my previous argument — is thus not simply on the level of *natures*. It is a real union of *persons*, as is implied by the image of the church as bride. The church is, more specifically, the body of Christ *because* she is his bride. This means, as we have seen, that she comes forth from his side as the new Eve of the new Adam. This primary meaning of the church as bride does not however exclude that *she really gives herself to Christ* as a bride is given to her bridegroom. She is, in other words, not only the personification of the temple, in which (or whom) there dwells the glory of the Lord, but also of Daughter Zion, the Lord's covenant partner. "The Bridegroom [of Eph. 5, that is to say, Christ] is the one who loves," comments John Paul II. "The Bride is loved: *it is she who receives love, in order to love in return*."[86]

In no way is this to be interpreted as an exhortation to women to be submissive to their husbands, for the pope insists upon the "mutual subjection" of spouses out of reverence for Christ "and not just that of the wife to the husband."[87] Of significance in this passage is, rather, the fact that the love of the divine Bridegroom is always primary vis-à-vis his bride, the church (and the Christian in the church), as is expressed in the letter to the Ephesians: "Christ loved the church and gave himself up for her, that he might sanctify her, having cleansed her by the washing of water with the word" (5:25-26). It is the sacrificial love of the divine Bridegroom — even unto death[88] — that makes his bride *lovable*, that bestows upon her the dignity of having been chosen and beloved; and it is this love that invests her with the power — indeed with the vocation — to love in return, which is to say that "we love, because he first loved us" (1 John 4:19).

---

84. See Council Vatican II, *Gaudium et spes*, #22.

85. "[T]he whole redeemed city, that is to say, the congregation or community of the saints, is offered to God as our sacrifice through the great High Priest, who offered Himself to God in His passion for us, that we might be members of this glorious head, according to the form of a servant" (Augustine of Hippo, *De civitate Dei* 10.6; English translation by Marcus Dods, *The City of God* [New York: Random House, 1950], p. 310).

86. John Paul II, *Mulieris dignitatem*, #29, emphasis John Paul's.

87. John Paul II, *Mulieris dignitatem*, #24. Reference here is made to Eph. 5:21.

88. "Christ has entered this history and remains in it as the Bridegroom who 'has given himself.' 'To give' means 'to become a sincere gift' in the most complete and radical way: 'Greater love has no man than this' (Jn 15:13)" (John Paul II, *Mulieris dignitatem*, #25).

Of course, it might be argued that while priority in loving is necessarily granted to the divine Bridegroom vis-à-vis the church, his bride, the same is not necessarily true of the human bridegroom vis-à-vis his bride. Indeed, in almost poetic terms Hans Urs von Balthasar describes the reciprocity of marital love: "In the Thou, wife and husband are told and shown who he is, who she is, in truth. Love is creative for the fellow man; it produces an image of him with which the beloved would not have credited himself, and when love is genuine and faithful it gives him the power to come closer to this image or make himself like it. He does not want to disappoint; he wants to show himself grateful that someone takes him so seriously and expects so much of him."[89] This mysterious phenomenon of spousal love obtains its "full truth in Christianity," which is to say that "A Christian never has his unity within himself; nor does he in any way seek it in himself. He does not collect himself around his own center, but rather wholly elsewhere. 'The life I live now is not my own; Christ is living in me. I still live my human life, but it is a life of faith in the Son of God, who loved me and gave himself for me' (Gal 2:20)."[90] The point here, as above, is not only that God's love for us in Christ maintains a certain primacy, but also and especially that our response really is required. As a bride really gives herself to her bridegroom (and not just he to her), the Christian *really does offer himself or herself to Christ.* And this bride includes all of humanity — men and women — since "all are called to respond — as a bride — with the gift of their lives to the inexpressible gift of the love of Christ, who alone, as the Redeemer of the world, is the Church's Bridegroom."[91]

This self-gift of the human person in response to Christ's own extravagant gift of himself on the cross corresponds, the Second Vatican Council reminds us, to the baptismal priesthood of the faithful.[92] "[W]ith respect to salvation," Theodore the Studite argues, "everyone becomes his own priest."[93]

---

89. Hans Urs von Balthasar, *Convergences: To the Source of Christian Mystery,* trans. A. E. Nelson (San Francisco: Ignatius, 1983), pp. 128-29.

90. Balthasar, *Convergences,* p. 129.

91. John Paul II, *Mulieris dignitatem,* #27. See also his general audience of September 29, 1982, in *Theology of the Body,* pp. 330-33.

92. The baptismal priesthood of the faithful is, more specifically, that whereby both men and women alike "present their bodies as a living sacrifice, holy and acceptable to God (cf. Rom 12:1), give witness to Christ in every place, and give an explanation to anyone who asks the reason for the hope in eternal life that is in them (cf. 1 Pt 3:15)" (Vatican Council II, *Lumen gentium,* #10; cited in John Paul II, *Mulieris dignitatem,* #27).

93. Theodore the Studite, *Antirheticus* 1, *Adversus Iconomachos, Patrologia Graeca,* 96:693. Cited by Paul Evdokimov, *Woman and the Salvation of the World: A Christian Anthropology on the Charisms of Women,* trans. Anthony P. Gythiel (Crestwood, N.Y.: St. Vladimir's Seminary Press, 1994), p. 109.

Indeed, for Gregory of Nazianzus, "no one can participate in the sacrifice unless he has offered himself as a victim."[94] Similarly, Origen, commenting on Saint Paul's exhortation to the Romans to present their bodies "as a living sacrifice, holy and acceptable to God, which is your spiritual worship" (12:1), reasons: "All those who have received the anointing have become priests. Each one carries his sacrifice within himself, and he himself puts the fire on the altar, so that he becomes an endless sacrifice. If I renounce everything I own, if I carry my cross and follow Christ, I have made an offering on God's altar. If I deliver my body . . . and pursue the glory of martyrdom, I have offered a sacrifice on God's altar, and I become the priest of my own sacrifice."[95] Certainly any such reference to the baptismal priesthood of the faithful risks infuriating feminists who recognize therein an attempt by the church hierarchy to justify the exclusion of women from among their ranks. Granting women an honorary, which is to say a "lesser," place in the church — one for which bodily sex apparently offers no obstacle — the hierarchy and conservative theologians seek, it is argued, to pacify women. Of course, this important question of women's "place" and role in the church merits particular consideration.[96] To thereby dismiss the question of the sacramental significance of Christ's masculinity, especially in that which concerns his salvific mission, is however, as Joyce Little ably argues, to opt for a functional rather than a sacramental vision of the human person.

> For Christ's maleness, let us clearly keep in mind, is not the disclosure of some divine maleness (in God there is no gender), but the disclosure of Christ's relation to the Church. He is male because he is the relation of Bridegroom. The priest, because he is not just a functionary (no matter how many functions he is required to carry out) but the sacramental sign of Christ, in whose Person he acts, must be capable of entering into that relation which vis-à-vis the Church is explicitly male. To think that women can do this is to suppose, as we have already seen, that male and female are not relationally ordered to one another, but simply interchangeable with one another.[97]

94. Gregory of Nazianzus, *Oratio II, Apologetica* 95, *Patrologia Graeca*, 35:497B, cited by Evdokimov, p. 109.

95. Origen, *In Leviticum, homilia* 9.9, *Patrologia Graeca*, 12:522-23; cited by Evdokimov, p. 109.

96. For a more thorough treatment, see, for example, my article, "Therese, Woman in the Church," *Logos: A Journal of Catholic Thought and Culture* 3, no. 3 (Summer 2000): 122-51.

97. Joyce A. Little, "The New Evangelization and Gender: The Remystification of the Body," *Communio* 21 (Winter 1994): 776-99, cited at p. 798.

This, it seems to me, is exactly what is supposed when, for example, Susan A. Ross insists that "a feminist theology of ordained ministry takes seriously human embodiment" but argues in the next phrase that distinctions of sex are as "irrelevant" to this theology as those of race and class;[98] or when Mary Aquin O'Neill insists upon "the mystery of being human together"[99] but argues that sacramental realism requires "mothers as well as fathers at the altar."[100] If, on the other hand, we wish to maintain that this distinction is sacramentally — and thus theologically — significant, then we must also take seriously the objection posed by Ruether: the argument for an all-male priesthood based upon the sacramental significance of Christ as head and bridegroom of the church apparently contradicts the notion that male laity are "brides" within this symbolic pairing, that they — just as much as women — really must respond to the divine Bridegroom with a sincere gift of self.[101]

Women as Christ's Body and Men as His Brides: A Spiritual Likeness

In responding to this serious objection, we do well to recall Johnson's insistence that women as well as men are "christophormic." It is in precisely this sense that men as well as women are rightfully addressed as "brides," for the spiritual likeness referred to by Johnson between Christ and the Christian is implied thereby. This is particularly apparent in that the "marvelous exchange" of salvation is also understood in terms of a mystical marriage. In the analogy of Ephesians, the "one flesh" union of husband and wife, whereby she is addressed as his "body" and he as hers (cf. 1 Cor. 7:4), is compared to the spiritual union of Christ and the church: she is sanctified and cleansed by the Lord, who presents her to himself "in splendor, without spot or wrinkle or any such thing, that she might be holy and without blemish" (Eph. 5:27). Hence the patristic image of the church as the mystic Eve fashioned from the side of Christ, asleep in the slumber of death on the cross:

> From his side as he slept God took a rib; it was he indeed who slept, took his rest and rose again, for the Lord raised him up. And this rib of his is nothing but his power, his virtue. When the Soldier opened his side there came forth at once blood and water, which was poured forth for the life of the

98. Ross, p. 203.

99. This is the title of her contribution and the theme throughout. See O'Neill, "The Mystery of Being Human Together."

100. O'Neill, p. 157.

101. Ruether, *Sexism and God-Talk*, p. 126.

world. This life of the world is the rib of Christ, the rib of the Second Adam; for the first Adam was made a living soul, but the Second Adam a life-giving spirit. The second Adam is Christ and the rib of Christ is the life of the church. We therefore are members of his body, of his flesh, and of his bones; and it may have been of this rib that he said one day: "I know that virtue is gone out from me" (Lk 8:46).[102]

In the first instance "the woman," or bride, is the church, but the church exists concretely in her members who are male and female. "For just as the body is one and has many members, and all the members of the body, though many, are one body, so it is with Christ. For by one Spirit we were all baptized into one body — Jews or Greeks, slaves or free — and all were made to drink of one Spirit. . . . Now you are the body of Christ and individually members of it" (1 Cor. 12:12-13, 27).

Simultaneously one and many, the bride of Christ is formed from the body he assumed and offered on the cross, the body he even now communicates in a real but sacramental way in the Eucharist for the building up of his mystical body in each of his members. Hence, although the community dimension is emphasized in the marital analogy of Ephesians 5, this should not, Pope John Paul II argues, obstruct the personal dimension, which "pertains simply to the very essence of conjugal love." In that which concerns the biblical figure of the church, "every concrete 'I' should find itself in that biblical 'we.'"[103]

Women, like men, are referred to as Christ's body; men, like women, are referred to as his "bride." Evidently the sacramental meaning of the human body takes on a new dimension here. Even those who share in the ministerial priesthood are included in this "bride" to the extent that they too offer themselves to the divine bridegroom who offers himself through their ministry.[104] The marital symbolism is obviously less apparent in this case, especially when the same individual is regarded under two aspects: as priest and as member. These conflicting images serve, however, to clarify the important distinction between acting in one's own person and acting *"in persona Christi."*[105] In the

---

102. Saint Ambrose, *Exposition of the Gospel according to St. Luke*, bk. 2, #85-89. Cited in Henri de Lubac, *Catholicism: Christ and the Common Destiny of Man*, trans. Lancelot C. Sheppard (London: Burns and Oates, 1950), p. 270; cf. 1 Cor. 6:15-17: "Do you know that your bodies are members of Christ? Shall I therefore take the members of Christ and make them members of a prostitute? Never! Do you not know that he who joins himself to a prostitute becomes one body with her? For, as it is written, 'The two shall become one flesh.' But he who is united to the Lord becomes one spirit with him."

103. John Paul II, general audience of September 29, 1982; *Theology of the Body*, p. 331.

104. On this see John Paul II, *Mulieris dignitatem*, #27.

105. See Vatican Council II, *Lumen gentium*, #28; John Paul II, *Mulieris dignitatem*, #26.

latter case, it is more correct to say that Christ acts in him, for the effect of his action is disproportionate to the act itself: the making present of the real body and blood of Christ in the form (under the appearance) of bread and wine by the pronouncing of the words of institution. These words — "This is my body . . . ; this is my blood" — are then "no mere narrative about the past; they are performative speech acts whereby Christ himself, through the priest, accomplishes the sacramental sacrifice. The shift to the present tense and the first person singular are therefore essential." In uttering these words, the priest "puts on the very person of Christ."[106] In virtue of the sacrament of orders, a priest ministering the sacraments is himself a "sacrament" — sign and instrument — of Christ who, through the instrumental mediation of the priest, offers himself and his bride-body to the Father.[107] This he does once and for all on Calvary, where the church is both created and joined to him in a spiritual "marriage." The effects of that one-time offering continue in time, however, through the ministerial priesthood whereby the sacrifice is made actual and the church is built up, as we have seen. The lay Christian, on the other hand, who participates in this sacrifice does so *in his own person,* which is to say that he or she really offers himself or herself to Christ, and in union with Christ to the Father.

The Christian joined to Christ as a bride to her bridegroom remains — in accord with the marital analogy — a free and, in this sense, an independent person.[108] To the extent that this person is united to the divine Bridegroom, however, he or she is actually *assimilated to him,* as is not necessarily true of the priest through whose ministry the lay Christian offers himself or herself. This assimilation, which is above all *spiritual,* exists primarily on the level of the will: the believer united to the Lord, as a wife to her husband, seeks to please him in all things (cf. 1 Cor. 7:34) by the power of his Spirit who is given to her. This is not simply to grant that the Christian is able to "anticipate" the divine will as a faithful wife, af-

106. Avery Dulles, "Gender and Priesthood: Examining the Teaching," *Origins* 25, no. 45 (May 2, 1996): 781.

107. See Vatican Council II, *Lumen gentium,* #28. It is thus possible to speak of Christ present in the person of the minister, "the same now offering through the ministry of the priest who formerly offered himself on the cross" (Council of Trent, Session 22: Decree on the Mass, chap. 2: *Denzinger* 940 [1743]). See also Congregation for the Doctrine of the Faith, Instruction on the Worship of the Eucharistic Mystery, *Eucharisticum mysterium,* May 25, 1967, #9. (English translation in *Vatican Council II: The Conciliar and Post Conciliar Documents,* ed. Austin Flannery [Collegeville, Minn.: Liturgical Press, 1975], p. 109).

108. Within the context of his commentary on Eph. 5, Pope John Paul II notes "that the essential bi-subjectivity of the husband and wife in marriage, which makes of them in a certain sense 'one single body,' passes within the limits of the whole text we are examining . . . to the image of Church-Body united with Christ as head" (general audience of August 25, 1982; *Theology of the Body,* p. 316).

ter many years of marriage, may be said to know the mind of her husband. The love which joins the believer to Christ is in fact entirely initiated by the divine Bridegroom, even to the extent that the Christian may be said to love Christ with the love *of Christ:* "God's love has been poured into our hearts through the Holy Spirit which has been give to us" (Rom. 5:5).[109] Because the divine Bridegroom lives in the Christian by his Spirit, the former's body becomes that of Christ in a way that no wife — however faithful and true to the intentions of her husband — may be considered "the body" of her husband. Similarly the church, existing concretely in her members — who are thereby the members of Christ — "is the sign and instrument of the presence and action of the life-giving Spirit."[110] In her, whom Christ established as his mystical body, divine life is communicated to believers, who are thereby rightfully referred to as "sacraments" of Christ. Through the sacraments proper, they are "united in a hidden and real way to Christ in his passion and glorification."[111] In the Eucharist, most especially, the Holy Spirit effects the strengthening of "the inner man" (Eph. 3:16)[112] whereby the body-bride is built up through the mystical transformation of each of its members into the image of her Head and Bridegroom. "For, 'the partaking of the Body and Blood of Christ has no less an effect than to change us into what we have re ceived.'"[113] Hence the continuation, noted by Theodore Mopsuestia, of the Spirit's transforming action exerted, first of all, upon the personal body of Christ at the resurrection, then upon the bread and wine in the Eucharist, and finally on those who are nourished for immortality by receiving it.[114] The Spirit's work is

109. Cf. John Paul II, *Mulieris dignitatem*, #27.

110. John Paul II, *Domininum et vivificantem*, #64.

111. Vatican Council II, *Lumen gentium*, #7.

112. John Paul II, *Dominum et vivificantem*, #62.

113. Vatican Council II, *Lumen gentium*, #26. "Let us believe from our hearts and proclaim it by our words that the power of Christ, which is invisible, works through the visible ministry of his priest, and creates out of material bread the true body of Christ. Let us also believe that all who are born again of water and of the Holy Ghost are, by partaking of this food, incorporated into Christ himself" (Adelman of Brescia, *Adelmanni ex scholastic Leodiensi episcopi Brixiensis, de Eucharistiae sacramento ad Berengarium epistola,* cited in de Lubac, p. 260).

114. "To keep alive we take nourishment in the form of bread — not that bread has this power of its own nature; it is only able to keep us alive because God decreed that it should have this power. This fact should convince us that we shall receive immortality when we eat the sacramental bread. For although it is not the nature of bread to produce this effect, once it has received the Holy Spirit and his grace, it can bring those who eat it to the enjoyment of immortality. . . . So too is it with our Lord's body, which the bread signifies: it received immortality and conferred it on others through the power of the Holy Spirit, even though it was quite devoid of immortality by its own nature" (Theodore Mopsuestia, Homily 15.12; First Homily on the Mass, in Edward Yarnold, *The Awe-Inspiring Rites of Christian Initiation: Baptismal Homilies of the Fourth Century* [Slough: St. Paul Publications, 1972], pp. 215-16).

thus described by Balthasar as forming "the mystical body of Christ by spiritually universalizing the historical Christ."[115] "The one loaf is the body of the risen Christ made present once again in space and time (see 1 Cor 10:16-17). Our sharing *(koinonia)* in this life is through a faith appropriated eating of the loaf that makes of all who share in it one body, the one bride of Christ, his flesh, and the one physical reality that gives expression to the unity established by our union with him."[116] It is this real incarnational presence of Christ transmitted in time — a presence that remains remarkably relational, both in his humanity and in his divinity — which is at stake, it seems to me, in the formula *in persona Christi.* Essential to the eucharistic symbolism are, more specifically, the mystical nuptials between the divine Bridegroom and his bride: the "one flesh" union of Christ and the church. In this celebration of the commingling of humanity and divinity in the reciprocal gift of persons — his partaking of her flesh and she of his — the bride really becomes the "body" of her Bridegroom.[117] She and each of her members, who are called to share in her bridal gift of self, are transformed through this eucharistic exchange into his image, becoming thereby a living "sacrament" of Christ.

The Sacramental Meaning of the Female Body-Person and the Assimilation of Grace

Beyond the important question, which has been treated in these pages, of the sacramental meaning of Christ's masculinity, there remains that of the sacramental meaning of the female body, including the question of its influence upon woman's role and place in the church. Hence the objection of O'Neill that even *if* a role were reserved in the church for a woman that could not be filled

115. Hans Urs von Balthasar, "The Word, Scripture and Tradition," in his *Explorations in Theology,* trans. A. V. Littledale with Alexander Dru (San Francisco: Ignatius, 1989), p. 17.

116. Francis Martin, *The Feminist Question: Feminist Theology in the Light of Christian Tradition* (Grand Rapids: Eerdmans, 1994), pp. 346-47.

117. "This communication of the Spirit of Christ is the channel through which all the gifts, powers, and extraordinary graces found super-abundantly in the Head as in their source flow into all the members of the Church, and are perfected daily in them according to the place they hold in the Mystical Body of Jesus Christ. *Thus the Church becomes, as it were, the filling out and the complement of the Redeemer, while Christ in a sense attains through the Church a fulness in all things.* Herein we find the reason why, according to the opinion of Augustine . . . the mystical Head, which is Christ, and the Church, which here below as another Christ shows forth His person, constitute one new man, in whom heaven and earth are joined together in perpetuating the saving work of the Cross: Christ, We mean, the Head and the Body, the whole Christ" (Pope Pius XII, *Mystici corporis,* June 29, 1943 [Boston: St. Paul Editions], pp. 46-47).

by a man — that of being the mother of God, for example — this role is not "symbolized in the official life of the church."[118] In so arguing she ironically insists upon the very hierarchical ecclesiology that many feminists refuse.[119] The importance of this debate does not however lie, it seems to me, in choosing between a Petrine and a Marian church, between the church as office and the church as communion; for both have their origin in Christ.[120] Indeed, this very tension points to the nuptial nature of the church herself. As the body of a married woman is simultaneously her own — being a constitutive part of her person — and that of her husband, in virtue of her self-gift to him, the church is both the body of believers and the body of Christ; it is both human and divine. This is not to say — and it bears repeating — that femininity might be equated with humanity and masculinity with divinity;[121] for Christ, who is both human and divine, is also fully male.[122] The sacramental symbol of the Lord as bridegroom of the church serves not so much to emphasize his divine nature as to reveal the truth concerning human nature as male and female, a truth founded in the human person's creation in the image of the triune God. By revealing, more specifically, the relational meaning of the divine nature through his sacrificial gift of self on Calvary — the fact that God is love (cf. 1 John 4:16) — Christ simultaneously discloses the relational meaning of human nature created in the divine image. When, for example, he prays "that they may all be one . . . even as we are one" (John 17:21-22), the Lord manifests "a certain parallel between the union existing among the divine persons and the union of the sons of God in truth and love." That is to say, he reveals that the human person "can fully discover his true self only in a sincere giving of himself."[123]

This gift of self, precisely as "nuptial" — whether in marriage or conse-

118. O'Neill, p. 157.

119. Ross argues, for example, that "[a] feminist eucharistic theology has its center in the ecclesial assembly not in the presider. When the focus is on the assembly, the Eucharist is a lavish gift to be shared, not scarce gold to be parceled out piecemeal only to those who qualify" (pp. 204-5).

120. "One can say that Christ, inasmuch as he represents the God of the universe in the world, is likewise the origin of both the feminine and masculine principles in the Church; in view of him, Mary is pre-redeemed, and Peter and the Apostles are installed in their office" (Hans Urs von Balthasar, *New Elucidations*, trans. Sister Mary Theresilde Skerry [San Francisco: Ignatius, 1986], p. 193). See also John Paul II, *Mulieris dignitatem*, #27.

121. Ross argues, for example, that the formula *in persona Christi* supports "the long-standing association of maleness with divinity" (p. 202).

122. The masculinity which is apparent in the symbol of the Bridegroom represents, John Paul II notes, "the human aspect of the divine love which God has for Israel, for the Church, and for all people" (*Mulieris dignitatem*, #25).

123. Vatican Council II, *Gaudium et spes*, #24.

crated celibacy — is the basis of what John Paul II calls "a certain 'iconic' complementarity of male and female roles," of "the 'Marian' principle and the apostolic Petrine principle" of the church. About women in particular he notes a "kind of inherent 'prophecy,' a powerfully evocative symbolism, a highly significant 'iconic character,' which finds its full realization in Mary and which also aptly expresses the very essence of the church as a community consecrated with the integrity of a 'virgin' heart to become the 'bride' of Christ and 'mother' of believers."[124] Women are, more specifically, icons of the church because they — as differing from men — are alone capable of entering into a spousal relationship *as brides* and thus also as mothers. They alone are able to so give of themselves as to let the beloved *literally enter within themselves* and to so receive the seed of that relation as to nourish and protect its fruit within their body-persons.[125] In virtue of this potentiality they are *images* — each in her own body-person — *of that which every human being is before God:* a creature destined for union with God and thus "equipped," as it were, with a certain capacity to receive him, that is to say, in the humble manner in which he chooses to give of himself: as the lowly child of Bethlehem, as the bloodied victim of Calvary, and as the bread of life offered in, and by, the hands of his ministers.[126]

In this sense the properly *feminine* relation of bride and mother takes on a particularly *spiritual* meaning, which is to say that it can — indeed it should! — be realized by men as well as women: "For whoever does the will of my Father in heaven," says the Lord, "is my brother, and sister, and mother" (Matt. 12:50; cf. Luke 11:27-28). In Augustinian terms, we were made for God, "and our hearts are restless until they rest in him."[127] "Resting in him" supposes, however, that God be received within the self; for it is in precisely this way that the human person is integrated into the Trinity: through the continuation of the Father's love for the Son in their common love for the disciples (cf. John 17:26).[128]

When, therefore, the pope describes the Bridegroom as "the one who loves" and the bride as *"she who receives love, in order to love in return,"*[129] he

---

124. John Paul II, "Letter to Women," #11, in *Origins* 25, no. 9 (July 27, 1995): 142.

125. For the sake of precision, I might add that this fruit is also very much their own.

126. On this subject see Michele M. Schumacher, "Vers une approche spirituelle de la pauvreté," *Nova et Vetera* 77 (January-March 2002): 51-63. English translation to be published in the fall of 2004 in the English edition of the same journal.

127. Augustine of Hippo, *Confessions* 1.1.

128. On this see Michele M. Schumacher, "The Concept of Redemption in the Theology of Hans Urs von Balthasar," *Theological Studies* 60 (March 1999): 53-71.

129. John Paul II, *Mulieris dignitatem*, #29.

seeks thereby to emphasize "the order of love": the fact, as we have seen, that human love has its measure and source in the divine love of Christ poured forth into our hearts by his Spirit (cf. Rom. 5:5). And this Spirit, it is important to point out, is given to us "at the price" of his passion and death, of his spousal gift of himself "to the end" (John 13:1). This is, in other words, a love which is first of all *received* before it is mediated further by way of a Christian vocation. As such it is always realized in the context of the mutual self-giving of Christ and the Christian, with the result that the question of the priority of a Marian church or of an apostolic-Petrine one is meaningless.[130]

Conclusion: The Sacramental Significance of the Human Body as Male and Female

From this perspective, which emphasizes the mutual relatedness of man and woman and the gifted meaning of human nature, it is difficult to admit an injustice, as does Susan Ross, in the need to "'import' a priest, often unknown to the community [of female religious], to ensure the 'validity' of the Eucharist."[131] On the contrary, there is good reason to agree with O'Neill that "this very inability to live a sacramental life without contact with men" may have saved women from certain "deformations" among male clerics and religious who are able "to separate themselves from women and create a single-sex world."[132] Deprived of meaningful relationships with women, such men are, she argues, thereby deprived of knowledge of themselves as sexually differentiated beings. Indeed, woman's revelation to man of his own masculinity by means of her femininity constitutes the most basic sacramental meaning of the female body-person. As such it is similar, in a complementary manner, to the role of masculinity in revealing the significance of femininity. Each manifests to the sexually differentiated other the "ecstatic" nature of human existence, the

---

130. "Who has precedence in the end? The man bearing office, inasmuch as he represents Christ in and before the community, or the woman, in whom the nature of the Church is embodied — so much so that every member of the Church, even the priest, must maintain a feminine receptivity to the Lord of the Church? This question is completely idle, for the difference ought only to serve the mutual love of all the members in a circulation over which God alone remains sublimely supreme: 'In the Lord, the woman is not independent of the man nor the Man of the woman. For just as the woman [Eve] comes from the man, so also the man [including Christ] comes through the woman; but everything comes from God' (1 Cor 11:11-12)" (Balthasar, *New Elucidations*, pp. 197-98).

131. Ross, p. 204.

132. O'Neill, pp. 154, 155.

vocation to realize oneself by becoming a gift for the other.[133] As Angelo Scola puts it, "unity is the full meaning of difference. Difference, or alterity, is a path to a more complete unity."[134]

Femininity and masculinity are thus natural expressions of the giftedness of the human person — of the fact that both men and women are called to realize themselves by giving themselves to others. On the most natural level this means that man and woman are orientated toward one another in the natural bond of marriage, which is to say that their bodily union is an expression of the spiritual union of their persons. Beyond this fundamental sense, both are orientated toward Christ as a bride to her bridegroom, whereby their marital union is itself a sign, or sacrament, of that to which each is called: a communion of love and life with Christ through his or her self-gift in response to Christ's own self-gift. It is thus possible to regard the spousal union of man and woman, by means of their mutual self-gift, as a *sign*, or sacrament, of the mutual self-gift implied in *the mystery of redemption;* for Christ's gift of self on the cross and in the Eucharist must be received by the believer in the form of his or her own self-gift. Indeed, the original unity of man and woman as portrayed by Genesis is, as we have seen, explained by and orientated toward the mystical nuptials of Christ and the church, which is to say that the Second Adam is united from "the beginning" to his body-bride, the church. "But it is not the spiritual which is first but the physical, and then the spiritual" (1 Cor. 15:46).

In the new economy of salvation, as in the original economy of creation, femininity is meaningful in relation to masculinity, as is masculinity in relation to femininity. "In the Lord woman is not independent of man nor man of woman; for as woman was made from man, so man is now born of woman. And all things are from God" (1 Cor. 11:11-12). Analogically, this means that although priority must be granted to the divine Bridegroom who "first loved us" (1 John 4:19), the believer really is called to receive this love and to respond as a "bride" to the divine Bridegroom. Indeed, the Christian's love for the Lord is itself his gift, for it is Christ's own love that fills his or her heart by his Spirit. Adorned with the treasures of his grace, the bride of Christ — whether male or female — is *spiritually assimilated to him,* in virtue of which she or he acts under the inspiration of his Spirit. As differing from the iconic resemblance of the

133. On this see Rousseau, "John Paul II's Letter on the Dignity and Vocation of Women"; Peter A. Kwasniewski, "St. Thomas, *Extasis,* and Union with the Beloved," *Thomist* 61 (1997): 587-603; Kwasniewski, "Solitude, Communion, and Ecstasy," *Communio* 26 (Summer 1999): 371-92.

134. Scola, p. 53. Similarly, John Paul II writes: "In the sphere of what is 'human' — of what is humanly personal — 'masculinity' and 'femininity' are distinct, yet at the same time they *complete and explain each other*" (*Mulieris dignitatem,* #25, emphasis John Paul's).

priest acting *in persona Christi,* theirs is the *likeness of holiness* to which all are called.

What is said of man with respect to woman is thus also true of the church — and of each member of the church — with respect to Christ, even though the latter always retains a certain primacy in the "order of love." As a woman's body may be said to belong to her husband in virtue of her free gift to him (cf. 1 Cor. 7:4), the Christian's body belongs to the Lord (cf. 6:20). The church, in turn, is "the fulness of him who fills all in all" (Eph. 1:23). Each bears the fruitfulness of the Bridegroom within herself so as to be not merely his vessel (cf. 2 Cor. 4:7), but also his beloved who really shares his wealth. The Bridegroom, writes Saint Cyril of Alexandria, forms us by his grace into his own image. "The beauty of this image shines forth in us who are in Christ, when we show ourselves to be good in our works."[135] The church is thus built up through the sanctification of her members. "Come then, dear God," cries Saint Ambrose, "and fashion this woman, this helper for Adam . . . for Christ. Not that Christ is in any need of help, but because we seek and long to find, through the Church, the grace of Christ. At this very moment the Church is a-building and taking shape; the woman is being fashioned and made. And so the Scripture makes use of a new term: we are 'built up upon' the foundation of the apostles and the prophets (Eph 2:20). At this very moment a spiritual building is rising into a holy priesthood."[136]

135. John Paul II, encyclical on the splendor of truth, *Veritatis splendor,* August 6, 1993, #73, with reference to Saint Cyril of Alexandria, *In Divi Johannis Evangelium,* vol 3, ed. Philip Edward Pusey, Brussels, Culture et Civilisation (1965), p. 590.

136. Ambrose, *Exposition of the Gospel according to St. Luke,* bk. 2, n. 85-9 (*Patrologia Latina,* 15:1666-68); cited in de Lubac, p. 270.

The Teachers of Man, for the Church as Bride

Anne-Marie Pelletier

> *In the mystery of his designs, the Father bestowed a Bride upon his only Son and presented her to him through prophetic signs. Out of love, he built an immense palace for the bride of the one who was light, and on the walls of the abode he painted various pictures of her Husband.*
>
> *Then came Moses who drew with an expert hand a picture of the Bride and Groom and covered it with a veil. He wrote down in his book that man would leave his father and mother and cling to his wife so that the two might truly be one. Thus, the prophet Moses speaks of man and woman to announce Christ and his Church. Moses, with a veil over his face, contemplated Christ and the Church; the one he called man and the other he called woman, to avoid revealing to the Hebrews this reality in its fullness.*
>
> *After the nuptial festivities came Paul. He saw the veil drawn over their splendor and removed it. He revealed Christ and his Church to the entire universe, showing them to be those described by Moses in his prophetic vision.[1]*

In these lines that come to us from the distant fifth century, Jacob of Sarug considers the church in the light of faith. This church is close to us, a familiar part of reality, which is often problematic as well. The church is decried, misunderstood, and is in fact difficult to understand even for Christians themselves. Where our ordinary impoverished and functional apprehension sees merely an institution regulated by human designs, the great hymnographer of the Syrian

---

1. Jacques de Saroug (Jacob of Sarug), "Homilie sur le Voile du Visage de Moïse," *Dieu vivant* 12 (1948): 55-62, at pp. 55-56.

church points to a mystery. The church is deeply rooted in the eternal thought of God. She is a person come forth through the will of God and destined, before time, to be the Son's beloved. This sumptuous Eastern theology also seeks, by means which may seem surprising, to lead us to the heart of the church, where she may be seen as a mystery of grace, inseparable from God's eternal plan and thus also from the blessed Trinity.

Certainly the designation of the church as "the bride of Christ" is current in Christian writings of both the patristic and medieval periods. "You know the Bridegroom, Jesus Christ. You know the Bride, the Church. Give glory to she who is espoused just as to him who espouses, and thus, you will be their children,"[2] preaches Saint Augustine to the Christians of Hippo, while Saint Gregory declares that "the Father brought about the wedding of the King, his Son, when, by means of the Incarnation, he united him with the Holy Church."[3] Jacob of Sarug, however, is not content to elaborate upon this rich traditional title and brings out the anthropological reality to be used as a reference and starting point. He brings to light man and woman who, in their union, even before the fullness of revelation, already allude to the mystery of the church. He recognizes in the human couple the *figure* of God's eternal plan, a figure inscribed within the lives of human societies and realized at the heart of the history of Israel, "in our own time, the last days," in the person of the church, body of Christ.

This perspective of placing mystical and divine reality within the same framework as anthropological reality evidently confers to the human couples a very singular importance and dignity. This is confirmed by the fact that the covenant, which lies at the heart of biblical revelation and will become the strongest expression of the relation God establishes with Israel, comports a nuptial meaning. We may recall here that the covenant, in its beginnings, may be interpreted as a type of contract between political powers of the ancient Near East, in which one party would become the protectorate of another. With the prophet Hosea, however, its meaning takes on a new aspect and is colored by a reference to conjugal life and to the loving ties formed between man and woman in a relation which calls for commitment in fidelity: "I will betroth you to myself for ever, betroth you with integrity and justice, with tenderness and love; I will betroth you to myself with faithfulness, and you will come to know Yahweh" (Hos. 2:10-20). Hosea's mission is to denounce the people's infidelity through his preaching and especially by the example of his life as a man ridiculed by an unfaithful wife. The words of the oracle cited above are nonetheless entrusted to him within this mission. The prophetic books continually orches-

---

2. Augustine, *Sermons au peuple* 90.6 (Edition Vivès, vol. 17, p. 57).
3. Gregory, Homily 38 on the Gospels, *Patrologia Latina*, 76:1283.

trate this promise that remains irrevocable, even in contexts charged with the vocabulary of judgment. Through Jeremiah, God confirms, "I have loved you with an everlasting love" (Jer. 31:3). Through Isaiah he reassures his people that "my love for you will never leave you and my covenant of peace with you will never be shaken" (Isa. 54:10).

In such a way the prophet's words depict the reality of a covenant for which love is both the reason and end. In this they constitute the climax of revelation and are the very greatest expression of hope. The shrewd eye, accustomed to our contemporary anthropological debates, is however likely to point out the difficulties this biblical language presents. The problem with this theological approach lies in a dual pairing: the masculine and the feminine on one hand, the divine and the human on the other; femininity being a reference to what is human and masculinity corresponding to the divine. The unfortunate consequences, which may ensue, are apparent when we consider that God is holy and Israel is sinful. Masculinity is thus associated with the figure of God — creator, all-powerful, holy, faithful — while femininity bears a connotation that is doubly negative: the female spouse is the symbol of created humanity and of the human sinner. The dissymmetry, thus understood, seems to be carried on into the New Testament where the sexual reference continues to be solicited in designating the church as bride of Christ-Bridegroom, and it is from this point that Jacob of Sarug develops his theme. It is understandable therefore that in feminist theologies this type of thought is the object of critical suspicion, and we wish to place the following reflections within the framework of this very problem. These reflections will attempt to identify the role of femininity in biblical revelation, and thus also the significance of the nuptial motif, on the basis of several key references from the Old and New Testaments. Our purpose in so doing is to bring to light the reasons for using feminine symbolism to present the church as well as to indicate certain possible effects of this theological perspective on the relations between men and women.

A Nuptial Figure of the Chosen People

It would seem that the Old Testament books are directly exposed to criticism, which taxes the Bible with a negative view of femininity. The cultural background of a patriarchal society and its traditions explains why women in these books are commonly placed in a situation of dependency on men, are deprived of a series of rights granted to men, are confined solely to the social conditions of spouse and mother and are thus rarely apparent in the grand gestures of Israel's history.[4] Upon reexamination, however, the question proves much more complex. Femininity in the biblical tradition is far from associated with merely depreciative significations.

On Nuptial Symbolism

It is in light of this that the nuptial symbolism mentioned above must be correctly appreciated from the outset. At first glance, it is a symbolism that seems to express a dissymmetry and to confine the feminine to a secondary role, in keeping with a typology all too familiar to human cultures. The consideration, however, of the different metaphors brought into play by the biblical text to express the relations God establishes between himself and his people suggests another interpretation.

As we know, the Old Testament calls God by various names.[5] He is designated as "King" ("Yahweh our King and our saviour," Isa. 33:22), "teacher" ("what teacher can be compared with him?" Job 36:22), "shepherd" of Israel ("and we are the people he pastures, the flock that he guides," Ps. 95:7). He is also the winegrower of the vineyard, Israel ("Yes, the vineyard of Yahweh Sabaoth is the House of Israel," Isa. 5:7), "architect" of his people who declares, "I lay in Zion a stone of witness, a precious cornerstone" (Isa. 28:16). Each of these figures brings to light a particular aspect of God's solicitude for his chosen people, but also implies an inequality. With the spousal image, however, confirmed as of the eighth century, we leave aside this asymmetry. As André Neher writes in his study on conjugal symbolism in the Bible, the spousal metaphor has the advantage over all other covenant symbols of "creating a space in which the Divine and the human are not merely dependent on one another, but come together in an encounter." Neher shows that the Bible is careful to avoid the restraint of referring solely to the marital bond, which would, of itself, be very much in keeping with the idea of inequality. Instead, he goes on to explain, the Bible surpasses this inequality by associating the principle of love with the physical union of spouses, where, to use the words of Genesis, man and woman are but one body. He states in conclusion that "the union of partners is then perfect and each one is empowered with the same capacity to love."[6]

It is thus clear that the biblical texts that use the nuptial theme do not aim

4. See R. de Vaux, *Les Institutions de l'Ancien Testament* (Paris: Ed. du Cerf, 1976), esp. 1:52-56, 67-69.

5. Cf. "Dieu," in *Vocabulaire de Théologie biblique,* Ancien Testament (Paris: Ed. du Cerf, 1974), p. 283.

6. André Neher, "Le symbolisme conjugal, expression de l'histoire dans l'Ancien Testament," *Revue d'Histoire et de Philosophie religieuses,* 1954, p. 38.

at suggesting or arguing in favor of a hierarchy or dissymmetry between God and Israel. Their use of a particular lexical repertory is rather the unexpected means to a more profound understanding of the covenant. Although this latter bears traits of inequality in its beginnings — for it establishes relation, fundamental dissymmetry, between the divine and the human — the conjugal reinterpretation inaugurated by the prophet Hosea ends in the designation of two interlocutors: God and Israel who, through the grace of love, encounter each other face-to-face, as man and woman in their original state of awe (Gen. 2).

From the Unfaithful Wife . . .

This point is of major importance and will enable us to correctly rectify the interpretation of Israel's ulterior history, the drama that is due to the covenant being more than a contract; it brings love into play. For this very reason the words of the prophets are often crucial. When the prophet Hosea is ordered by God to marry a prostitute and to remain faithful to her, despite her infidelity, the purpose is to show that the covenant is founded by God in a love which is beyond reason, which is prepared to attempt all possible strategies in order to bring back stray hearts, prostituted to false gods. It is nonetheless indisputable that by this very fact, the tumultuous history of Israel never ceases to condemn the dissymmetry between the unfailing love of the Spouse and his bride's betrayals. The various "trials" which stand out throughout the prophetic books testify to the dramatic history of which Ezekiel 16, among others, is an enthralling summary. As the generations pass, the reciprocity of love, the most moving revelation of the covenant, is progressively overshadowed by the growing separation between divine fidelity, which is impossible to discourage, and human infidelity, whose only remedy appears to be an act of God re-creating the human heart.

It cannot be denied that femininity here — a metaphor for the people, designating both *men and women* of Israel — is often associated with Israel's negative history. The risk then exists for Israel's masculine population, not to mention readers of the Bible on a more general scale, to draw from this an argument used to accuse and burden the feminine portion of humanity. At the same time, what is conveniently forgotten is that the infidelity stigmatized in the female spouse figure is the infidelity of the entire people. In a closer reading of the texts, it may be sufficiently ascertained that beyond the use of the feminine metaphor, the prophetic oracles distribute condemnations and sanctions in a way that can hardly be said to spare the men of Israel. As an illustration of this, we have only to consider the first chapters of the book of Isaiah, where the prophet orchestrates the trial instituted by God on his people. Admittedly a long passage of the text is heavy-handed in its vehemence toward the daughters of Zion:

> Yahweh said: Because of the haughtiness of the daughters of Zion, the way they walk with their heads high and enticing eyes . . . the Lord will give the daughters of Zion itching heads and uncover their nakedness. That day the Lord will take away the ankle ornaments, tiaras, pendants, and bracelets, the veils, headbands, foot chains and belts. . . . Instead of scent, a stink; instead of belt, a rope; instead of hair elaborately done, a shaven scalp, and instead of gorgeous dress, a sack; and brand marks instead of beauty. (3:16-24)

It would nonetheless be an error to conclude that women are particularly at fault. Other oracles are even more forceful in denouncing the people's "princes" (1:23), "judges" (1:26), "sorcerers" (2:6), the folly of a society in which "raw lads rule" (3:4), where people "add house to house and join field to field" (5:8), "from early morning chase after strong drink" (5:11), and "call evil good, and good evil" (5:20). In addition, it is not certain that the above diatribe against the daughters of Zion is not to be interpreted metaphorically: daughters of Zion meaning people of God.

. . . to Holy Zion

There is still more evidence to be considered: the resolutely positive elaboration of the female spouse figure as evoked sporadically throughout the Old Testament, beginning with the return from exile on through what the prophet Jeremiah calls the "new covenant" (Jer. 31:31). Here too the book of Isaiah is exemplary. In its second part, which may be dated from the time of the exile, the book depicts in various oracles and as a counterpoint to the Servant figure the traits of a holy Zion, a Zion beautiful to an unimaginable perfection, mother of a numerous people, donned with the brilliance of holiness in which God rejoices:

> See, I have branded you on the palms of my hands, your ramparts are always under my eye. Your rebuilders make haste, and your destroyers and despoilers depart. Look round about you, look, all are assembling, coming to you. By my life — it is Yahweh who speaks — you will wear these as your jewels, they will adorn you as brides are adorned. . . . You will then say in your heart, "Who has borne me these? I was childless and barren, who has brought these up? I was left alone, and now, where do these come from?" (Isa. 49:16-18, 21)

This same city of Zion is mentioned in another oracle as a city rebuilt with splendor by God: "Unhappy creature, storm-tossed, disconsolate, see, I will set your stones on carbuncles and your foundations on sapphires. I will make rubies your battlements, your gates crystal, and your entire wall precious stones" (Isa. 54:11). What is more, it is again Zion who hears proclaimed: "For now your creator will be your husband, his name, Yahweh Sabaoth" (Isa. 54:5). "You are to be a crown of splendour in the hand of Yahweh, a princely diadem in the hand of your God. . . . Like a young man marrying a virgin, so will the one who built you wed you, and as the bridegroom rejoices in his bride, so will your God rejoice in you" (Isa. 62:3, 5). Israel-Zion declares in response, "I exult for joy in Yahweh, my soul rejoices in my God, for he has clothed me in the garments of salvation, he has wrapped me in the cloak of integrity, like a bridegroom wearing his wreath, like a bride adorned in her jewels" (Isa. 61:10). Here Zion is the perfect bride in whom the words of Hosea are fulfilled: "That is why I am going to lure her and lead her out into the wilderness and speak to her heart. . . . There she will respond to me as she did when she was young, as she did when she came out of the land of Egypt" (Hos. 2:14-15). We also see here why Zion, in one of the last oracles of Isaiah, is a mother who miraculously gives birth to an entire nation, a numerous people that reconstructs the unity of Israel and the nations (Isa. 66:8).[7] The city described as a person evokes at the same time a collective entity, symbolizing the people as a whole. It is, as may be said of the Servant figure, a corporate personality.

In this way true femininity, as the Old Testament knows it, culminates in the figure of Zion, which both supports and confirms that of the beloved fiancée in the Song of Songs. This other major text, first belonging to Israel's tradition and later to that of the church, portrays a woman who is free of all infidelity, of all sin,[8] weaving her song into that of her beloved. In beauty, she who expresses herself in this greatest of love songs surpasses imperfection. She is so beautiful in body, so beautiful in heart, that her fiancé is faint with love: "You are wholly beautiful, my love, and without a blemish. Come from Lebanon, my promised bride, come from Lebanon, come on your way. . . . You ravish my heart, my sister, my promised bride, you ravish my heart with a single one of your glances, with one single pearl of your necklace" (4:7-9). The praises of this same woman are sung in Psalm 45: "then the king will fall in love with your

7. On Jerusalem, daughter of Zion, see Christine Pellistrandi, *Jérusalem épouse et mère* (Paris: Ed. du Cerf, 1989), pp. 185ff.

8. Song of Songs 1:5, "I am black but lovely, daughters of Jerusalem," has a tendency to arouse discussion. In church tradition these words have often been commented on as alluding to a past of infidelity and sin. The Hebrew *vev*, however, does not imply the opposition that this understanding supposes.

beauty" (v. 11). In this vibrant, jubilant love no trace is to be found of that which, subsequent to the transgression in Genesis 3, altered the original partnership between man and woman, described in its fullness in chapter 2. In this text, more than ever before, a relation is to be found which is rigorously equal: the man and woman of the Song of Songs exchange as equals the words by which they mutually celebrate each other. Some commentators conclude from this — in a not impossible hypothesis — that a woman wrote the book.[9] What is essential, however, is that Israel has unceasingly interpreted these words as expression, by means of a human love song, of its own collective history, fashioned within the mystery of the covenant granted by God. The Midrash and the Targum, for instance, interpret the Song in this way, using words from the text in their commentaries of great moments in Israel's history.[10] Beyond actual life experience, the Song is also the expression of an impossibility which is promised: that Israel will at last respond fully to love, that she will truly be the beloved wife of her beloved husband.

After the return from exile, this feminine figure of the people will be brought out in the texts with increasing emphasis. This is certainly the way the "woman of worth" *(eshet hayil)* at the end of the book of Proverbs is to be interpreted: "A perfect wife — who can find her? She is far beyond the price of pearls" (31:10). An excessively hasty reading of the text often reveals a mere portrait interpreted as either a somewhat conventional eulogy of the industrious woman, attentive to her husband's interests, or the defense and illustration of a femininity which gains liberties and takes initiatives during the centuries following the return from exile.[11] The Jewish tradition was not in error however when seeing in this text a celebration of Israel in its various representatives. *Eshet hayil* is identified with both feminine (Sarah and Rachel) and masculine (Noah, Abraham, Moses, etc.) figures, and becomes in later interpretations a figure of the people as a whole, of each man and woman composing it. Anita Sanchez-Bourdin, in a detailed study of the text,[12] remarks that here *eshet hayil* is the entire people, the community of Israel, which is to God what a bride is to her beloved bridegroom, and stretching her interpretation even further, she adds, "In this woman, the Creator's perfection is so fully present that she can-

9. This is the case in particular of André LaCocque, "Cantique des Cantiques," in P. Ricoeur, A. LaCocque, *Penser la Bible* (Paris: Ed. du Seuil, 1998), p. 383.

10. See my work, *Lectures du Cantiques des Cantiques, De l'Énigme du sens aux figures du lecteur,* Analecta biblica 121 (Rome, 1989), pp. 383ff.

11. Concerning the historical context of this text, see Claudia V. Camp, *Wisdom and the Feminine in the Book of Proverbs* (Sheffield: Almond Press, 1985).

12. Anita Sanchez-Bourdin, *Le poème alphabétique de Proverbes 31:10-31* (Brussels: Institut d'Etudes Théologiques, 1994), *Pro manuscripto*.

not help but, in the end, bespeak him: EH[13] is the God of Israel caring for the needs of his people. The maternal images used by the prophets allow for this radical reversal of roles. EH resembles her Creator, and tradition encourages us to distinguish, symbolically present in her, his valorous acts, his countenance." This superb vision makes femininity the expression of the perfection of love to which all Israel is called and because of which humanity at last reproduces God's image, deposited within her at the moment of her creation.

At the Appointed Time

The feminine as expressed in the New Testament is naturally in the wake of this tradition. On one hand and at a first level of observation, it extends the sociocultural dispositions of the First Testament, for women in Palestine at the time of Christ continued to live in the shadow of men and in dependency on them, being ranked among the most vulnerable members of society. The part played by women in the recognition of Christ's resurrection provides an example of this inferior status. They are by no means excluded from encounters with the resurrected Lord. Faithful to the end at the foot of the cross, they are the first to be present — already at the break of dawn — at the tomb to embalm the body of Jesus; hence they are the first to discover the empty tomb. Only on the testimony of men, however, does the unbelievable event begin to gain credibility amongst the disciples, for whom the myrrh bearers' testimony is "pure nonsense" (Luke 24:11).

"God Sent His Son, Born of a Woman . . ."

Once again, however, the mildly attentive eye brings to light a discreet yet decisive participation of women in the history of the gospel and the work of redemption. Mary, mother of Jesus, is clearly the most eminent example of this, for, as Saint Anselm admirably puts it: "God is the Father of all things created and Mary is the mother of all things re-created. God is the Father of universal creation and Mary is the mother of universal redemption."[14] The biblical narratives strongly uphold this conviction in the Gospel of Matthew, whose first chapters make a point of emphasizing "the child and his mother," or in the

---

13. i.e., *eshet hayil* (our own specification).

14. Saint Anselm, Prayer to Mary, *Patrologia Latina*, 158:956, cited in J-R. Pouchet, *Saint Anselme* (Paris: Ed. du Cerf, 1970), p. 94.

Evangelist Luke's opening account of Christ's childhood, which is also a testimony to Mary's part in the incarnation. Paul masterfully expresses the same reality in this sedate verse of the letter to the Galatians: "When the appointed time came, God sent his son, born of a woman . . ." (4:4).

In Mary, daughter and woman of Israel, receptive to the divine word and faithful in keeping it, steadfast in the humble obedience of faith, we are given to contemplate not only a woman but also all of Israel. The entire people — men and women alike — is manifest in the holiness of the covenant lived at last.[15] The Zion image encountered in the oracles recalled above achieves its fullness in Mary, who is both an individual woman and the figure of the new people brought to life in her. She is both mother of Christ and mother of the church — from the moment on the cross when Jesus gives John and Mary to each other (John 19:26-27) — and at the same time she is the perfect expression of the church. In a sermon on the assumption, Isaac of Stella meditates on this mystery within the mystery of Christ:

> The unique Christ is the Son of one Father in heaven and one mother on earth. There are many sons; there is but one son. Just as the head and the body are the only son and many sons, Mary and the Church are the only mother and many mothers, the only virgin and many virgins. Both are mothers; both are virgins. . . . One, free from all sin, gave birth to the head for the body; the other brought to life, through the forgiveness of sins, a body for the head. Both are mothers of Christ, but neither of the two fully engenders him without the other.[16]

In the last chapter of his great work *The Splendour of the Church*, Henri de Lubac assembles a number of texts from tradition which expand upon the richness of meaning in the relationship and mutual interpretation of the virgin Mary and the church according to the medieval principle which recalls: "Mary is figured in the Church, and the Church is figured in Mary."[17] This precious study, describing what Scheeben calls the "perichoresis" of Mary and the church, might be cited in full. In one admirable passage where he allows the words and images of multiple authors to resound, Fr. de Lubac reexamines the

---

15. On this point see my article, "Marie *versus Israël* et mère de l'Eglise," *Christus* 183 (July 1999): 283-96. See also Ignace de la Potterie, *Mary in the Mystery of the Covenant,* trans. Bertrand Buby (New York: Alba House, 1992), and Aristide Serra, *Miryam Giglia di Sion, La Donna di Nazaret e il femminle a partire dal giudaismo antico* (Rome: Ed. Paoline, 1997).

16. Isaac of Stella, "Homily for the Assumption," *Patrologia Latina,* 194:1863.

17. This is Serlo of Savigny's expression, cited by Henri de Lubac, *The Splendour of the Church,* trans. Michael Mason (New York: Sheed and Ward, 1956), p. 248, or in a later edition by the same translator (Glen Rock, N.J.: Paulist, 1963), p. 205.

episodes of Mary's life, so discreetly alluded to in the Gospels. This text must be quoted at length:

> When the Word, becoming flesh in her womb, poured out all His treasures upon her, He was already wedding and endowing His Church in the person of His Mother. Mary's *fiat* was an acceptance of the full realization of promises on her own account but also for all — collectively — and that *fiat* was awaited as coming from all. And when she exulted in her joy before Elizabeth it was again in the name of the whole Church that she cried out prophetically: "My soul hath magnified the Lord." . . . And when she looked on the Son in Nazareth and worshipped Him in silence, she was anticipating the worship that He was to receive from all the saints to come, and thus held the place of the whole Church, which she represented before Him. When, as the "silent Mother of the silent Word" she held blindly to the mysteries of God, watching all things and keeping them and pondering them in her heart, she prefigured that long train of memory and intense meditation that is the very soul of the tradition of the Church. And finally on Calvary, through the three long hours, holding the Church's place at the foot of the cross, she received from her Son the definitive teaching — a teaching not of words but of act through which all words are illuminated.[18]

The Church's Countenance in Other Women

Although the church recognizes Mary's preeminence and in looking at her meditates upon her (the church's) own identity, she is not "the only one of her sex"[19] to be the figure of the church in the Gospels. Much interest has developed in "the women of the Gospels" in recent decades, often in order to rehabilitate women, to argue in favor of Jesus' particular attention to them, to plead for the feminine in opposition to the masculine, allegedly held in greater honor in the primitive church. This view of the problem is probably too narrow, however. We must look to Martha and Mary, the Canaanite woman, the woman suffering from a hemorrhage, Mary Magdalene, the crippled woman, the widow of

---

18. De Lubac, pp. 260-61 (pp. 213-14 of the Paulist Press 1963 edition). On this same subject see Cardinal Joseph Ratzinger and Hans Urs von Balthasar, *Marie première Eglise* (Médiaspaul and Pauline ed., 1987).

19. This is the expression of Caelius Sedulius, who declares that the Blessed Virgin is "alone of all her sex to have pleased God." These words have been used as the title of a book by Marina Warner, *Alone of All Her Sex: Myth and Cult of the Virgin Mary* (New York: Random House, 1983).

Nain, the widow of the temple, and so many others, not simply to know what role women play in Jesus' ministry or what unusual attention they receive from the rabbi of Nazareth, but rather to learn from them the thoughts and gestures which, in the lives of both *men* and *women,* lead to holiness (the baptismal vocation) and shape the church's countenance in each of its members.[20]

Here too we must go beyond certain clichés. The women remembered by the Gospels are at times sinners who, welcomed and pardoned by Christ, become joyful messengers for all of the salvation which reunites humanity in the person of the Son of God. This is the case, for example, of the Samaritan woman and of the sinful woman who comes before Jesus in Simon's house. Their testimony to merciful love in the new age of mercy inaugurated by Jesus is clearly of capital importance for the life of the church, whose primary proclamation bears upon the forgiveness of which she is herself engendered.

Women are also the bearers of other signs, essential to the life of the church. Such — to restrict ourselves to several, only too brief, illustrations — is the case of Simon's mother-in-law, whose healing is reported by the synoptic Gospels: "And going into Peter's house Jesus found Peter's mother-in-law in bed with fever. He touched her hand and the fever left her, and she got up and began to wait on him" (Matt. 8:14-15). In a way, the event is of slight importance. All three synoptic Evangelists, amidst a series of far more impressive miracles, nonetheless reiterate it; for in a few words the scene fully expresses the identity of the church. Having been brought to her feet by Christ's death, she serves the one who came to serve her. The same may be said of the scene known as "the widow's mite" reported by Mark and Luke. Here the context is the approaching passion. The Gospel account bears the traits of rising suspense that intensifies debate; the great, grave, and urgent questions of existence rush into the mouths of Jesus' interlocutors, inciting him to decisive instruction. Suddenly a narrative pause arises (Mark 12:41-44//Luke 21:1-4): "He sat down opposite the treasury and watched the people putting money into the treasury." Here again, the episode is minor: "A poor widow came and put in two small coins, the equivalent of a penny." The hasty reader sees in this no more than a brief, edifying scene on the generosity of the poor. In reality, in the context of Jesus' ultimate ministry in Jerusalem where the question of his sovereignty has just been solemnly addressed ("The Lord said to my Lord: Sit at my right hand . . ."), it is of far greater importance; it bespeaks a faith so bold as to act on absolute trust: "But she from the little she had has put in everything she possessed, all

---

20. France Quéré, in her work *Les femmes de l'Evangile* (Paris: Ed. du Seuil, 1982), clearly adopts this perspective. The book proposes an admirable series of portraits of the women of the Gospels.

she had to live on." This gesture expresses what it means to be a disciple of the one who will live this same trust in his upcoming passion. Who can give of himself in such a way without believing that God has the power to give him life? This poor widow is the church herself who, based on Christ's word and on faith in his resurrection, believes, even unto and including the trial of death, that one person alone is capable of giving her life.[21] We should of course mention along these same lines still other women of the Gospels: those who welcome Jesus into their homes; Mary, who listens with delight to the words he speaks; those like the Canaanite woman, so ably allying intrepidity and reverence, who cry out to him in their distress; she who anoints his body in anticipation of his passion the following day; or those who remain at the foot of the cross when all have deserted him.

Femininity beyond the Feminine

A revisiting of these familiar Gospel scenes reveals that these women express far more than anthropological femininity. Along with the Blessed Virgin, they make up the icon of Christian life in the Gospels, painted in everyday colors, the colors of life in its essence, lived in an awareness of the true value of things, of time, and of the treasures of love, more certain than the deceitful pomp of honor and power. These women are instinctively aware that their poverty opens the floodgates of God's grace. Not surprisingly, the Magnificat is the song of a woman and, at the same time, the church.

To merely establish a contrast between men and women in the Gospels would be to simplify things, for one might easily match the feminine figures mentioned above with their masculine counterparts: the blind man Bartimaeus is no less an expression of the church than is the crippled woman Jesus heals; the Roman centurion imploring for the life of his child no less than the Canaanite woman requesting her daughter's salvation. The real difference is not to be established on the basis of sex. It lies instead in a distinction between the poor — be they men or women — who confidently present Christ with their poverty and the self-sufficient who, because they do not need Christ, can receive nothing from him. It is a distinction between those who recognize their need for God's assistance and those enslaved by false self-mastery. In the former category, men as well as women find their place.

---

21. Cardinal Christoph Schönborn's commentary of this text in a recent conference given during Lent may be of interest to the reader. *Quel avenir pour l'Europe?, Des cinq continents, cinq temoins,* presented by Cardinal Lustiger (Paris: Presses de la Renaissance, 2001), pp. 41ff.

The women who cross Jesus' path do clearly appear to be more spontaneously conscious than men of their need for God. Their objective situation probably preserves them in part from spiritual pride, to which are captive many men of Israel who use the law to protect and justify themselves. Because they are accustomed to serving, the mystery of a Messiah-Servant, whose "state was divine, yet he did not cling to his equality with God" (Phil. 2:6),[22] is certainly also more readily accessible to women. It remains nonetheless true that *all men* are encouraged to adopt the attitude of the widow who gives her life to God; *all men* are to identify themselves with Mary Magdalene, who in loving desire searches for Christ on Easter morning.

As we have seen, femininity in Scripture reaches beyond the feminine to constitute a characteristic of humanity. It is a facet of the human by which humanity comes into the fullness for which it was desired and created by God. But why then, one might object, is it designated in a way that strictly relates it to a mere portion of this humanity? Why is there in biblical tradition an odd insistence on using words and metaphors from the feminine realm to designate the holy people, a people composed of both men and women? If we refuse the easy conclusion that it is all just a question of artificial and suspicious rhetoric, we must seek the theological significance of these dispositions.

In fact, to use the technical terminology familiar to modern language sciences, it is as if the feminine constituted in biblical revelation the nonexclusive but nonetheless preferred signifier of a signified which gathers men and women into the single entity of humanity as a whole. This consideration, of utmost importance, requires abstaining from any hasty association of the masculine with the divine and the feminine with the human. The masculine naturally finds its place within the *human,* signified by a femininity including both sexes, and this is what the people-bride metaphor in fact expresses. It is also what is implied in Ephesians 5, which makes ample use of the Christ-church and man-woman parallels in the well-known polemical terms encouraging women to "submit" to their husbands as the church submits to Christ, while men are called to "love their wives as Christ loved the church." Unless we recall that Saint Paul confirms here in unquestionable terms the unity of the Christian vocation — all are called to be children of God; all are called to holiness which is God's glory — we are clearly unable to penetrate the meaning of these texts. Only in verse 22 does Paul begin a detailed account of specific roles and identities, recommending that each person live the unique baptismal condition with the specificity by which he or she becomes the "sign" of one aspect of Christian life. In

22. The history of womankind testifies to this proximity that is both a vulnerability and a grace. See my work, *Le Christianisme et les femmes* (Paris: Ed. du Cerf, 2001).

this way man is called to become the sign of Christ for the woman who is, by her baptismal vocation, to be configured to Christ. On her part, woman is called to be the sign of the church for the man, the church that he both is and must learn to be. In other words, man who is, in his being, both church and member of the church, is also Christ by participation. By imitating the "senti-ments" of Christ, he must be, according to his abilities, the sign of Christ for the woman. This latter, who is also church, and thus body of Christ, is asked to live this in such a way that she *teaches* the man the attitudes of the church-bride.[23] What this means is that from Paul's text, correctly understood, it may be con-cluded that man *(vir)* cannot truly realize his divine vocation unless he con-sents to being taught. He must allow himself to receive knowledge, through woman's intermediary, of what he is before God and of what he is to become. On this condition he can, in the words of Jacob of Sarug, be the church that the Father wishes to present to the Son.

The reversal brought about by the views we have attempted to argue here may seem surprising. Might there be, in contrast to received evidence, a privi-lege for women in the recognition of Christ's church in her femininity, ex-pressed in particular by the traditional nuptial theme? We would fall back into the all-too-human simplifications of our controversy should we affirm this without some modulation. It is, however, not possible to exclude that element of both ancient and current thought according to which women hold an essen-tial pedagogical function. This theme, developed by the Fathers early on, fur-nishes discourses, which otherwise bear traits of misogyny, with a solid equilib-rium. Over the last decades John Paul II has emphatically returned to this theme, yet it remains uncertain whether he has really been heard by a great number of the church's members: "The moral and spiritual strength of a woman is joined to her awareness that *God entrusts the human being to her in a special way,*" he writes in *Mulieris dignitatem,* adding, further on, "If the human being is entrusted by God to women in a particular way, does not this mean that *Christ looks to them for the accomplishment of the 'royal priesthood'* (1 Peter 2:9), which is the treasure he has given to every individual?"[24]

---

23. Concerning the interpretation of Eph. 5:21-23, see my article, "Le signe de la femme," *Nouvelle Revue Théologique* 2, no. 113 (1991): 665-89. Concerning the church's femi-ninity on a larger scale, see Maria Teresa Pocile Santiso, *La Femme espace de salut* (Paris: Cerf, 1999).

24. John Paul II, *Mulieris dignitatem* (Boston: St. Paul Books and Media, 1988), #30.

In Conclusion

At the end of our inquiry we see that it could be disastrous for a sound ecclesiology to be drawn into contemporary views pleading for a *gender* that, in the end, neutralizes difference between man and woman. We also realize that it would be detrimental to confuse roles, to suppress the differences that articulate the reality of the ecclesial body, in the name of a vocation which, although in fact shared, is lived in diversity, and in particular in the primary and fundamental diversity found in sex difference. It certainly remains important for us today to reinvestigate, with the inspiration of our contemporary questions, the significance of the incarnation, whereby God comes to us in the person of a messiah whose humanity is masculine. Is it not fitting that a woman be saved through the masculinity of Christ, her femininity's *other,* and that she receive from man, also *her* other, the sign of Christ who saves her? In the same manner, is it not entirely fitting and significant that man *(vir),* saved by Christ in his masculine humanity, needs to pass through woman, more precisely, through women, in order to be what he is called to be: a child of God, learning the "sentiments" and gestures of Christ known only to the church-bride in the intimacy of her love? It may shed light on the dialectic of salvation, suggested by these dispositions, to recall that at the origin of sin in the history of human societies is the problem of pride. In ending, let us recall that the theo-rhetoric of sex difference is maintained in John's Revelation, where victory over evil and death is expressed in the figure of the "immolated Lamb" but also in that of the woman, "a great sign which appeared in heaven," present in chapter 12. And in the end, it is with the proclamation of a wedding feast that revelation reaches its climax and culmination: "because this is the time for the marriage of the Lamb. His bride is ready, and she has been able to dress herself in dazzling white linen" (Rev. 19:7-8).

PART III

ETHICAL AND PRACTICAL
CONSEQUENCES

Can Feminism Be a Humanism?

Sr. Prudence Allen, R.S.M.

This article is exploratory rather than definitive. My goal is to reflect upon several different feminisms, to consider which of them fail and which succeed in being an authentic humanism. I am particularly interested in personalist humanism, which focuses on the full development of all human beings. Thus it will not be surprising to discover that two, or at most three, of the several different kinds of feminisms considered turn out to be consistent with the above goal of personalist humanism. Furthermore, all those feminisms which succeed are rooted in a Christian form of humanism. Those which fail do so because at the same time as they focus on the development of women they also exclude a particular group of human beings from the goal of full personal development.

The methodology I use in this exploration involves an immersion in a wide range of historical sources. Each author offers a specific description of his or her understanding of humanism. Then within a particular humanist tradition, another author is selected for the promotion of a kind of feminism. While many other authors could also be considered in this exploration, the ones selected seem to best articulate a particular approach to the topic. It is my hope that by this close reading of historical texts we will be able to grasp the development of different forms of humanism and feminism, and better evaluate their premises and conclusions. With this brief introduction to the goal and method-

This paper was given as the Glasmacher lecture at the annual meeting of the Canadian Jacques Maritain Association, Saint Paul University, Ottawa, Canada, on October 31, 1997. It was first printed in *Études maritainiennes — Maritain Studies* 14 (1998): 109-40. We are very grateful to its director, Dr. William Sweet, for permission to reprint it here.

ology of the article, we can now turn to the fundamental question: Can feminism be a humanism?

I pose this topic as a question, and it is a question that will create for many people a kind of tension. For others who think it obvious that feminism *can* be a humanism, as well as for those who think feminism *cannot* be, the question poses no tension, as the answer appears to be either a tautology (feminism is the same as humanism) or a contradiction (feminism cannot be a humanism).[1] If the question produces no tension, then there probably will not be — as Lonergan would say — any insight which comes as a release to this tension.[2] Consequently, it seems important to try to stay open to the question of whether feminism can be a humanism and remain in its tension in the hope that, by pressing the tension forward, we may together be able to reach some new insights both about feminism and about humanism.

To help our inquiry it will be useful to offer at the outset some "heuristic" definitions of humanism and feminism. By "heuristic" I mean to capture a sense of the terms that is precise enough to guide our reflections but not so precise that it resolves the issue before any inquiry is undertaken. So I offer as a heuristic definition of humanism, "the organized thought and action about what a human being really is and can become." Similarly, a heuristic definition of feminism will be "the organized thought and action which aims at removing obstacles for a woman to become (as a woman) what a human being or a human person really is and can become."

This heuristic definition implies that feminism is critical, in the sense that it offers a critique of those conditions in society which are obstacles for the full development of women. In other words, feminism does not emerge in a vacuum, but rather as a response to perceived limitations to the freedom of women to develop their potential for full personal growth and perfection.

As a practical beginning to our search we need to consider the historical development of humanism and the corresponding feminisms which emerged at different times in history. By bringing feminism into conjunction with humanism, I am trying to set up a framework within which we can inquire to-

---

1. In the first case, feminism may be viewed simply as a method to achieve a humanist goal, while in the second, the goal of feminism to promote primarily the well-being of women is seen as contradictory to a goal of humanism, to promote primarily the well-being of all human beings. If the solution to the question, Can feminism be a humanism? seems to be self-evidently either yes or no, then there remains no tension of inquiry and the question ceases to have relevance.

2. The Canadian philosopher Bernard Lonergan has identified as the first principle of his theory that "insight comes as a release to the tension of inquiry." Bernard Lonergan, *Insight: A Study of Human Understanding* (New York: Philosophical Library, 1956), pp. 2-3.

gether about fundamental concepts concerning the human being and the human person, interactions between men and women, and the appeal to various forms of freedom in pursuit of what might be called "the common good."

Before analyzing feminisms which seem to want to be a kind of humanism, I would like to exclude two kinds of feminisms which do not want to be a humanism. Both kinds have a historical root in a specific antihumanistic philosophy, and are inherited kinds of conscious antihumanisms.

The first kind of antihumanism flows from Martin Heidegger's essay "Letter on Humanism." This essay proclaims the end of Western humanism, and argues that "humanism" is a word which causes damage by implying that there is a simple essence of human beings. Heidegger directly criticizes Marxist, Sartrian, and Christian forms of humanism by arguing that they offer a univocal or universal definition of man which is a false construct. Consequently he asks if we should engage in a kind of open resistance to "humanism," and "risk a shock that could for the first time cause perplexity concerning the *humanitas* of *homo humanus* and its basis."[3] Heidegger ends his essay invoking a new way of thinking that "gathers language into simple saying. In this way language is the language of Being, as clouds are the clouds of the sky. With its saying, thinking lays inconspicuous furrows in language."[4] So for Heidegger the concept of man, or human being, floats away like a cloud in the sky.

The radical feminist who follows Heidegger's way of thinking, but on her own terms, is Mary Daly. If we take just one example from a recent text entitled *Pure Lust: Elemental Feminist Philosophy,* we find her saying the following: "In this true and radical sense, feminism is a verb; it is female be-ing. . . . *Feminism* is a Name for our moving/movement into Metabeing."[5] Daly rejects all forms of humanism, and as Heidegger suggests, "lays furrows in language" to break open any essential notion of the human being. So Daly does not want her feminism to be a humanism.

The second kind of antihumanism excluded from our question is found in the work of Michel Foucault. In the last section of *The Order of Things: An Archaeology of the Human Sciences,* we find an explicit rejection of humanism. Foucault argues that "man is an invention of recent date. And one perhaps nearing its end." He suggests that if (and when) the structures of our thought were to change, "one can certainly wager that man would be erased, like a face

---

3. Martin Heidegger, "Letter on Humanism," in *Basic Writings* (New York: Harper and Row, 1977), pp. 190-242, here p. 225.

4. Heidegger, p. 242.

5. Mary Daly, *Pure Lust: Elemental Feminist Philosophy* (Boston: Beacon Press, 1984), p. 194.

drawn in sand at the edge of the sea."[6] For Foucault there is nothing stable, unified, or integral about the human being, and no humanism to draw upon for its development or fulfillment.

A postmodernist feminist in the tradition of Foucault is Monique Wittig, who rejects any linguistic foundation for gender differentiation, and thereby rejects any possibility for defining a feminism, as well as a humanism. In an article entitled "The Mark of Gender," she argues that "Gender is an ontological impossibility because it tries to accomplish the division of Being. But Being as being is not divided. . . . Gender then must be destroyed. The possibility of its destruction is given through the very exercise of language. For each time I say I, I reorganize the world from my point of view and through abstraction I lay claim to universality. This fact holds true for every locutor."[7] Wittig concludes that language ought to be constructed so that there should be no gender differentiation at all, and that women and men, "as classes and as categories of thought or language . . . have to disappear, politically, economically, ideologically."[8] Obviously, if there are no women there can be no feminism, and if there are no women and men, there can be no humanism. So for this form of postmodernist thought, the question raised at the beginning of the article is meaningless.

From what has been said thus far, then, two kinds of "feminisms" are excluded by the question I am asking. However, there are many other forms of feminism and humanism for which it is meaningful to ask whether a feminism can be a humanism. In fact, many feminisms want to be considered as a kind of humanism, and some today might argue that a humanism needs to be a feminism. I will now turn to some of these other views to consider how we might understand the issues involved. For the purposes of this article I will identify six different historical forms of humanism: Renaissance humanism, Enlightenment humanism, Marxist humanism, existential humanism, pragmatic secular humanism, and personalist humanism. I will show how the human being is defined in each form of humanism, what kind of feminism sprang up within that humanism, and then ask the question from the perspective of personalist humanism, about what particular form of feminism might be appropriate.

Each form of humanism has a slightly different set of concepts about the human being, and the corresponding feminisms also have different views about what obstacles interfere with women's freedom to be (qua woman) really hu-

6. Michel Foucault, *The Order of Things: An Archaeology of the Human Sciences* (New York: Vintage, 1970), p. 387.

7. Monique Wittig, "The Mark of Gender," *Feminist Issues* (Fall 1985): 6.

8. Monique Wittig, "The Straight Mind," *Feminist Issues* (Summer 1980): 108.

man. Each of these humanisms, however, understands differently how human freedom is an important characteristic of what it means to be really human. Accordingly, then, although other characteristics could have been chosen for comparison, I will focus especially on the feature of freedom.

Renaissance Humanism and Feminism

The first form of humanism to consider is Renaissance humanism. While Erasmus (ca. 1466-1536) is thought to be the first person to actually call himself "a humanist," Francis Petrarch has been described retrospectively as the "first great representative" of humanism because of his influence on the subsequent development of humanism.[9] The Latin term *humanus* includes three meanings: (1) whatever is characteristic of the human being (i.e., what is "really human"), (2) especially one who is benevolent ("humane"), and (3) one who is learned or uses speech well ("humanist").[10] In the works of Petrarch we find a further meaning, namely, (4) a person who has received and who gives a classical education. Central to what it is to be a human being in this latter sense is the study of classical Greek and Latin texts, the rejection of academic and scholastic education, and the adoption of new forms of writing in Latin and in the vernacular, in letters, in poetry, in dialogues, and in essays.

The Latin expression *humanissime vir* was the usual way to address humanist scholars. The gender association of *vir* as the male human being seems to imply the exclusion of women from this conception of an educated human being at the time classical Latin was in use. This term evolved in Christian Latin through the addition of *-ismos,* to signify an activity common to many people. This suffix came into English as the "-ist" applied to the word, indicating a learned human being. In a similar way *humanista* and *homme de lettres* became the Italian and French versions of a humanist.[11]

If we give a general description of the early Renaissance humanist concept of the human being, realizing that nuanced differences will be ignored for our purposes, it would include the following factors: (1) the human being is situated in relation to a transcendent (Christian) God, (2) true nobility consists in living a wise and virtuous life, (3) the emotions or passions are a natural part of the human being and need to be well integrated by exercise of the intellect and will,

9. Paul Oskar Kristeller, *Eight Philosophers of the Italian Renaissance* (Stanford: Stanford University Press, 1964), p. 5.

10. See Vito R. Giustiniani, "Homo, Humanus, and the Meanings of 'Humanism,'" *Journal of the History of Ideas* 46, no. 2 (April-June 1985): 167-95.

11. Giustiniani, pp. 168-71.

(4) men and women can help one another grow in wisdom and virtue through dialogue and example, (5) freedom is an important aspect of the human being which ought to be exercised well, and (6) love helps build up the common good. These views can be found in Petrarch, but also in other humanists. For example, Giovanni Boccaccio (1313-75) emphasized the naturalness of emotions in men and women as well as the place of dialogue, and Giovanni Pico Mirandola (1463-94) emphasized the place of freedom in self-development. (Pico's *Oration on the Dignity of Man* first articulates the view that the human being is responsible, through the exercise of his freedom, to determine his own identity. This human activity of self-definition should take place in a kind of dialogical relation with God, who has given the human being certain characteristics which make this free initiative possible.)

When we turn to the more specific question of whether a Renaissance feminism can be a humanism, we have to note first of all that the words "feminism" and "feminist" did not come into use until after the nineteenth century.[12] Certainly if we apply the words only to a movement or an ideology of political action of groups of women, then there is no Renaissance feminism to bring into conjunction with humanism. On the other hand, if we allow the words to apply to women (or men) who engaged in some public action specifically aimed at improving the situation of women in the world at that time by removing perceived obstacles to the exercise of women's freedom to become really human (as women), then we can say that there were Renaissance feminists. In Renaissance humanism, writing letters or dialogues that were widely circulated was considered a form of public action. Four women who wrote philosophical texts which contained discursive arguments in support of woman's identity can be considered as Renaissance feminists: Christine de Pisan (1363-1431), Isotta Nogarola (1418-66), Lucrezia Marinelli (1571-1653), and Marie de Gournay (1566-1645).[13]

I will look at one of these — Christine de Pizan — to demonstrate that her Renaissance feminism was a Renaissance humanism.[14] Christine received a

12. Beatrice Gottlieb, "The Problem of Feminism in the Fifteenth Century," in *Women of the Medieval World: Essays in Honor of John H. Mundy*, ed. Julius Kirshner and Suzanne F. Wemple (Oxford: Blackwell, 1985), pp. 337-64.

13. See also Joan Kelly, "Early Feminist Theory and the *Querelle des Femmes*, 1400-1789," in *Women, History, and Theory* (Chicago and London: University of Chicago Press, 1984), pp. 64-109. Kelly argues that "it is fair to call this long line of pro-women writers that runs from Christine de Pizan to Mary Wollstonecraft by the name we use for their nineteenth- and twentieth-century descendants. Latter-day feminism still incorporates the basic positions the feminists of the *querelle* were first to take" (p. 134).

14. See the broader debate found in Joan Kelly-Gadol, "Did Women Have a Renaissance?" in *Becoming Visible: Women in European History*, ed. Renate Bridenthal and Claudia

classical education through her father's library and the library at the Sorbonne. Her over twenty major texts were well written in the vernacular: they included dialogues, poetry, and collections of letters about specific issues.[15] In two of her major texts, the public dialogue of letters gathered into the *Querelle de la rose* and the imaginary dialogue entitled *The City of Women*, Christine developed numerous discursive arguments to defend woman's proper identity.[16] Her feminism is primarily a defense against unjust slander against women. By arguing that certain authors falsely accuse women of various forms of vice, she hopes to demonstrate that women are just as capable of wisdom and virtue as men. In the following example we find her arguing against a satirist's devaluation of women: "But if women had written these books, I know full well the matter would have been handled differently. They know they stand wrongfully accused, and that the sharing has not been done evenly, for the strong take the biggest share, and the one who does the dividing keeps the biggest portion for himself. Yet malicious slanderers who debase women in this way still maintain that all women have been, are now, and always will be false, asserting that they have never been capable of loyalty."[17]

This particular passage exemplifies Christine's approach: a clear statement of the specific example of injustice (i.e., wrongful accusation), a suggestion for a constructive change (i.e., that women write about their own experiences), and a statement of her goal of a virtue (in this case, loyalty to men). In addition, she identifies a typical difficulty with slander — that it makes universal generalizations. In contrast, in her own work Christine generally remains with particular judgments. In another passage she considers that a possible bias distorts her own perspective about women, but she provides reasons for distin-

---

Koona (Boston: Houghton Mifflin, 1977), pp. 137-64, and in David Herlihy, "'Did Women Have a Renaissance?': A Reconsideration," in *Medievalia et Humanistica,* ed. Paul Maurice Clogan (Totowa, NJ: Rowman and Allanheld, 1985), no. 13, pp. 1-22.

15. See Earl Jeffrey Richards, "'Seulette a part' — the Little Woman on the Sidelines Takes Up Her Pen: The Letters of Christine de Pizan," in *Dear Sister: Medieval Women and the Epistolary Genre,* ed. Haren Cherewatuk and Ulricke Wiethaus (Philadelphia: University of Pennsylvania Press, 1993), pp. 139-70. Richards claims that Christine "adheres completely to the humanist tradition" and that her "feminism is in many ways a profound form of humanism" (p. 148).

16. See Sr. Prudence Allen, R.S.M., *The Concept of Woman,* vol. 2, *The Early Humanist Reformation, 1250-1500* (Grand Rapids and Cambridge, U.K.: Eerdmans, 2002), chap. 7, pp. 537-658, where her discursive arguments are charted and analyzed.

17. Christine de Pizan, *Epistre au Dieu d'amours (Letter to the God of Love), La Querelle,* 37. The *Letter to the God of Love* also appears in a different translation in *Poems of Cupid, God of Love,* trans. Thelma Fenster and Mary Carpenter Erler (Leiden and Newark: Brill, 1990), pp. 418-31.

guishing the true from the false, as a way of building a common basis upon which men and women can agree.[18]

It can be said that Christine de Pizan agrees with all the general characteristics listed above for the Renaissance humanist conception of the human being. That is, (1) the relation of the human being to God is directly stipulated in many of her works, and the end of the *City of Ladies,* which focuses on justice, the city is ruled by the blessed virgin Mary; (2) the emotions are frequently identified in her works and integrated into the human being's life; (3) her letters and dialogues constantly invoke dialogue between women and men, and among women, with a goal of increasing their respective wisdom and virtue; and (4) she argues for freedom from slander and misjudgments, freedom from the rule of emotions which take one away from a virtuous life, and for freedom to enter into mature interpersonal relationships as well as a broader political freedom. The goal of her feminism is to encourage women and men to exercise their freedom in all areas of their lives.[19]

If we consider Christine's writings in relation to the first of the meanings of "humanist" identified at the beginning of this article, or "what is characteristic of the human being or what is really human," it is clear that the goal of her "Renaissance feminism" is to confront those things which interfere with women being able to become really human. In particular, she confronts the devaluation of woman by some men (satirists) who reduce her either to a passive object to be possessed (a rose to be plucked) or to an irrational animal-like being who is filled with vice. In either reduction, woman is considered not really human. All of Christine's arguments seek to demonstrate the falsity of the grounds for these assertions.

The grounds to which she appeals include logic (finding fallacies in her opponents' reasoning), historical authorities who cite examples of women who serve as counterexamples (Petrarch, Boccaccio, Plutarch, etc.), and God (e.g., she begins the *City of Ladies* by attempting to demonstrate, by a series of reductio ad absurdum arguments, that woman cannot be evil because she was created by God, who is a good artisan). The appeal both to historical authorities and to creation by God is common to the early feminist humanists as two prime foundations for women being as really human as are men. Christine also

18. In letter VI [24] of Christine de Pizan to Jean de Montreuil. In her texts Christine often uses logical arguments such as reductio ad absurdum, negating the consequent, clarification, relation of whole to parts, relation of cause to effect, counterexample, and so forth. See Allen, pp. 578-84 and 606-9.

19. One should note also that Christine wrote a number of other books, covering a wide range of subjects, such as the use of military weapons; she also wrote political tracts and other sorts of works.

includes multiple appeals to her own experience of women to back up her claims.

Christine de Pizan is an example of a feminist who is interested in the full development of all persons — all men, all women, and all children — though she emphasizes that women are most often blocked in their development as full human beings. This pattern of defense of a woman's human identity is found in other Renaissance humanists as well. Lucrezia Marinelli in her book, *On the Nobility and Excellence of Women* (1601), directly engaged the arguments of philosophers, such as Aristotle, holding that women were more virtuous than men and men were more vicious than women. Moreover, in 1622 Marie le Jars de Gournay (1566-1645) published *Egalité des hommes et des femmes*, a text which appealed to the authority of Plato and Socrates for equal rights for women and men. She also appealed to the creation story in Genesis to defend her claim that women and men's virtue is "one and the same thing."[20] Through appeals to authority, as well as to philosophical argument, these early feminists were able to make the claim that women are of equal dignity to men.

When we turn to the Enlightenment, we can identify two stages in the development of feminism and humanism. In general, however, we find a shift in the grounds for what it means to be a human being and for what the basis is for women and men to have the same access to an equal place in the world. Reason itself becomes a new ground for defense of human identity.

Enlightenment Humanism and Feminism

Descartes, I would argue, was the "founder" of both Enlightenment humanism and Enlightenment feminism. *Cogito ergo sum*, which he posited as the source of human identity — identifying the human being as primarily a reasoning being — was carried over into arguments by feminists of the modern period. Descartes's disciple, François Poullain de la Barre (1647-1723), appealed to human reason as the source of equality of women and men in his text *De l'égalite des deux sexes*, published in 1673. Here, even though Poullain appealed to God as the original source of the equality of men and women as human beings, he began to shift the argument for equality to another foundation — he argued that

---

20. Marie de Gournay, *Egalité des hommes et des femmes*, in *La fille d'Alliance de Montigne: Marie de Gournay* (Paris: Librarie Honore Champion, 1910), p. 70. In *Grief des Dames*, also published in 1626, she made the same twin appeal to the authority of Platonic philosophers and God to defend woman's dignity against what she perceived as the deprivation of her liberty and goods by some men.

the spirit, brain, and faculties were the same in women and men and, therefore, women and men were "equally capable of the same things."[21]

For Poullain, as for most "Cartesian feminists," custom (or tradition) was identified as the enemy of the freedom of women. He argued that the remedy for this was human reason, which was able to attack custom and overturn its shallow grounds for claiming that women are not as fully human as men. He argues that "[t]hese kinds of reasonings [which exclude women from certain spheres of activity] proceed from . . . a false notion which men forge to themselves of custom."[22] In this early stage of Enlightenment humanism, the primary solution to inequality was education. Cartesian feminism wanted women to have the same opportunity for education as men.

Mary Astell (1666-1731), again by making an appeal to the equal origin of women and men, proposed that educational institutions be established for women: "For since God has given Women as well as Men intelligent souls, why should they be forbidden to use them?"[23] In her *Serious Proposal to the Ladies for the Advancement of their True and Greatest Interest*, she also claims that custom is the enemy of the exercise of freedom by women: "As prejudice fetters the understanding so does custom manacle the will, which scarce knows how to divert from a track which the generality around it take, and to which it has itself been habituated. . . . Custom cannot authorise a practice if reason condemns it, the following a multitude is no excuse for the doing of evil."[24]

In a text published "by a lady" in 1696 (often attributed to Mary Astell), the goal of feminism — for women to become recognized as more fully human — is clearly stated. The writer wanted "to reduce the sexes to a level, and by arguments to raise ours to an equality at most with men."[25] After demonstrating that women's minds, brains, and faculties are the same as men's, she argues that the law should recognize women's equality as well. The grounds for this equality are, again, first the fact of the creation of women by God, but also the nature of female creatures and "their primitive liberty and equality with the men."[26]

It is interesting to note that this development of feminism, following Des-

21. François Poullain de la Barre, *The Woman as Good as the Man; or, The Equality of Both Sexes* (Detroit: Wayne State University Press, 1988), pp. 102-3.

22. Poullain de la Barre, p. 66.

23. Mary Astell, *A Serious Proposal to the Ladies for the Advancement of Their True and Greatest Interest* (New York: Source Book Press, 1970), p. 18.

24. Astell, *A Serious Proposal*, p. 73.

25. Mary Astell, *An Essay in Defence of the Female Sex* (New York: Source Book Press, 1970), pp. 7-8.

26. Astell, *Defence*, pp. 39-40. She was trying to defend women's ability to rule, which in England was prohibited by law.

cartes, is primarily Protestant, whereas the early Renaissance (e.g., Christine de Pisan) had been largely Catholic. Poullain de la Barre became a Protestant, and Mary Astell lived in Protestant England. The appeal of Descartes's argument became very much integrated into Enlightenment Protestant feminist work. Still, the Cartesian feminists were not all humanists. In particular, those philosophers (Descartes included) who appealed primarily to reason as a foundation for human development often neglected to consider the education and development of the whole human being.

There is, however, a second stage of Enlightenment humanism. Here we find the mention of two qualifications to the exercise of reason which became fundamental to the understanding of what makes someone really human: (1) that human reason ought to be integrated with nature, and (2) that human reason ought to stand on its own, away from direction from others.

This stage of Enlightenment humanism is often considered to have begun with Jean-Jacques Rousseau. Rousseau rejected the (scholastic) academic education which some Renaissance humanists had been interested in, because he held that such an education was incapable of properly forming a human being to become truly human. In *Émile* he describes in great detail how nature itself is to become the teacher of the new man. Everything is to be brought into harmony with natural tendencies.[27] Thus education through the study of written texts is viewed as something which "meddles" with man's basically good nature and possibly renders it evil.[28] Indeed, it shifts toward learning directly from nature rather than from classical sources or history. (And so, just as women are coming to be interested in getting an education, suddenly — with Rousseau and others — there is a shift away from the value of a higher education.)

Rousseau claims that "[t]he natural man lives for himself: he is the unit, the whole, dependent only on himself and on his like."[29] So a human being does not need schools or libraries to develop his mind. He only needs his own powers of observation and reasoning and a few informal teachers to keep his reasoning and judgments in the right direction.

Rousseau's Enlightenment humanism has many different consequences. By his identification of freedom with goodness, he concludes that the human being was naturally good. This goodness comes to be expressed in "natural rights" and not, as we have seen in Renaissance humanism, in the exercise of virtue and wisdom. So the human being, by itself, is virtuous simply by being free. A further moral freedom belongs to the participation of human beings in

27. Jean-Jacques Rousseau, *Émile* (London: Dent, 1984), p. 7.
28. Rousseau, *Émile*, p. 5.
29. Rousseau, *Émile*, p. 7.

building the common good with others in citizenship. Here the human being is good by submitting to a law that, though he shares it with others, he gives to himself.[30]

Immanuel Kant, in his famous essay "What Is Enlightenment?" echoes this view that the truly human person should reject others' directives: "Enlightenment is man's release from his self-incurred tutelage. Tutelage is man's inability to make use of his understanding without direction from another."[31] Here we find articulated the beginning of a fundamental characteristic of the second phase of Enlightenment humanism, namely, that the individual human being ought to use his reason and freedom *independently* of all external sources including God or other men. So wisdom becomes detached from history and from theology.

One difficulty with this description of the value of reason for the development of the human being is found in both Kant's and Rousseau's claims that women's proper virtue is not reason but sense or taste. Here a distinction is introduced between ways of being human which divided the capacities within the human being, and identified reason with the male and sensation with the female. Rousseau expressed it this way — that even though the "machine" or body and faculties are the same in women and in men, it works differently, so that "woman observes, man reasons" and the "sole end [of her learning should be] the formation of taste."[32] And Kant directly summarizes it: "[h]er philosophy is not to reason, but to sense."[33] Therefore it is not surprising that Kant suggests at the beginning of "What Is Enlightenment?" that "the entire fair sex" finds the rejection of tutelage to be very dangerous if not impossible.

Rousseau and Kant both argued that societies were formed by a social contract or by agreement of the will among several human beings who enter into a collective body or kingdom of ends. Rousseau defines the essence of the social contract: "Each of us puts in common his person and his whole power under the supreme direction of the general will; and in return we receive every member as an indivisible part of the whole."[34] The difficulty of this description is that it implicitly excluded all women from its range, so that civilized society in Enlightenment humanism implied that only men could be fully human.

---

30. See Leo Strauss, *Natural Right and History* (Chicago: University of Chicago Press, 1953), pp. 279-81, for a more detailed account of this aspect of Rousseau's humanism.

31. Immanuel Kant, "What Is Enlightenment?" in *The Foundations of the Metaphysics of Morals* (Indianapolis: Bobbs-Merrill, 1978), p. 85.

32. Rousseau, *Émile*, pp. 349-50.

33. Immanuel Kant, *Observations on the Feeling of the Beautiful and Sublime* (Berkeley and Los Angeles: University of California Press, 1965), p. 79.

34. Jean-Jacques Rousseau, *The Social Contract and the Discourse on the Origin of Inequality* (New York: Washington Square Press, 1967), pp. 18-19.

One practical consequence of the second stage of Enlightenment humanism was the birth of a new form of Enlightenment feminism. Both men and women began to argue that for a woman to be fully human, she had to be able to participate in the government of public society. It was not enough to simply have self-government in wisdom and virtue as the Renaissance feminists suggested, but to be fully human demanded freedom to participate in public life as well. Of course, most Renaissance humanists did participate in some form of public life, and there was an implicit understanding that virtue involved such public service. Christine de Pisan did participate in a de facto manner by her writing about war, peace, and other such issues. France had a female ruler, and we have the example of Joan of Arc during this same period, so Renaissance feminist humanists did not put forward arguments that women's freedom involved a need to participate in public life because they didn't see the issue as much of a problem. Enlightenment feminism, however, took on this particular issue as central to its concerns. The French Revolution provided the context, for here we find that women used an appeal to reason to demand the overturning of custom which denied them access to citizenship. Olympe de Gouges, in her "Declaration of Rights of Woman and the Female Citizen," declared in article IV that "Liberty and justice consist of restoring all that belongs to others; thus; the only limits on the exercise of the natural rights of woman are perpetual male tyranny; these limits are to be reformed by the laws of nature and reason."[35]

Another key example of Enlightenment feminism is seen in Mary Wollstonecraft's *A Vindication of the Rights of Woman.* The claim that woman's virtue is to sense — to develop taste — while man's was to reason, struck Wollstonecraft as a way of seriously inhibiting woman's freedom. She states: "If, I say, for I would impress by declamation when Reason offers her sober light, if [women] be really capable of acting like rational creatures, let them not be treated like slaves; or, like brutes who are dependent upon the reason of man, when they associate with him; but cultivate their minds, give them the salutary, sublime curb of principle."[36]

This appeal to reason is also an appeal to God, albeit within an Enlightenment understanding of the "divine," as the following passage attests: "I love man as my fellow; but his sceptre, real, or usurped, extends not to me, unless the reason of an individual demands my homage; and even then the submission

35. Olympe de Gouges, "Les Droits de la Femme," in *Women in Revolutionary Paris, 1789-1795: Selected Documents with Notes and Commentary,* ed. Darling Gay Levy et al. (Urbana: University of Illinois Press, 1979), p. 88.

36. Mary Wollstonecraft, *A Vindication of the Rights of Woman* (New York: Norton, 1975), p. 36.

is to reason, and not to man. In fact, the conduct of an accountable being must be regulated by the operations of its own reason; or on what foundation rests the throne of God?"[37]

Women's lack of freedom to develop their minds was frequently criticized by Wollstonecraft. She claims: "Liberty is the mother of virtue, and if women be, by their very constitution, slaves, and not allowed to breathe the sharp invigorating air of freedom, they must ever languish like exotics, and be reckoned beautiful flaws in nature."[38] In this context, Rousseau's *Émile* is directly criticized by Wollstonecraft.

Not all Enlightenment feminists were women. The Marquis de Condorcet strongly defended, by an appeal to reason, the importance of removing obstacles to women's exercise of freedom. In one key passage from *Sur l'admission des femmes au droit de Cité* (On the admission of women to the rights of citizenship), he states: "To show that this exclusion is not an act of tyranny, it must be proved either that the natural rights of women are not absolutely the same as those of men, or that women are not capable of exercising these rights. But the rights of men result simply from the fact that they are *rational,* sentient beings, susceptible of acquiring ideas of morality, and or reasoning concerning those ideas. Women having, then, the same qualities, have necessarily the same rights."[39] It is clear, then, from these few examples, that Enlightenment feminism focused on the ideal of women becoming full citizens, as that was what it was to be fully human.[40]

Later Enlightenment humanism spawned three different forms of humanism in the nineteenth and twentieth centuries which developed parallel to one another: Marxist humanism, existential humanism, and pragmatic (secular) humanism. Each one develops a slightly different aspect of Enlightenment humanism, and all three have corresponding forms of feminism. It is also important to recognize that while all these thinkers refined or redescribed what

---

37. Wollstonecraft, p. 37.

38. Wollstonecraft, p. 37.

39. Marie Jean Antoine Marquis de Condorcet, *The First Essay on the Political Rights of Women,* a translation of "Sur l'admission au droit de la cité" by Alice Drysdale Vickery (Letchworth: Garden City Press, 1912), p. 5.

40. It is also interesting to note, in passing, that "The first self-proclaimed 'feminist' in France was the women's suffrage advocate Hubertine Auclert who, from at least 1882 on, used the term in her periodical, *'La Citoyenne'*" (see Karen Offen, "Defining Feminism: A Comparative Historical Approach," *Signs* 14, no. 1 [1988]: 126). Shortly afterward a feminist congress was held in Paris, and the term gained more popular usage. So "feminism," as an official appellation of a movement to remove obstacles to women's freedom to vote, emerged out of Enlightenment humanism and its turn to natural rights.

"humanism" is, each still wanted to be known as a humanist. This appellation or designation was something very important to them.

Marxist Humanism and Feminism

Moving now from a developmental or historical account of humanism to a thematic account of the various forms of humanism which have occurred during the last two centuries, I wish to discuss, as the first kind of "contemporary humanism," Marxist humanism and the feminism which sprang from it. In his early essay "Private Property and Communism," Karl Marx proposed a new form of humanism. Here he explicitly develops the naturalistic aspect of Enlightenment humanism as follows:

> *Communism* is the *positive* abolition of *private property*, of *human self-alienation*, and thus the real *appropriation* of *human* nature through and for man. It is, therefore, the return of man himself as a *social*, i.e. really human, being, a complete and conscious return which assimilates all the wealth of previous development. Communism as a fully developed naturalism is humanism and as a fully developed humanism is naturalism. It is the *definitive* resolution of the antagonism between man and nature, and between man and man. It is the true solution of the conflict between existence and essence, between objectification and self-affirmation, between freedom and necessity, between individual and species. It is the solution of the riddle of history and knows itself to be this solution.[41]

Marx, then, aims at developing a new kind of humanism which describes the characteristics of a "really human being." The first way the human being is understood differently from both Renaissance and Enlightenment humanism is that, previously, grounds for humanism were found in the creation of the human being by a transcendent God; now the grounds are explicitly atheistic. Marx states:

> [A]theism as the annulment of God is the emergence of theoretical humanism, and communism as the annulment of private property is the vindication of real human life as man's property. The latter is also the emergence of practical humanism, for atheism is humanism mediated to itself by the annulment of religion, while communism is humanism mediated to itself by

41. Karl Marx, "Private Property and Communism," in *Early Writings* (New York, Toronto, and London: McGraw-Hill, 1964), p. 155.

the annulment of private property. It is only by the supersession of this mediation (which is, however, a necessary pre-condition) that the self-originating *positive* humanism can appear.[42]

Marx's call to revolution by the destruction of private property and of a class-based society provides the practical means by which he hopes to bring about his new "positive" humanism. As history has demonstrated, this kind of humanism did not apply to all human beings, but only to some — the working men of the proletariat class.

Marxist humanism also focuses on the alienation of the human being through work in which one's labor comes to be "owned" by another person. In this case it is work itself, and in many cases work augmented by technology, which leads to a human being becoming alienated from his real human identity. Marx identifies the various alienations as alienation from the product of the labor, alienation from other human beings, and self-alienation. He concludes that "the man (the worker) feels himself to be freely active only in his animal functions — eating, drinking and procreating . . . — while in his human functions he is reduced to an animal. The animal becomes the human and the human becomes animal."[43]

The question of feminism was raised by Marx and his collaborator and friend, Friedrich Engels.[44] Engels, for example, argued that "The overthrow of the mother right was the *world historical defeat of the female sex*": because monogamy was instituted, private property was established, and woman and children became the property of man.[45] Engels argues that the first of the historical divisions of labor was between men and women for the purpose of the propagation of children, and that the husband represents the bourgeois and the wife the proletariat in the family. So we have feminism emerging from the very first statement of the Marxist view.

While some Marxist feminists emerged at the beginning of the twentieth century, it was not until after the 1960s that large numbers of feminists began to think of themselves in this tradition. There are, of course, many different strands of Marxist feminism. I will reference just a few of them, to illustrate some common themes. What we find happening here is something different from what we saw in Renaissance or Enlightenment feminism, in that certain

42. Karl Marx, "Critique of Hegel's Dialectic," in *Early Writings*, p. 213.
43. Karl Marx, "Alienated Labour," in *Early Writings*, p. 125.
44. See Marx, "Private Property and Communism," pp. 153-54.
45. Friedrich Engels, *The Origin of the Family, Private Property, and the State* (New York: International Publishers, 1972), p. 120.

categories of human being come to be identified as an "enemy" for women or for men's full development.

In the work of Marlene Dixon, for example, we find a focus on two themes: that Marxist political movements in the United States excluded feminism as an issue, and that the women's liberation movement was predominately interested in middle- or upper-class issues, and so it excluded Marxist concern with the conditions of the working poor.[46] Dixon's work is significant because it clearly articulates several fundamental principles of contemporary Marxist feminism. In an article entitled "We Are Not Animals in the Field: A Woman's Right to Choose," we find the following argument: "The right of all women to control our own bodies includes the right to bear children only when we want. Abortion on demand is the right of every woman. If we cannot end an unwanted pregnancy, if we are forced to bear a child against our will, then our right to self-determination has been completely denied to us."[47] Dixon clearly perceives a developing human being as an enemy to a woman's freedom. Moreover, sometimes she says the state is the enemy that seeks to control a woman's pregnant body and at other times she argues that the husband is the enemy in the family who seeks to control his wife as his property.[48] What happens, then, is that as the movement to help women grows, others have to be pushed aside. It is clear, however, that in all these arguments Dixon does not view feminism as a humanism, which includes the development of all human beings equally.[49]

We find another kind of argument in those Marxist feminists who focus on the "premarket" or unpaid aspect of women's work in the home. (Their solutions range from arguing for "wages for housework"[50] to the total abolition of the family.) The family itself is here perceived as an enemy for the woman's freedom. Perhaps the most radical Marxist feminist proposal for the abolition of the family is offered by Shulamith Firestone in *The Dialectic of Sex: The Case*

46. See Marlene Dixon, "Public Ideology and the Class Composition of Women's Liberation — 1966-69," in *The Future of Women* (San Francisco: Synthesis Publications, 1980).

47. Marlene Dixon, "We Are Not Animals in the Field: A Woman's Right to Choose," in *The Future of Women*, p. 124.

48. Marlene Dixon, "The Right of All Women to Control Their Own Bodies," in *The Future of Women*, pp. 207-14.

49. For other examples of early Marxist feminist theories, see Charnie Guettel, *Marxism and Feminism* (Toronto: Canadian Women's Educational Press, 1974); Juliet Mitchell, *Women's Estate* (New York: Vintage, 1973); Sheila Rowbotham, *Woman's Consciousness, Man's World* (Harmondsworth: Penguin Books, 1973) and *Women, Resistance, and Revolution* (Harmondsworth: Penguin Books, 1972).

50. See the work of Selma James and Giuliana Pompei, *Wages for Housework* (Toronto: Canadian Women's Educational Press, 1972), and that of Selma James, Priscilla Allen, and Sylvine Schmidt, *Wages for Housework Notebook* (Brooklyn, N.Y.: New York Collective, 1975).

for Feminist Revolution. She views technology as ultimately liberating, and suggests that women will only achieve their fully human identity when they no longer have to give birth, and children are produced through "test tube incubation" or artificial reproduction. The enemy here is identified as "childbearing" itself. Firestone calls it "freedom from the tyranny of reproduction and childbearing."[51] She surmises that "Machines thus could act as the perfect equalizer, obliterating the class system based on exploitation of labor."[52]

Now we can ask: Can a Marxist feminism be a Marxist humanism? Significantly, none of the Marxist feminists use the word "humanism" to describe their views. So we could say that they do not view themselves as humanists, even in the Marxist sense. They do, however, often give a priority to reason, even at the expense of other aspects of human identity. Furthermore, they all reject "naturalism" as a basis. We can see this in their consistent policy in favor of abortion on demand. A developing human being and the pregnant body itself are both perceived as enemies of woman's freedom. The solution is to get rid of both at will. In an analogous way the state and husbands are also perceived as enemies to women's freedom, so the solution is also to get rid of both. In these moves Marxist feminism separates itself from the situation of all human beings and focuses instead on the development of some human beings instead of others. Therefore it can be said that Marxist feminism, at least in the forms outlined above, does not appear to be interested in supporting the full development of all human beings.

Existential Humanism

I turn now to existential humanism, which sprang out of Enlightenment humanism, and which began with Nietzsche's reaction to Enlightenment humanism. Jean-Paul Sartre is perhaps the best-known representative of this "school." In a 1945 lecture entitled "Existentialism Is a Humanism," Sartre attempts to redefine humanism "in his own image," as it were:

> But there is another meaning of humanism. Fundamentally it is this: man is constantly outside of himself; in projecting himself, in losing himself outside of himself, he makes for man's existing; and, on the other hand, it is by pursuing transcendent goals that he is able to exist; man, being this state of passing-beyond, and seizing upon things only as they bear upon this

51. Shulamith Firestone, *The Dialectic of Sex: The Case for Feminist Revolution* (New York: Bantam Books, 1971), p. 225.
52. Firestone, p. 201.

passing-beyond, is at the heart, at the center of this passing-beyond. There is no universe other than a human universe, the universe of human subjectivity. . . . This connection between transcendency, as a constituent element of man, . . . and subjectivity, in the sense that man is not closed in on himself but is always present in a human universe, is what we call existentialism humanism. Humanism because we remind man that there is no law-maker other than himself, and that in his forlornness he will decide by himself; because we point out that man will fulfil himself as man, not in turning toward himself, but in seeking outside of himself a goal which is just this liberation, just this particular fulfillment.[53]

The core idea in Sartre's defense of existentialism as a humanism is that the real nature of a human being is something other than an isolated form of quietism, a sordid view of human identity, or a form of relativism.[54] Sartre wants to defend the view that the existentialist, by his transcendent decisions, presents a model of the human being as a transcendent subjectivity, who projects himself by an absolute freedom, into the future by his acts, and who makes himself into a particular kind of human being precisely by these acts.

Like Marxist humanism, existential humanism situates the human being in a world without God. Nietzsche had proclaimed that God is dead in his prologue to *Thus Spake Zarathustra,* and Sartre is very explicit on the theoretical foundation for an existential humanism: "Existentialism is nothing else than an attempt to draw all the consequences of a coherent atheistic position."[55] So the human being is not primarily a being in relation with other beings, human or divine. As quoted above, existential humanism argues that the human being is "constantly outside himself." In this move to transcendence, the human being comes up against various enemies of freedom: the body and other people. The body interferes with freedom, according to Sartre, because it is an "in-itself" — a thing without consciousness; another person interferes with freedom because he or she is a "for-itself" — another free consciousness. In *Being and Nothingness* Sartre develops in detail how various enemies of human transcendence function. "The true limit of my freedom lies purely and simply in the very fact

---

53. Jean-Paul Sartre, "Existentialism Is a Humanism," in *Existentialism versus Marxism: Conflicting Views on Humanism,* ed. George Novack (New York: Delta, 1966), p. 84. Also published in *Existentialism and Human Emotions* (New York: Philosophical Library, 1957), pp. 50-51.

54. For an example of this criticism see Walter Odajyk, *Marxism and Existentialism* (New York: Doubleday, 1965). He states: "Existentialism, one of the most antisocial and egocentric philosophies ever to be developed by the mind of man, is not in any position to speak of humanism, socialism, and true human freedom" (p. 30).

55. Sartre, "Existentialism Is a Humanism," p. 84.

that an Other apprehends me as the Other-as-object. . . . This limit to my freedom is, as we see, posited by the Other's pure and simple existence — that is, by the *fact* that my transcendence exists for a transcendence."[56] Consequently, as Garcin exclaims in *No Exit*, "Hell is — other people!"[57]

The first articulation of existentialist feminism came from Simone de Beauvoir, in *The Second Sex*. (One might be able to argue that Lou Andreas-Salomé [1861-1937] did this in relation to Nietzsche, but Beauvoir provides the first "systematic" account.) In the prologue to this work, Beauvoir identifies the two threats to freedom mentioned above: the body and other people; but she ties these "enemies" in a unique way to woman's identity. First, the body: "Woman has ovaries, a uterus; these peculiarities imprison her in her subjectivity, circumscribe her within the limits of her own nature."[58] The very identity of the body as a female body appears to Beauvoir to come into conflict with woman's drive for transcendence — an externally projected subjectivity.

Second, woman also experiences other people, and in particular the transcendence of men, as an enemy to her freedom: "Now, what peculiarly signalizes the situation of woman is that she — a free and autonomous being like all human creatures — nevertheless finds herself living in a world where men compel her to assume the status of the Other. They propose to stabilize her as object and to doom her to immanence since her transcendence is to be overshadowed and forever transcended by another ego which is essential and sovereign."[59] Both Sartre and Beauvoir appear to believe that a kind of humanism is still possible in collective action (the we — acting together for a common cause) and in friendships between men and women. Beauvoir argues at the end of *The Second Sex* that "when we abolish the slavery of half of humanity, together with the whole system of hypocrisy that it implies, then the 'division' of humanity will reveal its genuine significance and the human couple will find its true form."[60]

In *The Ethics of Ambiguity*, Beauvoir invokes the Renaissance humanist "turn to history" as a source of liberation.[61] But when we look at *The Second Sex*, there is no doubt that she saw herself as doing both a new kind of humanism, which placed the highest emphasis on the absoluteness of human freedom,

---

56. Jean-Paul Sartre, *Being and Nothingness* (New York: Washington Square Pocketbook, 1956), pp. 672-73.

57. Jean-Paul Sartre, *No Exit and Three Other Plays* (New York: Vintage, 1949), p. 47.

58. Simone de Beauvoir, *The Second Sex* (New York: Vintage, 1953), p. xviii.

59. Beauvoir, *The Second Sex*, p. xxxiv.

60. Beauvoir, *The Second Sex*, p. 184.

61. Simone de Beauvoir, *The Ethics of Ambiguity* (New York: Citadel Press, 1976), pp. 92-93.

and a new kind of feminism, which sought to provide women with a history in order to escape the lack of transcendence they experienced both from being reduced to their bodily functions and being reduced by the consciousness of men to objects rather than actively being subjects. Nevertheless, she still appears to support a universal humanism, for after quoting Karl Marx's statement that "the relation of man to woman is the most natural relation of human being to human being," she concludes that the task of men and women is to "establish the reign of liberty" and that "by and through their natural differentiation men and women unequivocally affirm their brotherhood."[62]

In a series of interviews, first, with Alice Schwarzer between 1972 and 1982 and, second, with Margaret A. Simons between 1982 and 1985, Beauvoir clarified how her views about feminism developed as the women's liberation movement progressed and different positions were articulated. In these interviews she emphasizes two particularly important aspects of her position. The first is a clarification of her rejection of any essentialist view of human nature as such, and the second deals with her rejection of taking an essentialist view of woman's nature as a starting point. "[T]he base of existentialism is precisely that there is no human nature, and thus no 'feminine nature.' It's not something given. There is a presence to the world, which is the presence which defines man, who is defined by his presence to the world, his consciousness and not a nature that grants him *a priori* certain characteristics."[63]

Beauvoir has always maintained that she is interested in linking her feminism with class struggle of both men and women. She defines feminism with respect to the situation of women in the world as follows: "In my definition, feminists are women — or even men too — who are fighting to change women's condition, in association with the class struggle, but independently of it as well, without making the changes they strive for totally dependent on changing society as a whole."[64] Existential feminism then involves a set of actions of a being characterized as consciousness in the world. However, Beauvoir's existential humanism, like Sartre's, concentrates only on one aspect of human consciousness, or what they call the "for-itself."

This existential feminism is *not* a humanism in the sense that it rejects any view of the whole human being as a unified entity. It is also not a humanism in that it implies that human beings (either developing or fully developed) who interfere with the free project of a conscious being may be killed. Both

62. Beauvoir, *The Second Sex,* p. 814.

63. Margaret A. Simons, "Two Interviews with Simone de Beauvoir (1982)," *Hypatia* 3, no. 3 (Winter 1989): 19.

64. Alice Schwarzer, *After the Second Sex: Conversations with Simone de Beauvoir* (New York: Pantheon Books, 1984), p. 33.

Beauvoir and Sartre came to the conclusion that when someone is perceived as an enemy to one's freedom, it is all right to kill that person, even if the person is innocent. (Sartre said he would have carried suitcases containing bombs and left them in cafés. He supported terrorism against members of certain classes or nationalities and, for a time, became involved in Maoist political action. Beauvoir supported abortion, arguing that "the embryo, as long as it is not yet considered human, as long as it is not a being with human relationships with its mother or its father, it's nothing, one can eliminate the embryo.")[65]

On the other hand, Beauvoir has always argued that women ought to work together with men and that, in a certain way, her human identity (as consciousness) takes priority over her identity as a woman. In rejecting a "woman-identity" starting point, Beauvoir states: "Better that she identify herself as a human being who happens to be a woman. It's a certain situation which is not the same as men's situation of course, but she shouldn't identify herself as a woman."[66] Beauvoir offers as an example her rejection of a marriage proposal by Sartre, because she understood both childbearing and housework to be oppressive to women. These two situations of women reduce her, she claims, from her human transcendence into an enslavement. "I have escaped many of the things that enslave a woman, such as motherhood and the duties of a house-wife."[67]

Even though she argues that "Women, and men too, must become total human beings," the total — in "total human being" — includes primarily human consciousness projecting in creative ways into work and into political action.[68] The body, and especially differences between woman's body and man's body, is rejected as simply part of the given, waiting to be transcended. In this one could say that Beauvoir's feminism is an existential humanism, as Sartre defined the meaning of humanism — i.e., as being constantly outside of oneself, projecting oneself, and losing oneself in one's projects.

Pragmatic Secular Humanism and Feminism

The third offshoot from Enlightenment humanism was a new form of humanism that was articulated in England by the Oxford philosopher Ferdinand Canning Scott Schiller (1864-1937), and by the American pragmatist William

---

65. Simons, pp. 18-19.
66. Simons, p. 19.
67. Schwarzer, p. 36.
68. Schwarzer, p. 46.

James. This form characterized the human being vis-à-vis law, language, and truth. In "Pragmatism and Humanism" James describes it this way: "Law and languages at any rate are thus seen to be man-made things. Mr. Schiller applies the analogy to beliefs, and proposes the name of 'Humanism' for the doctrine that to an unascertainable extent our truths are man-made products too."[69] In other words, pragmatic humanism rejects one view of Enlightenment humanism — that there are some absolute truths (the Truth) that the human reason is able to discover — and instead suggests that truths "make themselves as we go."[70]

At the same time, pragmatic humanism accepts the place of human reason in determining truths in a historically progressing manner. James contrasts rationalism and pragmatism this way: "The essential contrast is that for rationalism reality is ready-made and complete from all eternity, while for pragmatism it is still in the making, and awaits part of its complexion from the future."[71] This rejection of Truth as "ready-made" has consequences for feminism, particularly since the Enlightenment feminists appealed to the common presence of reason in women and men as the basis for their natural equality, and ultimately as a foundation for an appeal to equal rights to education, citizenship, and so on.

James also associates pragmatic humanism with the notion of "good consequences" for any truths. In "Humanism and Truth" he differentiates the pragmatic method itself from pragmatic humanism: "All that the pragmatic method implies, then, is that truths should *have* practical consequences. In England the word has been used more broadly still, to cover the notion that the truth of any statement *consists* in the consequences, and particularly in their being good consequences. . . . I think that Mr. Schiller's proposal to call the wider pragmatism by the name of 'humanism' is excellent and ought to be adopted. The narrower pragmatism may still be spoken of as the 'pragmatic method.'"[72]

When this new "pragmatism" is developed further, we discover that the criterion of evaluation is human experience. "Truth thus means, according to humanism, the relation of less fixed parts of experience (predicates) to other relatively more fixed parts (subjects); and we are not required to seek it in a relation of experience as such to anything beyond itself."[73] This turn away from a

---

69. William James, "Pragmatism and Humanism," in *Pragmatism* (Cleveland: Meridian, 1963), p. 159.

70. James, "Pragmatism and Humanism," p. 159.

71. James, "Pragmatism and Humanism," p. 167.

72. James, "Humanism and Truth," in *Pragmatism*, p. 230.

73. James, "Humanism and Truth," p. 239.

realistic epistemology toward a practical emphasis on personal experience is shared by many contemporary feminisms. The emphasis on experience as the sole criterion for truth is emphasized by James: "[T]he concrete truth *for us* will always be that way of thinking in which our various experiences most profitably combine."[74] This pragmatic notion of truth has the further characteristic that truth changes with time. James identifies this as an essential characteristic of the new humanism he proposes: "The humanism, for instance, which I see and try so hard to defend, is the completest truth attained from my point of view up to date. But, owing to the fact that all experience is a process, no point of view can ever be *the* last one. Everyone is insufficient and off its balance, and responsible to later points of view than itself."[75]

In the United States pragmatic humanism evolved yet further into what is called *"naturalistic"* humanism, and its subspecies of secular humanism, scientific humanism, and democratic humanism. Corliss Lamont, in his extensive treatment of the subject, *The Philosophy of Humanism,* identifies the key components of this modern American humanism: "Humanism is the viewpoint that men have but one life to lead and should make the most of it in terms of creative work and happiness; that human happiness is its own justification; that in any case the supernatural . . . does not exist; and that human beings, using their own intelligence and cooperating liberally with one another, can build an enduring citadel of peace and beauty upon this earth."[76] It aims toward the removal of discrimination, and what Lamont calls "human-being-ism, that is, devotion to the interests of human beings, wherever they live and whatever their status."[77] This view has, over the years, become integrated into the American way of thinking.

In 1933 several writers, including the American pragmatist John Dewey, produced the Humanist Manifesto. This document articulated fifteen fundamental principles, including a rejection of belief in God, a rejection of religion as tied to the supernatural, an affirmation of methods of modern science, an acceptance of a goal of the complete realization of the human personality, and the acceptance of the premise that institutions exist solely for the purpose of the enhancement of individual human life. Underlying this new approach was Dewey's affirmation of experience as the prime measure of truth.[78] In *Reconstruction in Philosophy* Dewey explains that "Growth is the only 'moral' end" and "Happiness is found only in success; but success means succeeding, getting

74. James, "Humanism and Truth," p. 241.
75. James, "Humanism and Truth," p. 250.
76. Corliss Lamont, *The Philosophy of Humanism* (New York: Ungar, 1982), p. 14.
77. Lamont, pp. 15-16.
78. See John Dewey, *On Experience, Nature, and Freedom* (New York: Liberal Arts, 1960).

274

forward, moving in advance."[79] Furthermore, "growing, or, the continuous reconstruction of experience, is the only end."[80]

This priority given to experience was picked up within the women's movement which began in the United States in the 1960s. The initial aim of the movement, as with earlier humanisms, was to remove obstacles to women becoming "fully human." Betty Friedan described the anxiety, boredom, and what she called the "progressive dehumanization" that many American women felt in their comfortable suburban homes. She interpreted this wide-ranging experience as a disease that had no name — a malaise of conforming to a "feminine mystique." Women now had university degrees, citizenship and voting rights, and material comforts — all the goals previous feminists had struggled to attain — and yet many experienced their social situation as leading to dehumanization. Friedan described it this way: "Since the human organism has an intrinsic urge to grow, a woman who evades her own growth by clinging to the childlike protection of the housewife role will — in so far as that role does not permit her own growth — suffer increasingly severe pathology, both for her and for her children."[81] In this context children, male chauvinism, and discrimination in the workplace became perceived as the new enemies of women's freedom. The solutions proposed for these situations included abortion/birth control, consciousness-raising, and preferential hiring or affirmative action to enable women to work outside the home.

The formation of the National Organization for Women (NOW), concerned with providing a means for women to network politically, turned feminism into a broad-based American political movement, reflecting many of the aims of the pragmatic (secular) humanists. The original statement of purpose at the organizing conference of NOW included the following: "NOW is dedicated to the proposition that women, first and foremost, are human beings, who, like all other people in our society, must have the chance to develop their fullest human potential. We believe that women can achieve such equality only by accepting to the full the challenges and responsibilities they share with other people in our society, as part of the decision-making mainstream of American political, economic and social life."[82] This early statement of pragmatic feminism fits very nicely into the goals of growth expressed by pragmatic humanism.

79. John Dewey, *Reconstruction in Philosophy* (Boston: Beacon Press, 1960), pp. 177, 179.
80. Dewey, *Reconstruction in Philosophy*, p. 184.
81. Betty Friedan, *The Feminine Mystique* (New York: Norton, 1963), p. 279.
82. "National Organization for Women: Statement of Purpose (1986)," in *This Great Argument: The Rights of Women*, ed. Haminca Bosmajian and Haig Bosmajian (Menlo Park, Calif.: Addison-Wesley, 1972), pp. 190-91.

In 1973 a new Humanist Manifesto was published, incorporating a number of feminist principles along with its own restatement of seventeen humanist principles. Again we find an explicit rejection of belief in God, in eternal life, and an explicit affirmation. "We affirm that moral values derive their source from human experience. Ethics is *autonomous* and *situational* needing no theological or ideological sanction. Ethics stems from human need and interest."[83] At the same time, the document is filled with a new zeal for respect for the dignity of the human person, the use of reason and intelligence, the protection of civil liberties, the removal of all discrimination because of sex, the rejection of violence as a means of interaction, a rejection of nationalisms, and the hope for a new ecologically sound and democratic world cooperation among peoples.

Many of these themes had also been developed in various forms of feminist activity over the years, including eco-feminism, nonviolent protests by women against nuclear war, and the criticism of abuses of human rights throughout the world. Moreover, women's experience becomes the basis for new feminist epistemologies, and women's situations become the basis for new feminist ethics. And, as some aspects of feminist ethics become integrated into the political structures of pragmatic or secular humanism in the context of economic scarcity, we find an ironic pattern beginning to develop within this humanism. Preferential hiring of women over men has led to the situation in which men of the same working class, because they are competing with women for the same jobs, suddenly become perceived as the enemy of women who need to work in order to grow and develop. Inversely, women of the same working class become perceived as the enemy of men. No longer are women or men able to devote themselves to working for the good of all men and women but, rather, they begin to fight one another for their own interest. In addition, we begin to see political alliances being formed with others like them in order to establish power bases of lobbying and pressure groups to defend their own special interests. So now the humanist ideal of working for the good of all deteriorates, so that one works only for the good of a few — the particular few who share the same narrow interests one has. Consequently, this kind of pragmatic or secular feminism turns out to be unable to be a humanism even in the pragmatic or secular sense because it excludes the interests of large numbers of human beings.

The same point can be made if we look at the prominence secular feminism has given to abortion. If the "happiness, growth, and success" of women depends upon the termination of the lives of unborn developing human be-

83. In Lamont, appendix, pp. 293-94.

ings, then this kind of feminism also cannot be a humanism which claims to defend the rights of all human beings to full growth and development. Consequently, any feminism which either explicitly or implicitly advocates a primacy to women's development by excluding the interests of large numbers of unborn developing human beings cannot be considered a humanism.

Personalist Humanism

We turn now to the last form of humanism to be considered in this article. Between 1933 and 1937 a new form of humanism began to emerge among Jewish and Christian philosophers almost in a morphic resonance.

It is difficult to determine who first articulated its grounds. We note in France, in 1932, the founding of the personalist review *Esprit* in Paris by Emmanuel Mounier and Jacques Maritain. In 1934 Mounier and Maritain, along with Gabriel Marcel and Nicholai Berdjaev, met together in a philosophy group and published a "Personalist Manifesto." This document contained the first public articulation of the new personalist humanism. But we also find, as early as 1919 (in early drafts of *I and Thou*), the Jewish existentialist Martin Buber emphasizing the interpersonal nature of dialogue among human beings and with God, and the relation of person and community.[84] Buber argues that true community of persons is established not through the feelings or experiences one person has for another, but rather "all of them have to stand in a living reciprocal relationship to a single living center, and they have to stand in a living, reciprocal relationship to one another."[85] In these reciprocal relations, human beings are not a thing or a "what" for one another, but instead become a "who" in relation to one another.

We also have the example of Edith Stein (1891-1942), who, while having converted to Catholicism in 1922, had been born a Jew. Stein had been giving public lectures in Germany and Switzerland on women's emancipation and the women's movement since 1928,[86] and in her autobiography wrote that, from 1916 on, she had been working on "something which was personally close to my heart and which continually occupied me anew in all later works: the constitution of the human person."[87] (Though Stein is not normally considered a personalist, I would argue that she ought to be so understood. If one looks at

---

84. Martin Buber, *I and Thou* (New York: Scribner, 1970).

85. Buber, p. 94.

86. Edith Stein, *Woman* (Washington, D.C.: ICS Publications, 1987).

87. Edith Stein, *Life in a Jewish Family* (Washington, D.C.: ICS Publications, 1986), p. 197.

how she elaborates her reflections on woman, her views have many of the same components of personalism. There is some question of how much she knew of the personalist movement, as some of her work antedates that of Maritain and Mounier — though she was also contemporary with them.)

A basic theme in this personalist humanism is the distinction between the individual human being and the person. Briefly, the individual is described in terms of the building up of the ego by acts of self-determination and self-development. The individual is also one of a kind and, in the case of woman or man as an individual, is simply one of a human kind. A human person, on the other hand, is a being who transcends the self, by a gift of the self to another person. In this case the center of the self is shifted from oneself to another, by a free act or series of acts. Here the human being is no longer just a "what" but becomes a "who," in relation to another "who." Right from the beginning, then, personalist philosophers emphasized that the human being could not be fully explained as simply a material being. Instead the human person was understood to be an integral spiritual and material being.

Mounier, for example, argues that personalism "includes every human problem in the entire range of concrete human life, from the lowliest material conditions to the highest spiritual possibilities."[88] This basic orientation of all personalist humanisms marks it off from the previous three forms considered in this article. In other words, personalist humanism places the human being in an interpersonal set of relations with God and with one another. It takes on a particularly Christian form when the appeal to the ground for the spiritual identity of a person is placed both in the creation of a human person in the image and likeness of a personal God and also on the particularly redemptive identity of Jesus Christ, who, although divine, took on human nature when he became man.

In Spain, in 1934, Maritain delivered a series of six lectures at the University of Santandar on this new personalism. These lectures were published in book form in Paris in 1936 under the title *L'humanisme intégral* (*Integral Humanism* or *True Humanism* in English translations). Here we find the first articulation of the claim that the univocal understanding of the human being present in older forms of humanisms should indeed be rejected, as it understands human beings simply as individuals, even if self-defining within the existential model. But there is also an implicit rejection of understanding the human being or person in equivocal terms — as proposed in forms of antihumanism. Instead, Maritain suggests that the terms "human being" and "person" ought to

88. Emmanuel Mounier, *Personalism* (Notre Dame, Ind.: University of Notre Dame Press, 1952), p. 9.

be understood as *analogical* in their application to women and men. This central place for analogy provides a key to the renewed form of personalist humanism that Maritain and others adopt.

Returning to human freedom, we could say the free will and intellect are understood as part of human nature through creation in the image of God, but that the proper humanist use of intellect and will depends upon the redemptive integration of the faculties within the person and the degree to which the person is able to participate actively in building a common good. Grace, or participation in the life of God, is crucial to these two activities of integration and appropriate action. Therefore the human person is not an absolute center, but rather a constantly renewed center through being changed by cooperating with grace.[89] Furthermore, within this renewed understanding, freedom is not simply a freedom of individual choice (as found in pragmatic or liberal humanism), but rather is "the autonomous freedom of the person" who is both material and spiritual.[90]

Dangers to this freedom then include a militant atheism which makes this world an absolute rather than a relative end, on the one hand, or an otherworldly spiritualism which ignores the proper place of building up the temporal order, on the other hand. Another danger is found in an extreme form of totalitarianism, in which the person is subsumed into the state, or in an extreme form of individualism, in which the individual emphasizes his or her own rights to the neglect of the common good.[91] In these situations the person is reduced from a "who" to a "what," or a thing to be used or repressed. Maritain summarizes more positively the goal of human freedom in *The Person and the Common Good*:

> It follows from the fact that the principal value of the common work of society is the freedom of expansion of the person together with all the guarantees which this freedom implies and the diffusion of good that flows from it. In short, the political common good is a common good of human

---

89. Jacques Maritain, *True Humanism* (New York: Scribner, 1938), p. 87. See also his essay "Christian Humanism" (1942), republished in *The Range of Reason* (New York: Scribner, 1952), chap. 14, pp. 185-99.

90. Maritain, *True Humanism*, p. 172.

91. These forms are developed in a discussion of a more contemporary form of personalist humanism, by Andrew Woznicki, *A Christian Humanism: Karol Wojtyla's Existential Personalism* (New Britain, Conn.: Mariel Productions, 1980), p. x. Cardinal Paul Poupard has spoken and written extensively on John Paul II's Christian humanism in his capacity as prefect for the new Congregation of Faith and Culture. In particular, he builds upon the Second Vatican Council's affirmation in *Gaudium et spes*, #55: "We are witnesses of the birth of *a new humanism*. . . ."

persons. And it turns out that, in subordinating oneself to this common work, by the grace of justice and amity, each one of us is still subordinated to the good of persons, to the accomplishment of the personal life of *others* and, at the same time, to the interior dignity of one's own person.[92]

This characteristic of personalist humanism, of being both concerned with the interior dignity of one's own person and at the same time dedicated to the common good of the freedom of the expansion of other persons, is crucial to our study of whether a feminism can be a humanism.

There is a close relation between a personalist humanism and a personalist feminism. For example, in 1936 Mounier published in *Esprit* the first article focusing on the relation between personalism and woman's identity, entitled "La femme aussi est une personne."[93] And Jacques and Raïssa Maritain struggled with many of the same issues.

We can clearly identify the characteristics of this new personalist humanism in Edith Stein's essays on women. A particular concern of hers was: What is fundamental to women's and to men's identity? What can they learn from one another, and how can they work together so that they can remove obstacles to one another's becoming fully human?

Her work was exploratory, but it focused on trying to understand the complex inner structure of the human person, as man or as woman, and the call of each to interior perfection and exterior responsibility. Stein identifies three aspects of personal identity: membership in the human species, membership in the subspecies of man or woman, and identity as an individual. Dangers to freedom would include lack of insight into these aspects of one's identity, or lack of effort in educating oneself in characteristics of the other subspecies (i.e., a woman needs to make an effort to develop masculine characteristics and a man to develop feminine characteristics), and the lack of cooperation with the grace of Jesus Christ. She elaborates on the Christian dictum, that Christ will make you free. "We therefore achieve total humanity through Him and, simultaneously, the right personal attitude."[94] By her emphasis on education, and specifically on woman's education, Stein elaborates the philosophical parameters of her broader personalistic humanism.

In Stein's form of feminism, if we choose to describe it as such for the

---

92. Jacques Maritain, *The Person and the Common Good* (Notre Dame, Ind.: University of Notre Dame Press, 1985), p. 103; originally published, 1947. See also Maritain, *True Humanism*, pp. 127ff. Maritain here develops these characteristics with respect to the *communal* characteristic of true humanism and its *personalist* characteristic.

93. Emmanuel Mounier, "La femme aussi est une personne," *Esprit*, June 1936, pp. 292-97.

94. Stein, *Woman*, p. 252.

purposes of this analysis — and we can because she is concerned with removing obstacles to the full development of women as persons — women and men are two analogous ways of being human persons. She describes the hierarchical interior ordering of the person as involving biological, psychological, philosophical, and theological realities, with the higher order integrating the lower order. One danger to freedom for women is the lack of knowledge of their complex structure and how it is analogous to (i.e., similar to and also different from) the complex structure of men. She calls for women to engage in a phenomenological analysis of their human, woman, and individual identities. She resists reducing women and men to things or "what's" but argues that all human beings ought to gain insight into how their uniqueness relates to their commonness. And in particular she emphasizes the need to gain insight into how woman's identity and situation offer unique contexts for education and action which are similar to and yet different from men.

Stein's work was exploratory, and it predated Beauvoir's by fifteen years. So in some ways it was the first contemporary attempt at an interdisciplinary approach to woman's identity. At the same time, it has in its foundation key components of personalist humanism, and it offers the possibility for further development within this approach to the goal of full human development. In this understanding, if a woman views a man as simply a member of a univocal group "men," she reduces him from a "who" to a "what." This may occur, for example, in a context of preferential hiring, or affirmative action. Similarly, if a woman views a developing human being as simply a piece of material, she reduces the fetus to a "what" or thing, instead of a developing someone worthy of love. This occurs in many attitudes toward abortion, and especially the most common one, namely, that a woman has a right to control her own body. It also occurs in the context in which abortion is described as a right to reproductive freedom. The exercise of freedom in this way reduces the developing human being to a what to be destroyed instead of a who to be defended and supported into full human and personal development. So a personalist feminism would differ in approach regarding these two key components of most contemporary forms of feminism. It would follow that only a personalist feminism could be a personalist humanism.

In all forms of personalist humanism the main danger to human freedom is identified as the lack of mature integration within a person and the lack of genuine participation in interpersonal societies or communities of building up the common good. The specifics of these aspects are elaborated in great detail in the Polish school of personalist humanism, especially in the works of M. A. Krapiec and Karol Wojtyla (known now as Pope John Paul II) — who picked up the whole momentum of early personalist humanism. While outside forces reducing the person to simply an individual are significant, the mature use of human freedom is seen as the starting point for full development as a person. (Though the work of this "Polish school" of personalism largely follows the Second World War, it seems likely that there had been a long-standing interest in personalism in Poland, based on the work of Mounier and Maritain. In the 1920s there were a number of people — such as Max Scheler and Roman Ingarden — who traveled back and forth between France and Poland. Mounier's works were published in Polish, and in 1934 he published an article in a Polish review [*Wiadomosci Literackie*] explaining what was happening in France in the personalist movement.)

Wojtyla, in particular, developed the view that the full development of every human being is the goal of all persons — and he elaborates this in what he calls "the personalistic norm." This norm is that one ought always treat other persons as beings worthy of love, not as "things" or as entities that can be abused. Wojtyla has elaborated this personalistic norm in a very interesting way in relation to women's identity.

Wojtyla (like Edith Stein) notes that the female lived experience of the body prepares women in a certain way to receive another human being from puberty every month, through ovulation. Then if a woman does have children, the experience of having children increases that sensitivity toward the whole being. A woman generates within herself, while a male generates outside himself. Wojtyla and Stein argue that there is a propensity in women to be concerned with human beings. (Even some radical feminists, who otherwise would disagree with Stein and Wojtyla, would admit this point, though they would describe it as focusing on "caring.")

In fact, Wojtyla calls this orientation "woman's genius" and part of a "new feminism" which, he argues, if it can enter the workplace as well as the home, has the possibility of bringing in the personalistic norm — to evaluate whether a person is being treated as a someone worthy of love. This focus on "the genius of woman" is relatively new, and can be found in *Mulieris dignitatem, Evangelium vitae,*[95] and in recent statements of the American bishops, including their statements on the role of technology in life. One can also find some of this in Stein's essays on women. I would like to note one passage from *Evangelium vitae* that is quite striking:

> In transforming culture so that it supports life, women occupy a place in thought and action which is unique and decisive. It depends on them to promote a "new feminism" which rejects the temptation of imitating mod-

95. *Evangelium vitae,* encyclical letter on the value and inviolability of human life, March 25, 1995.

els of "male domination" in order to acknowledge and affirm the true genius of women in every aspect of the life of society and overcome all discrimination, violence and exploitation. . . .

A mother welcomes and carries in herself another human being, enabling it to grow inside her, giving it room, respecting it in its otherness.
Women first learn and then teach others that human relations are authentic
if they are open to accepting the other person: a person who is recognized
and loved because of the dignity which comes from being a person and not
from other considerations, such as usefulness, strength, intelligence, beauty
or health. This is the fundamental contribution which the Church and humanity expect from women. And it is the indispensable prerequisite for an
authentic cultural change.[96]

We see Wojtyla using such phrases as "new feminism" and "male domination"
— something quite unlike what many people expect to hear from him.

This shows that something is happening — that there is a new
personalistic norm, with a new feminism and a new humanism, which is based
on an understanding of what is truly human, and on what women's and men's
places are within that.

Conclusion

Can feminism be a humanism? If one perceives any people or kind of people
fundamentally as an enemy — if one can push them out of one's life (and, in
the extreme, kill them) — then this is not a humanism. Personalist humanism
requires that one ought always work, as far as possible, for the full development
of all human beings with whom one comes into contact. If one is a personalist
feminist, one is interested particularly in those ways that can remove obstacles
for women to become fully human persons. What specifically one does, of
course, depends on the context one is in.

The original feminism that was humanistic was, as we saw, Renaissance
humanism — a humanism that sprang up within a Christian context, and was
situated within a person's relationship with God and with people's relations to
one another. The first, early Enlightenment form was still Christian, and feminists who adhered to it were also interested in the development of all persons.
But once feminism explicitly separated itself from relations with God, and
when it set itself up in antagonism with organized religion, it began to think of

96. *Evangelium vitae*, #99.

getting rid of other people. It saw certain groups of people as enemies and saw nothing wrong in eliminating them.

Personalist humanism, which was reestablished through the Catholic tradition in France and in Poland, is a renewal of humanism. The feminist movement within that is also a renewal of feminist humanism. Christianity, then, has an important role to play in the articulation of a personalist feminism and humanism. In Christianity one can speak of the beginning, the fall, and the redemption as in some way beginning to come, and there is some recent interesting work that has come out of the question, Do women have a different role to play in this redemptive activity than men? And if so, what would it be? How would women's identity be fundamentally different from men's and how similar? And thus one point that both Stein and Wojtyla have identified focuses on the importance of one's attitude toward other human beings.

There are many areas in which a personalist feminism might be able to cooperate with other forms of feminism in the contemporary world. Some of these include: a critique of particular ways technology may lead to the reduction of women; a critique of the ways capitalism misuses women; a critique of the ways education does not help the full development of women; a critique of the ways the structure of societies may inhibit the possibility for women to engage in meaningful work outside the home; a critique of the ways women's health is not adequately cared for; a critique of the ways the family — as the original place in which a human being is discovered as a unique and unrepeatable "who" in relation to other "who's" — can be strengthened; and so on. These were issues on which the recent Beijing conference on women began to focus in cooperative ways — and through which many different forms of feminism sought to find a common ground for a variety of humanisms.

So we can answer our original question of whether a feminism can be a humanism by the following. If feminism is an ideology that places women's development as a value over the development of men or of developing human beings, then, no, it cannot be a humanism. If, on the other hand, a feminism is an organized way of thought and action that gives special attention to removing obstacles to the full development of women, but at the same time works for the full development of all human beings as persons, then it can be a humanism. In fact, I would probably make the stronger argument, that only a personalist feminism can be a humanism in this full sense; it recognizes that the person is a "who," that a woman, a man, and a child are analogous ways of being a person, and that persons can be fulfilled only by participating with one another in building up the common good of other persons. Indeed, the only way to become fulfilled as a person is by the repeated habit of the giving of self to other persons.

Ethical Equality in a New Feminism

Jean Bethke Elshtain

An urgent quest for equality and freedom lies at the heart of Western feminism. But in what does this equality consist? How is freedom understood? Despite attempts to promote one dominant version of equality understood as radical sameness or indistinguishability in identities, vocations, and roles between men and women and to define freedom as the maximization of individual rights, debates continue. Perhaps the best entry point into an exploration of a new ethical feminism and of Pope John Paul II's contribution to this project is the proclamation in Genesis 1:27: "Male and female created he them." The implications of the ontological dignity and simultaneity of creation of women and men in God's image are fundamental to this end.[1] If to this one adds Saint Paul's famous declaration that in God "there is neither Jew nor Greek, male nor female, free nor slave," but instead, that "all are one" (Gal. 3:28) in the new dispensation of Christ Jesus, you find transhistorical claims of universal significance that first bear on an international church (God's pilgrim people), and second, bear more general implications that bore fruit over the centuries.

Thus it is altogether unsurprising that the performative implications of Christian understanding are manifest in something new in the antique world as two groups previously excluded from the antique city — women and the poor — are now incorporated within the boundaries of the *civitas*. The great scholar of the late antique world, Peter Brown, argues that Christian women took on a public role previously denied them in relation to the poor and the sick. They

---

1. Biblical scholars have shown that "Male and female created he them," although it appears first in Scripture, is actually a later, and far more sophisticated and mature creation story than the Gen. 2:22 "Adam's rib" account that has been almost the entire focus of feminist dissent from scriptural understandings in this matter.

founded shrines and poorhouses in their own names and were able to pick some of their own kin — their special saints — and go into the public world out of devotion to these self-chosen kin; this was one visible outcome of the new dispensation.[2]

It was also remarkable that many of the qualities most often associated with mothering — giving birth to and sustaining human life; an ethic of responsibility toward the helpless, the vulnerable, the weak; gentleness, mercy, and compassion — were now enjoined on all. "We must love one another" was a core Christian commandment. We are, argued Saint Augustine, well advised to judge ourselves and others not by our acquisitions or our power to dominate and to compel, but by what we and others love. The new Christian community was available to any who had a hunger and thirst for righteousness. The city of God on pilgrimage is "set apart by a holy yearning," in Augustine's phrase, and that yearning includes hope — hope lodged in the capacity of human beings to long for something different; to examine the nature of their relationships with their immediate environment; above all, to establish their identities by refusing to be engulfed in the unthinking habits of their fellows. The Christian recognized — or was called to recognize — an intimate dependence on the life around him or her and to be aware of the tenacity of the ties that bind us. Men and women in this community are not competitors but friends. They are brothers and sisters in communion.

Male and female created he them, yes, but working out the implications for earthly life was no easy matter. Historically the male and female both in relation and separately have been understood in vastly different ways. Prior to Christianity, the philosophy and practices of the ancient world featured a number of claims about the natures of men and women, and such views — especially Aristotle's — continued to circulate in the Christian era. The material on this is vast and unwieldy unless one finds helpful categories to organize what would otherwise be an unmanageable mountain of texts. From the ancient world to modern feminism, three dominant possibilities have emerged. Sr. Prudence Allen, in her comprehensive treatment, *The Concept of Woman: The Aristotelian Revolution, 750 B.C.–A.D. 1250*, worked out typologies that I have found very useful — especially so in sorting out how and where the full implications of "created he them" evolved, fitfully, over time.[3] I begin with three typologies explored by Allen and then move to John Paul II's contributions to a new femi-

---

2. Peter Brown, *The Cult of the Saints* (Chicago: University of Chicago Press, 1993). To be a public woman in the antique city was to be an outcast, a prostitute.

3. Sr. Prudence Allen, R.S.M., *The Concept of Woman: The Aristotelian Revolution, 750 B.C.–A.D. 1250* (Grand Rapids and Cambridge: Eerdmans, 1997).

nism explicitly. I conclude the essay with a discussion of the implications of John Paul's theology of the body for a new ethical feminism.

A Triple Typology

Sex Polarity

One form of devaluation of women present in classical antiquity and circulating yet is the position of sex polarity that holds that male and female are unlike essences, something akin to different species in the strongest statements of this position. Although the antique view devalued the female in relation to the male, as, for example, in Aristotle's argument that woman is a kind of "deficient" male, wanting in full rationality, there is a mirror image of this devaluation in what might be termed *reverse sex polarity* lodged in hostility on the part of female to male with the latter devalued in the overall scheme of things. Within the world of sex polarity, one sex is necessarily "better than" or a "victim of" the other. If one begins from the presumptions of sex polarity in either of its varieties, the only view of equal rights and freedom that is consistent with this ontological position is equal rights as adversarial, as a weapon one sex can, or should, use against the other.

Sex polarists come in a number of historical and contemporary varieties. Whatever the source of philosophical inspiration, the outcome is an ontological and epistemological gulf with men and women construed as radically different. This invariably works to devalue one sex in relation to the other. In this regard there are even harsher versions of sex polarity than Aristotle's, already noted, that begin with strong anthropological presumptions of the inferiority or superiority of one sex on the level of being itself. For example, in contemporary discussions of men, women, and war, it is striking how frequently the assertion that men are "by nature" violent, disorderly, the destroyers and violators among us is presented as if it were simply a fact of the matter. By contrast, women are identified with care, peace-lovingness, and attunement with nature. In polemical versions of the sex polarist argument, the universe itself is said to be imperiled unless peaceful women triumph over violent men. In a world of harsh sex polarity, there is no room for mediating across the ontological divide. Denying that all human beings are marked by sin and fall short and that violence is not the exclusive purview of one sex only, those who make such arguments are caught within a master/slave narrative as their reigning category for human relationships, from marriage to politics. Some triumph; some lose. It is time for women to triumph and for men to lose.

This impugning of one sex to the advantage of the other is, as I have suggested, a long story, as older misogynist narratives attacking women amply demonstrate. The difference between earlier generations of male disparagers of women and the current women disparagers of men is that the language of equal rights and freedom was not available as a central category in the earlier rhetorical struggle. By attaching equal rights to a crude model of who has power over whom, sex polarists cannot think their way out of, or through, static formulations. Or, perhaps better put, they can get out of the oppressor/oppressed and master/slave pairing only through the obliteration of one category: thus men must be "feminized," and only then will the more virtuous sex — women — truly triumph.

Sex Unity

A second position — sex unity — would seem to solve this problem of proclaimed ontological inequality or polarity. Indebted to a literalist reading of book 5 of Plato's *Republic,* this position obliterates difference in favor of the identity or unity of male and female. There are no differences that matter if one abstracts from embodiment, strips mothers and children and fathers and children of particular ties to one another, and "mates" males and females of the elite Guardian class in Plato's text on principles of eugenic selection. A notion of equality flowing from sex unity implicates one in a terribly abstract understanding of equality, rights, and freedom as one part of a totalizing philosophy. We become equal to the extent that we are identical, with our individualities rubbed off and our sexual identities a matter of indifference.

Oddly enough, sex unitists sometimes wind up in a position similar to that of the sex polarists who must vanquish the opposition or totally transform him (all men are "feminized"; all fathers must become "mothers," as fathering is associated with nothing but domination; and so on): another form of triumph through effacement. That is, the homogenizing urge, present at creation, so to speak, extends to political and theological projects that foresee the elimination of the whole category of gender, even the recognition of difference. All are "one," not in communion or as a creedal body within which the distinctiveness of persons is preserved, but rather in a politicized entity (whether a family, church, or polity) in which we are utterly indifferent to difference, having abstracted from our bodies so successfully that they are no longer a source of identity, no longer the object of epistemological wonder and dialogue and mutual attempts to understand. Equal rights, then, pertain to generic beings with bodies that carry no ethical weight.

Sex Complementarity

This position puts forward a vision of male and female in relation that emerged with distinctiveness within the Christian tradition. Sex complementarity begins from a stance of ontological equality and equal dignity that is nonetheless compatible with different offices and vocations. Equality neither requires nor presumes homogenization; rather, sex complementarity affords a sense of partnership, of what it means to be in community and in communion. Framed with this understanding in mind, equal rights become signs of human dignity, marks of both "the same" and "the distinctive" simultaneously. This latter position is philosophically rich, but it complicates matters enormously, requiring, as it does, a more nuanced understanding of the way equality structures our identities both within and, at times, in opposition to the many social institutions of which we are part. The strength of the position is that rather than a presumptive abstraction from the body (sex unity), or a presumptive and destructive absolutizing of sex difference (sex polarity), one displays embodied beings in relation in the fullness of their dignity.

The social and cultural implications of the sex complementarity position are many. One would look to whether men and women are treated by definition as an inferior in relation to a superior; or as an identical being to others in a way that negates particularity and individuation; or, alternatively, as analogical beings who work out their identities over time in relation. Here, of course, one must part company with those among our Christian forebears who saw in the male the most perfect representation of what it means to be created "in the image of God." Sr. Prudence Allen, in an interesting article on "integral sex complementarity," writes: "It is in light of . . . contemporary understandings that the recent writings of Pope John Paul II are so illuminating, for he states explicitly that woman and man equally reflect the image of God."[4] Allen concludes that it is "hard to overestimate the significance of this shift in emphasis that Pope John Paul II is bringing to the Church's understanding of man and woman as persons."[5]

I will turn to John Paul II's thought in a moment, but first let me put just a bit more on the table concerning sex complementarity, using Sr. Allen's discussion of two quite different thinkers: Edith Stein and Hildegard of Bingen (1098-1179). Stein shares a great deal of philosophic ground with the current

4. Sr. Prudence Allen, "Integral Sex Complementarity and the Theology of Communion," *Communio* 17 (Winter 1990): 523-44, cited at pp. 542-43. See also her essay, "A Woman and a Man as Prime Analogical Beings," *American Catholic Philosophical Quarterly* 66, no. 4 (Autumn 1992): 465-82.

5. Allen, "Integral Sex Complementarity," p. 543.

pope, so it is no big surprise that their appreciation of human corporeality and male and female as analogical beings created in God's image should overlap. I will focus on Hildegard briefly because this helps show the historic lineage of the modern view. For Hildegard, men and women mirror one another. Hildegard establishes "a horizontal basis for complementarity between women and men, that is, that they are significantly different and simultaneously equal in dignity and worth."[6]

Hildegard insists that men and women help create one another, that each is "so involved with each other that one of them is the work of the other. Without woman, man could not be called man; without man, woman could not be named woman. . . . Neither of them could henceforth live without the other."[7] This is fascinating in part because Hildegard seems to be working with an appreciation of human powers as plural, *potentia* rather than *potestas*. *Potestas* is a political construal of power as rule or dominion: power over others. *Potentia* points us toward something more open, less codified, from which our notion of potential is derived.

The cocreation of man and woman in relation to one another (each as the "work" of the other, in Hildegard's terms) is not an image of blissful harmony, an unlittered landscape of indistinguishable oneness. Indeed, the latter view of oneness presupposes the sex unity posture that I am challenging. In the sex complementarity mode, we are equal in dignity but distinct from one another as well. This complementary relationship will, at times, be one of struggle as men and women "work" one another, grappling with sameness and difference. But within the particular community we call the church, this struggle is framed by a shared lineage, a deposit of centuries-old belief and tradition. That tradition can teach us yet, if we but let it. One who has helped bring Christian understandings of "male and female created he them" to bear is, as I have already noted, Pope John Paul II. It is to a discussion of but a few of his contributions that I now turn.

Pope John Paul II on the Dignity of the Human Person, Male and Female

John Paul II's understanding of freedom is at odds with the reigning Western notion of freedom as full self-possession. This makes it difficult for even the

6. Sr. Prudence Allen, "Sex and Gender Differentiation in Hildegard of Bingen and Edith Stein," *Communio* 20 (Summer 1993): 389-414, cited at p. 402.

7. Allen, "Sex and Gender Differentiation," p. 402.

sympathetic reader to apprehend it. In *Evangelium vitae* he writes: "If the promotion of the self is understood in terms of absolute autonomy, people inevitably reach the point of rejecting one another. Everyone else is considered an enemy from whom one has to defend oneself. Thus society becomes a mass of individuals placed side by side, but without any mutual bonds. Each one wishes to assert himself independently of the other and in fact intends to make his own interests prevail."[8] John Paul's integral anthropology is key here, and it cuts much deeper than what is usually meant when one observes that a thinker holds to a "social theory of human nature" by contrast to some atomistic or individualist alternative that denies that we are born to community. Theories or ideologies that oversocialize us by absorbing the individual into a collective, or by seeing the person as the mere sum total of his or her reactions to external stimuli, are problematic as well, denying human freedom and moral dignity. John Paul, by contrast, insists that our cultures do not exhaust our very selves: there is a surplus, a something which transcends particular, relative arrangements, and that is the human person. He also departs from all versions of an egalitarian project that stress the individual as wholly apart from social life in principle, as if the self could be his or her absolute principle of identity and legitimation. He criticizes those who worship the idol of the self and deny the Creator's gift of life: all who turn away from the "saving" presence of other persons who help make us who we are. For we are never kingdoms unto ourselves. Our identities take shape over time in relation to others and in the cultures of which we are a part. Unsurprisingly, advocates immersed in one or more of the projects "pressured" by John Paul's account find his position objectionable. Indeed, sadly, they often condemn the project before engaging it sympathetically and critically.

For John Paul II our sociality runs deep: it is the creation over time of the person in community. True human freedom is attained in and through relationships and requires, as well, an appropriate relationship between Creator and creature. For only under God's guidance can we open up our hearts to love, our minds to the reason that love, which has primacy, unlocks. When we flatten the moral horizon and make immanence absolute, we set up oppositions where there should be a dialectic: between freedom and nature, freedom and the law. We see nature as something to master and to overcome rather than to *realize*. We treat our bodies and those of others as means, and in this way we negate the "gift of self."

This, for John Paul, is one of the great tragedies and sins of late moder-

---

8. John Paul II, encyclical letter on the gospel of life, *Evangelium vitae*, March 25, 1995, #20.

nity. The body is the bearer of meaning. We are not just spirits. All of this adds up to the perspective of *the acting person,* not only the title, in translation, of Karol Wojtyla's major philosophical work, but the cantus firmus of his encyclicals, from *Redemptor hominis* through *Evangelium vitae.*[9] All of John Paul's beginnings flow from the human person in his and her concreteness. Most often he neither affirms nor negates what is sometimes called "the subject." He simply begins in another place, understanding, as he does, the perils of philosophies of consciousness or many historicist accounts that, in quite different ways, construct an abstract, even reified notion of the subject. It is a complex person, a wondrous, inexhaustible creature, male and female, that lies at the heart of the human drama as he depicts it.

John Paul II dedicated his papacy to Saint Catherine of Siena. He dedicated himself — "completely" — to Mary. Nearly all his papal speeches and writings end with canticles, prose poems to Mary. This, together with his reaffirmation of church teaching concerning birth control, abortion, and priestly ordination, is taken as evidence of a romantic or "mystical" antifeminism, even, in some militant quarters, as narrow-minded misogyny. From the beginning of his pontificate, when he began to rearticulate his theology of the body in a series of homilies but after he had published a collection of essays on marriage and parenthood entitled *Love and Responsibility,* this pope has been a target of feminist protest.[10]

On one level, of course, it is quite easy to understand this reaction if one privileges the premises of individual-rights dominant feminism, especially in its current, heavily legalistic versions. It is difficult to "read" John Paul's writings on men and women in a context in which rights are viewed as an adversarial possession of one against some other. The dominant feminist project implicated in this understanding of rights holds that equality equals identity; that there is no distinction to be marked between male and female for the pur-

---

9. See Cardinal Karol Wojtyla, *The Acting Person,* trans. Andrej Potocki (Boston: D. Reidel, 1979). See also Kenneth L. Schmitz, *At the Center of the Human Drama: The Philosophical Anthropology of Karol Wojtyla/Pope John Paul II* (Washington, D.C.: Catholic University of America Press, 1993). Schmitz describes this text as deriving from Wojtyla's "thoroughly modern knowledge of philosophy" and his assimilation of "one of its modern approaches — phenomenology — to his own thinking" (p. 30). In this text, deriving from lectures Wojtyla delivered in the 1970s, he "intends . . . to describe human action in such a way that it will be seen to manifest the reality of the person in and through his or her actions out of the living experience of those actions" (p. 40).

10. *Love and Responsibility* (New York: Farrar, Straus and Giroux, 1981). Originally published in Polish in 1960. This section reproduces, extends, and amends a section of a piece entitled "A Pope for All Seasons?" that appeared in Reinhard Hutter and Theodor Dieter, eds., *Ecumenical Ventures in Ethics* (Grand Rapids: Eerdmans, 1998), pp. 14-37.

pose of distribution of any good or goods and in the creation of any good or goods: it is a variant on the sex unity position. Also, what men have tradition-ally "had" is construed as a "power" position, one bearing all the marks of dom-inance by contrast to the possibility of stewardship or service. Women, in this scheme of things, are construed as powerless and victimized, never as being the bearers of authority in any sphere or to any end or purpose. Women's steward-ship is taken as a symbol of their victimization. It is, therefore, easy to under-stand the controversy. But it is therefore very interesting indeed to unpack an argument, like John Paul's, that sees men and women as absolutely equal in dig-nity, as sharing fully in the *imago Dei,* yet draws from that not identity but dis-tinction.

John Paul's position holds that human life, including the life of the church, is enriched, not impoverished, by the respective embodiments of male and female, distinctions that neither imply nor require discrimination against women of an invidious sort. Indeed, he puts it in stronger terms. To deny that women share fully in the *imago Dei* is a grievous sin. Most contemporary West-ern feminists (though not all) reject this argument for equality and distinct but overlapping callings, finding in any articulation of difference an invitation to inegalitarianism.[11]

The Theology of the Body

Let's deepen our engagement with John Paul's distinctive drawing together of ontological egalitarianism and distinction by meditating on his homily "Inter-preting the Concept of Concupiscence," delivered during a regular Wednesday papal audience on October 8, 1980.[12] The pope's teaching on this occasion led to him being condemned for sexual priggishness and for his repudiation of lib-erated sexual attitudes. This seems to me a willful misreading. What John Paul

11. There are, of course, radical feminist "difference" theorists, too, of the sex polarity type, but they are found in sizable numbers only in the academy: they do not prevail in public policy and political debates save, perhaps, in the arena of legal theory, where the difference idea now is so powerful it threatens to swamp the equality principle. This difference argument is radically opposed to John Paul's understanding of distinction, for it holds that men and women, quite literally, inhabit different epistemological universes. John Paul's Christian egali-tarianism would find this position perplexing, at best; an invitation to suspicion, enmity, and division, at worst.

12. This homily and others central to John Paul's theology of the body appear in *Blessed Are the Pure of Heart: Catechesis on the Sermon on the Mount and Writings of St. Paul* (Boston: St. Paul Editions, 1983), pp. 142-49. The parenthetical page numbers in the following text are to this work.

was doing instead was teasing out of the Sermon on the Mount an erotic imperative that helps form a nonutilitarian sexual ethic for husband and wife; indeed, the pope's logic in this and many other writings pushes him in the direction of an egalitarianism that cuts to the bone, for he begins with absolute ontological equality — equality on the level of being — between man and woman.

John Paul assumes a scripturally based equality of rights and dignity between men and women. His concerns, in light of this equality, are the right ordering of male-female relations as these revolve around sexuality, *especially* married sexuality. He states: "The moral evaluation of lust (of 'looking lustfully') which Christ calls 'adultery committed in the heart,' seems to depend above all on the personal dignity itself of man and woman. This holds true both for those who are not united in marriage and — perhaps even more — for those who are husband and wife" (p. 142). The pope urges Christians to "dwell on the situation described by the Master," one in which the man "commits adultery in his heart" by means of an interior act given exterior expression in a "look" (p. 143).

But the look is not one of longing or mutually aroused desire; it is, instead, a lust that aims to possess and to use. The look John Paul addresses springs from lustful, not sacred, eros, and its possessing aim is divorced from authentic recognition of the humanity of the other person, thereby changing "the very intentionality of the woman's existence . . . , reducing the riches of the perennial call to the communion of persons . . . to mere satisfaction of the sexual 'need' of the body (with which the concept of 'instinct' seems to be linked more closely)."

The woman, the person lusted after in this scenario (though certainly she, too, can lust in this way), is reduced through a possessive "look" to a thinglike status. This is an instance of loving in what Augustine would call a disordered way in which another human being is used to one's own ends rather than enjoyed through a rightly ordered love that culminates in love for God. The objectification of the other person exudes a corrosive acid that permeates the interstices of the male-female pair. "In this way," John Paul continues, "that mutual 'for' is distorted, losing its character of communion of persons in favor of the utilitarian function" (p. 144). A distorted interiority that does not usher into an explicit act is difficult, at best, to apprehend, to analyze, and to grasp in order that one might assess how and in what manner it can be transformed. This John Paul acknowledges. But he rejects as inadequate those solutions to objectified possession of woman that concentrate solely on a "purely psychological (or 'sexological') interpretation of 'lust.'" For such reductionistic accounts provide neither a "sufficient basis to understand the text" nor a pathway for redemption of the male and female in communion (p. 145). A transformation of spirit, a change so deep that vital performative consequences flow from it, including freeing the human eye from the literal shortsightedness of possession with its reduction of others to functions, is called for.

With his arguments against turning married sexuality into the utilitarian use of the woman (or man, as the case may be), John Paul articulates an egalitarian ethos that suggests a vision of human community which, in its conceptual heart, embraces powerful imperatives of human dignity and in what such consists. The ethos he calls for, here and elsewhere, is one that liberates the human heart *from* lust and for *love;* it is an impassioned plea for mutuality and for locating authentic human freedom within the protective constraints of a nonutilitarian community. The attitude implied in the lustful possession of the other in human intimate relations taints humanity in general. For the reduction of a human being to thinglikeness (including the woman in marriage, too often) fuels and legitimates possession over all. That casting of a shroud over the humanity of the female is similar to the ways we have devised to sanction the excision of others, whether black, poor, Jew, or handicapped, from the fullness of communion, and it forestalls the emergence of deep communal imperatives.

John Paul II hints at the broader applicability of his liberatory ethos when he states — and this theme later fuels *Evangelium vitae* — "Human life, by its nature, is 'co-educative' and its dignity, its balance, depends at every moment of history and at every point of geographical longitude and latitude, on 'who' she will be for him, and he for her" (p. 148). Societal change in sexual justice matters begins, then, with a transformation of the basic pair: he/she. To the extent that this relationship is one of domination, possession, and consumption, predatory and possessive relations are legitimized. It follows that a transformation at this most basic level would ramify, first, throughout the little commonwealth of the family and then radiate outward, sending forth tendrils of humanity into a world that is often hostile and uncomprehending but that could not remain wholly unaltered by this permeation and permutation from within.

John Paul insists that there are various models of human existence that are shameful or wrong-in-themselves (like the possessive master/slave model, for example) or are, at best, radically incomplete. He doesn't use this language, but it is apt: intimate and social relations based purely on contract are amputated relations at best and may be sinful if they legitimate possession of the other and preclude the vital cocreation of male and female in relation to one another. The moment of action, the moment when the intention moves to word/act, is that moment when the male-female pair, in its coming together, transcends any contractual pairing in order to more fully embody deep ethical imperatives. The transcendence is lost if the relationship is trapped in a deadly, repetitive dance of possessor/possessed.

With this powerful critique of the reduction of human existence to utilitarian calculations or relations of force and lust, John Paul links himself with vital themes embedded in what is best called *ethical feminism*. The words from John Paul's World Day of Peace Message, "Women as Teachers of Peace," 1994, are as good a place as any to conclude: "If, from the very beginning, girls are looked down upon or regarded as inferior, their sense of dignity will be gravely impaired and their healthy development inevitably compromised. Discrimination in childhood will have lifelong effects and will prevent women from fully taking part in the life of society."[13] This is a strong brief against invidious comparison and ill use. Ethical egalitarianism is a project that awaits further development, and it is one John Paul sees as central to the new culture of life he outlines in *Evangelium vitae*. Women are at the heart of this culture of life, not as romantic visions of endlessly self-abnegating material figures, nor as virtuous and remote figures above the fray, but very much as active participants in the human drama whose embodiment always holds forth the promise of life in situ, whether a woman commits herself to childbearing or not. Women's bodies speak to generative human possibility, and women's centuries-old tradition of tending to the daily requirements of life in community, especially through the hard, hands-on, practical work of care, is a great heritage. The pity is not that women have thus devoted themselves, but that this humanly necessary work has too often been belittled, ignored, or even served as occasions for women's social and political inequality. Pope John Paul II lifts up this heritage and the claim to equal dignity and equality with distinctiveness. For him, specific attention to women's dignity is not a new claim: it has been central to his thinking for decades, for he has for decades stressed the inexhaustible dignity of the human person, of every human person without distinction.

---

13. Pope John Paul II, "World Day of Peace: Women: Teachers of Peace," *Origins* 24, no. 28 (1994): 465-69, at p. 468.

Equality, Difference, and the Practical Problems of a New Feminism

Elizabeth Fox-Genovese

That we are in sore need of a new feminism can hardly be doubted, and the answer to why we need one could hardly be more disconcertingly simple: the old one has failed. But a wide gap separates recognition of the need from the prospects for meeting it. In recent years recognition of the need has only grown, especially among women of faith. Pope John Paul II has insisted upon its urgency in a series of reflections: his "Letter to Women," written to delegates at the opening of the Beijing conference; his collected Angelus reflections of 1995, *The Genius of Woman;* and his *Mulieres dignitatem.* Sadly acknowledging that "unfortunately even today there are situations in which women live, *de facto* if not legally, in a condition of inferiority," John Paul insists that the prevalence of injustice makes it all the more "urgently necessary to cultivate everywhere a culture of equality, which will be lasting and constructive to the extent that it reflects God's plan."[1] Catholic and other Christian women have been taking up the challenge, although most have focused more upon the theory — philosophy and theology — of the problem than practical programs. What I shall, with no disrespect intended, call the retreat to theory testifies to the daunting complexity of the cultural, political, and practical problems.

The mere suggestion that feminism has failed, much less that it has failed women, would outrage mainstream feminists, although they frequently complain that the gains of the movement are in imminent danger of being reversed. A significant percentage of North American and western European women

---

1. *Pope John Paul II on the Genius of Women* (Washington, D.C.: United States Catholic Conference, 1997), p. 22, passage from the Angelus reflections, June 25, 1995. See also Pope John Paul II's "Letter to Women," dated June 29, 1995, and released at the Vatican July 10, 1995; and his *On the Dignity and Vocation of Women: Mulieres Dignitatem,* released in 1987.

doubtless concur that, since the 1960s, feminism has decisively contributed to a dramatic improvement in the position of women as individuals, as it undisputably has, although some would legitimately argue that gains on the one hand have carried losses on the other. The gains have been so rapidly and thoroughly integrated into the social fabric of First World nations that there is no reason to reiterate the ways in which feminism has contributed to increasing the dignity and independence of women. Not counting myself among those who seek to return women to the bedroom and the kitchen — were such a return even possible — I have no wish to minimize the intrinsic value of those gains, which, in many respects, are setting a standard for the rest of the world. In much of the world, women face problems that are virtually unimaginable for many of us, and although many of those problems are specific to their devalued situation as women, many are common to the men and children of their communities. Feminists regularly remind us that more needs to be done if women are to attain genuine equality with men, and so it does, especially in the developing world, but it remains debatable whether much of what feminists view as necessary — notably, free access to abortion — will truly serve the interests of women.[2]

Any new feminism must necessarily build upon the "old," even as it struggles to redress its wrongs. Few would contest that feminism has done much to improve aspects of the lives of many women, but as those who seek to formulate a new feminism know, the "improvements" have often come at a daunting cost that feminists are loath to acknowledge. In the first instance, the old feminism has not equally improved the lives of all women — or even all aspects of the lives of the privileged women it has most directly benefited — and it has had demonstrably negative consequences for many aspects of the lives of many women. Yet more important, the strategies of the old feminism have seriously undermined essential features of our culture and moral life, notably our ability to value and nurture human life in all its diversity, our respect for a uniform

2. The heated debates over CEDAW (Convention on the Elimination of All Forms of Discrimination against Women) in 2002 focus precisely upon the different views of the programs that will benefit women and communities even as they reveal the intensity of opposition between the different sides. On October 15, 2002, Cybercast News Service reported that feminist groups, including the Religious Coalition for Reproductive Choice, the National Organization for Women, the National Abortion and Reproductive Rights Action League, hysterically protested President Bush's nomination of Dr. David Hager to the Food and Drug Administration Advisory Panel on the grounds that Hager might be in a position to roll back approval of RU486. On October 17, 2002, the Associated Press reported that following a speech at the Cooley Law School in Lansing, Michigan, Sara Weddington told the *Lansing State Journal* that if Republicans won the fall elections, there would be an imminent danger that *Roe v. Wade* would be overturned.

standard of justice, our willingness to honor any form of natural or divine authority (although other forms of authority are flourishing), our willingness to nurture children and protect childhood, and our ability always to see other persons as ends in themselves — never means to another end.[3]

At the center of this web, theory and practice meet in a union as inseparable as that of soul and body, and here they confront the abiding feminist conundrum — the challenge of reconciling women's difference from men with their equality to them. Increasingly, both secular and Christian theorists claim to have moved beyond this alleged impasse, which they impatiently dismiss as no impasse at all. Some Catholics have even followed the aggressively secular Joan Scott in arguing that we err in viewing difference and equality as opposites when the true opposite of difference is similarity and that of equality is inequality. Others, notably Pia de Solenni, are drawing upon classical Catholic theology to argue that the souls of women and men have always been equal in the eyes of God even as they have also been different and, consequently, called to different roles. The theorists who pursue these discussions from the ground of orthodox Catholicism (including respect for the magisterium and the pope) frequently invoke the analogy of Christ's relation to the church, his bride, or that of the virgin Mary, mother of the church and preeminent exemplar of faith.[4]

Both analogies command respect — nay, admiration — and both capture essential spiritual qualities that a new feminism must include, but spiritual significance notwithstanding, they offer neither an adequate answer to the claims of the old feminism nor an adequate foundation upon which to build a new feminism in the world. Yet more dangerous, they implicitly retreat from the real terrain of struggle, namely, the equality of women and men in the world. However much secular feminists have protested the opposition of equality and difference in theory, they have never freed themselves from it in practice. And for evidence of their abiding attachment to equality as sameness, we need look no

---

3. See my development of this argument in Elizabeth Fox-Genovese, *Women and the Future of the Family,* with responses by Stanley J. Grenz, Mardi Keyes, Mary Stewart Van Leeuwen, ed. James W. Skillen and Michelle N. Voll (Grand Rapids: Baker, 2000).

4. Joan Wallach Scott, "Deconstructing Equality-Versus-Difference: Or, the Uses of Poststructuralist Theory for Feminism," *Feminist Studies* 14, no. 1 (1988): 33-50; Pia de Solenni, "The New Feminism: Contributing to a Philosophical and Theological Renaissance" (paper delivered at the Pontifical College of the Holy Cross, November 9, 2001), and her "*Fides et Ratio:* A Context for Developing the New Feminism" (paper delivered at the Twenty-Fifth Annual Convention of the Fellowship of Catholic Scholars, September 28, 2002). See also R. Mary Hayden Lemmons, "Equality, Gender, and John Paul II," *Logos: A Journal of Catholic Thought and Culture* 5, no. 3 (Summer 2002): 111-30.

further than their unyielding defense of abortion on demand at all stages of a pregnancy, including after birth. Their desperate attachment to this demand reflects nothing more nor less than a commitment to guarantee women the same — "no fault" — sexual freedom they believe men have always enjoyed, which amounts to a covert demand to equalize the physiological difference between women and men. The danger for the prospects of a new feminism lies in the possibility that Christian feminists are effectively restricting their "reconciliation" of equality and difference to the realm of theory, and a viable new feminism must directly confront the realm of practice. For most women understand their lives within the context of the realm of practice or as mediated by its problems.

Equal but different has assuredly not satisfied dissident Catholic feminist theologians like Rosemary Radford Ruether and Elisabeth Schüssler Fiorenza, who are becoming ever more radical with the passage of time. Their demands begin with the sexual liberation of women, grounded in the right to abortion, and extend to women's ordination to the priesthood. They impatiently dismiss the pope's appeal to women "to promote a new feminism which rejects the temptation of imitating models of 'male domination,'" and they deplore his claim that "the experience of motherhood makes you acutely aware of the other person, and at the same time, confers on you a particular task."[5] Their vision of an egalitarian feminist future would leave as little of orthodox Catholicism standing as secular feminists have left of mainstream Protestant churches, respect for marital fidelity, and the two-parent heterosexual family.[6] But restiveness with difference between women and men, especially when it might call for differentiation of roles, much less women's deference to men, has permeated virtually all Christian churches and is leaving a clear mark on the thought of women who consider themselves faithful rather than dissident Christians.

The main Protestant churches, with the Methodists and Episcopalians in the lead, have spawned strong radical feminist movements within their ranks,

5. John Paul II, *Evangelium vitae*, #99.

6. "The Campaign for a Conservative Platform," *Conscience* 16, no. 3 (Autumn 1995): 11, 14, quoting *Evangelium vitae*. *Conscience* is the pro-choice Catholic journal edited by Rosemary Radford Ruether. See also Elisabeth Schüssler Fiorenza, "Feminist Theology as a Critical Theology of Liberation," in *Churches in Struggle: Liberation Theologies and Social Change in North America*, ed. William K. Tabb (New York: Monthly Review Press, 1986), pp. 46-66; Rosemary Radford Ruether, *Disputed Questions: On Being a Christian* (Nashville: Abingdon, 1982); Elisabeth Schüssler Fiorenza, *Discipleship of Equals: A Critical Feminist Ekklesia-logy of Liberation* (New York: Crossroad, 1993); and for a general discussion of feminist theologians' attitudes toward Mary and women's relation to the church, Maurice Hamington, *Hail, Mary? The Struggle for Ultimate Womanhood in Catholicism* (New York and London: Routledge, 1995).

as the series of "Re-imagining" conferences attests. The Presbyterians join the Methodists and Episcopalians in ordaining women, and many Protestant churches are revising their texts and liturgy in the direction of gender-neutral language and practice. Thus groups such as Christians for Biblical Equality, who apparently see themselves as devout and faithful Christians, express growing dissatisfaction with failures to promote full equality between women and men, whether within marriage or in the leadership of the church as pastors, deacons, and elders. Firm proponents of requiring biblical translations to use gender-inclusive language, they also oppose traditional notions of male headship in marriage.[7]

Many members of Christians for Biblical Equality, like many Catholic women who engage these questions, apparently reject a representation of themselves as radicals, much less as rebels against the teachings of their faith. Many claim to respect the value and significance of sexual difference. Problems only arise with attempts to discuss how that difference should play out in practice: What, if any, social, political, economic — or even familial — roles should be allotted according to sex? Or, to borrow loosely from *Annie Get Your Gun,* what is there that men can do that women cannot do as well or better? What is there that women do that men should not also be obliged to do? The mere posing of such questions underscores the prevailing assumption that men have had the better part — the powers, the thrones, the glory — from which they have unjustly excluded women. This quest for "biblical equality" constitutes a thinly veiled attempt to redress that imbalance, but to do so with Christian charity rather than anger.

Proponents of these and similar positions apparently see themselves as the pioneers of a new Christian feminism, but close examination of their ideas suggests that either they suffer from a breathtaking lack of realism or they are privileging the claims of feminism over those of Christianity by attempting to force Christianity to conform to feminist demands. More important, their at-

7. For a brief account of the 2002 meeting of Christians for Biblical Equality, see Judith Person, "Christian Meeting to Study Sex Roles," *Washington Times,* September 24, 2002, available online at http://www.washtimes.com/culture/20020924-21282920.htm. For examples of the Protestant arguments, see Mary Stewart Van Leeuwen, "Re-Inventing the Ties That Bind: Feminism and the Family at the Close of the Twentieth Century," and other contributions in *Religion, Feminism, and the Family,* ed. Anne Carr and Mary Stewart Van Leeuwen (Louisville: Westminster John Knox, 1996). See also Mary Stewart Van Leeuwen et al., *After Eden: Facing the Challenge of Gender Reconciliation* (Grand Rapids: Eerdmans, 1993). For similar arguments from a Catholic, see Regina A. Coll, *Christianity and Feminism in Conversation* (Mystic, Conn.: Twenty-Third Publications, 1994), and Corinne Patton, "Catholic and Feminist: We Are Called to Be Both — Response to Elizabeth Fox-Genovese," *Logos: A Journal of Catholic Thought and Culture* 2, no. 4 (fall 1999): 27-38.

tempts to reconcile difference and equality within a Christian context sadly misestimate the magnitude of the task, as much at the level of theory as at the level of practice.[8]

At the level of theory, the discussion must begin with the recognition that feminism originated as the handmaid of individualism and, from the start, has been tied to and informed by the ideals of individual liberty and the equality of individual rights. As an ideology, feminism, which did not receive its official name until late in the nineteenth century, has consistently focused upon securing women's legal equality with men, notably their right to hold property in their own name, to vote, to obtain a divorce and retain custody of children should it be granted, to attend institutions of higher learning, to enter any profession of their choosing, and more. Also from the start, many — although emphatically not all — women's rights activists have been hostile to organized and revealed religion, primarily because they have deplored traditional religious teachings about the appropriate roles of women and men and, especially, their inclination to favor men's domination of women.

Deep resentment of traditional religions' propensity to proclaim women's ordained subordination to men has often blinded women's rights advocates to Christianity's consistent teaching on the equality of all souls in the eyes of God, captured in the familiar words of Saint Paul: "There is neither Jew nor Greek, there is neither slave nor free, there is neither male nor female; for you are all one in Christ Jesus" (Gal. 3:28). By the same token, those who understand the ideal of equality tend to treat all lapses from the ideal as abuses or transgressions. Both perspectives thus slight the rich complexity of Christian — and especially Catholic — thought. The first perspective focuses upon embodied life in this world, while the second focuses upon the innate worth of disembodied souls. But Catholicism views body and soul as indissolubly linked, hence the insistence upon the resurrection of the body. This aspect of Catholic theology opens the door to an understanding of equal but different, but it does not begin to solve the difficulties and contradictions of women's position in the modern — or postmodern — world.

Historically, a comprehensive understanding of equal but different has only flourished in premodern or prebourgeois hierarchical societies, for they, unlike modern individualistic societies, cultivated a notion of difference as or-

8. For preliminary criticisms of these attempts, see Elizabeth Fox-Genovese, "Catholic and Feminist: Can One Be Both?" *Logos: A Journal of Catholic Thought and Culture* 2, no. 4 (Fall 1999): 11-26, and my "Response to Corinne Patton," pp. 39-48 in the same issue; Donna Steichen, *Ungodly Rage: The Hidden Face of Catholic Feminism* (San Francisco: Ignatius, 1991); and Francis Martin, *The Feminist Question: Feminist Theology in the Light of the Christian Tradition* (Grand Rapids: Eerdmans, 1994).

ganic interdependence. Consequently, while the absolute worth of individuals might be understood as equal — at least to God — their functions in the world were understood as highly differentiated and only under the most exceptional circumstances as interchangeable. Since the great bourgeois revolutions of the seventeenth and eighteenth centuries and the massive cognitive and epistemological revolution that simultaneously provoked, accompanied, and resulted from them, the understanding of equality and difference has undergone a sea change. The premises of individualism, with their emphasis upon autonomy, independence, and self-determination, have made it virtually impossible to imagine an equality grounded in difference, with the result that feminists who seek equality for women have almost invariably been led to deny or abstract from sexual difference.[9]

Here we need not linger over the intellectual convolutions, beginning with the substitution of gender (understood as a social construction rather than an innate attribute) for sex, by which secular feminists have sought to deny the relevance of female bodies to women's social roles and needs. Suffice it to say, they have produced an array of bizarre conclusions, ranging from the rejection of all claims of difference as invidious "stereotyping" to demands for aggressive affirmative action programs to "level" the playing field. Perhaps this contradiction affords their main lesson and offers a salutary caution to Christian women who seek to formulate a new feminism. Difference cannot be wished away, and attempts to legislate away its consequences invariably end in an ominous strengthening of the state that enforces the programs to eliminate it. Unfortunately, the problems that plague the efforts of secular feminists to reconcile equality and difference, plague those of Christian feminists as well.[10]

Notwithstanding a discourse of mutual love and respect between women and men, Christians for Biblical Equality cannot easily disguise its discomfort with traditional female roles. In recent years discussions of "servant leadership" have proliferated, apparently with a view to binding men to the roles of service traditionally performed by women. The challenge to present the role of servant as admirable and desirable has nonetheless proved daunting, especially since the very attempt to do so betrays the extent to which the secular disdain for service has penetrated Christian thought. It is difficult to ignore the powerful bonds between individualism and secular feminism on the one hand and a re-

9. For a discussion of the distinct character of individualism and feminism's relation to it, see Elizabeth Fox-Genovese, *Feminism without Illusions: A Critique of Individualism* (Chapel Hill: University of North Carolina Press, 1991).

10. The leading proponent of these arguments is probably Judith Butler, *Gender Trouble* (New York: Routledge, 1990) and her *Bodies That Matter: On the Discursive Limits of Sex* (New York: Routledge, 1993).

jection of authority, whether natural or divine, on the other. And if we recognize the force of those bonds, we are led, however unwillingly, to recognize that the rejection of authority — and binding covenants — lies at the core of feminism and of the individualism from which it derives. In this perspective we may grasp the emphasis upon self-realization, liberation, and all the rest as neither more nor less than the refusal to be bound by any obligation to God or man. Not for nothing did Elizabeth Cady Stanton devote the last years of her life to a bitter critique of the Bible, which she published as a revised version of the original, entitled *The Woman's Bible,* and entitle her last important piece "The Solitude of the Self."[11]

Catholic feminists have tended to embrace the goals and claims of secular feminists, and their attempts to introduce feminism into the church have constituted a protracted and increasingly insolent challenge to the magisterium on all fronts. Catholics who are seeking a new feminism in keeping with the wishes of Pope John Paul II have scrupulously attempted to avoid those challenges, but for the most understandable of reasons, their contributions to the discussions have tended to remain highly abstract. Doubtless they understand all too well that their invocations of the virgin Mary and the church as the bride of Christ will never satisfy those who view feminism as the defense of women's right to self-determination and self-realization. So, again for the most understandable of reasons, they dodge the tough practical questions: male headship in marriage, marriage as a sacrament, contraception, abortion, homosexuality, extra- and premarital sex, the responsibilities of mothers, and more.

However much Catholic theologians and philosophers, including Saint Teresa Benedicta of the Cross (Edith Stein), Hans Urs von Balthasar, and Pope John Paul II, have emphasized the equal dignity and worth of women and men, they have also consistently insisted upon the difference between them, invariably emphasizing women's special vocation as the bearers and custodians of life. Just as men embody a distinct — and often unmeasured — ambition for power and domination, so do women manifest a special vocation for the care of life, which requires a measure of self-denial and self-abnegation. Nothing in feminism suggests that a woman's true vocation lies in sacrificing her own interests and desires to those of others, and even devout Catholic women have not found it easy to ground a new feminism in women's willing renunciation of

11. Elizabeth Cady Stanton and the Revising Committee, *The Woman's Bible,* pts. I and II (Seattle: Coalition Task Force on Women and Religion, 1974; original ed., 1898). For a preliminary discussion of the radicalism of her religious views, see Elizabeth Fox-Genovese, "Contested Meanings: Women and the Problem of Freedom in the Mid-Nineteenth-Century United States," in *Historical Change and Human Rights: The Oxford Amnesty Lectures, 1994,* ed. Olwen Hufton (New York: Basic Books, 1995), pp. 179-216.

self. In this respect the early efforts to formulate a new feminism have been slow to challenge the old feminism's individualist premises. My point is not to minimize the difficulty of the task: individualism has so thoroughly permeated our culture that no sphere, including religion, remains immune to its influence.[12]

Catholic thought, notably but not exclusively on the nature of the human person and the culture of life, nonetheless offers opportunities, which have yet to be pursued, to break through the prison house of individualism. Pope John Paul II in particular has written extensively on the fallacies in understanding the human person as an autonomous or isolate entity. The human person, he insists, exists only in relation to others, just as the three persons of the Trinity exist in relation to one another. Throughout his philosophical writing and, since his ascension to the papacy, in his encyclicals and letters, he has explored the idea and substance of the person as the combination of subjective perception and objective position, and he has countered the abstract concept of the individual with attention to the role of action and choice in the development of the person. Drawing upon a theologically informed existentialism, he has consistently argued, "an existential metaphysics of actual being *(esse actu)* is required to situate the moral agent in the actual context in which one acts."[13] The focus upon action and its context underscores the embodiment of the person and his or her moral and social connection to others. Thus the person cannot be understood as idea or intent — or by extension, desire — in the abstract, but only as idea or intent (or desire) in action. In this perspective no person can be autonomous — "an island," to borrow from John Donne — for each of us remains bound by interdependency and mutual responsibility to all others, and those bonds impose distinct limitations upon the individual freedom of any person. If this identification of the person with action imposes constraints upon individual freedom, it also offers a rich new understanding of freedom, namely, the inherent respect for human dignity that dictates that each person be viewed as an end and never as a means.[14]

12. See James Davison Hunter, *Before the Shooting Begins: Searching for Democracy as the Culture Wars Rage* (New York: Free Press, 1994). See also Elizabeth Fox-Genovese, "How Abortion Has Failed Women," *Crisis* 18, no. 3 (March 2000): 32-37.

13. Kenneth L. Schmitz, *At the Center of the Human Drama: The Philosophical Anthropology of Karol Wojtyla/John Paul II* (Washington, D.C.: Catholic University of America Press, 1993), p. 126. For a thoughtful introduction to Karol Wojtyla/John Paul II's thought, see this work by Schmitz. See also Rocco Buttiglione, *Karol Wojtyla: The Thought of the Man Who Became Pope*, trans. Paolo Guietti and Francesca Murphy (Grand Rapids: Eerdmans, 1997), and George Weigel, *Witness to Hope: The Biography of John Paul II* (New York: Cliff St. Books, 1999).

14. For the development of Karol Wojtyla's thought on these questions during his years as a professor at the University of Lublin, see his *Person and Community: Selected Essays*, trans. Theresa Sandok, O.S.M. (New York: Peter Lang, 1993).

If the essence of the human person lies in the union of action and intent — makes subjective consciousness palpable in embodied action — the reality of the person depends upon and cannot be understood or lived without the limitations upon individual freedom imposed by the coexistence of others. Thus does a proper understanding of the human person's relation to freedom return us to the realm of moral authority or, in the words of John Finnis, "moral absolutes."[15] This logic inescapably leads to the conclusion that moral imperatives are linked to the essence of the human person, whose very existence depends upon the independent reality of others. The defense of individual autonomy, liberation, and self-determination that lie at the core of secular feminism reduces to little more than autism — the isolation and anomie of the disconnected.

Catholic theology offers innumerable examples of connection as the core of a living — and lived — faith. In various ways, countless saints have pointed to connection with God as the fulcrum of their being, implicitly echoing the words of Saint Augustine, "Our hearts are restless, O Lord, until they rest in you." This spirit of connection echoes the lessons of humility embodied in the life of the virgin Mary. For as Balthasar has written, "Faith is the surrender of the entire person: because Mary from the start surrendered everything, her memory was the unsullied tablet on which the Father, through the Spirit, could write his entire Word."[16] It is difficult to imagine a starker contrast with the secular feminist imperative that each woman should be free to construct herself — to choose the life she wants even at the cost of other lives. Bluntly put, the contrast opposes the woman who chooses to sacrifice herself for the good of others and the woman who chooses to sacrifice others for her own good. And until we plumb the depths of the contradiction, we shall have poor prospects for constructing a truly new feminism.

Among the many connections that figure so prominently in Catholic theology and faith, the connection between mother and child, as represented in Mary's motherhood of Jesus — Mary the Theotokos — and her motherhood of the church, enjoys a special place and provides a bridge to the lives of ordinary women. Secular feminists have generally deplored women's "imprisonment" in the responsibilities of motherhood and perhaps even more the identification of women with motherhood. In their canon, self-realization requires liberation from domestic servitude to others and the right to play an independent role in

15. John Finnis, *Moral Absolutes: Tradition, Revision, and Truth* (Washington, D.C.: Catholic University of America Press, 1991).

16. Augustine, *Confessions* 1.1; Hans Urs von Balthasar, *Mary for Today,* trans. Robert Nowell (San Francisco: Ignatius, 1996; original ed., 1987), p. 45.

the world. The defense of women's right to liberation from children fuels their passionate and uncompromising defense of women's right to abortion on demand, which amounts to a demand for women's liberation from connection.[17]

Secular feminists would vehemently protest the claim that they seek freedom from connection and no less vehemently deny that their ideal of liberation constitutes the cutting edge of the "culture of death." But any new feminism must begin with the recognition that both charges are true. As the bearers of life, women, including those who never bear a child, possess a special affinity for connection and, consequently, potentially embody a special gift for connection. Nowhere is it written that each woman will realize that potential, which must find its realization in specific actions within specific contexts. And we all know that women are capable of chilling cruelty as well as heroic and sacrificial love. In situations, like our own, that discourage any binding connection, the probability that many women will fail in the realization increases exponentially, and massive failures of connection are precisely what is signified by Pope John Paul II's evocation of the culture of death. That women's most fervent aspirations for themselves have taken the form of a revolt against binding connection represents a tragedy of staggering proportions. For if women reject connection, who will embrace it?

My point is embarrassingly simple: there may be innumerable "other" feminisms, but there will be no new feminism until there is a feminism of life. Countless women, including many secular feminists, will doubtless concur, insisting that they "support" the culture of life. Feminists for Life is forging the path and doing admirable work for which we should all be grateful. But for the best of reasons, members of this group emphasize their kinship with the ideals of Susan B. Anthony and Elizabeth Cady Stanton, both of whom opposed abortion but otherwise embraced the essentials of individualism. Even they seem reluctant to tell women that their support for life will frequently require the surrender of their autonomy — their right to choose in many areas. And herein lies our greatest challenge: those who view women's binding connection to the children they conceive as a form of enforced service are not wrong. Nor are those who point to the staggering difficulties of reconciling care for children with worldly success. Nor yet are those who protest that women's primary re-

---

17. See Jaroslav Pelikan, *Mary through the Centuries: Her Place in the History of Culture* (New Haven: Yale University Press, 1995), and my review of it, "The Evolution of Mary: From the Gospels to Mariology to Feminist Critiques," *Books and Culture* 3 (May-June 1997): 34-36. For an extreme — but starkly honest — version of the argument that women should not be burdened by responsibility for children and should treat an unwanted pregnancy as an invasion by a hostile intruder, see Cynthia Daniels, *At Women's Expense: State Power and the Politics of Fetal Rights* (Cambridge: Harvard University Press, 1993).

sponsibility to children reinforces their subordination to men, or at least precludes their complete equality with them. As Jesus instructed his disciples, "No one can serve two masters; for either he will hate the one and love the other, or he will be devoted to the one and despise the other. You cannot serve God and mammon" (Matt. 6:24).

Recognition of a binding obligation to others — especially children, but also husband and frequently other members of an extended family — usually forces a woman to adopt a new perspective on her job or career in the world and even, if only for a finite period, relegate it to second place, if not put it on hold for an extended period. This necessity inescapably undermines a woman's ability to compete equally with men in the public world, at least for the short term. A woman's choices for life and fulfilling obligations to others do not, however, necessarily bar her from one or another form of worldly accomplishment. Most women today may expect a significantly longer life span than their foremothers, and countless numbers are finding ways to move in and out of jobs and careers in conformity with the other priorities in their lives. The great secret of such intermittent and unorthodox careers is that those who pursue them frequently prove more successful than their sisters who pursue more conventional tracks.

We should never forget that a woman's experience in domestic life, especially if it includes a serious measure of reflection, self-examination, and meditation, may do more to prepare her for subsequent success in a job or career than innumerable years in a mind-numbing "rat race." There are no guarantees that all women will draw such benefits from running a house and caring for children, but there is a high probability that those who enter into those tasks from the foundation of a strong marriage and in a spirit of willing service and joy in the fostering of human life will. Much depends upon the maturity and faith that permit a woman to choose to assume those obligations for her own reasons rather than responding like the adolescent who is being coerced by her parents. In addition, it has become widely accepted among people of differing economic status that fathers as well as mothers may participate actively in the care and education of children. The difference lies in the inability of fathers to nurse infants and the special bond that pregnancy creates between mother and child. These considerations point to a primary responsibility for women during the first two or three years of a child's life, by which time patterns have been established, which easily lead to an extension of that sexual division of labor within families — especially if more children have been born or are desired or if the parents have decided upon homeschooling.

For feminists, any presumption that women will have primary responsibility for children, much less that they will compromise their careers (and they rarely attend much to the wishes of less affluent women who only hold mere "jobs"), represents a betrayal of women's needs and rights. Their positions on these matters reflect an underlying conviction that justice will free women effectively to become men. Typically those who have most actively opposed feminist positions on women's rights and needs have fallen into the trap of seeing women as fit only for motherhood and service to others. Tragically this unilateral opposition to everything feminism represents has resulted in a general failure to attend to the variety of options from which women may choose. In particular, it has led many of those who most sincerely attend to the needs of children and the fostering of a culture of life to slight the gift of women's vocations to a single life.[18]

The world has a crying need for the talents and dedication of women, who are more than capable of fulfilling innumerable public roles with distinction — and in a spirit of charity and fidelity as well. Single women may choose to live and work as members of religious communities, as independent laypersons in the secular world or in an intermediate status, as for example do the numeraries of Opus Dei and the consecrated members of Commune et Liberazione. In the latter cases they work in the secular world, sometimes living in a community and sometimes on their own, but take vows of fidelity. In any of these capacities, and others, single women bring unique and sorely needed gifts to a vast array of occupations, none of which should be closed to those who have the qualifications for them. The point is not to "condemn" all women to marriage and motherhood, which many women still regard as their highest vocation, but to imagine feminism as a mansion with many rooms and to understand that some choices preclude others — at least in the short run. A new feminism must encompass and honor vocations for single women, just as it must support the distinct vocations of women who are wives and mothers. Both vocations offer ways in which women can contribute to rebuilding a culture of life.

True dedication to the culture of life requires respect for authority, if only the authority of God's commandment not to kill. In practice, that dedication normally also requires respect for the authority of children's nonnegotiable needs and perhaps the authority of a husband — or at least of the sacrament of marriage. There can be no genuine dedication to the culture of life without the surrender of some of our "rights" and a large chunk of our "autonomy." The es-

---

18. For the ways elite feminists have ignored the concerns and interests of the majority of women, see Elizabeth Fox-Genovese, *"Feminism Is Not the Story of My Life": How the Feminist Elite Has Lost Touch with the Real Concerns of Women* (New York: Doubleday/Nan Talese, 1996). On the value of a distinct role for men as fathers, see W. Bradford Wilcox, "Religion, Convention, and Paternal Involvement," *Journal of Marriage and Family* 64 (August 2002): 780-92.

sence of the culture of life lies in our ability to see others as like ourselves and to see Jesus in each and every one of them. Secular feminism has uncritically embraced the dominant male version of success and insisted that women have an equal right to reap its fruits. This single-minded focus upon worldly success has blinded secular feminists to the understanding that the success they covet also embodies many, if not all, of the attributes and policies they otherwise deplore: brutal competition, the quest for domination, exploitation of the planet and its resources as well as of people, and more.

Edith Stein, a favorite student and assistant of Edmund Husserl, never doubted women's intellectual capabilities or the world's need for their dedicated participation in its work. Yet Stein, recently canonized as Saint Teresa Benedicta of the Cross, also believed the nature of women's contributions differed from those of men. Thus, she cautions, a man's "one-sided endeavor to achieve perfection easily becomes a decadent aspiration in itself; our desire for knowledge does not respect limits placed on it but rather seeks by force to go beyond these limits; human understanding may even fail to grasp that which is not essentially hidden from it because it refuses to submit itself to the law of things; rather, it seeks to master them in arbitrary fashion or permits the clarity of its spiritual vision to be clouded by desires and lusts."[19]

In emphasizing women's greater propensity to nurture human persons and the earth, Stein never restricted their roles to family responsibilities. To the contrary, she insisted upon women's independent right to vocations in the world and, especially, to the intrinsic value of those vocations. But her enthusiasm about women's vocations did not change her belief that woman's nature differs from that of man in important ways. Many contemporary feminists see any admission that women may differ from men in nature or needs as a shameful capitulation and betrayal of women's rights. On a purely empirical level, most women do not agree, and a new feminism must respect many women's desire to marry, bear and rear children, and anchor a web of binding and loving connections. Beyond the desires of individuals, however, the fate of our world now hangs in the balance.

Many will see a betrayal of justice — and assuredly of feminism — in any suggestion that women may bear a special responsibility to nurture the culture of life, which alone can protect our future. But those who do are, however inadvertently, acknowledging their own imprisonment in outmoded, and increasingly dangerous, ideas. No doubt the ideals of service and sacrifice run directly against the grain of our culture, but if we deny their claims we place ourselves at

19. Edith Stein, *Woman,* trans. Freda Mary Oben (Washington, D.C.: ICS Publications, 1987), p. 70.

high risk. Until now, feminism in general — and we all know there are marginal exceptions — has waged a fierce battle to permit women to behave like men and, in the areas in which they cannot, to guarantee them the same results as if they had. A new feminism requires that we muster the courage and the faith to reverse this paradigm. Women throughout the world are in desperate need of policies that respect and protect them as women — not policies that ensure their access to abortion so that they can become as "free" as men. A feminism grounded in the defense of a woman's right to "choose" to have an abortion is inescapably a feminism that promotes the culture of death.

It is never easy to go against the grain, especially when doing so exposes one to social and economic risks. But without the will to defy prevailing ideas, we will condemn ourselves to more of the same. Jesus, in time and place, was profoundly countercultural. A new feminism must follow his lead and direct women's efforts to formulating a new model of the way to be human. Who knows? If we succeed in defending a culture of life in which personhood is understood as mutual recognition rather than autonomy and no person is ever objectified as the means to an end, men — within the constraints of their differences from us — may follow.

A Creative Difference: Educating Women

Marguerite Léna

Translated by Esther S. Tillman
and Michele M. Schumacher

"Women are educated — who knows how?" it is stated in *Hegel's Philosophy of Right*. For if "the status of manhood . . . is attained only by the stress of thought and much technical exertion," women need only to meditate. Like the plant, "their development is more placid and the principle that underlies it is the rather vague unity of feeling." Given time, sunshine, and water, she will flourish on her own. But this privilege has its price; it places her outside the serious undertakings of existence. "Women are capable of education, but they are not made for activities which demand a universal faculty such as the more advanced sciences, philosophy, and certain forms of artistic production. Women may have happy ideas, taste, and elegance, but they cannot attain to the ideal. . . . When women hold the helm of government, the state is at once in jeopardy, because women regulate their actions not by the demands of universality but by arbitrary inclinations and opinions."[1] Hegel knew that the greatest minds cannot transcend their own time; as far as the status of women is concerned, he did not even try.

But *time* ironically has transcended the philosopher's convictions. Women have attained political power without the state having been endangered; "the highest sciences" are no longer an exclusively male domain. We also

---

This text is in part reprinted from an article which first appeared in the French edition of *Communio* 7, no. 4 (1982) and then in the English edition under the title: "The Education of Young Women." The author greatly thanks the director of *Communio* for his authorization to reproduce and modify this text. Both she and the editor are also indebted to the director of the English edition for permission to adopt the original translation.

1. *Hegel's Philosophy of Right,* trans. T. M. Knox (Oxford: Clarendon, 1945, 1953), addition to paragraph 166, pp. 263-64.

know better that "the requirements of universality" are themselves threatened by a male-dominated culture. Not only do these requirements become problematic from the simple fact that they exclude half of humanity, but by depending only on the other half they sometimes risk being denatured into abstract formalism, and "the ideal" risks degenerating into ideology. Hence the cultural and spiritual urgency of the education of women.

Case Dismissed on Insufficient Grounds?

Surely the expression "women's education" is outmoded and untimely. Fenelon wrote a treatise on the education of young women, but his day is past. On the contrary, everything tends these days either not to admit the problem or to suppress it. First, the general tendency is against academic institutions devoted to the education of women. If not for a few exceptions which elicit smiles from liberal progressives, most academic establishments are mixed. The situation is the same for leisure activities, sports, voluntary service groups, discussion groups, and Christian education groups. The education of women? Case dismissed.

What is more, an education designed specifically for women implies content and objectives that are its *own*. As long as young women did not have access to studies and careers open to young men, it was relatively easy to define by elimination these contents and objectives. The education of women of that day played a double role: one technical, preparing young girls for the family tasks that awaited them, the other ethical, developing in them "the feminine virtues." These virtues corresponded at one and the same time to an immobile social status and to an eternal feminine essence. But these two aspects of traditional education have again come forward: increasingly women have the same preparatory, university, and professional education as men. They have become liberated from the restraints of household activities, with technical progress a contributing factor. Freed to enter new fields of knowledge and power, they are finding new ethical demands as well. The traditional feminine virtues are incapable today of covering the actual field of women's responsibilities. There are even those who think the feminine virtues would be more likely to turn them away from assuming these responsibilities.

Finally, suspicion has entered in here as it has everywhere: women's education has been accused of active complicity in the enterprise of subordination of woman to man and has been denounced as the crucible in which this inequality is affirmed and institutionalized. Not only does this traditional education define the narrow limits of her condition by imposing on her a minor status and inferior tasks, but it is what actually determines what woman is. As a result, she is nothing but a cultural artifact set up on a pedestal as an eternal essence. Paradoxically, this explains the fact that feminist currents so seldom include in their claims a specific demand for education. The rebellion of the "second sex" against its condition is going through the process of women's education. We know with what bitter vehemence Simone de Beauvoir has indicted this process.[2]

Do we have to give up education of young women, then, for lack of place, object, and subject? I do not think so. Above all, I do not think this question can be answered by reports of sociologists invoking the evolution of customs and mentalities. These evolutions have rather the advantage of forcing us to enlarge the problem of women's education beyond a purely functional perspective, to which it has often been reduced, either the better to exalt it or the more surely to denigrate it. A sheltered education of women in Bergson's sense of the term, directed toward the protection and maintenance of the family and social group without taking into account the creative impulse of persons, is fortunately challenged on all sides. A greater freedom in the choice of roles and models, and access to the responsibilities of professional and public life — even if considerable discrimination still persists — constitute the attainments, probably irreversible, of the last decades. On the other hand, progress is being made toward a livelier consciousness of the *common* educative responsibility of the man and the woman in family life and beyond it. This seems to me to be infinitely more important than the generalization of co-education. Whatever its sex, a child needs the father's *and* the mother's presence, and this is important in different forms along the entire path to adulthood.

Education is neither technical mastery over things nor biological childbearing. Perhaps it is the privileged place of collaboration between man and woman. It calls for their complementarity, highlights their differences, tests their solidarity. Finally, the present evolution reminds us that the mystery of the person transcends sexual differentiation. "One could no more cut a world of persons into two hemispheres," emphasized Emmanuel Mounier, "than one could quantify that world." Thus we are brought back to the paradox of all education and to the *human* paradox of sexual difference.

2. Simone de Beauvoir, *Le Deuxième Sexe* (Paris: Gallimard, 1949). Translated into English by H. M. Parshley: *The Second Sex* (New York: Vintage, 1989; originally, Knopf, 1952).

A Double Paradox

It is a paradox of all education that the educator is forbidden in the same gesture neutrality and total control. He cannot postpone his choices until the evidence has appeared. He cannot shed his personal responsibility on society as a whole nor count on the fad of the moment. He cannot escape the risk of setting a precedent.

Whether conducted by men or women, in a mixed milieu or not, the education of young women is necessarily marked by the implicit choices and attitudes of which educators are often scarcely aware. Implied is a certain idea of man and woman which education actually contributes to reinforcing and propagating. A clearer awareness of these attitudes and ideas, therefore, allows these educators a more just course of action. But this action, no matter how lucid and considered, could not for all of that consist in educating the child intellectually the way one gives form to an inert material. For it is not a question here of an aim of technical order which can be attained by a given procedure or determined by a method. To begin with, the child is not inert material. One cannot claim to "form the man" — or woman — according to a totally controlled "educational plan." A thousand secret forces, asleep or muted or sometimes exiled, await the educator who will free the song. Therefore, the educator can only grope his or her uncertain way between the expectation, on the one hand, of making the child conform to an essence or play a role clearly defined by its sex and, on the other hand, of excluding from its education anything that relates to the difference between men and women. But a start must be made.

For what is true of the education of man in general, that is, in the abstract, is all the truer when we take into account the sexual difference which concretizes for each of us our membership in the human race. Because a person is man *or* woman, no one carries in his or her flesh the entire shape of the human condition. If this sexual difference were only biological destiny, the education of women would be pointless. The biological develops; only the human is educated. On the contrary, if woman's being were nothing but cultural artifact, the education of women, by perpetuating this artifact, would have to be denounced as an alienation. But here we must reject both the naturalism which places feminine identity outside culture, claiming that its development is achieved "in some indeterminate manner," and the culturalism according to which education determines everything, including woman. For they both misconstrue the paradox of man, carnal to the very spirit, spiritual to the very flesh. Bodily existence, in which the sexual difference is first noted, is not only that of a living being but also of a subject. Existence is no longer a simple game of chance, the meaning of which is determined by absolute freedom or a dominant ideology. Existence is always already given and already meaningful. But this gift, to be realized, calls for the generosity of another gift; for the meaning to be made clear, the collaboration of other freedoms is called for. I cannot reach my femininity without the educative mediation of others any more than I can achieve my humanity without it. Education alone permits the *human* elevation of the biological order — otherwise lying fallow and suspended — and its interpersonal transformation.

The Creative Difference

Therefore, women's education does not involve solely the condition of woman but also, as always in education, the condition of man's meaning and his history. It is striking to note that totalitarian regimes and political utopias, concerned with total takeover of the future of the individual and society, have bumped up against sexual difference as an irritating obstacle on the way to a total rationalization of human becoming. They have striven most often to minimize this difference by assimilating the woman as far as possible, by means of education, to masculine roles and reducing her femininity to the sole function of perpetuating the race or the nation.

One can bring up here the military concern, always strong in this type of society, but it is certainly beyond this explanation. Because it is *given,* sexual difference belies the proposition of autonomy of man by himself. Because it is a *difference,* it is contrary to reason to "equate the sexes" too quickly and to yield to the temptation of uniformity. Finally, because it puts into law the formidable power of *love* in its obscure physical and spiritual indetermination, it removes behavior from intelligent planning.

It is still necessary to reflect upon this difference. Like all decisive anthropological realities, it is a "mystery" and not a "problem," to cite the categories of Gabriel Marcel's philosophy. We cannot so externally objectify the elements as to render ourselves spectators from above. We are ourselves involved in the question which takes possession of our bodies and involves the singular commitment of our freedom. But the mystery is not a limit — no more here than in the theological order — to our search for understanding. On the contrary, the difference allows me to understand myself by discovering "myself" in the light of an "other" whose proximity, in turn, is only signified in respecting his difference.

One might here evoke the categories utilized by Father Gaston Fessard in following Saint Paul: master-slave, man-woman, pagan-Jew.[3] It is significant that the first of these distinctions is immediately marked by violence: in theological terms, it points to "structures of sin," to the alienation of both the political relation of authority and power and the economic relation of seizure and the mastering of nature. The third distinction points to the economy of salvation: it is with the election of Israel in the Abrahamic and then Mosaic covenants that it takes flesh before being assumed and surpassed in the mystery of Christ. The difference of man and woman, on the other hand, points us directly and exclusively to the order of creation: it lies within the "separations" constitutive of the creative act, as their summit, and even as the place where they receive their sense: not scission, but vocation to sustain, serve, and multiply life; not conflictual opposition, but the call to celebration and thanksgiving; not distancing from the Unique, but his image and likeness: "In the image of God, he created them; man and woman he created them."

This is certainly the reason why one cannot align the relation of man and woman with the single dialectic of domination of the master-slave type, as certain currents of feminism attempt to do. That this is indispensable for denouncing unacceptable situations is only too clear, even urgent. In thinking, however, or worse in living the man-woman relation as one of domination — whatever the sense in which it is exerted — the authenticity of this relation is neither seized nor restored. The human impoverishment that follows once the proper originality of this difference — simultaneously created and creative — is overshadowed is almost immediately perceptible.

This originality is also the reason why one cannot simply differentiate man and woman by an inventory of biological, psychological, and cultural characteristics nor objectify their sexual adherence in an "essence." "Original" difference, preceding our grasp of it, is immediately at work *between* our liberties. It situates and roots our liberties in the humility of the flesh. It precludes them from enclosing in upon themselves, but calls each one to understand himself or herself in the light of the other. It situates them within a consent to the limit and infinite openness to otherness. This is so much the case that the difference would be neither understood nor experienced in the absence of this vis-à-vis of liberties. Certainly it is not ours to choose our sex, nor for that matter and for the same reasons those of the children born of us. We can only understand and live our sexual identities in the choice that we make to assume and honor them in ourselves and in others as a gift and a call, that is to say, in living in an ethical mode, which is first of all offered to us in the biological mode.

---

3. Gaston Fessard, "Esquisse du mystère de la société et de l'histoire," in *De l'Actualité historique* I (Paris: Desclée de Brouwer, 1960), pp. 159-75.

Here again, here especially, the spiritual is first of all inscribed within the flesh and thus within time: in the duration and fragility of a history exposed to the "infinite disturbances of love."

A Decisive Ethical Stake

On a beautiful page of *Either/Or,* Kierkegaard has the assessor, Wilhelm, and a young seducer carry on a dialogue. It concerns the awakening in the latter of the desire for the decisive change which will make him pass from the moving play of his sensations, in which he takes intense delight, to the "baptism of the will" which will introduce him into the ethical order. The way Wilhelm describes the young man, and the injunction he gives him, have a prophetic value for our entire culture:

> [I]f you will continue to divert your soul with the trumpery of wit and the vanity of spirit, then do so, leave your home, travel abroad, go to Paris, devote yourself to journalism . . . and when wit grow mute there is water still in the Seine and gunpowder in the store and traveling companionship at every hour of the day. But if you cannot do this, if you will not (and this you neither can nor will), then collect yourself . . . respect every honest effort, every unassuming endeavor which modestly hides itself, and above all have a little more reverence for woman.[4]

The ethical value of a culture is perhaps measured by this respect. How can it be concretely inscribed within the educative task? How, in turn, can this task contribute to its promotion?

It is significant that today a number of our social problems and major ethical debates concern the family and the control of life and death, and therefore stand on thresholds of which woman is traditionally guardian. The example of abortion shows clearly how inadequate the maternal instinct is for the protection of life when social pressure, indifference, and permissiveness everywhere, and the weight of material or moral misery, run counter to it. In the face of these challenges, unprecedented in their scope, and of technical facilities never before possessed, are needed more lucidity and generosity than instinct insures, more autonomy and creative courage than the traditional virtues of woman ever required. What is needed is the intervention of conscience, of effort, of example given, of word risked. What is needed is education.

4. Søren Kierkegaard, *Either/Or,* vol. 2, trans. Walter Lowrie (New York: Anchor Books, 1959), pp. 210-11.

Up to now, it was a matter above all, for many women, of obtaining professional status even at the cost of going through studies first conceived by men for men. This necessity continues, but we have to go further. The more extensive women's intellectual, social, associative, and political responsibilities become, the more important it is for society and culture that they exercise them *as women* in order to display in the pertinent domain the anthropological richness of their difference. In our societies, characterized by the technical inspection of the real, the triumph of logico-mathematical formalisms, the growth of political complexities — characterized, in short, by a formidable force of objectivation, of assimilation, of identification — it is necessary to give full recognition to this irreducible, unassimilable, nonobjectifiable, noncomparable difference between the sexes. In our societies, tempted to transform differences into oppositions and oppositions into conflicts, and to resolve the conflicts by marginalization or violence, it is necessary to restore to the creative difference between man and woman all its power of inquiry and all its promises of life. To the question, "Is the object of the education of young women to surmount or to affirm the difference between man and woman?" my answer is: It must surmount the discrimination but liberate the difference.

If every birth attests the mystery of this difference by actualizing and magnifying it within the man-woman union, education, which deploys one's birth in time, is in turn its servant and witness. It in fact supposes both institution — the masculine manner of surmounting passing time — and childbirth, the feminine manner of so doing. Hence learning to speak requires both the institution of a common language and the birthing of a new sentence; a moral education supposes the institution of law and the birthing of freedom; education of the intelligence depends upon the institution of knowledge and the birthing of discovery. To help youth grow is to unceasingly move from one of these symbolic poles to the other. This coming and going is so much easier when men and women collaborate according to their complementarity without either exclusively occupying one of these poles.

In helping women to be women without aggression or complex, we shall reawaken in ourselves the forgotten meanings, the dormancy or activation of which govern the ethical: *the meaning of faces,* presence irreducible to representation, breach of vulnerability in the empire of force, emergence of the person in the mass of structures; *the meaning of fidelity,* which the ongoing mastery of time dulls, which the play of possibilities crumbles, but whose memory the woman guards in her body by the slow gestation of the child. Perhaps we shall find again, like a light in the hour of darkness, the mysterious alliance of suffering and love so impervious to understanding, but about which Christ, on the threshold of his passion, told the last parable: "A woman about to give birth is saddened because her hour has come; but when she has delivered the child she forgets the pain, in the joy that a human being has come into the world" (John 16:21). We shall restore that other alliance formed by justice and mercy, that "gentle pity" whose absence renders the right obdurate. We shall also recover the sense of shame, which keeps watch at the threshold of all interiority, which harbors the secret depths of the world and of life, inaccessible to our inquiries, impervious to public existence. For the woman, heir of a long tradition of presence in the private sphere of the family and home, finds herself henceforth more and more engaged in the public sphere. She is thus in a situation of mediation and "interchange" between these two spaces, each having need of the other so as not to perish, whether by closing in upon itself or by superficiality. Our societies must invent new manners of uniting the public word of boundless information and the silence which preserves the secret of the private life, the efficacy of success which fosters technology and the fecund choice of life that protects its meaning, the universalization of exchanges and the concrete rooting in a memory which guards the richness and weight of humanity. Finally, there must also awaken in us the sense of childhood and old age, without which our societies slowly progress toward the inhumane.

There is no recipe for forming and exercising these meanings. At the most, one might suggest that woman has, in this domain, a particular responsibility that she must assume at the level of the global society as she has in the intimacy of the family.

I like to think that the best service accorded us by literary studies resides in this refining of the heart, in this expansion of intelligence beyond utility, in the conversion of sentimental enthusiasm into depth of feeling, and of obscure and indecipherable intuition into an idea that can be enunciated and communicated. In shaping the spirit as universal power of knowing, choosing, loving, literary studies allow escape from a narrowly conceived and lived femininity. They serve and expand its authentic richness. One encounters in these studies so many nuances and faces; they require so much patience. But I notice that perhaps all this makes them still more necessary for men than for women! So let us give up establishing programs. Let us not pose exclusivities. Let us not reserve any territory. A "female culture" would be just as mutilated and mutilating as a purely male culture. Rather, let us work tirelessly at giving to the rich polyphony of the culture notes that are characteristically feminine. Our common humanity is at stake.

At the Living Springs of Grace

There is at stake the spiritual future of our world. The Bible knows this well. Far from removing history from these "infinite disturbances," it strengthens and transforms their meaning. This is why the question of women's education is no stranger at all to sacred history, that is, to the dimension which is the most interior and the only definitive one of our human history. If every Christian educator must be concerned not only with the calling to rationality and to freedom of those entrusted to him/her, but also with their supernatural calling as children of God, he or she cannot forget that there exists, from this point of view, a mystery and a ministry of woman in the plan of salvation. This mystery has to be respected; this ministry, prepared. As Evdokimov wrote: "The modern, profoundly masculine world, where the feminine charism plays no role whatsoever, is more and more a world without God, for it has no mother and God cannot be born in it."[5]

We read in the story of Genesis literally that the woman will be for the man "a *help against* him" (Gen. 2:18).[6] In its mysterious conciseness this formula profoundly suggests, it seems to me, women's role in the forefront of the spiritual combat. Here it is that grace and sin meet face-to-face; here decisive consents and refusals operate. Beyond temptress, woman is revealer of sin: woman as object of sexual desire exposes the man's appetite for pleasure just as woman as slave discloses his appetite for power. It is all too obvious that the simple reversal of this scheme of things is in no sense a liberation of woman. The immodest images of certain advertisements stripping women and, under different skies, the imprisoning veils up to the faces of other women are two symmetrical expressions of the same scorn. Feminist claims today have therefore an essentially spiritual stake. Well positioned for denouncing the ravages which pleasure and power, left to their sole logic of death, have set up as ends, women risk yielding in their turn to the same logic of death. Self-love to the point of scorn for the other is never a privilege and has nothing exclusively masculine about it.

Education of women, in the light of the paschal mystery, must therefore lean heavily on the spiritual fecundity of disinterestedness and service and not be afraid to recall constantly the cost of true love and the beatitude which is concealed and revealed therein at one and the same time. We have to educate

5. Paul Evdokimov, *Woman and the Salvation of the World: A Christian Anthropology on the Charisms of Women,* trans. Anthony P. Gythiel (Crestwood, N.Y.: St. Vladimir's Seminary Press, 1994), p. 251.

6. Cf. Renee de Tryon-Montalembert, "Quelques pistes de reflexion sur l'homme et la femme à partir de la tradition juive," *Contacts,* no. 110 (fourth trimester 1977): 277.

our young girls to take all their responsibilities, to display generously all their powers of initiative and creativity, to struggle energetically to attain and hold their place in society and in the church. But we must in the same spirit call on them not to hold back jealously anything from the position that makes them with perfect right the equals of men: to love without asking return and give without counting the cost. Not because they are women, but because such is the secret of existence and of all true spiritual fecundity.

Because of the historic weight of models of feminine subordination, this request is perhaps particularly difficult to formulate without equivocation, to honor without compromise. But I think we have no choice. We cannot wait for woman to be "liberated" to open up to her the paths of life. If she does not walk there first, others will perhaps never be able to follow. It is often thanks to the woman, who has sometimes been defined as "being for others," that the man becomes aware of this same vocation of "being for others," which he tries to forget in his striving for self-sufficiency. If this "being for others" is freely assumed and not undertaken in the bitterness of an imaginary inferiority, if it enters the church and becomes charity, then *"there is no longer man or woman"* (Gal. 3:28), but the true freedom of children of the kingdom.

Revealer of sin, woman also holds fast to the living springs of grace. In its highest light in Mary, woman's vocation symbolically and effectively gathers the work of the centuries of the promise, the slow education of the fiancée in the desert, that of the bride in the promised land, the secret maturation of wisdom in the time of Judaism. It is certainly not by chance that Saint John mentions the presence of Mary at the foot of the cross and situates the story of the passion between two scenes of feminine compassion: the tears of Mary of Bethany near the tomb of Lazarus, provoking those of Jesus, are echoed by the tears of Mary Magdalene, near the tomb of the Crucified One, which give rise to the angel's question and the manifestation of the Resurrected One. There is an order of realities perceiving more quickly those expressions crossed by tears — tears of pain or of joy — and women are sometimes more willing to surrender their faces to tears.

This is why the pressure of professional duties and public involvement must not turn women away from their properly spiritual responsibilities. Mary's *yes* is a clear decision, an irrevocable event in the history of salvation which marks the caesura between the new covenant and the old. But Mary's *yes* is prolonged in memory's faithfulness: "Mary carefully preserved all these memories and pondered them in her heart" (Luke 2:19). Her *yes* assumes the weight of duration and opens the living tradition of the church. It seems to me that this twofold aspect of the mystery of Mary — the instantaneous clarity of consent, the fidelity that spans time — invites us to a double vigilance. On the one hand we have, in the present state of the world, to insure the original fidelities. We know it is the women who have kept the faith alive for several generations in the communist regimes, and everything points to the fact that in our own homelands, too, this role has devolved upon us. "To bring forth God in ravaged souls" is no minor task, and it requires a slow preparation. But on the other hand, it is not enough to transmit gratuitously what we have gratuitously received. We have to enter decisively into the spiritual combat of the time. Our *no* must be *no;* our *yes, yes.* "Today," as Evdokimov still writes, "in view of the Third World, Africa, Asia and Latin America, in view of materialism, secularization, pornography and drugs — in view of all the elements of demoniac decomposition, of violence, of war, it is woman who . . . is predestined to say *no* in order to stop man at the edge of the abyss and show him his true calling as witness to God's mysteries."[7]

What this *no* costs and signifies, the women of the Middle East and of Algeria, as before the countless "Matriona" of the eastern countries, know better than we. In return, there are certainly influxes of grace today which are possible only if a woman's *yes* opens up for them access to our history, and this requires not only the courage of fidelity but also that of resourcefulness. For our church can also succumb at times to the double risk of private withdrawal or public dispersion which lies in wait for civil societies: private withdrawal, when the sap of the gospel no longer irrigates "the vast domains of economic and political systems, of the culture, of the civilization, and of development," no longer permitting Christ "to speak to man," according to the strong words of Pope John Paul II at the beginning of his pontificate; public dispersion when the grace of the Word is, as it were, diluted in the "elements of this world," measured by the length of its media effects or by majority opinion. It is thus necessary to invent a new modality of a feminine presence in the church, also in terms of an "exchange" between its public space of visibility and social fecundity and its private space of praying and loving interiority. Women today have the grace of circulating from one of these spaces to the other as the respiration of the Holy Spirit, whom the tradition of the church simultaneously refers to as the interior Master and the great "Exiler." I dare hope women consecrated in the religious apostolic life might bear this grace for the world. For if our call has situated us there, it depends upon us to prepare, in the long silence of the slow germination of all human growth, these yeses which are springs without which the desert will inexorably expand.

---

7. Evdokimov, *Contacts*, no. 110 (fourth trimester 1977): 273.

Contributors

Sr. Prudence Allen, R.S.M., is Chair of Philosophy at St. John Vianney Theological Seminary, Denver, Colorado, and Distinguished Professor Emeritus, Concordia University, Montreal. She received her Ph.D. from Claremont Graduate University in 1967. She is the author of a two-volume work, *The Concept of Woman: The Aristotelian Revolution, 750 B.C.–A.D. 1250* and *The Concept of Woman: The Early Humanist Reformation, 1250-1500*, published by Eerdmans. She has lectured widely in the United States, Canada, England, Poland, and Israel, and published in such journals as the *American Catholic Philosophical Quarterly, Maritain Studies, Dialogue, Lonergan Workshop, Feminist Studies, New Blackfriars, International Philosophical Quarterly, Thought,* and *Communio.*

Beatriz Vollmer Coles was born in Caracas, Venezuela, and has studied in several countries, concluding with her doctoral thesis in philosophy at the Pontifical Gregorian University in Rome. She has specialized in gender issues from a philosophical perspective and has participated in various conferences both in Europe and in the United States. In addition, she was assistant professor of philosophy at the Gregorian University as well as professor and dean of the faculty at the archdiocesan seminary in Caracas. Her family has moved to New York, where she is currently a "stay-at-home mom" for Alberto ('99) and Helena ('01).

Jean Bethke Elshtain is the Laura Spellman Rockefeller Professor of Social and Political Ethics at the University of Chicago, where she teaches in the Divinity School, the Department of Political Science, and the Committee on International Relations. Her many books include *Augustine and the Limits of Politics,*

Democracy on Trial, Who Are We? Critical Reflections, Hopeful Possibilities, and most recently, *Jane Addams and the Dream of American Democracy.*

Elizabeth Fox-Genovese is the Eléonore Raoul Professor of the Humanities and Professor of History at Emory University, where she was the founding director of the Institute for Women's Studies. She also serves as editor of the *Journal of the Historical Society.* She is the author of *Women and the Future of the Family* (2000), *"Feminism Is Not the Story of My Life": How the Feminist Elite Has Lost Touch with the Real Concerns of Women* (1996), *Feminism without Illusions: A Critique of Individualism* (1991), and *Within the Plantation Household: Black and White Women of the Old South* (1988). She coedited *Society Reconstructing History: The Emergence of a Historical Society* (1999) with Elizabeth Lasch-Quinn. She writes widely on women's issues, as well as religion, contemporary culture, education, and social issues, and served as an expert witness for the VMI and Citadel cases.

Hanna-Barbara Gerl-Falkovitz was born in Bayern, Germany, in 1945 and studied philosophy, German literature, and political science at the University of Heidelberg and the University of Munich, where she received her doctorate and habilitation in philosophy. There, at the Romano Guardini Institute, she also worked as an advanced assistant and substitute professor. In 1989 she was named professor of philosophy in Weingarten (Baden-Württemberg), and since 1993 has been the chair of philosophy of religion and comparative religious sciences at the Technical University of Dresden. Her specialties include the religious philosophies of the nineteenth and twentieth centuries, with a concentration upon Romano Guardini, Edith Stein, and philosophical gender research. She has also specialized in Renaissance philosophy, especially Italian humanism. Among her publications is a biography on Romano Guardini (4th edition in 1995), and her most recent book is *Eros, Glück, Tod und andere Versuche im christlichen Denken* (Resch-Verlag, 2001). She currently serves as an adviser for the complete works of Edith Stein in German.

Marguerite Léna was born in 1939, and since 1961 has been a member of the St. Francis-Xavier apostolic community, a community of consecrated life founded by Madeleine Daniélou and dedicated to the formation and evangelization of youth. She teaches philosophy at the high school level and literature at Sainte-Marie de Neuilly and is also dedicated to the formation of seminarians for the diocese of Paris. She is the author of *L'Esprit de l'éducation* (Paris: Desclée, 1991), *Le Passage du Témoin* (Paris: Parole et Silence, 1999), and various articles in *Communio, Christus,* and *Etudes.*

Robert Francis Martin was born in New York City in 1930 and ordained a priest at St. Joseph's Abbey in 1956. He holds degrees in theology (S.T.L.) and sacred Scripture (S.S.D.), both from Rome. He has taught at St. Joseph's Abbey, the École Biblique in Jerusalem, Steubenville University, the Catholic University of America, and the John Paul II Institute, and presently holds the Chair of Catholic-Jewish Theological Studies at the John Paul II Intercultural Forum in Washington, D.C. His scholarly and popular works extend over many fields, and some of his more recent writing has been in the area of feminism.

Anne-Marie Pelletier, doctor of religious sciences, teaches biblical exegesis at the Ecole Pratique des Hautes Etudes in Paris and at the Ecole Cathédrale of the diocese of Paris. Her publications include *Lectures du Cantique des Cantiques, De l'énigme du sens aux figures du lecteur,* Analecta biblica 121 (Rome, 1989), *Le christianisme et les femmes* (Paris: Cerf, 2001), and numerous articles, some of which are listed in the bibliography of this book.

Michele M. Schumacher, born in 1964, is the mother of four young children and an external research collaborator at the University of Fribourg in Switzerland, where she received her licentiate in theology in 1991. She also holds a doctorate in theology (1994) from the John Paul II Institute in Washington, D.C., where she studied mediation in the theology of Hans Urs von Balthasar. Before moving to Europe after her wedding in 1996, she worked for two years as the director and founder of the Office of Family Life and Social Justice for the diocese of Yakima, Washington, and taught as an adjunct professor in a master's program in theology offered by the Archdiocese of Portland in conjunction with the Religious Institute for Religious and Pastoral Studies of the University of Dallas. She has published numerous articles in the areas of theological anthropology, Christian feminism, and dogmatic theology, and is currently studying the anthropology of women in the works of the Swiss mystic Adrienne von Speyr for the Swiss National Scientific Foundation.

Sibylle von Streng was born in Belgium, where she studied philosophy at the University of Louvain-la-Neuve, concluding her studies with a memoir comparing the concept of truth in the works of M. Heidegger and H. U. von Balthasar. As an assistant at the University of Geneva, she studied and translated the texts of such young phenomenologues as Edith Stein, M. Geiger, A. Pfaender, and D. von Hildebrand. She is presently married with three young children and living in Switzerland. Within the context of the family home, she is engaged in philosophical research bearing principally upon the anthropology of woman in the works of Edith Stein.

Further Reading: A New Feminist Bibliography

Alveré, Helen. "A New Feminism: The Holy Father's Call to Christian Women." *Liguorian,* May 1997, pp. 4-11.

Caldecott, Léonine. "Sincere Gift: The Pope's 'New Feminism.'" *Communio* 23 (spring 1996): 64-81.

Conde, Gloria. *New Woman.* Translated by Karna Swanson and with foreword by Mary Ann Glendon. Hamden, Conn.: Circle Press, 2002. Original: *Mujer Nueva.* Mexico City: Editorial Trillas, 2000.

Glendon, Mary Ann. "A Glimpse of the New Feminism." *America,* July 6, 1996, pp. 10-15.

Hendrickx, Marie. "Un autre féminisme?" *Nouvelle Revue Théologique* 112 (1990): 67-79.

John Paul II. *The Genius of Women.* Washington, D.C.: NCCB/USCC, 1999. This is a compilation of his 1995 Angelus reflections on women and other papal writings from that year addressing the same subject.

——. "Letter to Women." June 29, 1995. In *Origins* 25, no. 9 (July 27, 1995): 137-43. This is also included in *The Genius of Women.*

——. *Mulieris dignitatem.* Apostolic Letter on the Dignity and Vocation of Women. August 15, 1988.

——. "Women: Teachers of Peace." World Day of Peace Message, January 1, 1995. *Origins* 24, no. 28 (December 22, 1994): 465-69. This is also included in *The Genius of Women.*

Schumacher, Michele M. "Women in the Teaching of John Paul II." In *The Wisdom of John Paul II,* pp. 64-74. London: Catholic Truth Society, 2001.

On the Anthropological Theology and Philosophy
Founding This New Feminism

Allen, Prudence. *The Concept of Woman.* Vol. 1, *The Aristotelian Revolution, 750 B.C.–A.D. 1250.* Grand Rapids and Cambridge, 1985.

————. *The Concept of Woman.* Vol. 2, *The Early Humanist Reformation, 1250-1500.* Grand Rapids and Cambridge, 2002.

————. "Integral Sex Complementarity and the Theology of Communion." *Communio* 17 (Winter 1990): 523-44.

————. "Sex and Gender Differentiation in Hildegard of Bingen and Edith Stein." *Communio* 20 (Summer 1993): 389-414.

————. "A Woman and a Man as Prime Analogical Beings." *American Catholic Philosophical Quarterly* 66, no. 4 (Autumn 1992): 465-82.

Ashley, Benedict. *Justice in the Church: Gender and Participation.* Washington, D.C.: Catholic University of America Press, 1996.

————. *Theologies of the Body: Humanist and Christian.* Braintree, Mass.: Pope John XXIII Medical-Moral Center, 1985.

Bouyer, Louis. *Woman in the Church.* San Francisco: Ignatius, 1979.

Chervin, Ronda. *Feminine, Free and Faithful.* San Francisco: Ignatius, 1986.

Clark, Stephen. *Man and Woman in Christ: An Examiniation of the Roles of Men and Women in Light of Scripture and the Social Sciences.* Ann Arbor: Servant Books, 1980.

Evdokimov, Paul. *Woman and the Salvation of the World: A Christian Anthropology on the Charisms of Women.* Translated from the French. Crestwood, N.Y.: St. Vladimir's Seminary Press, 1994.

Hauke, Manfred. *Women in the Priesthood? A Systematic Analysis in the Light of the Order of Creation and Redemption.* Translated from the German by David Kipp. San Francisco: Ignatius, 1988.

Hourcade, Janine. *La femme dans l'Église. Étude anthropologique et théologique des ministères féminins.* Paris: Téqui, 1990.

————. *Des femmes prêtres?* Paris: Mame, 1993.

————. *Pourquoi la femme?* Paris: Desclée, 1992.

Iouriev, Xénia. *L'église et les femmes. Vers une anthropologie trinitaire à la lumière de la théologie orthodoxe.* Lausanne: L'age d'homme, 2001.

John Paul II (Karol Wojtyla). *Love and Responsibility.* San Francisco: Ignatius, 1993.

————. *The Theology of the Body: Human Love in the Divine Plan* (Boston: Daughters of St. Paul, 1997).

Lacroix, Xavier. *Le corps de chair. Les dimensions éthiques, esthétiques et spirituelles de l'amour.* Paris: Cerf, 1992.

Lehmann, Karl. "The Place of Women as a Problem in Theological Anthropology." *Communio* (English edition), Fall 1983, pp. 219-39.

Lemmons, R. Mary Hayden. "Equality, Gender, and John Paul II." *Logos: A Journal of Catholic Thought and Culture* 5, no. 2 (Summer 2002): 111-30.

Little, Joyce A. "The New Evangelization and Gender: The Remystification of the Body." *Communio* (English edition) 21 (Winter 1994): 776-99.

May, William E. *Marriage: The Rock on Which the Family Is Built.* San Francisco: Ignatius, 1995.

McInerny, Ralph, ed. *The Catholic Woman.* Papers presented at a conference sponsored by the Wethersfield Institute, New York City, September 28, 1990. San Francisco: Ignatius, 1991.

Martin, Francis. "Male and Female He Created Them: A Summary of the Teaching of Genesis Chapter One." *Communio* 20 (Summer 1993): 240-65.

Militello, Cettina. *Donna in Questione. Un itinerario ecclesiale di ricerca.* Assisi: Cittadella Editrice, 1992.

Miller, Monica Migliorino. *Sexuality and Authority in the Catholic Church.* Scranton, London, and Toronto: University of Scranton Press and Associated University Presses, 1995.

Moll, Helmut, ed. *The Church and Women: A Compendium.* San Francisco: Ignatius, 1988.

Pelletier, Anne-Marie. *Le christianisme et les femmes. Vingt siècles d'histoire.* Paris: Cerf, 2001.

———. "Il n'y a plus l'homme et la femme." *Communio* (French edition) 106 (March-April 1993): 35-45.

———. "Masculin, féminin, le sens d'une tradition. l'occasion du débat sur l'ordination des femmes." *Nouvelle Revue Théologique* 117 (1996): 199-216.

———. "Le signe de la femme." *Nouvelle Revue Théologique* 113 (1991): 665-89.

Pissarek-Hudelist, Herlinde, ed. *Die Frau in der Sicht der Anthropologie und Theologie.* Düsseldorf: Patmos Verlag, 1989.

Quay, Paul M. *The Christian Meaning of Human Sexuality.* San Francisco: Ignatius, 1985.

Rousseau, Mary. "Pope John Paul II's *Letter on the Dignity and Vocation of Women:* The Call to *Communio.*" *Communio* (English edition) 16 (Summer 1989): 212-32.

———. "The Primacy of Gender." *Proceedings of the American Catholic Philosophical Association* 66 (1992): 11-12.

Santiso, Maria Teresa Porcile. *Con Occhi di Donna. Identità, Ministero, Spiritualità, Contemplazione, Parola.* Bologna: Edizioni Dehoniane, 1999.

———. *La femme, espace de salut. Mission de la femme dans l'Église. Une perspec-*

tive anthropologique. Paris: Cerf, 1999. This is a translation from the original Spanish. There is also an Italian edition.

Schindler, David L. "Catholic Theology, Gender, and the Future of Western Civilization." In David L. Schindler, *Heart of the World, Center of the Church: Communio Ecclesiology, Liberalism, and Liberation,* pp. 237-74. Grand Rapids: Eerdmans; Edinburgh: T. & T. Clark, 1996.

————. "Creation and Nuptiality: A Reflection on Feminism in Light of Schmemann's Liturgical Theology." *Communio* 28 (Summer 2001): 265-95.

Schumacher, Michele Marie. "The Prophetic Vocation of Women and the Order of Love." *Logos: A Catholic Journal of Thought and Culture* 2, no. 2 (Spring 1999): 147-92.

Scola, Angelo. "The Dignity and Mission of Women: The Anthropological and Theological Foundations." *Communio* (English edition) 25 (Spring 1998): 42-56.

Shivananden, Mary. *Crossing the Threshold of Love: A New Vision of Marriage in the Light of John Paul II's Anthropology.* Edinburgh: T. & T. Clark, 1999.

————. "Feminism and Marriage: A Reflection on Ephesians 5:21-33." *Diakonia,* 1996, pp. 5-22.

————. "The Pope, Man and Woman." Occasional Papers, Oxford University Catholic Chaplaincy, Oxford, 2001, pp. 19-26.

————. "Subjectivity and the Order of Love." *Fides Quaerens Intellectum* 1 (Winter 2001): 251-74.

Solenni, Pia Francesca. *A Hermeneutic of Aquinas's* Mens *through a Sexually Differentiated Epistemology: Towards an Understanding of Woman as* Imago Dei. Rome: Apollinare Studi, 2000.

Stein, Edith. *Essays on Woman.* Translated by Freda Mary Oben. 2nd ed. Washington, D.C.: ICS Publications, 1996.

On the Practical Implications of a New Feminism

Belleggia, Concetta, F.S.P., ed. *Real Women: Advice, Commentary, and Encouragement for Women Today.* San Francisco: Ignatius, 1994.

Glendon, Mary Ann. "Vatican Delegation in Beijing." The Beijing Women's Conference (September 4-15, 1995). *Origins: CNS Documentary Service* 25, no. 13 (September 14, 1995): 203-6.

————. "Vatican Stance: Women's Conference Final Document." *Origins: CNS Documentary Service* 25, no. 15 (September 28, 1995): 233, 235-36.

Hourcade, Janine. *Les deaconesses dans l'église d'hier . . . et de demain?* Lausanne: Saint-Augustin, 2001.

John Paul II. "Appeal to the Church on Women's Behalf." *Origins: CNS Documentary Service* 25, no. 12 (September 7, 1995): 185, 187.

————. "On Fully Fostering Women's Roles in the Church." *Origins: CNS Documentary Service* 25, no. 13 (September 14, 1995): 201, 203.

————. "Women: Teachers of Peace." World Day of Peace Message, January 1, 1995. *Origins: CNS Documentary Service* 24, no. 28 (December 22, 1994): 465-69.

Joyce, Mary Rosera. *Women and Choice: A New Beginning.* St. Cloud, Minn.: LifeCom, 1986.

Matlary, Janne Haaland. *Il Tempo della fioritura. Per un nuovo femminismo.* Milano: Mondadori, 1999. An English edition coauthored by Helen Alvaré is in preparation.

Murphy, Cornelius F., Jr. *Beyond Feminism: Toward a Dialogue on Difference.* Washington, D.C.: Catholic University of America Press, 1995.

Steinfels, Margaret O'Brien. "Obstacles to the New Feminism: Look Before You Leap." *America,* July 6, 1996, pp. 16-21.

A New Feminism from a Spiritual Perspective

Balthasar, Hans Urs von. "Die Würde der Frau." *Internationale katholische Zeitschrift: Communio* 11 (1982): 346-52.

Blaquière, Georgette. *La grâce d'être femme.* 12th ed. Paris and Fribourg: Saint-Paul, 1993.

Croissant, Jo. *La femme sacerdotale ou le sacerdoce du cœur.* 5th ed. Nouan-le-Fuzelier: Éditions des Béatitudes, 1992.

Hausman, Noëlle, ed. *"Comme elles l'avaient dit." Être femme aujourd'hui.* Namur: Vie Consacrée, 1996.

Heller, Karin. *Et couple il les créa.* Paris: Cerf, 1997.

Schumacher, Michele M. "Therese, Woman in the Church." *Logos: A Journal of Catholic Thought and Culture* 3, no. 3 (Summer 2000): 122-51.

Speyr, Adrienne von. *Handmaid of the Lord.* Translated by E. A. Nelson. San Francisco: Ignatius, 1985.

————. *Three Women and the Lord.* Translated by Graham Harrison. San Francisco: Ignatius, 1986.

Teresa (Mother) of Calcutta. "Spiritual Poverty and the Breakdown of Peace." Speech at the U.S. National Prayer Breakfast (February 3, 1994) in *Origins, CNS Documentary Service* 23, no. 35 (February 17, 1994).

Vanier, Jean. *Man and Woman He Made Them.* Mahwah, N.J., and New York: Paulist, 1985.

See also *Contacts: Revue française de l'orthodoxie* 29, no. 100 (1977). The entire issue dedicated to the Orthodox and Jewish vision of woman.

Critiquing Traditional Feminism

Crittenden, Danielle. *What Our Mothers Didn't Tell Us: Why Happiness Eludes the Modern Woman.* New York, London, and Sydney: Simon and Schuster, 1999. This is a more popular than scholarly account.

Fox-Genovese, Elizabeth. "Catholic and Feminist: Can One Be Both?" *Logos* 2, no. 4 (Fall 1999): 11-25. And in the same issue, her response to Corrine L. Patton ("Catholic and Feminist: We Are Called to Be Both — a Response to Elizabeth Fox-Genovese"), pp. 39-48.

————. *"Feminism Is Not the Story of My Life": How Today's Feminist Elite Has Lost Touch with the Real Concerns of Women.* New York: Doubleday, 1996.

————. *Feminism without Illusions: A Critique of Individualism.* Chapel Hill and London: University of North Carolina Press, 1991.

————. *Women and the Future of the Family.* Grand Rapids: Baker, 2000.

Hitchcock, Helen Hull, ed. *The Politics of Prayer: Feminist Language and the Worship of God.* San Francisco: Ignatius, 1992.

Martin, Francis. *The Feminist Question: Feminist Theology in the Light of Christian Tradition.* Grand Rapids: Eerdmans, 1994.

McMillan, Carol. *Women, Reason, and Nature: Some Philosophical Problems with Feminism.* Princeton: Princeton University Press, 1982. Although this is somewhat dated, her excellent arguments remain timely.

Oddie, William. *What Will Happen to God? Feminism and the Reconstruction of Christian Belief.* San Francisco: Ignatius, 1988.

Steichen, Donna. *Ungodly Rage: The Hidden Face of Catholic Feminism.* San Francisco: Ignatius, 1991.

Index

Abortion: existentialist feminism and, 272; gender feminism and, 57; Marxist feminism and, 268; personalist feminism and, 281; pragmatic secular feminism and, 90-92, 276-77, 299-300; Wojtyla/John Paul II on, 77-79, 91-92, 93

Achtemeier, Elizabeth, 176-77

The Acting Person (Wojtyla), 65, 69, 73, 76, 77, 94

Adam: and image of God in Genesis, 142-50, 160, 161-62; and relations between man and woman, 157-58, 208-9, 222-23

Aertsen, Jan, 35n., 37n., 41n.

Agrippa, Henry Cornelius, 72

Allen, Prudence, ix-x, xiv, 286, 289. *See also* Humanism and feminism; John Paul II and new feminism

Alvaré, Helen, 68n.

Ambrose, 142n., 223n., 231

Andreas-Salomé, Lou, 270

Anselm, 174, 240

Anthony, Susan B., 307

Aquinas. *See* Thomas Aquinas

Aristotle, 63, 69, 71, 74, 87, 164, 259, 287

Astell, Mary, 85, 260-61

Atheism, 90n., 265-66, 279

Auclert, Hubertine, 80n., 264n.

Augustine of Hippo, 41, 160, 191, 195, 202, 219n., 233, 286

Badinter, Elisabeth, 58-59n., 60, 62, 62n., 97n.

Balthasar, Hans Urs: on Adam and Eve, 208; on Christ's masculinity, 213; on "dual unity," 162, 215; on equality and difference, 304; on faith, 174, 174n., 185, 188-90, 195-96, 306; on gender feminism, 59; on marital love, 220; on Mary, 49, 195-96; on precedence in the church, 229n.; on "world without women," 33

Baptismal priesthood of the faithful, 220n., 220-21

Barr, James, 144

Barrett, Michele, 24n.

Barth, Karl, 145

Beauvoir, Simone de: and conceptions of the body, 8, 14; direct opposition to Christ/God, 101, 101n.; on the essence of woman, 4, 27-28, 271; and existentialist feminism, 86, 96, 270-72; on men and women, 17, 60; on nature and freedom, 27-28; on nature-nurture dualism, 25; and new phase of feminism, 53, 60

Becker, Gary, 135

Beijing Conference on Women (1995), 81, 284, 297. *See also* "Letter to Women" (John Paul II)

Benoit, Pierre, 159